AF437782

Cover Images:

Front: KZN/KSL photo of Latter-day Saint President Heber
J. Grant at the opening night dedication of the radio station,
May 6, 1922, on the roof of the Deseret News Building in Salt
Lake where the station was located.

Upper Left: KDYL photo of Ira J. Kaar who constructed the
radio station that first aired in Salt Lake on May 10, 1922.

Upper Right: KFUR/KLO photo of Harman Peery who owned
KFUR/KLO that first aired in Ogden on January 28, 1925

ON THE AIR
IN THE BEEHIVE STATE

ON THE AIR
IN THE BEEHIVE STATE

The Pioneers of
Utah Radio & Television
Broadcasting & Cable TV

Tim Larson

Printed in the United States of America

ISBN: 979-8-21825-505-3

DEDICATION

To the memory and legacy of Ira J. Kaar

TABLE OF CONTENTS

Acknowledgments

The genesis of this book, or more accurately my interest in Utah broadcasting history, harkens back four decades to my introduction to the indefatigable efforts of Ira Kaar, who as a precocious radio amateur was omnipresent in pioneering Utah radio broadcasting. Kaar and some 100+ other Utah broadcasting and cable pioneers graciously shared their personal stories with me. A special thanks to Kaar, John Baldwin, Sid Fox, Arch Madsen, Ben Larson, Frank Carman, Howard Johnson, Leland Perry, Reed Bullen, George Hatch, Jack Gallivan, Alvin and Lena Marie Pack, and the Earl Glade family.

Professionals at the National Archives in Suitland and College Park, Maryland, and at the Utah State Historical Society provided essential documents. Two colleagues at the University of Utah J. Willard Marriott Library, Gregory Thompson and the late Roger Hansen, gave me in-person and financial support for the last several decades. And, of course, I mined the Marriott Library's large Utah Broadcast History Collection and the Everett L. Cooley Oral History Collection for documents and remembrances.

I thank Don Gale, Bonneville International Corporation executive (ret); Robert K. Avery, University of Utah Department of Communication professor (ret); and the late Malcolm Sillars, College of Humanities Dean and Communication Department faculty member, for reading and critiquing early manuscript versions of this book and for their editorial support and encouragement over the last several decades. In addition, I thank the several hundreds of people, who are named in the book for their unique contributions to Utah broadcast history.

And special appreciation goes to Craig B. Wirth, U of U colleague, Utah history documentarian and a Utah broadcast history aficionado. He has an ongoing five-decade long broadcast journalism career and provides incomparable oversight of my work.

I am grateful to Les Roka who faithfully provided timely and exceptional editorial support; helping me write a book accessible to the general public and pleasing to the family and friends of the pioneer Utah broadcasters I hopefully have honored. Nick Cockrell, a prodigious photo editor, graphic artist and digital media expert, prepared the photo gallery and the book covers.

Lastly, I am greatly indebted to Anne Holman, co-owner of King's English Bookshop in Salt Lake City, and manuscript editor Joanie Packard whose expertise helped me prepare this book for publication.

I am solely responsible for the content presented here, but, undoubtedly, with the dizzying amount of information presented, some inadvertent misinformation may have been proffered. Please alert me to needed relevant and material corrections.

Thank you for engaging this book.

Tim Larson
tim.larson@utah.edu

FOREWORD

I am amazed by the powerful influence radio has had on our lives, crafted by people, often bright teens, who beginning in the early decades of the last century pioneered Utah broadcasting. These radio pioneers didn't pretend to be sociologists or cultural or electronic geniuses but were dreamers, promoters, risk-takers -- entrepreneurs -- and newspaper publishers who with government guidance shaped Utah radio's market structure and safeguarded its sustainability. They discovered Utah radio, which has entertained, informed, and given us nostalgic memories, and, indeed, behaviorally changed us in many respects.

Tim Larson has spent decades gathering inside information from the people who first pioneered Utah radio and later television broadcasting and cable television. He garnered personal stories, procured government documents, poured over newspapers, accessed countless hours of recordings, and traveled the country to engage those pioneers in order to tell a unique inside story of their efforts. No one has assembled and mined the volume of important first person stories and primary research about Utah radio and television pioneers, as has Tim for this book. It now is impossible to replicate his research efforts. Without Tim's passion for discovering the beginnings of Utah broadcasting and cable television, the pioneers' stories would be lost and go untold.

Tim, my colleague and friend, has readily shared his research with others and me and helped to enlighten my broadcast history documentaries and television programs. I am honored to introduce this very accessible scholarly account of Utah's radio and television pioneers and the beginnings of the first Utah broadcasting stations and cable television systems they fostered. This book also makes an exceptional contribution to Utah history.

Craig Wirth
Communication Director, Episcopal Diocese of Utah
Producer, *Wirth Watching*
Salt Lake City

PREFACE

What follows below is a brief personal journey map telling my story of how this book came to be. It was born in the late 1970s when as a new mass communication professor at The University of Utah I sought out practicing Utah broadcasters in an effort to develop some town-and-gown relationships. In doing so, I contacted and listened to the stories from working broadcasters who told me about earlier broadcasters who had mentored and encouraged them in their careers.

One Utah broadcaster's name seemed to pop up the most in Utah broadcasting lore. Sidney S. Fox still was a Utah radio broadcasting legend in the 1970s even though he had not been active in Utah broadcasting for decades. He was the ultimate promoter in and out of radio and was unfailingly generous to his friends and colleagues. His story is related in several chapters.

Impressed with Fox's historical omnipresence in early Utah broadcasting, a graduate student and colleague, Patrick Boyles, became interested in Fox's story. In 1981, Boyles started work on his master's thesis about Fox. Fox was unavailable because he was recovering from a pedestrian/car accident. But Boyles contacted John M. Baldwin, who had been Fox's longtime KDYL engineer, beginning in 1928. His wife, Marie Baldwin, also contributed details about the Fox legend.

We learned greatly about Fox from the Baldwins but more importantly for the origins of this book, John told us about his first days at KDYL in the late 1920s. We learned from him of Ira J. Kaar, a name that had been inscribed on the station's first transmitter. Kaar, a gifted amateur radio operator, had constructed one of Utah's first two radio broadcasting stations: KDYL AM for the *Telegram* newspaper in 1922 and had put his name on the transmitter.

In March 1982, Bob Lee, host of KSL's *Public Pulse* program, invited me on his show to discuss Utah broadcasting history. Lee asked me to identify some early Utah broadcasting pioneers. I named some people including Kaar, adding that many pioneers likely were deceased, having been involved as teens and young adults six decades earlier with the founding days of Utah radio broadcasting. Ira Kaar, then 80, subsequently contacted me to say he was very much alive. He evidently had heard me on *Public Pulse* on KSL 1160 AM, from his home in Laguna Hills, California.

Kaar consented to an interview at his home scheduled for the next day. Pat Boyles and I left Salt Lake City for California in his small pickup truck at four p.m., drove all night, and, even after running out of gas near Cedar City, met Kaar as scheduled at nine a.m. at his California Leisure World home the next morning.

Kaar was slightly built, maybe 5'6" tall, with a reddish clean-shaven face and white hair combed straight back. He had a clear, deep and confident voice, was articulate and easily chose his words, very much a gentleman. Quite alert, he seemingly still was current in the field, even subscribing to engineering journals, nearly 15 years after he had retired.

Kaar initially seemed somewhat wondrously curious about our interest in him but was cordial and quickly engaged us with early Utah radio broadcasting stories and his career at the General Electric Company in Syracuse, New York. We chatted with him for several hours, left in the late afternoon and drove all night back to Salt Lake City, in possession of Kaar's large personal photo album and 35 three-ring notebook binders. The thick binders documented the 35 plus years he was at General Electric. Every page in each binder logged his daily research, with meticulously handwritten entries, witnessed in order to preserve findings for possible patents, of which Kaar had accumulated many. These three-ring binders now are held in reserve in the Special Collections at The University of Utah Marriott Library.

After our visit with Ira Kaar, I was hooked on Utah broadcasting history and now have dedicated decades to it.

Kaar and I became noteworthy friends: Kaar, ever the scientist and I, the humanist. I visited Ira frequently over the next decade, discussing and recording recollections of his Utah broadcasting activities when he was in his teens and early twenties. One special visit in 1983 involved my flying to California and driving him back to Salt Lake City in his Cadillac, to be inducted into the Utah Broadcasters Association Hall of Fame. I recorded many hours of conversations with him on that round trip.

Ira Kaar's was one of the first of some 100-plus oral history interviews I've conducted over the years, mostly of early Utah broadcasting pioneers; the people who began Utah broadcasting and who form the basis for this book.

In early drafts, I used the oral history interviews almost exclusively to inform the book's content. I showed one early draft to Floyd O'Neal, then director of the American West Center at the University of Utah, seeking an assessment of my work. His response after examining the draft was: "Don't try to stretch a rat's ass over a rain barrel." I took O'Neal's "suggesting" more elicitation to heart. I realized I didn't have sufficient primary records and needed to explore sources beyond the important oral histories and bring my findings to bear. O'Neal pointed me to the National Archives in Washington, D.C. for documentation.

I traveled five times to the Federal Records Center in Suitland, Maryland, and the National Archives in College Park, Maryland. I copied original Utah broadcast license applications, transcripts of Federal Radio Commission and Federal Communications Commission hearings and rulings, relevant congressional and other government documents, and extracted information from the papers of important stakeholders involved in early Utah broadcasting.

I copied some 3,000 pages at the Federal Records Center in Suitland, manually inserting 10 cents in the copy machine for each page. The record center did not provide change, so I acquired dimes beforehand. To give an apt visual of the apparent importance of the documents I sought at the Federal Records Center, a female security guard, in uniform and carrying a billy club, monitored my use of them. Only one document at a time was allowed at my desk and approval was required for every document before photocopying it. Only two photocopy machines were available, and, based on demand for their use, a patron could use a machine for only 10 minutes each hour. In addition, records had to be requested a day in advance, although one retriever I befriended did disregard that rule, to my benefit.

Unknown to me, just before my fifth visit to the Suitland National Archives Federal Records Center (NARC), federal documents pertaining to U.S. and Utah broadcasting were transferred from the Suitland Center to the newly opened National Archives in College Park, Maryland, adjacent to the University of Maryland. I went to the College Park National Archives a short time after it opened on January 4, 1994, and was pleased to see it had many photocopy machines that took credit cards in a very large research room that hosted no uniformed guards carrying billy clubs. That was the good news. The bad news was that the accession numbers for the broadcasting documents had not yet been sent from Suitland in the records transfer, and the young College Park employees were completely oblivious to the location of federal broadcasting records in the new Archives.

An employee asked me if I knew the group number under which the broadcast records had been indexed back at the Suitland Center. I did, in fact, know. The employee directed me into the stacks to retrieve the Utah broadcasting documents I sought. I was given unsupervised access to the inner holdings of this massive National Archives storage facility, measuring 1.8 million square feet. The movable stacks, which stretched almost entirely from the floor to the ceiling, could be compressed on tracks to maximize space. I pictured myself being forever squeezed between immense movable stacks, if somebody unaware of my presence pushed a button to get access to any adjacent stacks. The research room at the National Archives in College Park is open to the public, but research visits now may require an appointment and a virtual consultation prior to an onsite visit.

This book still depends heavily on Utah broadcasting pioneers' accounts of their contributions to the beginnings of Utah broadcasting. I acquired names, dates, personal and public documents, references, quotes, biographical sketches, even minutiae from them to integrate into a story that hopefully honors the enormous efforts of the pioneers who breathed life into Utah broadcasting, beginning more than a century ago.

I was fortunate to have had the opportunity to interview many of these pioneers before they passed. Their stories are fascinating. They epitomize a cultural dynamic that many have pinned on Utah's peculiar unconventionality as the nurturing ground for entrepreneurship and creative enterprise. At the time that pioneers such as Kaar and Fox cranked up the momentum to bring radio to Utah, the state was far less populated and definitely less urbanized than today.

As readers will note, some of the pioneering radio stations engaged here were founded in parts of Utah other than Salt Lake City. In addition to the first three television stations, there also was the founding of a cable network enterprise that would become the nations largest. Utah always has punched well above its weight class, metaphorically speaking, when it comes to achieving distinction in numerous areas of business, arts, technology and research. The story of Utah's broadcasting pioneers is no different.

The large documentation of their work is now housed in the Marriott Library Utah Broadcasting History Collection. These archives now are available to an interested public and can be mined by future historians.

INTRODUCTION

In the early 1900s, Utah, although its population was spread out broadly across the state's large expanse of territory, was growing at a pace not much different from what had happened in the early 2000s. The 1920 U.S. Census revealed that Utah's population was 449,396, representing a boost of more than 20% within the prior decade. Meanwhile, true to Utah's quintessential pioneer spirit, there were visionaries who embraced the possibilities of the newfound medium of radio and gave the state's residents plenty of options to enjoy the benefits of wireless entertainment and access to news from every imaginable point on the planet.

This chronicle of Utah's broadcasting history, from its earliest points, starts with the antecedents of a foundation that proved resilient and adventurous through the golden age of radio and into the possibilities of broadcast television. Undertaking such a history is somewhat risky because the significance of the human experience is often found in the contextual fabric that defies a printed account. The process of selecting what properly belongs in chronicling the history of broadcasting in Utah necessarily excludes people and events that may have contributed substantially to the story as told. Recognizing that, what follows is a historical reconstruction, circumscribed as the story of the beginners and the beginnings of Utah's first ten commercial radio and three television broadcasting stations and the first major cable television system. As this is the first substantial chronicle of Utah broadcasting's beginnings, it is the hope that others will expand upon it and enrich the story with details, events and recollections from many others who contributed as broadcasting pioneers.

Radio pioneers as Utah broadcasting unfolded and blossomed over several decades, beginning in the 1920s, determined what it would become, defined what it accomplished, and owned what it became. Some of these same people later pioneered Utah television broadcasting and cable television. This is a history of enterprise and the impulse to risk everything to achieve material success, economic freedom and self-governance, showing that the true added-value capital of Utah radio and television broadcasting and cable television was not only about money, equipment and enterprise but also of entrepreneurial mind and innovative spirit – the signature values of Utah pioneer culture.

Although treated here individually, it is argued the selected pioneers were united in a distinctive entrepreneurial mindset. Examining these individuals and their decisions reveal a cohesive history of the first decades of Utah radio and television broadcasting and cable television. Thus, seemingly disparate and disconnected individuals are tied together in a longitudinal narrative of achievement and vision.

During the period from the early 1900s going into the 1950s and beyond, selected broadcasting and cable pioneers established businesses that became the foundation for a market structure of the Utah broadcasting and cable industries that has endured with commendable resilience in an age of digital, immersive media consumption.

This story of the evolution of Utah's first ten pioneer radio and three television stations offering a broadcasting service is based on a plain premise. Utah broadcasting was not the result of haphazard, isolated or distinct events over time. Broadcasting in America and in Utah was the result of government regulations and policy imperatives. It also encompassed a social process involving pioneers, early adopters and opinion and influence leaders engaged in the activities of discovering, inventing and innovating, and then communicating – that is, making common and fully accessible discoveries, inventions and innovations.

The chronicle starts with the period of 1900-1922, a prehistory, so to speak. The discussion opens on the scientific, technical and economic setting in which Pittsburgh's KDKA, America's first station to provide an enduring radio broadcasting service, emerged. This brief account of the people and their activities on the national scene provides a contextual foundation for relating the history of Utah broadcasting.

The story then turns to Utah and its first radio amateurs, who were active before and after World War I. This engages the 1916-1922 period and the 1922 founding of KZN and KDYL radio broadcasting stations in Salt Lake City, and, later, KFUR/KLO in Ogden. These three broadcasting stations were the only ones to survive the 1920s, and the discussion focuses on why these stations survived while others fell by the wayside. KZN and KDYL had similar beginnings, thanks to amateurs who secured financial backing from two Salt Lake City newspapers

Amateurs also were responsible for establishing Ogden's KLO in 1925. After its start, KLO developed with the financial backing of the Peery brothers, owners of "Ogden's Leading Amusements," and later received support from capitalist Abe L. Glasmann of the *Ogden Standard Examiner*. After he gained control of KLO in the early years, Glasmann provided the means for his sons-in-law, George C. Hatch and Cecil Heftel, to launch their broadcasting careers.

The happenings at KDYL and KZN/KSL from 1924 through the time when television was established also are chronicled. In 1924, after only two years, the respective newspaper owners of KZN and KDYL became disillusioned with radio and subsequently relinquished control to interim operators of the two stations, and eventually to promoters Earl J. Glade (who later would become mayor of Salt Lake City) and Sidney S. Fox. These men, who likely would have been comfortable and successful pitching any hard-to-sell product, fortuitously chose radio broadcasting, because, at the time, it represented the most fertile ground for their promotional talents.

The book continues with stories and recollections of other pioneers in Utah's broadcasting markets. John N. Cope and his family formed the Radio Service Corporation (RSC) as the parent to KZN, and changed its call sign to KFPT. Glade later joined KFPT and persuaded the LDS Church and the *Salt Lake Tribune* to collaborate and take over the Radio Service Corporation, which introduced the KSL call letters – perhaps the most widely recognized and familiar signal in Utah even in the 21st century. Glade's versatile entrepreneurial talents had a major impact on KSL's transition from an operation that relied heavily on the smart instincts of strong-minded

entrepreneurs to a formal enterprise directed by a corporate board of
directors. Another major personality is J. Reuben Clark, Jr., appointed RSC
president, whom in the late 1930s removed Glade from his key post at KSL – a
controversial decision that reverberated poorly and negatively in discussions
by several generations of Utah broadcasters. Glade was removed from KSL's
daily operations to RSC's corporate offices, after Clark hired Ivor Sharp, his
son-in-law, to take over management of the station. This act of nepotism is put
in context, and details surrounding the events leading to Glade's KSL ouster
are told publicly for the first time in nearly 80 years. Of course, KSL's foray into
television, beginning in 1949, is discussed extensively as well. KSL's television
origins came about through the efforts of a triumvirate that included engineer
Vince Clayton, with oversight by Sharp and Clark.

Other pioneers shaped Utah's broadcasting history as well. Sidney S. Fox's
promotional efforts anchored KDYL's place in the emerging broadcasting
market, beginning in 1926. Fox looked consistently at other business platforms
so he hired managers, engineers and others to strengthen KDYL operations,
especially as he later looked toward establishing Utah's first television station.
Fox and John Baldwin, KDYL's chief engineer, gave a pilot TV demonstration
in 1939, and put the experimental television station W6IX/KDYL on the
air nine years later. But, Fox switched paths in 1952, selling all his KDYL
broadcast holdings, worth $4,000 when he acquired the station in 1925, to
Time-Life, Inc., for $2.5 million, which would be worth approximately $21
million in today's value.

Radio grew at a healthy yet steady pace from 1927 to World War II,
which coincided with the enactment of the Radio Act of 1927 and the
Communications Act of 1934. As the discussion shows, radio's expansion
in Salt Lake City branched out to rural areas in the state, especially in Utah's
agricultural, mining and tourism communities.

At every key step as the state's broadcasting industry evolved, there always
were individuals destined to push Utah forward, including Frank Carman and
his Intermountain Broadcasting Group, which came online in the midst of the
Great Depression. It was a formidable undertaking in 1935, as details about

the difficulties in putting Salt Lake's KUTA on the air indicate. Carman, also a Utah television pioneer, founded KUTV-TV in 1954, in partnership with the Kearns-Tribune Corporation. But, he could not carry the burden of the financial risks in a new market venture and shortly after sold his share of the station to the Abe Glasmann family.

Other Utah broadcasting pioneers persevered during the Depression. In 1936, Sam G. Weiss, the son of a Uintah Basin pelt trader, established KEUB in Price, Utah but soon sold it to program director Jack Richards, whose extended family would own the station for more than 75 years. Meanwhile, in Cedar City, Leland Perry and Harold Johnson set up KSUB in 1937. KSUB struggled for stability from its earliest days and misfortunes would plague the operations for decades. Perry's story about sustaining the station through many crises adds depth to the enormous efforts Utah pioneers put into giving the state's residents plenty of broadcast options. In 1939, Clifton A. Tolboe, a contractor who collaborated with Arch L. Madsen, launched KOVO, Provo's first radio station, and the Bullen family made application for KVNU in Logan. At the same time, the beginnings of the initial Intermountain Network took shape, and would eventually comprise KLO, KOAL and KOVO.

During World War II, no new stations would be founded, but two new radio stations would come online either near the end of the war or in the postwar period – KNAK and KALL, representing the ninth and tenth pioneer stations, respectively. Among the leading figures was Howard D. Johnson who initially led the postwar expansion in radio broadcasting. Six years after he had applied for the broadcasting license, Johnson finally secured it in February 1945, just months before the end of the war, and was now permitted to put KNAK online in Salt Lake City. Other key postwar figures were George and Gene Hatch, whom with Abrelia Hinckley, obtained permission from the federal War Production Board to go forward with constructing facilities for KALL. The station was on the air in 1945, soon after the war ended.

The postwar sections of the book turn toward the stakes set for Utah's first three television stations and the first major cable television system. Some of the names are familiar to many who closely follow the state's history. The first generation of television and cable in Utah was made possible by personalities such as George Hatch, Jack Gallivan, Bob Magness and John Malone.

The final section concludes with a summary of Utah broadcasting/cable present ownership status, spanning the decades after World War II and going into the first two decades of the current century. A snapshot of the current broadcasting landscape in Utah is accompanied by projections for broadcasting and cable in the state, which is among the fastest growing in the country in terms of population. Certainly, a discussion would not be properly contextualized without accounting for shifts in government regulations and rules regarding station ownership, the continuous advancements in communication technology and the immersive presence and convergence of digital media, which has augmented new paths of convenient and immediate access to news and entertainment. Utah's 21st century broadcasting landscape resiliently portrays how the work of its pioneers from nearly a century before has stood up remarkably well.

SECTION I

THE PREHISTORY OF UTAH RADIO

CHAPTER 1

THE PRE-HISTORY OF AMERICAN AND UTAH RADIO BROADCASTING

The stories of the birth and development of radio broadcasting in Utah often have been told as anecdotes, which adds to the romanticized perceptions of visionaries being sparked by lightning-like flashes of inspiration. But, the state's broadcasting pioneers were much more grounded and pragmatic. Before a station came online, the pioneers were well aware of the work going into experimenting, proving concepts and building an infrastructure of technological knowledge. Genius was fortified not only by an acute sense of enterprise but also about the search for what pioneers in wire and wireless media were accomplishing many miles from Utah.

The prehistory is important for laying the foundation. There were three interactive dynamic social forces to bring about broadcasting in America and in Utah: science, technology and economics. Thinking about each of the forces in a social perspective is key. Science thrives on a community of peers dedicated to the methods of discovery and the empirical affirmation of new knowledge. Technology thrives on the ongoing process of invention to put new scientific knowledge into practice and widespread acceptance. Economics as a social force is served by the fruits of innovation, which makes the values of sustainability critical in the viability of market economics and the central concern of economic policy, which is efficiently allocating scarce resources for maximum output and impact. Hugh Aitken outlined these social forces in his 1965 book *Explorations in Enterprise.* The end results of the sequential interaction of these three primary social forces were new consumption patterns, expanded options for consumer behavior, the rising importance of mass media and the value of advertising, marketing, promotions and public services. Aitken emphasized that the social forces are not characterized by a linear relationship, especially as the individuals who pioneered broadcasting had roles that overlapped all three forces (science, technology and economics).[1] But, the pioneers who launched the first Utah radio and television broadcasting stations and cable systems arguably followed a discernable linear relationship. Outside of a few exceptions, they were entrepreneurs looking to maximize the economic social force by leveraging existing science and technology to build broadcasting stations and cable systems.

The pathway to radio started nearly 90 years before the first radio station came online. In 1832, Samuel F.B. Morse invented the electric telegraph and sent an electrical impulse along a wire, through which he activated an electromagnet, resulting in audible clicks. By means of a code that Morse developed, these clicks were translated into symbols and words. In 1875, Alexander Graham Bell invented the telephone, which converted words and sound into electricity, a major advancement from the dots-and-dashes vocabulary of telegraphy. The problem with both telegraphy and telephony, however, was the requirement of a wire connecting the sender and the receiver. People who were not online could not directly communicate.

Developments in broadcasting technology spread rapidly. Faraday, Maxwell, Popov, Hertz, and other scientists advanced electromagnetic radio wave knowledge essential to wireless radio development, allowing expert engineers such as de Forest, Armstrong, Fessenden, Marconi and others to develop wireless technology essential to radio broadcasting. They also played on the economic end of the spectrum of the three social forces. Marconi provided technology and economic direction for RCA's David Sarnoff, General Electric's Owen Young, and Westinghouse's Harry P. Davis. Marconi would later advise government regulators about the policy framework for advancing a radio broadcasting service.

Utah broadcasting pioneers would adapt the national template to their needs. At the turn of the century and in the early years of wireless telegraphy, the only known way of generating radio waves was by a spark-gap device. A voltage charge strong enough to jump across a gap resulted in the classic

---

1   Aitken, Hugh G. J. , ed., Explorations in Enterprise, (Cambridge, Mass.: Harvard University Press, 1965), p. 9.

snapping and clicking sounds that were coded into dots and dashes. Before WWI, a cleaner form of wireless emerged, thanks to Lee de Forest's audion tube and continuous-wave technology. Continuous radio waves, also known as unmodulated electrical waves, were interrupted with a switch that replaced the spark-gap in the communication process. It then became possible to transmit voice and music using wireless radio.

With continuous wave technology available as early as 1914, it is argued that before WW1, everything was scientifically and technically in place for radio broadcasting in America to begin. Why did it not begin until 1920? The answer lies in the economic dimension of the social process. Before WWI, the U.S. government used wireless technology for marine and war purposes while Marconi paved the road for commercial services, and amateurs used the technology as a hobby. Nearly all government, commercial and amateur radio communication prior to World War I by wireless telegraphy was accomplished using "tap-type" devices that, in the hands of skilled telegraphers, produced coded messages. However, the sending and receiving of coded messages was not the stuff by which radio broadcasting could succeed. The vast majority of Americans were unfamiliar with and uninterested in "taps radio." To be economically viable, radio had to be transformed from a communication medium used for encoded and private messages sent point-to-point, to a medium offering a broadcasting service point-to-multipoint, thereby reaching a large, heterogeneous and anonymous public audience.

After the war ended in 1919, the transformation unfolded quickly. Businesses capitalized on radio's major wartime liability – lack of security and privacy. During the war, radio was not used to send secret messages because the wireless airwaves, unlike wires, were not private, and anybody with radio receiving equipment, including the enemy, could intercept signals. After the war, this serious wartime flaw emerged as radio's major virtue in America. Thus, the evolution to a point-to-multipoint mass communication medium was complete.

Sarnoff, who helped shape the market structure of American broadcasting, explained the transformation[2]:

> There were [those] who saw in this very limitation [lack of
> privacy] radio's greatest opportunity. They envisaged the possibilities
> of a new system of mass communication by radio, which would
> enable a single voice to be heard at the same instant by countless
> millions everywhere. ... It was a method by which a liability was
> converted into an asset. The very non-privacy of the radiotelephone
> gave to it universality of application. Had our telephone messages
> over the air been confined to secret and private use, we might never
> have had any radio broadcasting.

For obvious reasons, the U.S. government controlled all uses of radio
during WWI. But after the war, if radio was to provide a broadcasting service
to the general public, it was preferable to return control of it to the private
sector. The U.S. government's inclination was to do just that, except, in doing
so, ownership of American radio would be put in the private hands of the
British-controlled Marconi Co.

At the end of the war, Marconi negotiated with Young of General
Electric for the exclusive rights to the Alexanderson Alternator, a powerful
radio transmitter. If General Electric approved exclusive rights, the Marconi
Company could have effectively controlled American radio/wireless
communication. But, Young, along with members of Congress as well as two
future presidents (Franklin D. Roosevelt, who then was acting secretary of the
U.S. Navy, and Secretary of Commerce Herbert Hoover) opposed such a move.
The story is more complicated, but on November 20, 1919, Young successfully
established the Radio Corporation of America (RCA), a consortium of
American companies, and bought out the stockholders of the Marconi
Company in America.

In Utah, RCA's absorption of the American branch of Marconi was given
little press, which belied the immense significance of Young's accomplishment

---

2   Sarnoff, David. "A lecture before The Franklin Institute," Philadelphia, Pa., November 18,
1936; published in the RCA Review, "Three Decades of Radio," 1936.

for the future of broadcasting in America and Utah. In an article on the third page of the November 21, 1919 edition of the former *Salt Lake Herald*, it was reported:

"Stockholders of the Marconi Company of America voted today in favor of the company's absorption by the Radio Corporation of America. The Radio Corporation has the financial support of the General Electric Company in this project, the latter contributing $2,500,000, partly for acquisition of American Marconi shares." Soon, AT&T, the United Fruit Company, with its receiver and antenna patents, and Westinghouse joined the RCA pool and provided the market structure for radio broadcasting in America.

With the formation of RCA and the advent of Pittsburgh's KDKA in 1920, science, technology, economics, politics and regulation were melded, by design and good fortune, to reincarnate radiotelephony into radio broadcasting. KDKA, identified as America's first radio station to offer a broadcasting service, clearly was not the result of any new scientific discovery or technological invention. In fact, during the war, Westinghouse staff already had designed, equipped and operated two radio stations. One was at the Westinghouse Plant in East Pittsburgh (2WM), and the other (2WE) was at engineer Frank Conrad's home in a residential district about five miles away. The work of both radio stations during the war was tied to serving the U.S. Signal Corps.

But, those stations did not offer a radio "broadcasting service."

After WWI, in September 1919, patent restrictions were again imposed, and Westinghouse looked for ways it could "broaden, popularize and commercialize" radio in order to recoup its investment. It first pursued the idea of a regular news service for ships at sea, using its ship-to-shore stations. This idea met with considerable negative reaction in the commercial radio marketplace and Westinghouse abandoned it. In the meantime, Conrad, with his relicensed amateur station 8XX, continued experimenting from his home. Instead of point-to-point, "private" communications, he regularly provided programming for the general public, albeit, a small audience, which had the proper receiving sets. In the early 1920s, a Pittsburgh department store, the Joseph Horne Company, placed newspaper advertisements, that highlighted its stock of radio receivers, which could be used to receive Conrad's programs. These ads were credited with boosting sales of these sets and developing an audience for Conrad.

Conrad's activities motivated Davis, then vice-president at Westinghouse, to revamp his thinking about radiotelephony, which helped him realize that confidential, private uses of radio to generate revenue were ill-advised and would not be a sustainable revenue stream. Instead, Davis concluded that broadcasting to the general public listening at home was the future of radio, as he recalled later in a recorded oral history[3]:

> It was felt that here was something that would make a new public service of a kind certain to create epochal changes in ... everyday affairs, quite as vital as had the introduction of the telephone and telegraph, or the application of electricity to lighting and to power. We became convinced we had in our hands, in this idea, the instrument that would prove to be the greatest and most direct mass communication and mass education means that had ever appeared.

Perhaps, Davis overstated Westinghouse's public versus economic interests in broadcasting, but epochal social changes in everyday life did come about as an artifact of Westinghouse employing existing radio technology. More important, however, for the purposes here, were the market changes. Westinghouse redirected its human, scientific, technical and economic resources into a radio broadcasting service, moving away from wireless telephony and establishing a market structure for the American broadcasting industry that even with the introduction of digital radio has lasted for more than 100 years.

Radio historians rely on five criteria for determining the date a radio station first went on the air to offer a "broadcasting service." A radio

---

3   National Record Center, Record Group #173, FCC Accession # 54-A-145, Record Center Location #17-81-42-1-5, Box 2, KDKA file.

broadcasting station must: (1) utilize radio waves, (2) to send non-coded sounds by speech or music, (3) in the form of a continuous program service, (4) intended to be received by the public, and (5) if after 1912, be licensed by the government.[4]

Government records confirm that a Westinghouse broadcasting application for Pittsburgh's KDKA, received by Radio Inspector S.W. Edwards at the Detroit office of the U.S. Department of Commerce on October 10, 1920, was approved, making it the nation's first officially licensed radio station offering a "broadcasting service." It was a Class 2, limited commercial license. With this provisional government license, on November 2, 1920, KDKA aired the Harding-Cox presidential election returns and became the nation's first licensed broadcasting station to begin a continuous broadcast program service intended to be received by the public.

This compact summary of the pre-history of commercial radio broadcasting sets up the next section to discuss Utah's own contributions to the prehistory in the state's new radio market.[5] To reiterate, the approach here is event driven with a focus on the impressive individuals who pioneered the first 10 Utah radio stations as well as the first three television stations and cable systems for broadcasting. It is, above all, the story of the beginnings of Utah radio broadcasting, aided predominantly by prescient entrepreneurs who fostered, promoted, nurtured and solidified the foundation for the broadcasting industry that continues to this day.

---

4   Sterling, Christopher H., and Kittross, John M., Stay Tuned: A Concise History of American Broadcasting. California: Wadsworth, 1978, p. 58.

5   For excellent accounts of the development of RCA, the patents pools, and Westinghouse, see: Davis, H.P., "The History of Broadcasting in the United States." A speech made before the Harvard University, Graduate School of Business Administration, April 21, 1928; and Sterling, Christopher H., and Kittross, John M., Stay Tuned: A Concise History of American Broadcasting. California: Wadsworth, 1978, pp. 52-58.

CHAPTER 2

IRA JOHNSTON KAAR AND
THE UTAH RADIO AMATEURS

In January 1909, with the formation of the Junior Wireless Club of New York City, and with another similar organization started by Hugo Gernsback, publisher of *Modern Electrics* magazine, wireless amateurs banded together in national radio organizations. Soon after these national clubs were formed, local wireless clubs followed. The first such local wireless club in the entire U.S, was the Radio Club of Salt Lake City, Utah, founded in September of 1909. By 1912, Salt Lake City amateurs numbered among the estimated 3,000 operators nationwide.[6]

From 1912 to 1915, Utah amateur radio thrived. Even the so-called Regulation Fifteenth of the Radio Act of 1912, which limited amateur transmissions to wavelengths not exceeding 200 meters, didn't seriously hamper Utah amateurs. Frequencies below 200 meters were considered inferior, because they supposedly didn't propagate as well as those above that threshold. In general, Utah amateurs weren't much affected by the radio law, because the U.S. Department of Commerce and Labor, under whose authority radio licenses were granted at the time, moved slowly to process inland amateur license applications. There was a greater possibility of interference to commercial traffic from coastal stations, so the government accordingly focused on applicants from seaboard states:[7]

> Amateurs in the seaboard States should write to the examining officer in their vicinity [for an amateur license]. ... Amateurs in the inland states will follow the same course, but they are requested to be patient,

---

6   Clinton B. DeSota, Two Hundred Meters and Down: The Story of Amateur Radio. (Connecticut: The American Radio Relay League, 1936), 24-25.
7   Department of Commerce and Labor, Bureau of Navigation, Regulations Governing Radio Communication, Edition September 28 (Washington D.C.: GPO, 1912),13.

as licenses probably cannot be issued to them as operators or to their
apparatus before November or December [1912]. Where application
has been made for a license and the Department has not been able to
act, through lack of time, steps toward imposing penalties of course
will not be taken.

This was a pivotal event for the future of radio broadcasting in Utah and in
all of America. From 1912 to 1915, inland amateurs, including those in Utah,
used their unlicensed code stations on nearly any frequency and at any power
they chose, to relay non-essential information to each other and to ships at sea.
If federal regulators had not exempted the unlicensed and uninspected stations
of the inland amateurs, allowing the amateurs to mostly ignore the dictate
to operate below 200 meters, there would not have been as strong a private
sector radio presence before the U.S. entered WWI. As a result, after the war,
a government monopoly of radio might have continued longer than it did and
would have inhibited the introduction of a privately-owned radio broadcasting
service to America:[8]

It is almost a certainty that, had enforcement during the first years of
the radio law been adequate, amateur radio would have been nearly
extinct by the time of America's entry into World War; and that after
the war amateur stations would never have been allowed to reopen.

Early on, because Utah amateurs had not caused any problems with their
unlicensed stations, the government did not issue any licenses to operators in
the state until 1915. The first amateur government licensee of record in Utah
was George W. Cook of Ogden with station 6CW. Stephen Besley II of Salt
Lake City with 6PA, Philip B. Stone of Murray with 6PW, Russell Moelris of
Murray followed him with 6RC, and Howard D. Harris with station 6AJA at
Ogden High School.[9] These were provisional licenses, which meant they were
issued without government inspection and without testing the operators.

When the U.S. entered the war, the government took control of all uses of

---

8   DeSota, 35.
9   Department of Commerce, Bureau of Navigation, Radio Stations of the United States,
Edition July 1, 1915, Washington, Government Printing Office, 126.)

radio, and amateurs nationwide were instructed to shut down their stations. Those amateur operators who were skilled in code often became the wireless operators needed by the government to process war communications. During WWI, one Utah amateur, Julian G. McCollom, who began his unlicensed experimental amateur station in 1908, and who was believed to be one of a few Utah active radio amateurs at that time, was a U.S. Army captain in charge of a radio company in France. After returning to Salt Lake City, he resurrected his amateur Special Land Station (6ZV). He became a radio manager for the Inter-Mountain Electric Company and, in 1922, experimented with a radio mounted in a Jewett automobile, reporting good reception of a KZN concert from the summit of Parley's Canyon.[10]

In 1917, McCollom was one of thousands of American men who used their amateur skills and were trained to help in the war effort:[11]

> As soon as war was declared, plans were made for the training of radio operators on a scale never before known. Preliminary schools were established in the various naval districts and served as feeders for the main schools at Harvard and Mare Island. The Harvard school has a capacity of nearly 4,000 students, men being graduated at present at the rate of about 180 per week. This large supply of operators made it possible for the Navy to supply radio operators to all trans-Atlantic merchant vessels, in addition to the large number of operators required for naval vessels and naval shore stations.

The reference above to male graduates of wireless schools underscored the reality of the times. Wireless, whether it was amateur, commercial or government, was regarded as turf reserved for men. The official policy of the U.S. Department of Commerce and Labor's Bureau of Navigation, however, was that "...women are eligible as applicants for licenses of any class or grade upon the same conditions as men."[12]

---

10   Deseret News, June 3, 1922, sec. 3, 1.

11   U.S. Congress. House. Committee on the Merchant Marine and Fisheries. Government Control of Radio Communication: Hearings before The Committee on the Merchant Marine and Fisheries on H.R. 13159, Testimony of Secretary of the Navy Josephus Daniels. 65th Cong., 3rd Sess., 12 December 1918, 7.

12   Department of Commerce and Labor, Bureau of Navigation, Regulations Governing Radio

Earlier, in support of discouraging women from radio service during wartime, a letter from the Director of Naval Communications to the Commissioner of Navigation contained the following:[13]

> The Naval Communication Service will appreciate the co-operation of the Department of Commerce in discouraging women from studying radio telegraphy. ... At present it is quite impossible to utilize women as radio telegraphers [in the Navy]. ... Just recently this office has had occasion to call the attention of the Editor of a popular magazine to a very misleading article which appeared (to intimate) that the Navy was planning to place women in charge of important shore radio stations.

So, despite the official affirmation of women in radio during peacetime, war was different. A release from the Division of Women's War Work reiterated the ban for women telegraphers:[14]

> Radio inspectors of the Department of Commerce have been instructed to advise women who are ambitious to become radio telegraphers to study Morse (wired) telegraphy instead. Because of a great shortage of competent telegraphers at the present time the Western Union Telegraph Co. is so anxious to get operators that it undertakes their instruction and pays them while learning.

No Utah woman of record applied for amateur or commercial status during the war or, in fact, before the 1930s. Only one woman in the entire U.S. was believed licensed as a commercial radio operator on shipboard during WWI.[15] She was Elizabeth Lansdale DuVal of Baltimore, Maryland, who

---

Communication (Washington D.C.: GPO, 28 September 1912, 13.

13   Navy Department, Naval Communication Service, Office of the Director, Washington, D.C., Letter to the Commissioner of Navigation, Department of Commerce, from D. W. Todd, Commander, U. S. N., Director Naval Communications, November 10, 1917.

14   Department of Commerce. Committee on Public Information, Division of Woman's War Work. Release from Helen Randall, 19 February 1918. File 907NR. National Archives. Washington, D.C.

15   Department of Commerce. Committee on Public Information, Division of Woman's War Work. Release from Helen Randall, 19 February 1918. File 907NR.

obtained a first grade commercial license and was employed on the HOWARD of the Merchants and Miners Line, having been assigned as junior operator on December 4, 1917, several months after the U.S. declared war against Germany. Duval was in sole charge of the wireless station from one until six o'clock every afternoon and on watch each night from half past one until eight in the morning. She was the daughter of Edmund Brice DuVal and the great granddaughter of Judge Gabriel DuVal, one of the early justices of the U.S. Supreme Court. Possibly her influential family helped her to successfully secure a radio position aboard ship when all other women were discouraged.

Even if women of record were not involved in Utah wireless, four women were at the heart of early Utah wired telegraphy. In 1866, when "men couldn't make enough money" in telegraphy to support their families, four Utah women became skilled operators: Elizabeth Claridge, Belle Parkes, Hetty Grace, and Mary Ellen Love.[16] These women worked in telegraphic relay offices from St. George to Nephi, often working out of their homes while raising families. They were close friends and stayed in touch by chatting in code after business hours. These women accomplished in wire communication in 1866 what no Utah woman chose or was allowed to do in amateur wireless.

After WWI, some amateurs began to use voice, instead of code. But, the voice-operators were perceived by code-operators as not maintaining high standards. According to amateur code-operators, radiotelephony required no operator skill and no commitment to the community of amateurs, whose reason for existence was to master code technique for public service. Voice operators were perceived as too chatty and a threat to the amateur wireless culture. In addition, a phone or voice station was not considered efficient because it took five times the scarce spectrum space of a code station to operate. This conflict, however, did not expand because the overwhelming number of amateurs in Utah and across the nation operated code instead of phone stations, well into the 1930s. Nevertheless, this was an important part of the social process that provided another clue in explaining why radio broadcasting developed as it did.

---

16   Department of Commerce. Committee on Public Information, Division of Women's War Work. Release from Helen Randall, 19 February 1918. File 907NR.

Using more powerful and sophisticated technology, both of these amateur factions in America planted seeds in the electronic global village and lost their insularity. Voice station operators often used their stations to transmit to the general public, much like broadcasters soon would be capable of operating. At the same time, code amateurs clarified and solidified their public service role by turning to experimenting with long distant and transoceanic communication. Both amateur factions achieved a status in communication that nobody else achieved: They became "...the only class on earth capable of communicating beyond the range of their own senses without paying a toll to some governmental agency or commercial corporation."[17]

Ira J. Kaar

After the war, some Utah amateurs followed radio-related careers in engineering, manufacturing and sales, but many did not directly apply their wireless experience to radio broadcasting, sans a continuous program service. One significant exception was Ira Johnston Kaar, a particularly important Utah amateur in the 1910s and 1920s because of his ubiquitous technical and operational presence in the development of nearly every Utah radio broadcasting station in the early 1920s. Kaar was born October 17, 1902, in Dunsmuir, California, to Homer O. and Margaret Johnston Kaar. The family moved to Salt Lake City in 1906, and Ira's father began as an apprentice and worked his way up to foreman of one of the largest automobile garages in Salt Lake City. He later sold Jordan and Mercer automobiles. In 1919 he began commuting from Salt Lake City to Denver as vice president of the Victor Clutch and Motor Company.[18]

As a young man, Kaar was not gregarious and did not particularly enjoy the company of those who did not share his passion for or knowledge of science and engineering:[19]

---

17   DeSota, 3.
18   Salt Lake Telegram, November 12, 1919, Automotive Section, 3.
19   Mervin Hogan, Telephone interview by Paul Rose, May 20, 1990, Salt Lake City.

He was not a mixer with any of the students. He was a very mature
individual. There was no horsing around. Very business like. Ira
Kaar was one of those rare individuals who had the judgment to
listen to other, older men advise him that you start at the bottom [of]
something that's expanding and are prepared for the steps. He was a
tremendously capable individual.

From an early age, Kaar (who went by the nickname 'Ike') was interested
in electrical engineering and applied research. He was influenced by the work
of the German educated Charles P. Steinmetz and later he even emulated
Steinmetz by going to General Electric to work. Another influential personality
was Michael I. Pupin, who had moved the electrical engineering field from
a craft toward a profession. Steinmetz and Pupin represented a new breed of
electrical engineers whose aim was to maximize the professional influences on
the field and minimize industrial and business pressures. In May 1912, when
pressing business influences in the prestigious American Institute of Electrical
Engineers (AIEE) threatened the professional integrity of scientific work, some
members left to form the Institute of Radio Engineers (IRE). Membership
standards were aimed at making IRE a highly exclusive, international
professional fellowship:[20]

[A person wanting to join IRE] … had to be at least 27, a professional
electrical engineer in active practice for at least five years, and
in "responsible charge" for at least two years. Most important of
all, the candidate had to be qualified to design as well as direct
electrical engineering works. These requirements effectively
excluded businessmen and managers who were not fully qualified
engineers. The close kinship of electrical engineering with science was
recognized by an alternate qualification of having done original work
of value to electrical science.

Although not yet 27 years old or a practicing engineer, Kaar easily
subscribed to the admission requirements, standards of excellence, and the

---

20   Edwin T. Layton, Jr., The Revolt of the Engineers: Social Responsibility and the American
Engineering Profession, Baltimore: The Johns Hopkins University Press, 1986), 39. Note: These
requirements were those of the AIEE before 1912, but were adopted by the IRE after it was formed.

professional versus commercial orientation of IRE. As a teenager, he aspired
to become the kind of scientist-engineer – the kind of human being he thought
worthy of IRE membership. What started for Kaar as an amateur hobby soon
became the essence of his personal and professional identity and the reason for
his very existence.

In 1912, at the age of 10, Kaar first showed the spirit of enterprise in the
field that would become his lifelong career. With Art Johnson, a boyhood
friend and neighbor, he constructed a receiver that consisted of a coherer, a
device used by Marconi in his early experiments. Kaar described the apparatus
as:[21]

> [A] a glass tube filled with iron filings with two electrodes at the
> ends. It was struck by the tapper of a doorbell. When a signal was
> received, the iron filings would cling together and pass a current that
> could operate a telegraph sounder. Then the clapper would strike the
> coherer and dislodge the iron filings and the thing would be open
> again for a new signal.

During this time, Kaar and his friend also successfully constructed
a telegraphic line between their neighboring houses on 700 South Street
near the downtown area of Salt Lake City. But, that was merely for wired
communication and for Kaar, as he described it, "that fad soon passed away."
Kaar's attention shifted exclusively to wireless over the next couple of years.
He employed the Ford spark coil – so named after the Ford automobile that
used the device in its ignition system – to produce the critical spark across a
gap. In conjunction with a galena (sulphide and silicon) crystal detector and a
radiating antenna, Kaar used the spark coil to communicate by wireless code
with, among others, a young amateur, Jack Ensign, who lived more than a mile
away near the State Capitol Building in Salt Lake.[22]

In 1916, at age 14, with four years of amateur experience, Kaar obtained
his first amateur radio license – for station 6QQ. Like other Utah amateurs,

<hr>

21   Ira J. Kaar, Interview by Tim Larson, 21 April 1986, tape nos. U-456 and U-457, transcript,
Everett L. Cooley Oral History Project, Marriott Library, University of Utah, Salt Lake City, UT, 3.
22   Ira J. Kaar, Interview by Tim Larson, 3.

he had been active for several years without a license. Kaar's 6QQ was a
typical code station in that it initially employed a stationary spark gap and
later a rotary spark gap system. Kaar was resourceful in scrounging up parts
and materials for his amateur station. His rotary spark gap device employed
a disk on which studs were mounted. The disk turned at a high rate of speed
past stationary electrodes, and the spark would take place on contact with the
studs and then would be interrupted when the studs passed the electrodes.
One problem existed with the rotary spark gap device, however. The disk had
to turn at about 15,000 RPM and finding a motor to turn at that speed was
difficult at the time. Kaar explained how he solved this problem:[23]

> The answer came in the use of a vacuum cleaner motor, which I took
> from [junk] and mounted on a new base, provided it with the spark-
> gap disk, and I was in business.

Kaar also scrounged up photographic plates to build the condenser for
his amateur station:[24]

> I found a photographer on State St. who was willing to sell to me
> plates, which had been used and were in his files. But to make sure
> that I didn't use the image, he scratched it all off before he sold me
> the plates. He charged me, I think, ten cents each for those plates. I
> covered them with copper foil and stacked them up, inserted the
> whole assembly into a tank of transformer oil, and I had a good
> condenser to use with the spark gap.

Obviously confident in his enterprising skills, Kaar built an antenna and
attached one end to a wooden extension on a power pole and the other end to
pulleys and supports he installed in a tree in the yard of his parent's home on
700 South in Salt Lake City:[25]

> Later I abandoned the power pole at the rather urgent invitation of
> the power company and built a double two-by-four mast with guys at

---

23   Ira J. Kaar, Interview by Tim Larson, 4.
24   Ira J. Kaar, Interview by Tim Larson, 5.
25   Ira J. Kaar, Interview by Tim Larson, 4.

four places. This mast stood sixty feet high, and I was very proud of
it indeed.

Kaar was focused and impassioned, and the nucleus of his existence soon
became the pursuit of hard sciences and mathematics. He gravitated to the
scientific and the natural laws of physics and away from the humanistic and the
supernatural. In 1916, Kaar entered the Latter Day Saints University, which,
despite its name, was primarily a high school. LDSU was the descendant of
the LDS Business College, itself the progeny of the Salt Lake Stake Academy
founded in 1886. LDSU was located on Main Street in the city's downtown, on
the property presently housing the gardens between the old Hotel Utah (now
the Joseph P. Smith Building) and the LDS Church Office Building in Salt Lake
City. In 1916, the main entrance to LDSU was fronted on North Temple.

LDSU was, in part, supported by the LDS Church and had a great interest
in the moral and religious training of its students. The school offered religion
classes and held devotional services, but these amenities were not what
attracted Kaar to LDSU. He chose it because it had the best laboratories of any
of the high schools in Salt Lake City, and because it had a very good library of
books on wireless telegraphy. Here is where Kaar was introduced to the work
of Fessenden, Hertz, Popoff, Pierce and many other pioneers of electricity and
wireless. Regarding the superior laboratories at LDSU, Mervin Hogan, a friend
and LDSU classmate of Kaar, relates:[26]

> When I left the LDS High School in the spring of '23 and registered at
> the University of Utah, I ventured into engineering and I tell you their
> laboratories and facilities were pretty shabby in the sciences, [or]
> chemistry and physics, compared with LDS High School.

At this time, some of the original Utah amateurs applied for special
licenses to allow them to use frequencies above 200 meters. In January, 1916,
as mentioned earlier, McCollom obtained one of the first amateur Special Land
Station licenses in Utah for station 6ZV, and in August Beasley obtained the
second for 6ZI . That same month, Conrad obtained his license in Pittsburgh

---

26   Mervin Hogan, Telephone interview by Paul Rose.

for Special Land Station 8XK, which was the forerunner of KDKA, the nation's first radio broadcasting station.

Kaar didn't have a Special Land Station license, but he communicated by code on 6QQ until April 1917, when, like McCollom, Beasely and all the amateur and commercial radio station operators, received a letter from the U.S. War Department instructing him to dismantle his wireless transmitter and receiver for the duration of the war. Obviously, he complied.

In 1919, while the wartime ban was still in effect, Kaar was instrumental in forming a society at LDSU that took on the acronym S.S.S. As Kaar penned in the LDSU student newspaper, *The Gold and Blue,* in April 1919, "S.S.S. did not stand for 'Sunday School Sharks' or 'Scientific Singers of Songs,' but for the 'Saints Scientific Society.'"[27] The S.S.S. was an organization for LDSU students interested in photography, chemistry, physics, electronics and, of course, wireless. Kaar served as vice-president and later as president of the S.S.S.

Meanwhile the U.S. government lifted the ban on radio receivers on April 15, 1919, but maintained it on transmitters. In September of that year, in anticipation of the lifting of the transmitter ban, Kaar began constructing an amateur radio station at LDSU for S.S.S. members. It was a 50-watt code station that he built in the physics lab housed in what is now known as the Joseph Smith Memorial Building. As Kaar recollects, two students could carry the simple transmitter up to the movie projection room in the gallery of Barratt Hall, an auditorium where the whole student body met for religious services, news and announcements. From the small projection room, a thick antenna wire was hoisted to the top of a nearby flagpole and the station was in operation. The situation in late 1919 at LDSU looked like the following:[28]

> Ira Kaar, head of the radio Division, is ably assisted by Marvin
> Andelin, who was an operator on board ship for some months, and
> can therefore tickle the old key until it itches. Brother Howells has
> been imbibing radio wisdom all summer at the Leland Stanford

---

27   The Gold and Blue, (Latter Day Saints periodical), April 1919, 148.
28   The Gold and Blue, (Latter Day Saints University periodical), November 1919, p. 52.

University of California, and will assist Kaar, so some of these nearby radio stations are very apt to hear some awful "Howelling" in the near future from some of the amateurs.

Marvin Andelin and Thomas Howells also were radio amateurs. Andelin, with amateur station 6JT, was an older LDSU student than Kaar, while Howells, head of physics at LDSU, was the S.S.S. faculty advisor. By 1922, Howells simultaneously held licenses for 6BBF, the LDSU station which later became broadcasting station KFOO, and for one at his home, station 6BAL at 1777 Crystal Avenue in Sugar House. Despite the above allusion to Howells "imbibing radio wisdom," he was a Stanford student working on his doctorate in psychology, and his S.S.S forte was in the photography area, not radio engineering. As Andelin said: "Kaar was the one who knew radio."[29]

Mervin Hogan corroborated Andelin's words:[30]

> Ike Kaar was a one-man deal. He was the trouble-shooter, the operator, and the what-not. He ran the whole thing. It wasn't a matter of having any help. He had to program it and everything. You just can't imagine it. There were some people with great ability in those days and Ike Kaar certainly stands as one of the greatest products of the LDS High School and the University of Utah.

After the transmitter ban finally was lifted in late 1919, Kaar applied for his own Special Land Station license. In January 1920, he was given the call letters 6ZA. Special Land Station call letters in the western states began with the "6-Z" prefix, with "6" designating the Sixth-District, and "Z" designating an amateur Special Land station. A letter of the alphabet beginning at "A" and going in order then followed these two designations. With the "6-Z-A" call letters, it would appear that after the war, Kaar obtained the first Special Land Station in the Sixth District, which included California, Nevada, Utah, Arizona and the Hawaii territory. This may not be accurate, however, because even though he obtained 6ZA, it is not known if after the war some amateurs requested some

---

29   Marvin S. Andelin, Interview by Tim Larson, 23 July 1990, Salt Lake City, UT.
30   Mervin Hogan, Telephone interview by Paul Rose.

semblance of their pre-war call letters. Nevertheless, Kaar certainly was among the first in the Sixth District to receive a Special Land station license after the war. He was given "special" rights and exemptions with 6ZA:[31]

> In the case of special amateur stations, wave length in excess of 200 meters is permitted for the special amateur relay work, or emergency work such as that performed in the flood districts, and ordinary communications between special amateur and special amateur station should not in any case be conducted on wave lengths in excess of 200 meters ... or power in excess of one-half kilowatt or one kilowatt, depending upon the location of the station.

It was important for Kaar to be exempted from using 1-kilowatt of power on wavelengths below 200 meters because of his involvement in the American Radio Relay League (ARRL), an organization formed in May 1914, by amateur guru Hiram Percy Maxim of Hartford, Connecticut. In January 1920, Kaar began using 6ZA as an Intermountain nexus in the highway of ARRL stations that relayed messages back and forth across the U.S. and around the world.

At the time, this kind of radiotelephone relay work, not broadcasting, was thought to represent the future for wireless. The July 1914, issue of *Popular Mechanics* echoed the views of the ARRL founders:[32]

> The coming of wireless telegraphy has made it possible for the private citizen to communicate across great distances without the aid of either the government or a corporation, so that the organization of the relay league actually marks the beginning of a new epoch in the interchange of information and the transmission of messages.

Kaar was involved with ARRL from its inception in 1914, and became its assistant manager for the Rocky Mountain District after the war and Andelin became ARRL manager. In these positions, Kaar and Andelin not only relayed messages but also were the official ARRL local inspectors of amateur stations,

---

31   Bureau of Navigation, Department of Commerce, Radio Service Bulletin, Washington, D.C.: GPO, 1 March 1917, 10.
32   DeSota, 40.

because, as stated above, few inland amateur stations were ever inspected:[33]

Lionel Cornwell, who became a nationally respected sound engineer, related that he and "Johnny" Cope in the early 1920s couldn't get their amateur station to operate correctly, so they called their friend and ARRL "government-man, Ikie Kaar," who tuned it and made it work perfectly.

When Art Johnson, Kaar's friend and next-door neighbor on 700 South Street., set up his Special Land Station for use by the Air Mail Service at the Fairgrounds in Salt Lake, he also earned Kaar's approval. In a March 1, 1921, telegram to the Commission of Navigation, Washington, D.C., Johnson wrote:

> SPECIAL AMATEUR LICENSE WAS APPLIED FOR APPROVED AND FORWARDED BY LOCAL DISTRICT RADIO INSPECTOR ABOUT A MONTH AGO DESIRE TO START OPERATION AT ONCE AND AM HOLDING UP COMMISSION OF STATION PENDING RECEIPT OF LICENSE WOULD APPRECIATE YOUR EXPEDITING ACTION IN THIS MATTER KINDLY ADVISE.

Kaar was the "local district radio inspector" for ARRL to which Johnson referred in his telegram. On March 3, 1920, Johnson's license was issued and he began operating the Salt Lake radio link for the Air Mail service. Johnson was even said to have guided a plane to a safe landing in a blinding snowstorm using radio.

ARRL also published a monthly magazine called *QST* – which is amateur radio shorthand for "Calling all stations" or "Calling all Ams (Hams)." *QST* was started in December 1915, to keep the amateur wireless operators of the country in touch with each other and to maintain high standards of amateur operation.

The June 1920 issue of *QST* included a description and photograph of Kaar's 6ZA Special Land station. It was this code station that Kaar modified

---

33   Lionel Cornwell reminisces on tape, circa. 1960.

for voice and turned into the KDYL broadcasting station two years later. The QST article read:[34]

> 6ZA is the station of the Assistant Manager of the Rocky Mountain Division [of ARRL], Mr. Ira J. Kaar, at Salt Lake City, Utah, and this photograph shows it to be excellently outfitted. The transmitter is a 1 K.W. 'Thor', knife-edge rotary gap. ... [It] constitutes splendid arrangement and makes for increased efficiency. We don't see how it could be improved. The receiver consists of the conventional tuning apparatus with single step amplifier ... [and] ... a short wave regenerative set. ...On the right will be noticed a DeForest panel telephone set. 6ZA can work nearly all the west coast amateurs, also 5ZA and 9JE to the east, and is doing excellent relay work. Communicating record to date, 850 miles; receiving record 8000 miles. Pretty good.

In early 1920, ... "Da--da da --da-a -- and the first official wireless message ever sent from the L.D.S.U. flashed through space. Ralph Baker of South Ninth East ... answered back, 'Science controls the universe, with it nothing is impossible.'"

After he constructed the station at LDSU, Kaar was not much interested in it because he considered it to be unsophisticated. Instead, he would often transmit from his home using his Special Land Station, 6ZA, for the benefit of those operating the S.S.S. station at LDSU:

> The S.S.S. radio division, Eugene Pack in charge, got in communication with Kaar, who was at home, who played several phonographic selections for our benefit, which were transmitted to us over the radio phone with which he is experimenting. Brother Thatcher was listening and called for classical music at first, but finally decided that jazz carried better.

---

34   QST, Kenneth B. Warner manager and editor, published by the American Radio Relay League, Inc. Hartford, Conn. , Volume III, No. 11, June 1920, 39

Eugene Pack later became a highly talented and respected broadcast engineer at KSL and was technically responsible for several Utah stations.

Kaar graduated from LDSU in the spring of 1920 and prepared to enter The University of Utah that fall. It had been only three months since his thirteen-year-old brother, Dean, was killed in a shooting accident, and he wanted to get away for the summer. For several years Kaar had been hearing messages on 6ZA from steamships, and he had an interest in being a wireless operator on a ship, just like Andelin, his friend:[35]

> I went to San Francisco, took the examination for a commercial operator's license, and then haunted the docks for, it seemed to me, weeks, before I finally found a job on the steamship "Newport", a ship which I had heard many times on my station in Salt Lake. When I went aboard this steamer, I had no idea where we were going. I was satisfied that I had a job, that I was going to eat and have some place to sleep, and that I was going to return to San Francisco.

The steamer U.S.S. Newport went to Panama, through the canal and back, and returned up the west coast. It was a mail carrier that stopped at all the ports along the coast of Central America. Many of these port cities have now become big tourist destinations, but they were not very inviting when Kaar visited them. He remembers Mazatlan, for instance, as very unattractive with whitewashed adobe huts and a sanitation system consisting of sewage ditch which ran down the middle of the street. A stop in Acapulco, however, was especially memorable because he was invited aboard the U.S. warship Cleveland, to see the radio room:[36]

> It was a very welcome trip to me because I saw some modern radio equipment. It was a tube transmitter ... using the Bell Lab's tube. I think it was a VT2. One of the operators, sensing my interest, presented me with two of those tubes, courtesy of the U.S. Navy, which I guarded carefully and took home with me to [6ZA] my

35   Ira J. Kaar, Interview by Tim Larson, 6.
36   Ira J. Kaar, Interview by Tim Larson, 7-8.

station. When I got home, I built a transmitter around those two tubes. It had power output of five watts, but it did transmit a voice signal to my amateur friends around Salt Lake City, and I don't know how much further its range would be because I didn't hear from anyone else.

Upon his return from sea in September 1920, Kaar enrolled at The University of Utah and pursued a bachelor of science degree in electrical engineering. Over the next four years, he took dozens of classes in engineering, math and the hard sciences, as well as English and other subjects. His grade record shows that his head and heart were in the engineering, math and English courses, in which he earned "A's" and "B's," and not in shop-practice and physical education, where he received "C's."

He did have one course in engineering, however, in which he reportedly had trouble. As indicated above, Kaar was focused on electronics to the near exclusion of everything else in his life and, by the time he reached The University of Utah, was also quite confident in his abilities. When asked about it, Kaar did not remember this encounter, but his classmate Hogan clearly remembered that Kaar was taking a surveying class and had a near disastrous encounter with the civil engineering professor teaching it:[37]

Ike was never an individual that fiddled around – a very mature individual. ... He had one individual that he locked horns with and that was Howard L. Baldwin who taught surveying, and who was in the civil engineering department. ... He was a young buck – thought he was pretty damn smart himself – and he and Ike just locked horns. Ike couldn't see why he should spend afternoons making a fake survey of the railroad line up through Dry Canyon. That didn't amount to anything to him. He let Baldwin know that he didn't give a damn about surveying or anybody who surveyed – there were other things in life and in engineering besides surveying. Baldwin was just inflamed – they locked horns. Kaar almost didn't graduate.

---

37   Mervin Hogan, Interview by Tim Larson, August 17, 1990, Salt Lake City.

In the summer of his freshman year, Kaar took what he called a vacation with the U.S. Forest Service in the Coeur D'Alene National Forest in Idaho. His job was to erect antennas, to build small shanties and to install radiotelephone equipment for the purpose of reporting forest fires. The Forest Service had an unsatisfactory telephone system, consisting of wires strung on fence posts and hung through the trees. When a fire or a storm would occur, trees would fall severing the wires, and there would be no emergency communication:[38]

> The chief forester thought that perhaps radio communication would serve their purpose better. He obtained an appropriation and bought some equipment from General Electric. The receivers and transmitters that were purchased were designed originally for the NC4 seaplanes of the United States Navy. These were the planes that made the first trips across the Atlantic Ocean, and this was the equipment they carried. By a change of wavelength, we adapted these sets for the Forest Service use, and they worked very well.

Kaar and McCullough, his friend from his boyhood days and fellow University of Utah engineering student, worked together that summer and installed stations in McCall, Warren, Coeur D'Alene, and several other places in Idaho. Kaar says of the adventure: "Anyway, these transmitters worked very well besides providing a very interesting and pleasant vacation."[39] Arch L. Madsen and Cutler R. Miller, Utah amateurs who later became broadcasting professionals, had a similar U.S. Forest Service experience a decade later.

Also during college, Kaar was employed for a period at the Baldwin Loud Speaker Company in Holladay, at 3474 South 23rd East. The Nathaniel Baldwin Company made superb ear phones used in conjunction with early wireless components. Nathaniel Baldwin reportedly started the company when he was struck with the difficulty of hearing in the Salt Lake Tabernacle. He then sought to invent a system to amplify sound. In 1910 he patented an amplification system that he incorporated into a receiver headset. Within each earphone was coiled a mile of fine copper wiring and a mica diaphragm, giving

---

38   Ira J. Kaar, Interview by Tim Larson, 21 April 1986, 9.
39   Ira J. Kaar, Interview by Tim Larson, 9.

the Baldwin headset the most sensitive reception yet possible.[40]

In the beginning Baldwin had difficulty persuading others about his invention, but in anticipation of the war breaking out, the U.S. Navy tested the earphones and placed large orders with him for all its ships. This was the main reason for Baldwin's early success. At its height in 1922, the Baldwin Company employed 150 men and women on an around-the-clock schedule, turning out 150 headsets per day for customers all over the world:[41]

> Baldwin products were recognized throughout the country and in
> a number of foreign lands as the highest grade of radio receiver on
> the market. Customers apparently agreed because the comparatively
> expensive equipment was in heavy demand. It has been said that
> ... Baldwin was offered over a million dollars for his company but
> declined for fear that the business would be moved out of state and
> that local residents would be robbed of employment.

In the early 1920s, after broadcasting became popular, Baldwin added a horn to his earphone to make it a loudspeaker so more than one person could listen at a time to radio. But despite his significant invention, Baldwin is not acknowledged as important to radio broadcasting in Utah or the nation because his earphones were stand-alone components and were not incorporated into the sets of any large radio receiver manufacturers. Nonetheless, Baldwin earphones were considered essential for any transmitting or receiving station around the country in the early 1920s. While working for Baldwin, Kaar made for himself a silver-plated earphone headset that remains today as the only working item from his 6ZA amateur station and the wireless era. Kaar gave me the Baldwin headset he made for himself while working at the company.

Kaar had many amateur friends but no wireless equals, either among his peers or elders. Even at the age of 20, he was the mentor of many Utah amateur radio enthusiasts who later went into broadcasting, including KDYL's

<hr>

40   Merrill Singer, "Nathaniel Baldwin, Utah Inventor and Patron of the Fundamentalist Movement," Utah Historical Quarterly, 47 (Winter, 1979), 48.
41   Merrill Singer, 49.

Harold Mailander and Everett (Hap) Seeley; KZN's H. C. (Harry) Wilson; John N. Cope and Lionel Cornwell, and KSL's Eugene Pack. For some like Frank Carman, who in the 1930s engineered KOAL in Price and constructed KUTA in Salt Lake, Kaar was more than a mentor – he was an idol. Carman said that "...his interest in communication was stimulated by his admiration for such radio pioneers as Ike Kaar and the late Everett Seeley – somewhat older Salt Lake boys who had the 'radio bug.'"

In 1921, Kaar was approached by A. L. Fish, publisher of *The Telegram* in Salt Lake City, to construct a broadcasting station for the newspaper. Kaar began broadcasting for *The Telegram* from his parent's home on May 10,1922, using the KDYL call letters. While constructing KDYL, Kaar regularly helped fellow amateur H. Carter Wilson with engineering problems at KZN, which went on the air on May 6, 1922, four days earlier than Kaar officially opened KDYL. The events surrounding the opening of KZN and KDYL in 1922 are discussed in more detail in the next chapter.

To round out Kaar's story, in early 1923, while a university engineering student, Kaar constructed a radio broadcasting station at The University of Utah. The students in the School of Mines and Engineering operated KFUT, and Kaar secured its first license in June 1923. It became the forerunner of K-UTE, the campus radio station that was launched in the 1990s and continues to this day. However, KFUT had not been in continual operation since 1923.

Kaar, having completed his degree in 1924, was hired by General Electric and moved to Schenectady, New York, to work in the company's research lab. He went with a strong recommendation from H. T. Plumb, General Electric's manager in Salt Lake City and Kaar's mentor:[42]

> The bearer of this letter, Mr. Ira J. Kaar, recently has entered our testing department. I would like him to become acquainted with some of our leading engineers at Schenectady, and take the liberty of asking you to be interested in Mr. Kaar and help him to meet other

---

42   H.T. Plumb, General Electric Company, Salt Lake City, Letter to Dr. S. Dushman, Research Laboratory, General Electric Co., Schenectady, New York, November 5, 1924.

scientific men who may assist in his advancement. Mr. Kaar, who is a graduate of the University of Utah, has been very much interested in radio for a number of years and I believe has considerable potential ability along that line.

General Electric, founded in 1892, was a perfect place for the scientist-engineer Kaar who was employed there for decades. New discoveries and the introduction of new products in new markets was the General Electric norm. This was why the General Electric Research Laboratory and the Engineering Laboratory existed; it was why great scientist-engineers such as Charles P. Steinmetz (Kaar's boyhood idol), Willis R. Whitney, Ernst F.W. Alexanderson, William Coolidge and Irving Langmuir came to General Electric, and why they stayed there.

Kaar's legacy fortunately has been preserved, as the extensive volumes of his professional papers and correspondence are housed in The University of Utah Marriott Library's Special Collections. The archives are open to the public and many of the records have been digitized for convenient access. Indeed, Kaar had the foresight to ensure that the stories of the flourishing start to Utah's broadcasting era and the hard-working entrepreneurs who made it possible would never be lost. It is a fitting parallel to their recognition of radio as a medium that would burrow deep roots in modern society and even the most distant and rural communities in Utah.

The story now turns to the rapid evolution of Utah radio broadcasting station services beginning in the early 1920s, with the help of the radio amateurs who so far have been discussed in this book.

CHAPTER 3

UTAH SETS THE FOUNDATION FOR RADIO BROADCASTING

The Landscape in 1922

In 1922, terrorism in Belfast, Ireland and its environs again assumed massive proportions. In Washington, D.C. President Warren G. Harding dedicated the Lincoln Memorial. Near Orem, Utah, the Timpanogos Cave was preparing to open. In Salt Lake City, at Wandamere Park, workers were preparing a golf course to be named after Bishop Charles W. Nibley, who donated the grounds. The Salt Lake Commercial Club placed ads in 20 publications nationwide touting, "See Salt Lake City, the Center of Scenic America." Fifty responses were received nationwide and the Club proclaimed, "Advertising pays and brings results."

In May 1922, 54 daily newspapers across the U.S. had radio broadcasting licenses and were broadcasting news. Two newspapers in Salt Lake City added to that by putting radio broadcasting stations on the air. The *Deseret News* put KZN, which later assumed the KSL call sign, officially on the air on May 6. *The Salt Lake Telegram* put KDYL on the air on May 10. Both stations had been heard testing prior to their inaugural broadcasts. From the top of the Deseret New Building H.C. Wilson tested KZN, and I. J. Kaar from his parent's home at 234 East 700 South tested KDYL.

As noted earlier, in recounting radio history and pointing to the development of radio broadcasting in Utah, one might look at it as if it was created and had a life of its own, without considering the implications of human intervention or contribution. Early radio broadcasting was governed by federal regulations enacted and enforced by officials who, enabled by engineers, strived to evolve this technology to serve the "public interest, convenience or necessity." The new radio broadcasting service evolved from a private point-to-point service into a public point-to- multipoint broadcasting service.

In the chapters to follow, the successful applicants involved in the first 10 pioneer Utah radio broadcasting stations are compared to the applications from those individuals who sought broadcasting licenses but failed to acquire them. The history starts with the first three Utah radio stations, KZN, KDYL and KFUR, and their pioneering founders. Then beginning in the mid-1930s, the stories of the seven other applicants who comprise the pioneering group of 10 stations in Utah are recounted. Later in the book, the reader will note that essentially the same people who pioneered the first three Utah radio stations also founded the first three Utah television stations.

Emerging Policy and Regulations

Regulations governing the radio broadcasting industry and to a great extent regulations setting ownership standards have surely helped to mold the market structure of the broadcasting and cable industries, possibly more than the market based advertising structure. Since the early 1900s, Congress has enacted radio regulations that introduced prodigious cultural and significant technological changes as radio evolved from a point-to-point personal telephone-like service into a point-to-multipoint public broadcasting service.

Radio broadcasting station ownership regulations have progressed significantly since the first 10 Utah pioneer radio founders filed their broadcast station license applications. Some of the laws shaping radio broadcasting's market structure early on, however, were not enacted specifically for radio broadcasting. For instance, government antitrust laws applied to the radio industry, including the Sherman Antitrust Act (1890) which dealt with unfair competition locally and nationally; the Clayton Act (1914), which dealt with monopoly behavior; and the Federal Trade Commission Act (1914) and Wheeler-Lea Act (1938), which dealt with unfair or deceptive acts or practices in commerce.

Antitrust laws likely did not much concern the first three enduring Utah broadcasting station applicants (KZN, KDYL, KFUR). But, applicants in the 1930s had more concern. Antitrust laws were tied to radio broadcasting in Sections 313 and 314 of the Communications Act of 1934, expressly stating that when such laws are violated, it could result in denying broadcast licenses.

But, the applicants for the first three stations, beginning in 1922, primarily were subject to the Radio Act of 1912 that updated the Wireless Ship Act of 1910. The next paragraphs summarize this early period of enacted legislation.

Wireless Ship Act of 1910

The first U.S. radio communication regulation, the Wireless Ship Act or the Radio Act of 1910 (July 24, 1910) required a ship carrying 60 passengers, and traveling 200 miles from a U.S. port, to have wireless radio equipment with a range of at least one hundred miles. It did not require a license or assign operating frequencies. It was the first time Congress seriously entered radio's regulatory dominion.

Radio Act of 1912

On April 14,1912, near midnight the RMS Titanic luxury ship hit an iceberg and sunk in the North Atlantic. Although the Titanic sent distress signals, rescue ships in near range had shut off their wireless equipment, and operators at this late hour were not on duty. Interference from wireless operators on land also confounded the distress signals, so they were not immediately answered.

This disaster prompted Congress in May to pass the Radio Act of 1912. President Taft signed the law on August 13, and it became effective in December. This Act essentially amended the Radio Act of 1910 to license wireless radio operators, including allotting lower frequencies to amateur operators, mandating two radio operators on ships 24/7 to ensure a continuous watch, and allocating a separate and distinct distress frequency to avoid interference in emergencies.

While a license was required from the Department of Commerce and Labor (Department of Commerce after 1913), the Radio Act of 1912 gave no discretionary power to regulators to determine who was issued a license and on what discrete frequency they could broadcast. Licenses were ruled to be available for-the-asking.

Initially, all radio broadcasting stations nationally were assigned to operate on a single frequency, 833 kilohertz (kHz). By August 1922, two more frequencies were added: 619 kHz and 750 kHz. But even with three frequencies made available for broadcast use, in Utah and across the nation the interference problem was not alleviated. Radio station operators essentially failed to voluntarily share broadcast time on those frequencies, and interference among them remained a major problem.

The 1912 Act regulated point-to-point wireless communication. But, it was insufficient for allocating scarce frequencies and avoiding the headache of signal canceling interference among users when radio broadcasting, a service meant for point-to-multipoint distribution, became available. From 1922 to 1927, regulators sought to solve the interference problem, but it was not until Congress enacted the Radio Act of 1927 that the issue was satisfactorily resolved.

Radio Act of 1927

The Radio Act of 1927 established the Federal Radio Commission (FRC). In Utah and nationwide, as explained above, many wireless radio operators in the early-to-mid-1920s were issued broadcast licenses to operate on a limited number of frequencies, causing significant interference. The Radio Act of 1927 was enacted to mitigate interference and to more equitably allocate frequencies and power.

It required stations nationwide to justify their licensing in the public interest, and the FCC "tried to bring order out of chaos" by reassigning 732 broadcasting stations to specific frequencies, including KSL, KDYL and KFUR/KLO. Radio station quotas for each state were promulgated based on population. As a result, Utah's quota limited the state to only three stations offering a radio broadcasting service, so KSL, KDYL and KLO were FRC approved. Thus, only three radio broadcasting stations were permitted to operate for the nine years following the passage of the Radio Act of 1927. More licenses became available in Utah, beginning in 1936, after the Communications Act of 1934 allowed applications for low-power 100-watt stations. The 1927 Act introduced the Public Interest Convenience or Necessity (PICON) clause to broadcast licensing, and it was carried over to the Communications Act of 1934. But there was a slight change in the 1934 Act, referencing instead Public Interest, Convenience and Necessity (PICAN). "And" was substituted for "or" ---PICON to PICAN-- for some reason. Today, "Public Interest" simply is used for the most part, sans "convenience and necessity." The 1934 Act applied to all 10 pioneering radio stations in Utah.

Communications Act of 1934

The Communications Act of 1934 established the Federal Communications Commission FCC), replacing the Federal Radio Commission with some of the regulatory functions previously conducted by the Radio Act of 1927 and the Interstate Commerce Commission. Where the Radio Act of 1927 regulated only wireless radio licensing and operations, the Communication Act of 1934 regulated interstate and foreign communications by wireless, wired and common carrier communications, including by radio, telegraph, telephone, later television, and eventually satellite. The FCC does not regulate Internet networks, not even in the Net Neutrality realm. Adjusted by amendments and court rulings, the 1934 Act largely governed wired and wireless communication in the U.S. until, for the first time, major ownership regulation changes were enacted in the Telecommunications Act of 1996, which will be discussed later.

There were two ways to obtain a radio broadcasting station: Buy an existing station or apply for a license and put a new station on the air. The 10 Utah pioneer stations could engage only the latter option, as there were no existing Utah stations for sale. Applicants for the first three Utah radio broadcasting stations — KZN (KSL) and KDYL in 1922, and KFUR (KLO) in 1925 — faced no appreciable competition for their respective broadcast licenses, essentially available for the asking. But, they also fought for listeners, first on one and then on a maximum of three designated frequencies to overcome interference. For the remaining seven stations in Utah's first wave of radio broadcasting stations, the FCC, empowered by the Communications Act of 1934, was charged with determining if an applicant was qualified to hold a license and serve PICAN, a nebulous construct. Also in competing applications, the FCC was charged with determining which applicant was best qualified to hold the license and to serve PICAN.

Fort Douglas Radio, Salt Lake City

The first public demonstration in Salt Lake City of a radio broadcasting station occurred on May 10, 1922, when members and guests at a Commercial Club luncheon heard a phonographic concert sent from the U.S. Army radio station at Fort Douglas, east of downtown and located on the present-day campus of The University of Utah. The concert was picked up on the Commercial Club's newly installed receiving station and was played over loudspeakers. Three hundred people attended the demonstration and another two hundred who could not be accommodated returned after the luncheon to witness the broadcast.[43]

Interest in radio for the novice, the amateur, and for those in the radio business was very high at the Commercial Club that day. Four days earlier, the Deseret News put KZN on the air, Utah's first recognized radio station offering a broadcasting service, and the Salt Lake Telegram was scheduled to launch its new radio broadcasting station that very evening. Commercial Club members were invited back that night (May 10) to hear the inaugural broadcast of KDYL, Utah's second officially recognized radio station offering a broadcasting service.

The Fort Douglas radio station, call letters WYCJ, was licensed in October, 1921, and put into service long before the May 1922 inaugural broadcasts of either KZN or KDYL. Why then are KZN and KDYL recognized as Utah's

---

43   Salt Lake Telegram, May 10, 1922, p. 11.

first two broadcasting stations when WYCJ existed prior? The answer lies in defining a radio "broadcasting service." In 1922, all radio stations — amateur, commercial, government or privately owned — used broadcast means to transmit a signal, but all did not provide a radio broadcasting "service."

For example, the Fort Douglas station was not licensed to provide a radio broadcasting service, even though that was the novelty demonstrated at the Commercial Club on May 10. The normal use for the Fort Douglas station was reserved for the War Department as a long-distance wireless telephone link between Washington, D.C. and San Francisco. The Fort Douglas station used broadcast-means to send and receive communications, but it didn't provide a "broadcast service" and wasn't a broadcasting station in the sense attributable to KZN and KDYL.

It is no surprise that at the Commercial Club luncheon, Captain Clay I. Hoppaugh, in charge of the Fort Douglas radio station, said the future of radio for government use depended largely on ensuring secrecy in the sending of messages.[44] From his perspective, this was true. The Army used radio to send and receive secret messages across America, and the government was saving $500 per month ($8,200 when adjusted for inflation) by using the radiotelephone network to skirt by paying commercial wire rates.[45]

Hoppaugh's focus was not on turning a liability into an asset, as per KDKA and Sarnoff's dream discussed earlier, or in making radio more accessible to the public. His focus was on coded messages and on limiting public access to them. He clearly did not envision that radio communications would soon be sent to "whom it may concern," or that it would become an important factor in the social and commercial life of the country for endless decades to come.[46]

Unlike the Fort Douglas station, KZN and KDYL were not established to facilitate the private exchange of messages. KZN and KDYL were "sending-stations" only, licensed to scatter signals over the land for anybody to receive, much like as a farmer broadcasts seeds over their land. They were licensed

---

44   Salt Lake Telegram, May 10, 1922.
45   Salt Lake Tribune, April 4, 1922, p.18
46   Salt Lake Tribune, May 11, 1922, p. 10

to disseminate radio communications — wireless electromagnetic radiation — intended for reception directly by the public. In short, the Fort Douglas station was a medium of interpersonal communication, while KZN, KDYL and the Utah broadcasting stations that followed them became media of mass communication.

The important point here is that the difference between radiotelephone stations, like the one at Fort Douglas, and radio "broadcasting service" stations, like KZN and KDYL, is not so much a technical one as an institutional feature, an industry and a process difference.[47] Understanding this difference guides the reader to appreciate that the entrepreneurs who started KZN and KDYL were true innovators. They put existing science and technology together, under regulatory imperatives set out in the Radio Act of 1912, and created an institution, an industry and a process resulting in new economic behavior and a radio broadcasting service emerged.

Two enterprising individuals were responsible for initiating the efforts to license and build KZN and KDYL broadcasting stations. They were Melvin R. Ballard, general circulation manager of the Deseret News and Arthur L. Fish, publisher of the Salt Lake Telegram. These men had a vision to involve their respective newspapers in radio broadcasting; an entrepreneurial venture they believed would sell newspaper subscriptions and advertising, and likely result in an electronic version of the newspaper.

Pioneers but not Founders: Earl J. Glade and Sidney Fox

The stories of radio's broadcast origin in Utah start with two of the state's most important pioneers who were not necessarily founders of their stations: Earl J. Glade at KZN and Sidney S. Fox at KDYL.

In 1923 the original newspaper owners of KZN and KDYL, the Deseret News and the Salt Lake Telegram, respectively, became disillusioned with radio broadcasting after barely a year of operations. Radio hadn't displaced

---

47   Christopher H. Sterling and John M. Kittross, Stay Tuned: A Concise History of American Broadcasting (Belmont, California: Wadsworth Publishing Company, 1990), 13.

newspapers as people had believed, and KZN, in particular, had not become an effective proselytizing medium as some high-ranking leaders in the Church of Jesus Christ of Latter-Day Saints had anticipated.

Ownership changes occurred quickly. The Telegram owners of KDYL turned the station over to the Newhouse Hotel and James Waters, its manager, to operate. After a short time, it was sold to Fred Provol, who, with his mother, Eva, owned the retail Hudson Bay Fur Company in Salt Lake City. Eva was married to Fox, who, in 1925, purchased KDYL from his stepson, Fred. The Deseret News, with KSL, followed a similar ownership path. John N. Cope, an amateur enthusiast, who formed the Radio Service Corporation of Utah (RSC) in 1924, as the corporate parent to the station, acquired what would become KSL. Glade became involved and subsequently persuaded the LDS Church and the Tribune Company to invest. Glade became KSL manager, and the LDS Church assumed a controlling interest in the RSC.

Glade and Fox had different personalities and styles. Fox was as candid and impulsive as Glade was poised and deliberate. Fox was rough; his language was full of "Foxisms," or words he concocted. Glade was smoother; his language was proper. Glade's voice became a fixture on KSL, but Fox appeared only infrequently on KDYL. Each was charming and persuasive in their unique ways.

Fox and Glade also shared a few traits. Neither was a broadcaster by goal or plan. They were, first and foremost, promoters and salesmen, and broadcasting simply became the most fertile promotional ground for their efforts. Prior to going into broadcasting, Glade taught business classes at Brigham Young University and at the University of Utah and worked at the Gillham Advertising Agency in Salt Lake City. He later formed his own public relations and advertising company. Fox, prior to going into broadcasting, dropped out of school, promoted and distributed films to Intermountain movie theaters, and became part of the California and Florida real estate booms after WWI. Fox and Glade had the stomach for risk in pursuit of great financial return. They were confident in their selling abilities, and each was said to have been the highest grossing salesperson at his respective station during the 1920s and 1930s. Each spent more than 30 years in and around the Utah broadcasting business.

Neither Fox nor Glade actually founded, established or was involved in his respective station, when it began operations in 1922. They were not the "founding-fathers," despite the allusion to such in dozens of newspaper articles over several decades, including their respective obituaries. Each man joined his station several years after it first went on the air. Although not the founders, Fox and Glade still had no template for operating a commercial radio broadcasting station. There were no examples of successful radio broadcasting stations in Utah to emulate when these entrepreneurs started in the broadcasting business in the mid-1920s. They made it up as they went along.

In addition, neither Glade nor Fox was the astute business decision maker as legendary chronicles have attempted to portray. Instead, they used their promotional skills, public relations abilities, self-confidence and personal charm to deftly turn deals and generate large personal incomes in the enormously difficult times during the Great Depression.

Essentially enjoying carte blanche as manager during the 1930s, Glade and Fox used entrepreneurial strategies and aggressive promotional tactics to lead KSL and KDYL to profitability. They used creative financing and tax-avoiding strategies to expand operations and, on the way, convinced Salt Lake City businesses of the value of advertising on radio. Radio was essentially depression-proof. Unlike the movies, it required a single, albeit relatively large, investment for a receiver, and the programs were free after that. KDYL and KSL produced popular local programs and affiliated with national networks, thus becoming vitally important to their listeners and advertisers.

The purpose here is to relate the significant entrepreneurial skills of both Fox and Glade, but at the same time to say, starkly, that these "emperors had no clothes." In nearly every mention of Fox or Glade, whether in a newspaper, magazine article, book or speech, only their successes are mentioned, as if they came easily and without mistakes, and without gut-wrenching worry and overwhelming risk. The significant abilities of these two men are chronicled, but their human sides also are discussed, in an effort to show that they operated in a real world, had great strengths and weaknesses, and had to overcome personal and corporate difficulties in making KDYL and KSL successful.

Fox owned KDYL and essentially did whatever he wanted personally at the station. But, this was not the case for Glade at KSL, who early on acquired a corporate board giving oversight to his personal and management decisions. After making KSL a success through his entrepreneurial efforts and hard work, he and his wife, Sarah Elizabeth Rasband Glade, initially did everything at the station, including sweeping the floors at night after everybody else had gone home. Glade was removed from the seat of power at KSL and replaced through, what some have called, an act of nepotism by a high-ranking LDS Church official. Meanwhile, Fox sold his KDYL holdings in 1953 and retired from active participation in Utah broadcasting.

They were pioneers in demonstrating all of the potential and pitfalls of a medium, which was operating metaphorically in blue ocean territory. Their stories are instructive for comparing to those individuals who took on similar roles as immersive digital media technology in the 21st century promulgated a new communications medium of channels. And, their pioneering efforts emphasized how radio remains resilient a century after the pioneers set stakes in the broadcasting landscape.

Section II chronicles the founding and the operations of Utah's first 10 radio broadcasting stations.

SECTION II

THE TEN PIONEERING RADIO STATIONS
IN UTAH

CHAPTER 4

THE STORY OF KZN AND KSL RADIO IN SALT LAKE CITY

KZN's historical precedent was made two years before the station went live but its initial path was anything but a "broadcasting service." Melvin R. Ballard, circulation manager for the Deseret News, was introduced to radio in 1920 when he teamed with Harry Carter Wilson, the International News Service telegraph operator for the newspaper, to use a wireless station on top of the Deseret News Building to teach Morse Code to the Boy Scouts. Early on, the plan was for the Boy Scouts to communicate by code with their peers in other parts of Utah. Ballard suggested that the Deseret News could send news and information by code to Boy Scouts in different parts of the state, and they could decode and disseminate it. He also envisioned a communications link between the Church of Latter-Day Saints headquarters in Salt Lake City and each of the churches throughout the state.

On October 8, 1920, Wilson sent a letter to the Bureau of Navigation in Washington, D.C., requesting permission to broadcast on higher wavelengths than 200 meters allowed regular amateurs. He wrote:[48]

> There are no government stations, to my knowledge, closer than the Pacific coast, to us, and would be pleased to have you consider this and if possible to issue us a permit for a special license, after proper forms are properly filled out. ...We've taken this matter up with the Radio Inspector [J.F. Dillon] at San Francisco, ...but was informed [by him] to take it up with you.

Six days later, A. J. Tyrer, acting commissioner of navigation, gave the

---

48   Department of Commerce, Bureau of Navigation.
"Letter from H. C. Wilson to Commissioner of Navigation." 8 October 1920. File 1109-6NR. National Archives. Washington, D.C.

green light to Wilson for operating his amateur station on the 375 meters wavelength, as well as on 200 meters.[49] For giving Wilson the variance, Tyrer was scolded by his subordinate, J. F. Dillon, the 6th District radio inspector in San Francisco:[50]

> I would state that the inspector has more or less difficulty in limiting the number of special stations, including those desiring to transmit the signals and press matters, which is of doubtful interest to amateurs in general. For instance, Mr. Wilson, among other things, desires to transmit time signals at 9 o'clock, Mountain Time, which corresponds to 8 o'clock Pacific Time. At that time the Naval Station sends out weather reports and if the Deseret News transmits time signals and bulletins, all amateurs desiring to obtain weather reports, an important item for a majority of them, will be interfered with. It would help matters materially if the Bureau [of Navigation] could consistently refer such applications to this office for recommendation before committing themselves regarding the granting of special licenses.

The back and forth continued. Tyrer replied to Dillon's November 3 letter, in which he scolded the Bureau for not referring Wilson's application to him in San Francisco:[51]

> It was the opinion of the Bureau that a station located this distance from the Coast could safely use a wavelength of 375 meters and should not prevent amateurs receiving the time signals and weather reports from the Pacific Coast Naval Station which it is understood uses the wave length of 2,400 meters for this purpose. Mr. Wilson stated in his letter that he had taken up this matter with you and was

49   Department of Commerce, Bureau of Navigation. "Letter from A. J. Tyrer, Acting Commissioner of Navigation, to H. C. Wilson, Manager, Telegraph Department, The Deseret News." 14 October 1920. File 1109-6NR. National Archives. Washington, D.C.
50   Department of Commerce, Bureau of Navigation. "Letter from J. F. Dillon to Acting Commissioner of Navigation, A. J. Tyrer." 3 November 1920. File 1109-6NR. National Archives. Washington, D.C.
51   Department of Commerce, Bureau of Navigation. "Letter from Acting Commissioner A. J. Tyrer to Radio Inspector J. F. Dillon, San Francisco." 15 November 1920. File 1109-6N/R. National Archives. Washington, D.C.

told that the matter of using a wave length in excess of 200 meters should be taken up directly with the Bureau.

The start of 6ZM

Today, the incident likely strikes the reader as nitpicking but a century ago, no one had any idea just what the impact of bureaucratic oversight would have on the viability of a medium that was on the verge of expanding rapidly into virtually every American household. It is not clear why Dillon would chastise Tyrer for approving Wilson's 200-meter variance if he, in fact, directed Wilson to take up the matter with the Bureau. Regardless of the confusion, Wilson had acted fortuitously by going directly to Washington, D.C. instead of the less sympathetic inspector in San Francisco. With the Deseret News cleared to operate at 375 meters wavelength, the news operation subsequently opened 6ZM, a Special Land amateur station, on November 22, 1920. The *Deseret News* touted itself as ... "the first newspaper in this part of the country to install a wireless set to broadcast press and weather reports."[52]

This was the same time when Frank Conrad in Pittsburgh put KDKA on-the-air, the nation's first broadcasting station. But unlike Conrad and KDKA, Wilson did not propose a broadcasting "service" as such or seek a broadcast license. He wanted to use his amateur station to transmit press and weather reports by code. Broadcasting by voice was not his intention with 6ZM, nor was it technically feasible for him at the time.[53] This was consistent with what most radio amateurs were interested in doing at the time. Coded news sent by Wilson on 6ZM was a project shared by a brotherhood of amateurs and was not designated a radio broadcasting service in the sense accomplished by Pittsburgh's KDKA.[54]

The goal of sending-out information to amateurs did not change for Wilson, Ballard and the Deseret News over the next two years. In a letter

---

52   Deseret News, March 4 and March 6,1922, p. 1.
53   Department of Commerce, Bureau of Navigation. "Letter from H. C. Wilson, Manager, Telegraph Department, Deseret News, to Acting Commissioner of Navigation, A. J. Tyrer.
54   Erik A. Barnouw, A Tower in Babel: A History of Broadcasting in the Untied States, Volume I --to 1933 (New York: Oxford University Press, 1966), 70.

to the U.S. Department of Commerce a few days prior to February 6, 1922, Ballard continued to support the "transmitting-to-amateurs" interpretation over a "broadcasting-to-the-general-public" purpose for 6ZM. Ballard also contemplated some other uses that could be promoted to their advantage:[55]

> In this connection [referring to press, weather and police information] we thought that perhaps we would work to a certain extent with local police and sheriff organizations in chasing down criminals and others who were endangering the community and by distributing this information broadcast, [to] the local amateurs, which we now have a list amounting to nearly 200, could pick up the information and communicate with their local town sheriff or constable. In framing regulations governing the wireless, of course we would appreciate it, if it could be arranged to give the greatest latitude possible as the only object we have in conducting a wireless telephone or telegraph station is for service to the public and it reacts on us as a good advertising medium and enables us to be of some service to the public and enables us to be of some service to the community and at the same time attract favorable comment.

In early 1922, 6ZM was still seen as a radio station aimed at amateurs, and through them, giving access to the police and on to the public. As late as February 8, 1922, less than three months before a broadcasting station license was issued to the Deseret News Company, Wilson and Ballard did not contemplate broadcasting to the general public. But, there also was interest in its advertising potential.

Ballard wrote a strongly worded complaint to the U. S. Weather Bureau about the strict radio regulations enforced by the Bureau of Navigation in the U.S. Department of Commerce. He wondered about how difficult it was to negotiate a license to broadcast something as innocuous as weather

---

55   Department of Commerce. Bureau of Navigation. "Correspondence between C. F. Marvin, Chief of the Weather Bureau, United States Department of Agriculture, and D. B. Carson, Commissioner, Bureau of Navigation, Department of Commerce," 6 February 1922; and, "Letter from D. B. Carson to M. R. Ballard, Circulation Mgr., Deseret News," 8 February 1922. File 1179-6. Record Group 173. National Archives, Washington, D.C.

forecasts. Unbeknownst to Ballard, his letter would immediately lead to KZN, a broadcasting station providing a broadcasting service to the general public. Ballard wrote:[56]

> We are in hopes that some time the government regulations could be such that it would permit a newspaper to not only operate and broadcast information to amateur operators and use same for publication in our columns without the restriction of both of us taking out a commercial license. I don't understand a great deal concerning wireless regulations, but thus far I can see that before a newspaper or others in the country can develop it very far and make it of practical use to all concerned, great latitude will have to be allowed regarding this item.

Ballard's words were prescient without a doubt. C. F. Marvin, chief of the Weather Bureau, forwarded Ballard's letter to D. B. Carson, commissioner of Navigation, and Carson wrote back suggesting a different tack than what Ballard suggested:[57]

> This office sees no objection to granting you a license to carry on the broadcasting service contemplated. It will be necessary to assign the wave length of 360 meters for broadcasting police reports, news items or entertainment, if desired, and a wave length of 485 meters for broadcasting Government reports such as the market reports and the weather forecasts. As your station will come under the jurisdiction of the Radio Inspector, Customhouse, San Francisco, California, it is suggested that you take up with him the matter of obtaining a license for your station.

---

56   Department of Commerce, Bureau of Navigation. "Correspondence between C. F. Marvin, Chief, Weather Bureau, Department of Agriculture, and D. B. Carson, Commissioner, Bureau of Navigation, Department of Commerce," February 6, 922; and, "Letter from D. B. Carson to M. R. Ballard, Circulating Mgr., Deseret News," February 8, 1922. File 1179-6 N/R, Record Group 173. National Archives, Washington, D.C..

57   Department of Commerce. Bureau of Navigation. "Correspondence between C. F. Marvin, Chief, Weather Bureau, Department of Agriculture, and D. B. Carson, Commissioner, Bureau of Navigation, Department of Commerce," February6, 1922; and, "Letter from D. B. Carson to M. R. Ballard, Circulating Mgr., Deseret News," 8 February 1922. File 1179-6 N/R, Record Group 173. National Archives, Washington, D.C.

Now it was Ballard's turn to take up the matter with the radio inspector. No longer would Ballard merely seek variant uses for Wilson's 6ZM Special Land amateur station. He would now apply for a broadcasting station license to provide a broadcasting service on two frequencies, 360 and 485 meters. By early March, the proposed new station was described in the *Deseret News* as being able to send up to 1,500 miles by code (telegraphy) and 1,000 miles using voice (telephony).[58] Wilson would dismantle his 6ZM amateur spark set as soon as the radiotelephone set was ready for operation.

The launch of KZN

Ballard left the Deseret News Company on April 1,1922, leaving Wilson, by virtue of his amateur experience the only person with any significant technical knowledge, to proceed with the broadcasting station application. Ten days later, the radio inspector in San Francisco received Wilson's application. The license was granted on April 21, and KZN call letters were assigned. After this, all efforts and expertise" were pooled at the Deseret News Company to get the station on the air as quickly as possible:[59]

> At this same time, Nathan O. Fullmer, the *Deseret News* business manager, and Elias S. Woodruff, its General Manager, were trying to locate for Wilson some broadcasting equipment at an inexpensive price. On April 25, Woodruff wired Wilson from New York and told him to buy the radio set for which he [Wilson] was negotiating in San Francisco.

But even after the KZN broadcasting license was granted, Woodruff and Fullmer did not have any enthusiasm or optimism for KZN as a stand-alone entity:[60]

---

58   Deseret News, March 4, 1922.
59   Heber G. Wolsey, Ph.D. diss., Michigan State University, 1967) p. 62. Quoting Elias S. Woodruff letter of April 25,1922 to Nathan O. Fullmer.
60   Wolsey, 62

Radio is a real problem. I believe we will never be able to broadcast except in a small way. Nevertheless, it is good for Wilson to get the set for the amount he is spending. We may have to stop after a while, and if we do we will not be out much. The publicity will be worthwhile.

The first broadcast over KZN, Utah's first official radio station offering a "broadcasting service", occurred on May 6, 1922, at 3 p.m., when Wilson went on the air with, "Hello; Hello; Hello; This is KZN; KZN the Deseret News, Salt Lake City, calling; KZN calling.[61] This was followed at eight that night with greetings of dedication from the Church of Jesus Christ of Latter-day Saints and government officials, speaking from atop the Deseret News Building in downtown Salt Lake City. At the dedication, LDS Church President Heber J. Grant, in "characteristic, ringing voice," read a solemn passage from the LDS Doctrine and Covenants. However, Hilda Augusta Winters Grant, wife of the president, using a lighter tone and less formal words, likely better reflected the spirit of those gathered on the rooftop and those few listening at home to KZN that night:[62]

I think this is one of the most wonderful experiences of our lives. I am glad I live in this age when everyday --almost every hour, brings us some new invention. I would not be surprised if we were talking to the planets before many years. This is one of the most wonderful inventions of this or any other age.

The Deseret News immediately began using KZN to promote the newspaper. After KZN had been on the air for only five days, with great confidence the Deseret News challenged readers with: "Bring the World Into Your Home. Without radio you are out of touch with the world. Radio has become a necessity and The DESERET NEWS wants to see a dependable Receiving Set in every home. Hence this great free offer."[63] The advertisement went on to explain the particulars of the free receiver give-away:[64]

---

61   Deseret News, May 8, 1922, Sec. 2, 1.
62   Deseret News, May 8, 1922.
63   Deseret News, May 11, 1922, 10.
64   Deseret News, May 11, 1922.

Here's the Way to Get your Radiophone Free This complete
Radiophone Receiving Set – consisting of Tuner Cabinet and
Headpiece Set with double receiving phones, will be given away
absolutely free for: 6 twelve month subscriptions, 12 six month
subscriptions, 24 three month subscriptions, or 36 two month
subscriptions. Any combinations of the above making the equivalent
of 72 months subscriptions to the Deseret News.

There is no indication in subsequent weeks how successful this promotion
was. Also, there is no available evidence that this promotion was ever aired
over KZN. But when the Deseret News put KZN on-the-air, it put pressure on
its competitor, the Salt Lake Telegram, to get a station of its own in operation.
Left unchallenged, the Deseret News station could be used to promote
newspaper subscriptions and to scoop the Telegram in reporting up-to-date
news.

Meanwhile, John Cope and Lionel B. Cornwell launched radio station
KDYV, which was licensed to operate at 360 meters (this would compare
today to about 830 KC on AM radio). Like KZN, KDYV would transmit news,
concerts, and market and weather reports. Cope and Cornwell also became
associated with the Western Radio Sales Company, a radio receiver sales
business, when it opened in Salt Lake City on June 24, 1922, with six offices
in surrounding states. The announcement cited that Cope and Cornell were
"among the best radio men in the west, and assure reliable service."[65]

KDYV was one of the local stations whose concerts and other programs
were played daily in the Western Radio Sales "commodious" offices located in
the McIntyre Building in Salt Lake City. Western handled the products of the
Radio Service Corporation of America, General Electric and Westinghouse,
and Cope and Cornwell would install and service receivers that were sold.
Cope and Cornwell were in their late teens in 1922 and had a collective vision
that radio broadcasting could become a profitable business enterprise if only
radio receivers would become widely distributed. During 1922 and 1923,

---

65   Deseret News, Saturday, June 24, 1922, 2

they operated KDYV from Cope's parent's home at 1138 Michigan Ave. using the reportedly, but unlikely that height, a 100-foot tower and antenna system located in the Cope household's backyard. A loudspeaker placed on Cope and Cornwell's tower on Michigan Ave. could be easily heard in Liberty Park, five blocks away.

Radio's allure was fleeting for some. Despite the formal welcome in the spring by LDS Church leaders, the church lost interest in KZN after Elias Woodruff left his post as Deseret News general manager. After B.F. Grant, brother of the church's first president, took over Woodruff's spot, Heber Grant indicated "he would have nothing to do with radio."[66]

B.F. Grant did not share Cope and Cornwell's optimism about radio broadcasting's future. Wilson, the Deseret News telegrapher and the original engineer for KZN continued through 1923 as troubleshooter for the station. But he was not very successful in keeping the station in good working order. Subsequently a very depressed KZN operation and facilities were offered to Cope and Cornwell. They had no money, but the Deseret News Company gave them use of the KZN shack on the roof of its Main Street Building, in hopes that the two young men could rebuild the station and operate it from income they generated. Cope and Cornwell shut down their KDYV station and combined its good working equipment with KZN's and the station's performance improved dramatically.

In conjunction with R. S. Howells, general manager of Western Radio Sales, Cope and Cornwell recruited University of Utah students to sell radios in the evenings and buyers were encouraged to tune into KZN. Many sets and earphones were sold, and musicians from all over the area came to KZN and were put on the air free of charge in order to provide entertainment for people who purchased radio receivers. But, there were few regular commercial advertisers as yet to support other programming.

---

66   Interview with Nathan O. Fullmer, June 20, 1967; and an undated handwritten article concerning early days at KSL written by Earl J. Glade; both as reported in Heber G. Wolsey, The History of Radio Station KSL from 1922 to Television, Ph.D. thesis, Michigan State University, 1967, 73.

Years later, in the 1960s, Cornwell mentioned in a recorded conversation that one day in 1923 he and Cope were demonstrating a radio broadcast at the University of Utah, as they were watched by Earl J. Glade, the future mayor of Salt Lake City who was then a 38-year-old University of Utah advertising instructor. Cornwell said that Glade was full of questions about everything, and that he was so interested in radio that he asked to join the Cope and Cornwell Company as a salesperson. He would work on commission. Cornwell reminisced about how things spread rapidly in 1923. Glade immediately went to the J.G. McDonald Chocolate factory, then located near downtown, next to where Squatter's Brewery and condominiums are now located, to secure a commitment from them to sponsor a weekly KZN performance of the J.G. McDonald Orchestra. Cornwell said that he and Glade were invited to the McDonald home that evening.

Mrs. McDonald reportedly requested that KZN play for her dinner guests *By the Waters of Minnetonka*, a popular love song by Thurlow Lieurance, which he based on a recording he took from Sitting Eagle, a Crow Indian. But, there was a hitch. At the same time, the song and the McDonald announcement also had to be heard by a friend, Mr. Jones, owner of Jones Drug Store in Los Angeles — some 600 miles away — who was standing by at his store. Cornwell, who was at the McDonald house five blocks away from his station, called operator Charlie Hays and Cope (who were at the station) and relayed Mrs. McDonald's request. Cope tweaked the equipment to obtain the maximum signal out of KZN's 250 watts. Fifteen minutes after the recorded song was played, Jones called McDonald at his home and said the reception in Los Angeles was great. According to Cornwell, McDonald signed a contract that evening, Glade's first day selling for KZN, and he reported that Glade was magic from the very first day and the station expanded.[67]

The power of promotional prowess is what brought Glade into the pioneer's circle for broadcasting, thanks to the happenstance interaction of

---

67   Lionel Cornwell reminisces on tape, circa 1960s.

the advertising instructor observing two ambitious men young enough to be college students hawking radio set receivers for KZN. Cornwell likely became less involved with KZN daily operations and went on to develop a successful audio-sound business, although he mentioned in his oral history that he still was involved with KSL when it aired the first Mormon Tabernacle Choir program in 1929.[68] Cope changed KZN to the KFPT call letters on June 13, 1924 and the station became the darling not only of the Deseret News Company, which proudly hosted the station on the rooftop of its Main Street building, but also brought then Mayor C. Clarence Neslen to officially open the new station, followed by music.

In 1924, Cope, along with his father Francis W. Cope and Heber C. Johnson and S.E. Mulcock founded the Radio Service Corporation of Utah (RSC), This would be the corporate parent to KFPT. Francis Cope, who was an RSC director in its earliest years, was not directly involved with station operations. He was one of Utah's first CPAs, operating the Audits and Office Systems Company with offices at 703 Deseret Building in 1921 and later in the Templeton Building on South Temple in downtown Salt Lake City. The elder had had many accounts including the LDS owned Hotel Utah. The younger Cope was president of RSC, with Johnson as the business manager, and Mulcock, who was in home construction, was a director. At the November 17, 1924 meeting of RSC, Mulcock was appointed general manager of the corporation and Johnson resigned as business manager. Charlie Hays was appointed to replace Johnson as business manager, at a salary of $160 per month. His duties included accounting and program supervision and he was expected to fill in as on-air announcer if no other talent was available. Cope also was RSC's technical director, also at a salary of $160 per month. He was the point man for all daily operations of the radio station.

Glade, who had been so inspired by the prospects for the new medium, managed to keep his university teaching job while becoming the station's sales manager and contract's face value, based on the actual cash payments RSC received. He also was paid a $25 per month retainer fee, a modest sum even at that time. It was a do-or-die performance agreement. If RSC believed that

---

Glade had not been attending to the challenge of beefing up sales revenue for the fledgling station, the company executives could end his employment. Glade would eventually go on to become quite a force in Utah's new radio broadcasting scene, which also would give him the visibility to enter local and state politics.[69]

Glade was cut perfectly to suit the role in leading Utah's nascent radio industry to staking solid roots. Born in Ogden to an LDS family on December 2, 1885. He learned his work ethic from his father, who was a baker and would eventually move the family to Park City where they lived for about ten years. During that time, he had his first "real" job — as a "mudder," a "mudhen" and "oiler" in the Daly West Concentrating Mill, an operation for working with ore. His job was to keep the sluice valve open so the mud and ore could slip through. Sometimes, he would report later, the mud would "accidentally, of course," slip through and splatter on Salt Lake City highbrow student visitors. It might have been hyperbole on Glade's part. But, Glade to tens of thousands of Utahans would become known for his utmost sense of grace and civility in business as well as in politics.

Glade served a mission for the LDS Church in Germany and attended BYU, graduating in 1914 and heading the department of business education at BYU for a time. In 1915, he moved to Salt Lake City from Provo and organized a direct mail advertising service. From 1916 to 1918, he worked at the L.S. Gillham Advertising Agency. Just 33, he began teaching in the University of Utah's business school and introduced courses in advertising and selling. His civic career was launched when on December 4, 1919, Glade was elected president of the Salt Lake Kiwanis Club at the first annual election of officers held in the Newhouse Hotel. In 1921 he went in business with John D. Giles, and they formed the Glade and Giles Advertising, Sales Promotion and Business Counsel Company with offices at 54 South Main Street, today the site of the City Creek Shopping Center.

---

69   A summary developed from the actual agreement as reported in the minutes of the Board of Directors meeting of the Radio Service Corporation of Utah held November 17, 1924.

In 1924 Glade joined station KFPT and continued when the call letters were switched to KSL on June 25, 1925, which has remained the same now for nearly a century. For the moment, he continued his university teaching job. The change in call letters came after Glade persuaded the LDS Church to acquire RSC stock in turn for 51% ownership and voting control at the station. This cleared the way for the RSC founders, including Cope, to resign their executive positions on April 21, 1925.[70]

Also, at about this time, the station moved to LDS Church owned offices in the basement of the Vermont Building in Salt Lake. Cope remained as the technical director while Glade was made an RSC director and KSL general manager.

Although the Copes and the other RSC founders sold their stock interests in the corporation by the end of the 1920s, RSC remained the parent corporation over KSL for the next 38 years, until in the 1950s when the KSL AM-FM-TV Company and later Bonneville International Corporation (BIC) assumed ownership of all the RSC holdings.

A complex triumvirate of management: RSC, KSL, LDS Church

Another prominent figure in the early years of KSL was John F. Fitzpatrick, secretary of the Salt Lake Tribune Publishing Company. In 1925, he invested $1,050 in KSL, and on December 4, 1928, became an RSC director and vice president after Cope resigned. The directors also approved a fivefold increase of RSC capital stock (from $30,000 to $150,000), primarily due to The Tribune's increased stock ownership. The LDS Corporation owned 49% of the stock, with the Salt Lake Tribune Publishing Company, under Fitzpatrick's direction, becoming the second largest stockholder, holding 20%. The remaining 31% of stock ownership was spread out in smaller chunks among shareholders.

---

70   Reported in the RSC Board of Director minutes, April 21, 1925.

Fitzpatrick unofficially assumed a financial oversight role and became part of the contract negotiations for KSL and its network. He helped make KSL a profitable radio station over his twenty-year tenure before, in 1945, he sold the Tribune's RSC interest to invest in KALL radio. With Fitzpatrick's infusion of Tribune money and Glade's ability to attract other stock investors, KSL expanded quickly both in revenue and facilities.

Because of LDS ownership interests in KSL, LDS Presiding Bishop Sylvester Q. Cannon was elected President of RSC on June 9, 1926, a position he would hold for the next 12 years. The primary duties of the Presiding Bishopric are to oversee the temporal affairs --buildings, properties and commercial corporations-- of the church as well as the bishoprics of congregations throughout the world. Cannon, who had an engineering degree, was employed in the mining industry and was the Salt Lake City engineer prior to his appointment as LDS Presiding Bishop.

The RSC presidency was one of several similar positions he held. Cannon was well known in many circles during the 1920s and 1930s. He served as board of trustees president of the Dr. Groves LDS Hospital in Salt Lake City, the Dee Hospital in Ogden and the Idaho Falls Hospital, all of which were owned by the LDS Church. At various times during this period he was also president of the LDS Business College, Zion's Aid Society, Deseret Gym, McCune School of Music and Art and the Deseret News, as well as Radio Service Corporation of Utah (KSL). He was also treasurer of the Uintah Basin Construction Company, as well as being a supervisor of Salt Lake County Draining District #2 and a director of ZCMI, Zions Securities Corporation, Utah Hotel Company, Amalgamated Sugar Company and U.S. Fuel. He was also appointed by state office holders to serve on many committees and councils.

With Cannon's many other commitments while he also was serving as RSC president, it was Glade who carried the responsibilities at KSL and had great latitude in running the station. Over the next decade, Glade developed at least three companies within KSL: Radio Broadcasters Inc. (RBI), the KSL Public Address Service, and an Artists Bureau. Each was informally perceived as a KSL business, but in their early years they had little financial accountability to the RSC and instead they were directed to Glade. Clearly there were no improprieties on Glade's part, and RSC directors were content to give him full rein involving KSL in intra-station businesses with very little oversight and accountability. Nevertheless, these auxiliary operations within KSL provided additional compensation to select KSL employees, who often used KSL telephones, studios and some equipment to conduct business.

Glade first set up Radio Broadcasters, Inc. (RBI) to develop programs and sell advertising on a contract basis for the station. RBI was responsible for local programming and advertising sales during strategic parts of the KSL broadcast day. When on December 4, 1928, John F. Fitzpatrick became a director and vice president of RSC, he expressed concern that the accounts of Glade's RBI and those of the station should be separated, and that each should have separate bookkeepers.[71]

This was the first mention of many in the years to come expressing concern over the existence of RBI. The discussions didn't center on the propriety or accountability of RBI, but, rather, if it would be more advantageous for KSL to put Glade on salary instead of commission and to have KSL take over the programming and sales efforts that RBI conducted. Inherent in these discussions was the assumption that Glade would work equally hard for KSL on a salary basis as he had on commission for his wholly owned RBI. At the July 26 and November 26, 1929, meetings of the RSC board, members asked that RSC's contracts with Glade be studied for their effect on the station. The schedule of payments to Glade for the resale of time by RBI was adjusted but not significantly changed as a result. Again, on November 15, 1932, the RSC Board questioned Glade's intra-company practices, among other concerns. Glade continued to operate on a commission basis and to broker or resell KSL time using RBI for six more years. During this time, Glade received part of his salary from KSL and part from RBI.

The second business, Public Address Service, operated more informally. This gave some technical staff members the opportunity to earn extra income

---

71   RSC BOD Meeting minutes, December 4, 1928.

while using KSL's public address equipment for external jobs. Engineer Eugene Pack carried on the business, with others, in the KSL engineering department. For instance, engineer Mel Wright spent Tuesday of each week, his day off at KSL, installing and operating the public address equipment for Rotary Club meetings.

The organizations served by the Public Address Service paid the KSL employees. As such, no accounting records were kept by KSL during this period, even though it was an operation using KSL equipment. The existence of the Public Address Service was known to Glade, but not generally to other RSC directors. Nothing improper was going on and Glade did not receive payment from the public address services provided by KSL employees. KSL obliquely benefited from the public address services provided to organizations to which Glade belonged and for those where he was a frequent speaker. The Public Address Service was officially taken over by KSL in 1939 when Glade was no longer the station manager.

Another attempt by Glade to stay involved in the operations side of broadcasting came with The Artists Bureau. Its purpose was to develop and organize talent for radio and to provide entertainers for other performances. The Artists Bureau, the third company-within-a-company at KSL, was ideal for KSL, according to Glade, because then the public would think of KSL whenever they wanted out-of-station entertainment of any sort.

The RSC board was concerned about Glade's intentions, especially after he expressed a financial interest in Ogden's KLO, discussed later as another Utah pioneering radio broadcasting station. The board directors believed that it was not a wise business practice to sell time that affords an opportunity of competition with Glade as KSL manager. Yet, despite the board's inclination to take up the matter at a forthcoming meeting, no record could be found that the board, in fact, did just that or why the matter was dropped without further discussion.[72]

KSL's culture and the continuance of Glade's position at KSL abruptly

<hr>

72   RSC minutes of the Board of Director meeting held on November 15, 1932.

changed when in August 1938, J. Reuben Clark, second counselor in the LDS First Presidency, was appointed RSC president to replace Cannon. Unlike Cannon, Clark was a hands-on KSL administrator, and one of his first actions was to appoint Ivor Sharp, his son-in-law, as his assistant.

Sharp had just bought a home in Manhasset, Long Island, and was bound to take a considerable loss when he sold it. His pension rights, insurance program and seniority would also be at risk. But, when on September 15, 1938, Clark arrived in New York City with the KSL job offer, Sharp became Clark's assistant and eventually moved on to becoming KSL manager. This would marginalize Glade in his day-to-day KSL operational responsibilities and eventually the change relegated Glade to the auspices of the RSC board.

Clark visited the ailing LDS Church President (Heber J. Grant) at home several times each week to keep him informed of his activities:[73]

> If Clark ... conducted any major business without advance approval by President Grant, he quickly announced the fact to the President. Therefore, <u>after</u> Clark hired Sharp, he apologized to Grant ... for not consulting him before a K.S.L. stockholders meeting ... [and he] told him about putting Ivor Sharp on board of Directors; told him about the condition of the company.

To curtail criticism of his actions, Clark didn't hire Sharp directly to replace Glade, although that was his ultimate intent. Clark knew attempts to replace Glade would be very unpopular inside and outside the station, even if replacing him was believed to be the ideal circumstance for KSL and the RSC stockholders.

Ushering in KSL's second era of development

Preparing for Sharp's arrival, Clark's first major change was to dissolve KSL's contract with RBI. Glade had built a hefty revenue stream for RBI by virtue of RSC's contributions. In 1937, RBI accounted for $72,459 of KSL's

---

73   D. Michael Quinn, J. Reuben Clark: The Church Years, BYU Press 1983, 85.

gross business earnings, nearly 20% of the total of $387,540. At the October 12, 1938 RSC board meeting, even before Sharp arrived at KSL, the board significantly readjusted Glade's employment at KSL. As stated, the RSC board said, "Radio Broadcasters [RBI] will write no more time after October 1."[74] When RBI was dissolved, Glade was put on a fixed salary and incurred the biggest impact. From 1930 through 1939, Glade's KSL earnings through RBI had averaged $25,000 per year, reaching a high of $42,000 in 1937. During the four years after RBI was dissolved, his KSL earnings were reduced to an average of only $11,000 per year.[75]

Sharp focused on ushering in KSL's second chapter. That first creative, free-wheeling first chapter ran from June 9, 1924, when the RSC articles of incorporation were filed through 1938. During the first era at KSL, there was an exciting start-up period, followed by a decade of incredible growth, both in terms of revenue and influence. Glade proved an exceptional entrepreneur as well as performer, salesman and promoter for the station. The second chapter opened with Glade being ousted from the seat of power, the dissolution of Glade's three intra-company organizations at KSL, and with the simultaneous hiring of Sharp to reorganize KSL and make RSC into a major corporation.

Sharp's first day on the job at KSL, as "assistant" to RSC President Clark, was November 4, 1938. Sharp met with Glade, Auditor Dan H. Vincent, Technical Director Eugene Pack and others and, over the next few days, began reviewing KSL financial records, accounting procedures, reports and other operating statements. Sharp abruptly concluded that the station's business methods were unduly involved, obsolete, inadequate, without real direction, and unworthy of an important station like KSL. The only effective way to correct conditions, he thought, was to start reorganizing.

After working under these conditions for two years and apparently disappointed with how his sphere of influence and control had shrunk to his only post as a member of the RSC governing board, Glade resigned on

---

74   RSC Board of Directors minutes for October 12, 1938, dated November 3, 1938, 1.
75   Principal Activities and Accomplishments of Radio Station KSL during the period August 1938 to August 1943," prepared for President J. Reuben Clark, Jr. by Ivor Sharp, August 12, 1943, Tab 1, 2.

December 23, 1940. The next day at the KSL employees' Christmas party, Glade ..."regretfully, and with some bitterness, bade farewell to those present."[76]

The KSL Artists Bureau, however, remained intact, but as this was the first time in more than 15 years that Glade was no longer associated with KSL as a formal employee, the Bureau was on the verge of vanishing. With a loan from RSC he endeavored as a private individual to make the Artists Bureau profitable and provide him his major source of income. Glade never filed the Articles of Incorporation for the Artists Bureau and very soon realized reconstitution was hopeless.

On January 27, 1941, Glade told Clark that he was having difficulty establishing the Artists Bureau on a paying basis. Clark met with Glade a month later and suggested that he might want to give up the Bureau and return to KSL full time.[77] On March 19, Glade accepted Clark's offer and two days later sent formal notice to him, acknowledging he no longer would pursue the Artists Bureau.[78]

Glade returned to KSL and mostly assumed community affairs responsibilities and represented KSL in the national arena working with the National Association of Broadcasters to produce a *Code of Good Practice* for broadcasting stations nationwide. Sharp, who continued well into the 1950s as an RSC and KSL executive, would expand his own imprint, including KSL's FM counterpart and KSL television in the 1940s.

Glade seemed always to survive not on the strength of his business acumen but instead upon his warm, gracious, and cordial nature, on his radio training and speaking voice, and on his intellect and command of the English language. It was these same qualities that would make him a successful politician. On September 22, 1943, Glade announced his candidacy for Salt Lake City mayor. He won election and served three terms from 1944 to 1956

---

76   Sharp typed explanation entitled 'KSL Artists Bureau Glade Artists Bureau and Continental Broadcasting Company' in Sharp's personal files, written sometime in 1943, p. 10.
77   Letter from Clark to Glade dated May 23, 1941
78   Glade letter to Clark dated May 21, 1941

as Salt Lake City's 25th mayor. He continued as an RSC director and received a KSL consulting fee of $350 per month during the entire 12 years he was mayor.

In 1961, Arch Madsen, the newly appointed president of KSL AM–FM-TV by LDS Church President David O. McKay, brought Glade, whom he greatly respected, back to KSL as vice president of community Affairs. Glade was put on-the-air on KSL TV after a 23-year hiatus from KSL radio. He continued working with KSL until his death in 1966.[79]

Undeniably, Glade was the father of Utah radio, remembered as Utah's first professional radio broadcasting pioneer. He shaped the enduring market structure of Utah radio broadcasting and confirmed its sustainability through advertising supported operations. He turned Utah radio broadcasting from a hobby practiced by amateurs to a business enterprise staffed by professionals. His belief in advertising was inviolable and came from his strongly held faith that honored self-improvement and work. To Glade, advertising was sacrosanct:[80]

> Advertising at its best is one of the most potent elevators of living standards in the world today. Further, it is the world's champion builder of payrolls. What this means to humanity is possibly most appreciated by those who know the significance of work as a true friend of man. As an energizer to achievement and to improvement; as a stimulant to constructive activity, advertising is incomparable.

Incidentally, Glade's life and times are chronicled in *Earl J. Glade: An Inside Story of Church and State, Politics and Media*, by Tim Larson and Craig Wirth.

---

79   For a comprehensive look at Glade's endeavors inside and outside of KSL, see: Earl J. Glade: An Inside Story of Church and State, Politics and Media, by Tim Larson and Craig Wirth, 2019.
80   Earl J. Glade, "Advertising at its Best," New Improvement Era, 1937.

CHAPTER 5

KDYL: SALT LAKE CITY

As mentioned previously, Arthur L. Fish's entrepreneurial efforts were instrumental in the founding of KDYL, Utah's second radio broadcasting station, which like KSL also has endured. Prior to coming to Salt Lake City, Fish worked as a representative for the *Los Angeles Times* in San Francisco and as business manager of the *Oregon Journal* in Portland before joining the Army during World War I. He came to Salt Lake after the war and became the publisher of the *Salt Lake Herald* on January 1, 1920. One of Fish's earliest entrepreneurial decisions came on July 18, 1920, when he suspended publication of the *Herald*, and then assumed control and became publisher of the *Salt Lake Telegram*.[81]

In the winter of 1922, Fish contacted his friend, Dr. H. T. Plumb, the Salt Lake based General Electric representative, to inquire about applying for a radio broadcasting station license. Plumb was interested in high-frequency phenomena, and he often discussed radio with Ira Kaar, who was studying engineering at the University of Utah. Plumb suggested that Fish and Kaar meet. Fish had already briefly met Kaar two years earlier when he gave Kaar, who was then 18, a check for $100 (the inflation adjusted equivalent of about $1,200 today) for winning a nationwide radio contest that was locally sponsored by the *Telegram*.[82]

Later, Fish and Plumb visited Kaar at his parent's home to examine Kaar's 6ZA Special Land amateur station and find out if Kaar could do for the *Telegram* what Frank Conrad had accomplished for Westinghouse at KDKA in Pittsburgh more than a year earlier.[83] Kaar had a provisional license for a

81   N. Malmquist. The First 100 Years: A History of the Salt Lake Tribune, 1871-1971 (Salt Lake City, Utah: The Newspaper Agency Corporation, 1971), 287
82   Salt Lake Telegram, "S. L. Amateur First in U. S. Radio Contest," 8 May 1920, Sec. 2, 1.
83   Ira J. Kaar, Interview by Tim Larson, Everett L. Cooley Oral History Project, Tape Nos.

Class-5, Special Amateur station, which he previously renewed a year earlier on December 29, 1921. This experimental license authorized him to transmit ordinary amateur communications at 200 meters (1499 kilocycles) and to experiment with other communications at 375 meters (approximately 800 kilocycles). "Provisional' meant the license, although an official one, was issued without the station being inspected. It was not inspected on-site because it was considered too remote from the headquarters of the radio inspector in San Francisco and, as explained earlier, did not represent an interference problem for private commercial or government wireless operations.

Fish asked Kaar if his station could transmit voice and music. Kaar said it was possible but it would have to be modified considerably if they wanted to transmit over great distances such as what was possible at Pittsburgh's KDKA. Remember that Kaar had built a five-watt transmitter using the vacuum tubes he obtained when, in 1920, he visited the radio room on the U.S.S. Cleveland, a navy ship docked in Acapulco. Kaar recalled its capabilities:

> It had [a] power output of five watts, but it did transmit a voice signal to my amateur friends around Salt Lake City, and I don't know how much further its range would be because I didn't hear from anyone else.[84]

Fish asked what modifications were needed on 6ZA, how extensive they were, and how much they would cost. Apparently satisfied with Kaar's answers, Fish then asked him if he would modify his 6ZA transmitter to temporarily transmit voice and music for the *Telegram*, while Kaar built a permanent broadcasting transmitter for the newspaper. Kaar agreed and the seed was planted for what became KDYL.

Kaar modified his 6ZA amateur station by first installing high power vacuum tubes obtained from General Electric by Dr. Plumb. Fish and Kaar then went to San Francisco to purchase necessary equipment to change 6ZA to a broadcasting station. Kaar completed the modifications on his 6ZA

U-456 and U457, April 21, l986. Transcript, 13.
84   Ira J. Kaar, Interview by Tim Larson, 21, 7-8.

transmitter and tested it by sending a signal across town to fellow amateur Hap Seeley. Thus, he began broadcasting at 200 meters.

Fish asked Kaar if he could broadcast some programs, which the *Telegram* would organize and do so under the auspices of the *Telegram* newspaper. Kaar agreed and the Telegram had planted the roots for broadcasting. The transformed 6ZA continued to be located in Kaar's parent's home on 700 South Street in Salt Lake City. Kaar recalled:[85]

> My generous and kindly parents permitted me to revamp the parlor
> of our home into a studio. The *Telegram* news department hired a
> program director that engaged artists to visit my home and put on
> programs, which were transmitted from my equipment on the second
> floor.

KDYL obtains its full broadcast license

Fish next asked Kaar to apply for a broadcasting license while Kaar continued to broadcast for the *Telegram* on 6ZA at 200 meters. Toward the end of April 1922, Kaar finished the application, signed it with "A.L. Fish, Pres." at the bottom and sent it off for approval. Kaar inked the entire license application in cursive and when Fish's signature is compared to one known to be his, the "A. L. Fish, Pres." signature on the application is clearly revealed to have been penned by Kaar and not Fish. Obviously, the forgery was with Fish's consent and the license application was recommended for approval on May 1, 1922, by inspector J.F. Dillon in San Francisco.[86]

The intention of KDYL to "cooperate with other broadcasting stations," as specified in the license, in the zone referred not only to Utah's first radio broadcast station (KZN) but also to the several other broadcast licensed stations that went on the air about the same time. Utah amateurs had moved quickly from licenses to send code and voice using their spark and CW (continuous wave) amateur stations, to broadcast licenses using the same.

---

85   Ira J. Kaar, Interview by Tim Larson, 14

86   Department of Commerce, Bureau of Navigation, "License for Land Radio Station, Limited Commercial, No. 453." (Washington, D.C.: Department of Commerce, May 1, 1922.

Many point to KZN, which evolved from H.C. Wilson's 6ZM amateur station, and KDYL, which resulted from I. J. Kaar's 6ZA amateur station, as the only two pioneer Utah radio broadcasting stations, when, in fact, there were several others started by amateurs at the same time in 1922. They included KDZL in Ogden, licensed to Rocky Mountain Radio Corporation, and KDYV in Salt Lake City, licensed to amateurs John N. Cope and Lionel Cornwell. KDYV was broadcasting from Cope's home at 1138 Michigan Avenue and had been on the air only a few days after KZN and KDYL began operations in May 1922. By February 1923 the original four were joined by still two more stations: KFCP in Ogden, licensed to amateur Ralph W. Flygare, and KFLH in Salt Lake City, licensed to the Erickson Radio Co. Suddenly Salt Lake City and Ogden had a germinating radio market. These stations within a short time were licensed, like KZN and KDYL, to broadcast music, concerts and lectures on 360 meters, and were licensed for market or weather reports on 485 meters.

The expansion continued through the mid-1920s. In 1924, Utah amateurs pioneered three more broadcasting stations. Salt Lake City's KFOO, licensed to Latter Day Saints University, was transformed to a broadcasting station from LDSU teacher Thomas Howell's amateur station. KFUT, another broadcasting station built by Kaar was licensed to the University of Utah and KFPH, licensed to amateur Harold C. Mailander operated in Salt Lake. In 1925, amateur Glen Garner helped construct two Ogden stations: KFUR, which later became KLO (discussed in the following chapter), and KFWB. Also, in 1925, amateur Laurel Cole constructed KFXD in Logan.

KZN (which later became KSL), KDYL and KFUR (which later became KLO), however, were the only three stations offering a continuous broadcast service that were sustained beyond the 1920s. KZN and KDYL initially survived because of their respective newspaper connections and the promotional advantage provided by those connections. KFUR, although not initially under newspaper ownership, soon benefited greatly when the owners of the *Ogden Standard Examiner* took over the station. The critical factor of success appears to be that KZN and KDYL were launched for boosting sales of newspapers while several other stations were established for raising sales of radio sets. Many newspapers and radio stations across the nation appeared to value the symbiotic relationship:[87]

> That it [newspaper ownership of radio] pays is obvious by a glance
> at the advertisements, and an appreciation of the keenness of the
> competition in such cities as Detroit, Atlanta, Salt Lake, and New
> Orleans, where practically all dailies vie with one another for
> both news space and broadcasting excellence. To date, none of the
> 56 broadcasting dailies [nationally] has cancelled its license and
> newspapers are taking out licenses at the rate of about two each week.

Likely prompted by possible competition from other stations, specifically
the Desert News' KZN station which debuted on May 6, 1922, Fish officially
commissioned Kaar's 6ZA as the *Telegram's* broadcasting station:[88]

> Preparations for what will probably mean the greatest service
> ever offered by any newspaper in the intermountain region were
> practically completed Sunday [May 7, 1922]. A temporary radio
> transmitting set is being installed for the Telegram. Tests were made
> Sunday afternoon and evening on 200 meters from station 6ZA.
> The voice and music were perfect. … By Tuesday or Wednesday the
> transmitter will be ready for The Telegram to begin broadcasting on
> 360 meters.

On KDYL's inaugural night, Wednesday, May 10, 1922, Kaar changed
his 6ZA amateur station, which he had been broadcasting on 200 meters to
one broadcasting on 360 meters for the *Telegram*. A major radio concert was
planned for opening night on KDYL:[89]

> Phonograph records will be played between other selections to be
> furnished in diversified ways. For instance, there will be operatic
> aria, the reading of bedtime stories and the transmission of news
> bulletins. Between 7 and 8 o'clock tonight, members of the Dunbar
> Opera company will charm over the [KDYL)] service with selections

---

87   Deseret News, July 29, 1922, Sec. 3, 12.
88   Salt Lake Telegram, May 8, 1922, Sec. 2, 1
89   Salt Lake Telegram, May 10, 1922, Sec. 2, 1.

from that old and lovely opera, "The Bohemian Girl," Lee Parvin, the manager, having made arrangements for them to appear at The Telegram's sending station.

Initially, the station call letters were promoted as KDL, sans the Y. The following appeared in the Telegram:[90]

Join with the throng that tonight will listen to The Telegram's classic concert to be broadcasted from its station, KDL. ... From the KDL of The Telegram will be broadcasted tonight a concert par excellence.

The call letter issue is a bit of a historical novelty. The license was granted on May 8, 1922, by then U.S. Secretary of Commerce Herbert Hoover, but for some reason the *Telegram* newspaper thought that the assigned call letters for the station were KDL, even though KDYL was clearly assigned to the station in the license grant signed by Hoover. Nevertheless, for the entire month of May, the *Telegram* erroneously used KDL instead of KDYL in reference to its station. It is likely that notification of the license grant was first sent by telegram from the U.S. Department of Commerce, and it is possible that a telegraphic error resulted in the KDL call letters. It was the end of May before the actual license was received by mail and the error was discovered and corrected in the *Telegram.*

KDYL establishes its foothold in Utah's new radio market

May 1922 was an exciting period for the launch of radio broadcasting in Utah, as we know it today. Along with the demonstration at the Fort Douglas Club on May 10 (discussed in an earlier chapter), other organizations and businesses provided listeners the opportunity to hear KDL's concert par excellence on opening night. For instance, the Newhouse Hotel, where Kaar would two months later locate KDYL's high power station, invited the public to join the festivities on May 10:

Indication of the interest being manifested is furnished at the

---

90   Salt Lake Telegram, May 10, 1922.

Newhouse hotel, where James H. Waters, the manager, proposes to
install receiving sets so that the guests may hear the news, concerts
and other features which will be broadcasted from the Telegram's
elaborate station. ... To meet the demand of the public, to satisfy its
large family, to bring light from darkness, to interest, to educate and
to amuse is the purpose of The Telegram in taking this advanced step,
and mark another rung in the ladder of progress in Salt Lake City and
Utah.[91]

Ever the newspaper entrepreneur, on the day after KDYL went on the air,
Fish immediately saw the potential of exploiting the young Kaar's engineering
expertise to create goodwill and sell newspaper subscriptions for the *Telegram*.
To wit: free advice in solving the mysteries of radio was offered:[92]

The Telegram has decided to establish a bureau where information
relative to radio will be disseminated free to the subscribers of this
newspaper. As a consequence, Ira Kaar, radio expert, has been
engaged. [He] may be consulted in room 115, Keith Emporium
Building, the same building that houses The Telegram's establishment.
If you are in doubt as to any intricacy in the manipulation of the radio
telephone, if you need advice regarding the establishment of receiving
sets or require information regarding the installation of radio
equipment, you should get in touch with Mr. Kaar, whose knowledge
of the many factors which enter into the new science will be imparted
to all those who wish to avail themselves of the offer here made.

Over the next several months, while continuing to operate KDYL from his
parent's home, Kaar built a new facility for Fish on the roof of the Newhouse
Hotel. On August 28, 1922, the new KDYL station officially went on-the-air.

Kaar designed and oversaw the construction of the KDYL antenna system,
the transmitter, the power supply, the operating room and the studio on top of
the Newhouse Hotel. The transmitter was "of the latest type known to science,"

---

91   Salt Lake Telegram, May 9, 1922, Sec. 2, 1.
92   Salt Lake Telegram, May 21, 1922, Sec. 2, 1.

as noted in the press. The studio was constructed so that no echo or distortion would reach the several sensitive microphones, which Kaar installed to pick up music from all kinds of instruments and from large or small groups:[93]

> Tonight [August 28, 1922] at 7 o'clock the Telegram's new K.D.Y.L. broadcasting station will start sending its radio telephone concerts. No expense has been spared in equipment, and one of the most modern and latest stations of its kind is found on top of the Newhouse Hotel. Ira Karr [*sic*], engineer and operator in charge has worked for months getting everything ready and has designed a special transmitter.

The *Telegram* continued to own the station, and Kaar, while attending the University of Utah, continued to operate KDYL for the next two years. Kaar was chief engineer and was responsible from May 1922, to February 1924, for filing every three months, under the Radio of Act of 1912 requirements, the renewal for KDYL's license. Even after the Telegram Publishing Company began leasing KDYL to James H. Waters, manager of the Newhouse Hotel, on February 19, 1924, Kaar remained at the station. But with his college graduation approaching, Kaar left KDYL in May 1924, and H.C. Mailander became the chief KDYL operator and the person responsible for license renewal applications. Everett J. (Hap) Seeley joined Mailander a year later. Seely was a KDYL operator and engineer, as was C.W. Hays another KDYL employee. Seeley and Hays were well-known amateur contemporaries of Kaar in the previous decade.

The arrival of Sidney S. Fox

In 1925, Fred Provol purchased KDYL radio station and formed the Intermountain Broadcasting Corporation (IBC) on July 19, 1926, as parent to KDYL, and on November 1 the KDYL license was transferred to IBC, whose principal shareholder was Provol. IBC's purpose was "to operate broadcasting stations and other 'amusement' enterprises."[94] Everett J. Seely and C.W. Hays

---

93   Salt Lake Telegram, August 28, 1922.
94   IBC incorporation papers, July 19, 1926.

joined Provol in forming IBC. Provol, who was running his mother Eva's Hudson Bay Company apparel and fur businesses, turned over KDYL to Seeley and Hays to operate in 1926. Provol saw the station as little more than an interesting sideline and likely saw it as having no worthwhile practical or financial viability.

But, more consequently, Provol's mother was married to Sidney S. Fox. He was not involved when IBC was formed but would acquire the Intermountain Broadcasting Company/KDYL from Provol in late 1926. Fox had an upbringing that early on suggested a keen instinct for business. At age seven, in 1896, Fox went into partnership with a St. Louis neighborhood friend on a lemonade stand. His partner furnished the water and the ice and Fox furnished the lemons and the sugar. While he might have been too young at the time to comprehend the significance of product value, he proved to be a quick learner. In subsequent business ventures, he nearly always provided the metaphorically cheaper water and ice, while others supplied the more expensive lemons and sugar.

Above all, Fox wanted to be in show business. A good tap dancer, he debuted in a St. Louis vaudeville act at age 14 but, by his own admission, "had no voice." The vaudeville act dissolved and about the same time he quit school. At his parent's insistence, he continued in night school while he ushered at a vaudeville theater. After a short period, he became a copy boy for the *St. Louis Post Dispatch* and then a sample clerk for a large nut and fruit company. His next job was as a single-entry bookkeeper for a St. Louis shoe company.

At 17, he went to Denver, arriving at the Seventeenth Street railroad depot one Sunday morning in 1906. Almost immediately he met a young man whom would become a lifelong friend. Abe Hirschfeld was a little older than Fox, streetwise and "somebody for a young guy to talk to." He made Fox feel at home.

Fox never forgot his first day in Denver. He said he went there for health reasons, and he knew he had to make it on his own. His father was having financial difficulties and would be in no position to help him. Hirschfeld introduced Fox to other young people in the Jewish community and he immediately fit in with his new friends. Even then, Fox was well groomed and a good dancer. Socially he was a hit.

Hirschfeld also gave Fox his first Denver job. "Well, I'll tell you what you do, Sid, you might as well go out and represent me and take orders for cards." Hirschfeld was in the business-card printing business, and he used a small hand press to print cards on the spot for customers. Fox said he went down to Denver's assignation district where the dance halls and saloons were located and where Colorado miners came for "entertainment." Fox found that there were 500 "girls" in the district who were soliciting sex. These prostitutes worked in crib-like boxes located in an eight-square block area. Fox noticed that each of the women had her name in her crib window: "St. Louis Sadie, Kansas City Betty, Chicago Lou." It struck him that these women all had individual "businesses" of their own and could use business cards. According to Fox, he sold "business-cards" to about 200 of the prostitutes with printed "information suggested by the business owner" on each card. Fox kept half of the money from the cards he sold for Hirschfeld, which became the seed investment for his Denver business activities.

That was in 1906. Hirschfeld, who often was called A.B., married in1907 and went on to become a state legislator and a "community pillar." He died in April, 1957 and his rabbi eulogized ... "the forceful, dynamic civic stalwart who rose from obscure handset printer to eminence in lithography, as a great and good man, ... a distinguished and honored citizen."[95]

Hirschfeld's philosophy of life was, "As long as you are living, do good. If you don't do good, you are not living." It was that philosophy, with a qualification, that Fox took to heart. Fox "did good" with his money and was compassionate to those who needed money, but he also was not a counselor or somebody to whom you went to discuss a personal problem, unless that problem could be helped by money. He was mostly interested in his own pleasures. With a few significant exceptions, Fox kept company with those who were flamboyant like him and relished living in a flamboyant world.

---

95   4th of Nison, 5717, Denver Colorado, April 5, 1957, Vol. XLIV, No. 14.

Fox was an easy touch for those less fortunate and when KDYL prospered, his generosity became legendary. He paid hospital bills for friends, employees and their children, threw parties for the children at Shriners Hospital, lent money to friends with no expectation of it being repaid, picked up the tab for parties in Las Vegas and Reno, looked after his mother Sallie Fox and sister Jessie Loeb, and showered his employees and their kids with gifts at Christmas. For instance:

> The station resembled Santa's workshop at Christmas time. Fox even hired extra help to wrap the gifts. Kids remember meeting Fox and getting change or a dollar bill from him, like other people might give gum or candy. [96]

After his initial Denver printing job with Hirschfield, Fox went into the newly emerging moving-picture industry, working for Pathe and Selig-Essenay, among the early pillars of Hollywood's Studio Era. As he would later find with radio broadcasting, Fox saw great potential in this developing industry. He acquired distribution offices in the Denver and Salt Lake territories and for the next 14 years was in business for himself on the road distributing such "super colossal" movie releases of the time as *Mickey, Civilization, The Garden of Allah* and *Raffles.*

Fox gained some friends in Salt Lake City and was socially active. In 1920, on a trip to Pocatello for the grand opening of a summer garden owned by a friend, Fox met Eva Provol in the hotel dining room. As mentioned earlier, she lived in Salt Lake City and owned the Hudson Bay Fur Company. After a short courtship, they were married. In 1921, Fox was listed in the *Polk Directory* as general manager of a company called All Star Productions. Soon after, Provol turned over the Hudson Bay Fur Company operation to her son, Fred, and she and Fox went to Los Angeles to take advantage of the real estate boom and then on to Florida for the same reason. In 1925, Fox returned to Salt Lake, and the *Polk Directory* then listed his employment as "real estate."

---

96   KDYL's engineer John M. Baldwin biographical sketch of Fox, [circa 1978].

Upon his return, he helped his stepson (Fred Provol) at the Hudson Bay Fur Company. In classic Fox mannerism, Fox sent Hudson Bay employee, Coleman Creel, with furs to clothing stores in small towns throughout Idaho and Utah. Creel placed furs in these stores on consignment and these stores became representatives of the Hudson Bay Fur Company. Fox capitalized on friendships he had established in these small towns during the 14 years he spent in the film distribution business.

This was classic Fox because throughout his adult life Fox consistently added value to ordinary products through distributorships, product representations, stock-lettings and syndication. In the marketing scheme, Fox was the quintessential master of place (one of the classic 4 Ps) in marketing. He knew how to move products to customers. From his lemonade stand days going forward, Fox always was a risk taker, speculator and a gambler.

In late 1926, Fox acquired KDYL, along with the controlling stock from Fred Provol, a switch, which was amended accordingly in the IBC charter. The reason Fox acquired KDYL was not only to bailout his stepson but also to replicate the sweet financial deal he had observed with Glade at KSL. Fox observed that Glade's company, Radio Broadcasters, Inc. (RBI), was making "big $" by operating KSL for the Radio Service Corporation of Utah, the KSL licensee. Fox intended to set up a similar arrangement with the IBC, the KDYL licensee. Thus, Fox entered the field of broadcasting to become like what Glade had accomplished at KSL, at least from a personal financial standpoint.

No compensation for Fox was recorded until July 1, 1927, after which he began to take $400 per month, appropriating all KDYL's profits each month for the remainder of 1927. His salary from July 1, 1927 through 1928 averaged a little over $400 a month, a figure not inordinately high to the Internal Revenue Service. However, in 1929, his salary began averaging over $1,000 per month and in 1930, over $1,600 per month. These figures were perceived as inordinately high to the IRS. The IRS concluded that, "reasonable and true compensation is only such amount as would ordinarily be paid for like services by like enterprises in like circumstances."[97]

In Fox's defense, there were few "like services" or "like enterprises" in "like circumstances" to which the IRS could compare. On the other hand, in defense of the IRS, Fox likely went overboard by offsetting all IBC profits with salary payments to him. The tax rate likely was lower on personal income than on corporate income and Fox took advantage of it. Fox argued that his "management and ability" were responsible for the progress of the corporation and that he was entitled to the entire amount of compensation taken. Fox made the point that he was not an officer and manager in name only, but that he also expended efforts in building the business by personally securing business that other sales people failed to secure.

Nevertheless, the IRS was not sympathetic to Fox's argument. It held that the amounts paid Fox were "relatively much higher than paid by other corporations coping with the same limitations and coming within the scope of this taxpayer."[98] The IRS allowed Fox to declare only a $10,000 KDYL salary (equal to $140,300 today) for each year of 1929 and 1930. IBC, which was nearly totally owned by Fox, had to pay higher corporate taxes on the perceived overpayment to him.

Curiously, if the IRS had used Glade's income as manager at KSL for 1929 and 1930 to make "like" comparisons, they would have found that Fox was not overpaid. In those two years, Glade averaged $18,373 per year while Fox averaged only $18,200. However, Glades' direct salary from KSL was only $62 in 1928 and $7,050 in 1929. The remainder came from his Radio Broadcasters, Inc. (RBI), which caused no known stir at the IRS. Indeed, Fox still had things to learn from Glade's acumen for this new industry. Fox could have taken some of his income through IBC stock dividends and the IRS likely would not have protested his total income from both salary and stock, but he yet wasn't that sophisticated. It wasn't until 1931 that he began to derive income from both sources, and this quieted the IRS.

---

97   IBC IRS Tax Audit, 1931, Schedule 5A, 9.
98   IBC IRS Tax Audit, 1931, Schedule 5A, 10.

In those early years, the IRS also examined Fox's methods for determining the value of IBC capital stock, but found there were no IBC tax liabilities associated with his methods. Under the Radio Act of 1912, a license was available to any applicant for the asking because the government had no discretionary power in issuing broadcast licenses. Thus, when Fox acquired KDYL from Provol in 1926, the "operating license" was of no real value; it was essentially worthless.

This changed when, on February 23, 1927, President Calvin Coolidge signed the Radio Act of 1927 into law. The Act set up a five-member Federal Radio Commission (FRC) and gave it discretionary power to license stations, classify radio stations, prescribe the nature of the services they would render and assign bandwidths, power, and operating frequencies. After the Radio Act of 1927 was passed, the KDYL license suddenly became a precious, highly valued instrument as a scarce resource.

Fox knew nothing of the subtleties of the Radio Act of 1927 and what a "scarce resource" meant to him, but in discussions with his Denver broadcasting friend, Eugene O'Fallon, Fox discovered that the KDYL license carried substantial "goodwill" value, so he declared the KDYL license as an asset and issued stock on its value. After KDYL liabilities were subtracted from assets, on July 1, 1927, Fox determined the net value of KDYL to be $4,000. Fox then set up an asset called an "operating license", in the amount of $11,000, and issued capital stock in the amount of $15,000 to cover the total net asset value of the station. Fox owned $14,980 of the stock while the stock Creel and Provol possessed was valued at $10 per share. On December 31, 1927, Fox increased the value of the "operating license" and issued $3,000 more in stock. By December 31, 1928, he had increased the value of the license by more than six fold to $26,500 and the net value of IBC was now set at $52,500.

Because the value of the license represented the value of Fox's share in IBC, he controlled a majority of the stock in the corporation and could manage KDYL as he wished. As shareholders paid cash for KDYL (IBC) stock and steadily carved into Fox's majority position, he responded by merely increasing the value of the license. To gain permanent control, Fox doubled the value of the license and by December 31,1930, the "operating license" – valued at $98,832 and nearly totally controlled by Fox – represented 90% ownership of IBC. Fox likely never paid a single dollar in cash for any of his IBC stock. He had learned to provide the proverbial water and ice while other assets provided the lemonade and sugar.

Fox's team and leadership style

Fox spent minimal time with daily station operations, except in dealing with advertising sales. KDYL was on the air for only four hours each day from 8 p.m. to midnight, when he took over from Provol in late 1926. Fox immediately extended the broadcast day to ten hours (from 2 p.m. to midnight), ready to capitalize on a revenue stream of selling more commercial time slots to advertisers. In early 1927, in an FRC license application, Fox declared KDYL to be "the only station in this district operating in the daytime, thousands of radio fans and dealers dependent upon us for amusement, educational talks, market reports, weather for[e]casts time signals etc."[99]

With a distinction of one word that might seem trivial to the uninitiated, Fox demonstrated his promotional prowess. KDYL could have been the only station in the "district" operating in the daytime if there actually was such a thing as a radio "district." It was Fox's invention. If he meant "zone," then KDYL clearly was not the only station in the 11 western states and the territories of Alaska and Hawaii to operate in the daytime. KDYL then wasn't even the only one in Salt Lake. For Fox, "district" could have meant KDYL's neighborhood. This was classic Fox hyperbole and typical of his paucity of candor in correspondence with government agencies over the years, even those like the Federal Radio Commission that was only a month old when he wrote the above in his first official radio license application. The sovereign Fox over the years snubbed institutions like the FRC/FCC and the IRS, yet each of these government agencies overlooked his eccentric input in hearings.

In the years he owned KDYL, Fox did not like being alone or doing things

---

99   Application for Radio Station License to the Federal Radio Commission, Intermountain Broadcasting Corporation, dated March 30, 1927 and signed by S.S. Fox, Pres. & Gen. Mgr..

alone, so whether he was gambling in Las Vegas, going to the doctor for a nose pack, or taking a massage, he often had somebody in his cortege with him. Several men and women, certainly not sycophants, could be included in this group, but three people were especially close to Fox: Harry Golub, Freddy Horowitz and Manny Drucker. Like Fox, all three were Jewish. Golub was an affable "show business type," barrel-chested with a rich baritone voice. His rendition of *Ol' Man River* on KDYL reportedly was an audience favorite. Golub came to Salt Lake City to manage the Orpheum Theatre, across the street of the Ezra Thompson Building in downtown. Golub and Fox did some promotional ventures together, and the flamboyant Golub eventually became a KDYL salesman.

Horowitz and Drucker also were KDYL salesmen and Fox's personal friends and confidants. Neither of these men were flamboyant, although they did well in Fox's flamboyant world. Horowitz was focused on straight selling – no discounts, no frills. He and the hard-nosed Drucker were said to have had no time for business lunches and schmoozing. One either bought KDYL on its merits or they didn't buy from Horowitz or Drucker. Like Fox, Drucker's ubiquitous cigar was his trademark. Although these men were Fox's personal soldiers, all three were superb salesmen and they earned their keep. Meanwhile, Drucker's son-in-law, Aaron Bournstein, and granddaughter, Jan Bournstein, followed him into broadcast sales. Ms. Bournstein eventually rose to marketing director for KTVX, television, the modern day KDYL.[100]

Although a superb promoter, Fox was not a visionary, nor a "student" of future broadcast developments. Almost every broadcasting idea he developed came from somebody else. His stepson got him into radio, his very first "Trip-to-Paris" radio promotion in 1927 came from his wife's cousin, and his radio engineer, John Baldwin, fostered his experimentation in Salt Lake City television in 1939. What Fox did best was to sell and to promote new and risky ideas thought up by others. He would leap with the force of his and others' money into a venture while others were still calculating risk. He was almost uniformly successful with these quick deals. Although his long tenure as owner

---

100   Jan Bournstein interviews by Tim Larson, August 24 and 29, 1989, Salt Lake City; Aaron Bournstein interview by Tim Larson, February 3, 1990.

of KDYL seems to belie it, his nature was to get in, make a deal and get out as quickly as possible with a big profit.

Beginning in 1927, Fox handpicked people who could profitably run KDYL for him. These men, however, would not be part of his retinue. Knowing little about the broadcasting business, Fox again called on Eugene P. O'Fallon, his Denver friend and owner of KFEL, to find someone with experience to manage KDYL. O'Fallon suggested Philip G. Lasky. Fox convinced Lasky to come to Salt Lake City as KDYL's assistant manager, reporting to Fox, who was the general manager. In June 1927, Lasky came to Salt Lake City at somewhat less money than he was making at KFEL, with the understanding that he would participate in KDYL's success. He signed no contract and arrived on Fox's oral promise that he would prosper as KDYL would prosper. Lasky joined KDYL as an engineer, announcer and assistant manager but later became station manager, secretary of IBC and acquired 100 shares of IBC stock. Lasky describes Fox as a fine, compassionate and benevolent man who kept his word. When Fox sold the KDYL stations in 1953, Lasky, although he left Salt Lake City 18 years before, was still an IBC stockholder. He received a check for $8,924 ($96,629 today).

Lasky had been a wireless amateur in his teens and became a favorite of Dr. W.D. Reynolds, a dentist, who was the most experienced of a coterie of wireless amateurs in Denver after WWI and in the early 1920s. Reynolds taught Lasky all about building radio stations from scratch. Lasky's wireless amateur station, 9DHI, was later absorbed by Doc Reynolds' 9ZAF experimental voice station. In 1923, Lasky quit high school after his sophomore year and with the $60 he had saved, he went to San Francisco to go to sea as a wireless operator. He was 17 years old and he never lived at home again, and his formal education was continued only through extension courses. After a time at sea, Lasky went to work for the U.S. Airmail Service which was using old Federal Telegraph 2-kilowatt arc transmitters to guide airmail planes across the western states. Wireless stations were located in San Francisco, Reno, Elko, Salt Lake City, Cheyenne and Omaha. Lasky was assigned to the Cheyenne station and his job was to use the wireless to keep track of planes as they were flying from station to station. There was no communication with the pilots who were flying WWI DeHaviland fighter planes:[101]

> These wireless stations used to keep track of the airplanes that were
> flying. These were two-seated open cockpit planes, with a bag of mail
> in one seat and the pilot in the other, flying the railroad tracks as their
> navigation system.

Lasky worked this job for about a year and then went to Omaha's *World
Herald* and then to the *Denver Post* as a newspaper reporter. Lasky improved
his writing and oral communication skills as a reporter, but his passion
was still for radio. It was 1926 and Lasky was 21 years old. In Denver, Doc
Reynolds' 9ZAF had become broadcasting station KLZ in 1922, General
Electric had built KOA in 1924, and Eugene P. O'Fallon had recently founded
KFEL located at East 15th Avenue and Grant St. in Denver. Lasky went to
work at KFEL and had his own little radio show. He was also the engineer, the
announcer, general handyman and designer, builder and equipment installer.

Before hiring him, Fox told Lasky that there were two KDYL employees,
from the Telegram Newhouse Hotel and Fred Provol days, that he was going
to release. They were operator Seely and operator announcer Hays. As stated,
Seeley and Hays were two of the organizers, with Fred Provol, of the IBC.
Seeley and Hays and Mailander had kept KDYL on the air for three years after
Kaar left for General Electric early in 1924. But, Fox told Lasky that KDYL
would start clean when he took over: "Here's the station, run it." Seeley
and Hays met Lasky his first day in Salt Lake City and reportedly were not
enthusiastic at his arrival.[102]

On December 31, 1927, IBC tax records show that Seeley and Hays each
were issued $1,000 in IBC stock for services they had rendered. This would
have represented 25% ownership of IBC between them if Fox hadn't boldly
declared KDYL's "operating license" to be worth $40,500, which then would
have made Seeley and Hays stockholders, each with a 1.9% stake, and just
for 3.8% for Fred Provol, 7.6% for Eva Provol and himself as holder of a 77%

---

101   Lasky interview by Tim Larson and Gregory Thompson, May 4, 1984; and with Tim Larson
April 12, 1988, at Lasky's home in Hillsborough, California.
102   Lasky interview by Tim Larson, April 12, 1988, at his home in Hillsborough, California, 53.

share. Reportedly, it was Seeley's contention that he was not fairly treated by Fox's handling of the capital stock account, and he understandably was not complimentary of Fox. In Fox's defense, he took over KDYL when the station generously had only $4,000 in net value, even after Seeley and Hays had been running it for a significant period of time where the value had not appreciated considerably.

Within a short period, Fox put a $97,000 value on the KDYL operating license and goodwill. When asked in a 1935 FCC hearing about that figure, Fox replied:[103]

> That item [operating license] is an original entry made by our accountant at the time in setting up our books. It has been carried along from year to year, and as a matter of fact is nothing more than, I would say, just a general item that does not mean anything in our setup.

Clearly, Fox did not believe the operating license did "not mean anything." He had put none of his own money, only $4,000 of his wife's cash, into KDYL. Yet, he controlled 77% of IBC by virtue of the increased value of the operating license. It was this ownership that allowed him to dismiss Seely and Hays, who were major IBC stockholders before Fox had ballooned IBC's value by using the operating license as leverage. In plain words, Fox's 1935 testimony was not, putting it kindly, totally forthright.

Much later, it became commonplace for broadcasting stations to declare their operating licenses as a valued intangible asset. Fox applied the idea in Utah in 1927, seven years before it became a nationally accepted accounting practice. He was fearless when it came to "innovative" financing and, in 1935, government legislation and his irreverent methods perfectly meshed to his advantage.

When Lasky took over KDYL in June 1927, the transmitter was not in ideal working order. All of the equipment was housed in a small partitioned

---

103   FCC Transcript of Hearings, testimony of Sidney S. Fox, January 30, 1935, 14.

space with a window at one end of the studio. The 50-watt transmitter, about
the size of today's television set, sat on a table next to a window out of which
trailed the antenna wire. The nameplate on the front carried Kaar's name. It
was evident that this transmitter had many of its vital parts transplanted after
Mr. Kaar moved to GE three years before.[104]

Lasky's first task was to visit the Fort Douglas station and borrow some
replacement 50-watt tubes from the U.S. Army Signal Corps to put into the
transmitter Kaar had built for Fish and the *Salt Lake Telegram* many years
before. Lasky then hired Jack Albert for additional technical help. Albert
was experienced with audio equipment, but knew little about broadcasting
equipment per se, particularly transmitters. He came to KDYL from many
years in AT&T's long lines department and, as such, was quite knowledgeable
of amplifiers and switching gear. Albert and Lasky built all new studio
equipment and put things in "pretty good working order." Fox trusted Lasky to
start from scratch with employees, programming, equipment and offices. They
then moved the station to the Ezra Thompson Building at 143 South Main
Street in downtown, and KDYL continued to improve.

Promotional and talent prowess

In the summer and autumn of 1927, while Lasky was hiring people,
developing talent and programs and updating equipment, Fox was desperately
trying to get Main Street merchants interested in buying commercial spots on
KDYL. It was nearly impossible, until he exploited an idea given to him by his
wife's cousin, Frank Algage. In Denver, Algage told Fox of an American Legion
movement whereby cities across the U.S. would send WWI veterans to Paris
for a ten-year reunion. Algage told Fox all about the idea, hoping he would
implement it in Denver. Instead, Fox came back home with the idea and began
to develop it in Salt Lake City. Fox executed a landmark promotion that had
a lasting change on Salt Lake City merchants' attitudes about the viability of
radio advertising.

---

104   Philip Lasky: Remarks to the members of the Utah Broadcasters Association, August 2,
1986, Park City, Utah, upon induction into the Utah Broadcasters Hall of Fame.

Fox had nearly a million "Free-Trip-to-Paris" voting certificates printed and he gave them to more than 40 Salt Lake City merchants who had to purchase spots on KDYL to be a part of the promotion. Each merchant was enlisted to buy 35 spots at one dollar per spot during the period of July 2 to August 20, 1927. Merchants advertised on KDYL that they were participants in the "Free-Trip-to-Paris" campaign and that voting certificates could be obtained with each purchase. For every ten cents that a customer spent at a participating store, the individual was given one voting certificate. Fox established the "Free-Trip-to-Paris Company of Utah" and opened store front offices on Main Street as voting headquarters. He took out full-page ads in the local newspapers and he personally sold the campaign in visits to merchants. Customers made purchases and then went to FTP Headquarters to cast votes for their favorite WWI veteran. A list of 500 WWI veterans was compiled and 200 signed up and received votes:[105]

> With every ten-cent purchase they got a vote. The three men who got the most votes would go to Paris. Well, now I [Fox] had to have the backing of the American Legion, the Commander in Charge, and I had to get a number of servicemen to participate in wanting to go to Paris. So, I had to open a voting headquarters where I put ballot boxes, and I had to have merchants buy these votes, and give them out with a ten-cent purchase, see. Now that was before trading stamps, and the result was that I put across a deal that probably netted me, in the overall. I must have made about five thousand dollars net on the deal.

While Fox thought up other station promotions, Lasky continued to develop local talent. There were some high school students having a pep rally in the studio one day, and Lasky recalled that a "particularly glib, personable and handsome student" who was doing an imitation of Maurice Chevalier singing *Louise* caught his eye. It was G. Bennett Larson. He called the teen's mother who worked as a dietician for Utah Power and Light and asked for permission to hire her son as an announcer. With assurances that employment

---

105   Sidney S. Fox Collection, Marriott Library, S.S. Fox recollects, date unknown, [circa 1975], 22.

would not detract from her son's schooling, she approved.

Ben Larson, soon after being hired, became a huge success as Uncle Ben, hosting a children's show. A studio was rebuilt to house his *Kangaroo Club*, complete with junior scale furniture. The show aired weekdays at five p.m. and the KDYL corridors each afternoon were packed with children and their mothers. The Club Motto was "SAS" – "Save and Succeed." Little banks were given out to kids for their savings. "Cousin" Lil Frank, the late Salt Lake City clothier Alan Frank's mother, played the piano for the Kangaroo Club, as did Fox's stepson Robert Provol and Tom Brown, a mail carrier. Soon, the Kangaroo Club Band was formed and a bandmaster was hired to teach the kids about music. As Lasky reported, "Not much went on in Salt Lake City that didn't include the Kangaroo Band, resplendent in their black and orange colored uniforms."

Larson began at age 16 in 1927 and continued performing as Uncle Ben until late 1929 when he went to the National Broadcasting Company (NBC) in New York, which was then just in its third year of operation, as a producer and director. Over the next five years he became responsible for shows featuring at that time some of the nation's best-known celebrity entertainers. These included Ed Wynn's *Fire Chief* shows, Eddie Cantor's *Chase and Sanborn Hour* and Rudy Vallee's Thursday night shows. In 1932, Larson was involved in the debut of Al Jolson, already famous for his Broadway performances, on NBC radio. A collection of Larson's marked-up scripts from the shows he directed is housed in the Marriott Library Special Collections at The University of Utah. From 1934 to 1945, Larson worked at several major New York advertising agencies and then moved on to manage and/or own radio and television stations in Washington, D.C., Philadelphia and New York City.[106]

With the move to broadcasting, radio's engineers and operators needed to upgrade their credentials. Lasky had a 1st class operators license but needed someone with a commercial operator's license. George D. Snell got his FRC operating license in 1925 for his amateur 6AKM station and later a 2nd Class

---

106   Interview with G. Bennett Larson by Tim Larson, August 4, 1985, at his Los Angeles, CA, area home.

Commercial License. Lasky at KDYL hired him in 1927, becoming one of KDYL's earliest employees. Snell was a good operator who could send and transcribe international code "with the best of them", but he also was soon found to be a gifted writer and announcer, and these abilities were quickly utilized. Snell later married Lasky's secretary, Althea Pederson. He also became KDYL's Uncle Ben in 1929 after Larson went to NBC. In 1934, Snell published his first novel, *The Great Adam*, and the first copy of the first edition, complete with autograph and inscription, went to Lasky.[107]

Snell worked at KDYL for 17 years until 1945 when he left to write and produce programs for KPO in San Francisco. B. Floyd Farr, a friend and former fellow KDYL broadcaster, hired Snell at KPO, NBC's flagship station in San Francisco. In Utah, Farr, a college graduate, had been a Weber High School teacher as well as a live commercial announcer at Ogden's Paramount Theatre during movie reel changes. He moved to announcing at Ogden's KLO radio station and then to KDYL 1320AM in Salt Lake. In 1935, a KPO executive heard him on a KDYL NBC Network remote feed and offered him an announcing position at the San Francisco station. After a short time, he became KPO's chief announcer while also carrying the same duties when called upon from the West Coast for the NBC Network. On December 7, 1941, when Pearl Harbor was attacked and the U.S. entered World War II, he used a telephone hookup to KPO from Pearl Harbor, and was the lead-in announcer from KPO for the NBC Network for covering the breaking news.

In 1947, Snell and Farr, with financial assistance from George Mardikian, owner of the Omar Khayyam Restaurant In San Francisco, obtained a permit and built KEEN radio in San Jose, which became a successful station with a country-western format. Snell, Farr and their families owned and operated several stations in the West and Hawaii for several decades, including KBAY, KVEG, KFIG, KFOA and KHAU, among others. In honor of his enormous contributions, Farr was elected to the Bay Area Radio Hall of Fame in 2018.[108]

---

107   Tim Larson and Greg Thompson interview with George Snell, May 3, 1984, at his Northern California home; Tim Larson and Craig Wirth interviews with Keith B. Farr, 1986 through 2015, at his Lodi, CA, home.

108   Keith B. Farr, Bay Area Radio Hall of Fame: https://bayarearadio.org/sf-radio-history/ farr. Documentation from and conversations with B. Floyd Farr's daughter, Nancy Delgado, and extensive interviews with Keith B. Farr, Floyd's nephew, who worked at Utah's KLO and at the

Another of Lasky's important hires at KDYL was announcer Richard T. Harris. At about this time, the Salt Lake newspapers refused to run radio schedules in their newspapers, fearing radio competition would reduce newspaper sales. Harris was one of those appointed to develop a KDYL program schedule for distribution. "The Voice of KDYL" developed into a bimonthly newspaper that carried the "news of KDYL programs." Harris was listed with Lasky in the masthead of the paper as an editor. The "Voice" continued to be published even after the Salt Lake newspapers again resumed publishing the daily radio schedules. Harris continued to announce and contribute to the publication after George Provol took over as its associate editor. Robert Provol became its circulation manager in the early 1930s. Nepotism prevailed as both employees were Fox's stepsons.

Harris left KDYL in 1938 and formed the Richard T. Harris Company, a full-service advertising agency. Later it became Salt Lake City's iconic Harris and Love Advertising Agency, which, in turn, morphed again into the Riester-Robb and then the Riester Advertising Agency. Harris had very fond memories of his KDYL days and had high regard for Fox and Lasky.

Lasky hired many people who continued at KDYL even after he left in 1935 for San Francisco, but of those he hired, Larson, Snell and Harris were his favorites. Lasky was not much older than his colleagues, but he nonetheless was a father figure for the three men: "These are … the three for whom I have special regard. I considered them as my 'kids'. Perhaps 'brothers' would be more apt. They were high-grade persons, very intelligent and talented. All were creative, Dick and George as writers, Ben as a showman."[109]

Fox's 'extended family'

In 1928, a "real" engineer was needed. KDYL couldn't get its new transmitter on 3300 South, outside of downtown Salt Lake City, to work properly. In August 1928, the transmitter was not on the air, although

---

Snell/Farr stations in Las Vegas and in Lodi, California, provided important information over several years about the two long-term friends.
109   Lasky interview with Tim Larson [transcript], April 12, 1988 in his home in Hillsborough, California, 46.

installation had begun several months prior. Snell, Lasky, and Victor Vettel were licensed operators but not broadcast engineers so Fox needed a skilled engineer who could finish installing the transmitter and put it on-the-air. That person also was expected to maintain the equipment and complete the changeover from using composite (homebuilt) equipment to regular Westinghouse manufactured equipment. It was essential if KDYL had any intentions of expanding its broadcast services and satisfy the Federal Radio Commission's professional engineering standards.

Fox went again to his Denver friends for suggesting a name, which turned out to be John M. Baldwin, who was working in Texas in the geophysical department of the Marlin Oil Company. Baldwin was responsible for exploding dynamite in the ground and using radio to measure the time interval it took for the sound waves to go down and come back up. which effectively located oil reserves for the company. But, Baldwin was laid off when Marlin closed out the entire department in July 1928. He went back to Oklahoma City and found KDYL's letter offering him a job and started work a month later.

Baldwin was born October 11, 1905, in Washington, D.C., and as a young boy played with radio as a hobby. In the early 1920s, he moved to Oklahoma City to work in an electric store as a salesperson. But, selling was not his best skill so he transferred to the workshop, making radio receivers, where he was a natural. He also helped build a radio transmitter for a station in Ardmore, Oklahoma, and then went to Chickasaw to build a 20-watt radio station. But, the original owners lost interest in that station and the Oklahoma College for Women paid Baldwin to move the station to the stage of its campus auditorium and run it. Surrounded by velvet drapes, Baldwin played records at night and continued working in the store building radios during the day. After leaving Oklahoma, Baldwin worked for KOA radio in Denver as an engineer.

Baldwin was Fox's second major hire after Lasky. As with Lasky, Fox picked Baldwin as much for his self-confidence and independence as he did for his engineering abilities. Fox needed no sycophant, and Baldwin certainly did not become one. Baldwin had a gift for leading Fox to focus on matters important to the station and get him to listen. Plainly speaking, Baldwin looked after Fox, rather than the other way around.

Baldwin's first task at KDYL was to put the new 3300 South transmitter on the air, and he immediately discovered why the tubes continued to blow: "It seems the engineer they had didn't realize that the tubes they used in the transmitter required pure water [to cool them]. They piped well water which was very heavily laced with alkali into the tubes and, naturally, it blew them all up."[110]

Baldwin corrected the cooling problem with distilled water and put the finishing touches on the transmitter. Six weeks after he arrived, KDYL began broadcasting using 1,000 watts of power, up from the original 100 watts it had been using. KDYL's slogan in 1928 was "On-the-air-Goes-Everywhere," which might have been a little exaggerated for 100 watts of power, but when it was boosted to 1,000 watts the slogan seemed more appropriate. He was promoted to vice president in charge of KDYL engineering. He later became an IBC stockholder and officer.

Fox hired the services of a third essential person in those early years – his lawyer, Calvin W. Rawlings. Whenever he put any financial deal together, he called on Rawlings who was a partner in the Rawlings, Wallace & Black law firm. Like Fox and Lasky, Rawlings was always impeccably attired and dapper looking. He was said to present a portrait from Park Avenue – in a word, "class." Rawlings became a successful antitrust attorney and for several years in the 1970s was City Attorney for Salt Lake. He served on the University Board of Regents and Institutional Council, and was vice president of the Utah Symphony, an honorary member of the Utah National Guard and was involved in Boy Scouts for 35 years.

He was actively involved in politics both locally and nationally and rose in the Democratic Party to become chairman of its national credentials committee. Of politics, Rawlings said, "I've always been as proud of being a

---

110   Interview with John M. Baldwin and wife Marie in his Salt Lake City home, May 9, 1979. Interviewed by Patrick Boyles and Tim Larson.

politician as I am of being a lawyer. Politics is an honorable profession with many dedicated men and women [involved]." One of Rawlings dearest friends was James A. (Big Jim) Farley, the "kingmaker" from the Democrat's New Deal days.

With a self-effacing sense of humor, Rawlings belied the usual impression of a "hick" from way out there in Utah. One day he was riding with President Truman in Provo and pointed out his boyhood home to the President: "There's my home when I was a boy. I didn't dream at that time I'd be riding with the President of the United States. President Truman reportedly drawled, "When I was a boy and growing up around a house like that I didn't dream I'd be President of the United States."[111]

Rawlings represented Fox and KDYL from the early days, and on Christmas Eve in 1942, Rawlings wrote Fox a brief note of deep appreciation not just for the professional relationship but the one they enjoyed as friends:[112]

> I have told you many times how I valued our friendship, but I want to put in writing that I think you are one of the greatest friends that any man has been privileged to have. There is nothing more valuable than friends Real friends who will stand by you when the going gets tough. Sid, I consider you such a friend and this though gives me much pleasure and contentment. You have put yourself out many times in many many ways to help me and make me happy. Don't think I do not appreciate everything you have done for me and my family. ... Someday an opportunity may present itself which will permit me to show to you my appreciation of our friendship. Until then always have in mind that I am standing ready to reciprocate for the many courtesies you have extended to me.

Rawlings remained Fox's personal lawyer even after he sold the KDYL

---

111   From an article in the Salt Lake Tribune. April 6, 1975, Sec. 2, 1, which was written by Clark Lobb about Rawlings' political involvement with the Democratic Party.
112   Letter to Fox from Rawlings dated December 24, 1942, in the Fox Collection at the Marriott Library at The University of Utah. Fox biography, [circa 1970] p. 8; and Tim Larson conversation with Fox when he was in a Salt Lake City nursing home after being hit by a car for the second time. [circa 1980]

station in 1953, often not even charging for his legal services. By all accounts, Rawlings did reciprocate in their friendship many times over, thus, entirely keeping his 1942 Christmas Eve promise to Fox.

Fox employed Lasky, Baldwin and Rawlings for their respective competencies, and they became part of his extended family. He also employed members of his immediate family, seemingly out of obligation. Through the years, at times, Fox's stepsons – George, Robert and Myron Provol – worked at the station. Fred Provol, the oldest stepson, although he once owned KDYL, seldom, if ever, worked there. Most of his adult life was spent in retail businesses associated with his mother's Hudson Bay Fur Company. Miriam, Fox's only stepdaughter, never officially worked at KDYL either. She was part owner, with Fox, in Miriams, a Salt Lake City women's clothing store.

Myron and Miriam, the youngest of Eva Provol's children, were actually the only two Provol children officially adopted by Fox. They even assumed the Fox last name. Meanwhile, the older three "unofficial" stepsons kept their birth father's name. Myron Provol Fox attended military school and reportedly worked not too successfully as a salesman at KDYL. In the early 1940s, he went to California and became successful in the ceramics business. He died at age 37 in October 1953, the same year Fox sold the KDYL stations. Myron died of diabetes, which he had inherited from his father, Jacob H. Provol. Myron's father died from the disease in 1916, the year Myron was born and four years before his mother, Eva, married Fox.

George Provol was hired in 1928 and, except for a stint at a Colorado Springs station, worked in various administrative positions at KDYL until Fox sold the stations in 1953. In 1930, he was listed as a KDYL announcer, and in 1931 was listed as a KDYL "assistant." In 1934, he was the associate editor, under Lasky, of *The Voice of KDYL*, a station newsletter. In 1939, he was production manager. In 1944, he was listed as the commercial manager with 16 years of radio experience at KDYL. In 1945, he was listed as IBC vice president and KDYL national sales manager, and in 1949 was given the title of sales manager. He had many jobs at KDYL over the years, and in 1953 received $17,620 for his 0.5% ownership of KDYL. He later operated the George

Provol's Hudson Bay Fur Company of Ogden.

Robert Provol, who dropped in and out of KDYL employment, was an artist and musician and played piano on the Kangaroo Club for a time. He painted his hair purple and his appearance, which would not be unusual today, struck many as outrageous at the time. He was listed as circulation manager for *The Voice of KDYL* in 1934. From what is known, he was a nice person but, like his brother Myron, was deemed different for his times, or perhaps well ahead of his time.

Indeed, 1928 was the momentous year for KDYL Many years later, Lasky, speaking in 1986 when he was indicted in the Utah Broadcasters Hall of Fame, said, "1928 was a pivotal year [for KDYL]. Aside from moving its studios, KDYL increased power to 1000 watts, built a new transmitter at 33rd South and 9th West Streets, changed frequencies [and] ...began operating from 6 a.m. until midnight."

Meanwhile, in the late 1920s, Fox continued to sell "moving pictures" and to delve into quick deals to supplement KDYL's advertising revenue, while Lasky continued to develop and improve the station. Lasky instituted remote broadcasts from dance halls to showcase KDYL's talent. For instance, the Haymond sisters, a trio of musicians, were regulars on KDYL. The Evans Sisters, another trio of singers, had preceded them on KDYL. The Haymonds became good friends of Lasky, and, like him, also ended up in San Francisco where they formed a successful talent-booking agency.

Lasky sometimes went to Hollywood for talent in those early years, where many ambitious and experienced announcers could be found. There he found Jack Carrington, who brought his sophisticated, British accented voice to KDYL in the early 1930s and was a superb announcer. During Prohibition, Carrington reportedly made gin in his hotel room next to the former Lamb's Grill restaurant in downtown Salt Lake City. Fox liked Carrington's accent and was sorry to see him leave KDYL.[113] Eddie Marbel, another Hollywood recruit, who was a rotund guy who also sang and announced, periodically providing

---

113   Lasky interview with Tim Larson, 46.

KDYL broadcasts with live entertainment.

Another radio celebrity was Ted Rogers, who came to KDYL from a socially prominent Utah family. The son of a judge, he was widely known to be intelligent and well educated. For a while he was married to one of the Steiners, whose father was the head of a successful linen supply company that provided linens for hotels and restaurants. Rogers was a "Joe College" type, a good dresser and a great announcer. He left the radio business to join the Steiner family business and later moved on to importing goods from Mexico. His brother, Craig, a smart and able individual, had also worked at KDYL as traffic manager.

Announcer Jack Gregson became an important play-by-play sports voice and was the Mutual Network's sports department manager before retiring from broadcasting and moving to Richmond, Virginia. Frank Austin and Al Priddy were also announcers, with Austin calling sports news broadcasts. Announcer Tom Barbre came from Denver's KLZ. Others pursued different careers after their time at KDYL. Lee Taylor, an early KDYL announcer became a lawyer after he left radio. Elwyn Quinn came to KDYL from Shelly, Idaho, and went on to put KVON in Napa, California, on the air.

Emerson Smith became chief announcer at KDYL radio and went over to KDYL television in 1948. Fox promoted Smith after a short tenure, recognizing his talents as an announcer. Smith was the only announcer/reporter who covered the first execution at the new Utah State prison, which was located at the Point of the Mountain along the Wasatch Front, in 1951. Eliseo Mares was executed by firing squad, but the execution didn't go completely as planned, however. Five gunmen, positioned about 15 feet away, missed twice, hitting Mares in the stomach and hip, and it took several minutes for the prisoner to die. Yet, what Smith's reaction to this was has never been known nor did he speak publicly about it. A consummate professional, Smith came to KDYL from NBC's flagship station KPO in San Francisco.

Another important KDYL employee was Eugene Jelesnik. Fox hired him as radio music director in August 1945, and he assumed the music director position for KDYL television in 1947 when that station was launched. Jelesnik inherited the KDYL orchestra and was the accomplished impresario for it and the associated Salt Lake Philharmonic that he resurrected in 1946. With years of musical experience in New York City prior to coming to Salt Lake City, the indefatigable entertainer, conductor and concert planner and broker was KDYL's greatest emissary, producing hundreds of public and free musical performances a year in the community. However, Fox, while allowing a near total freehand with his public efforts, didn't fully take advantage of Jelesnik's past entertainment and leadership experience in New York. Instead, he relegated him to menial tasks at the stations and used him as a lackey, errand runner, and gofer – a dutiful minion. The employer and employee clearly didn't get along. One person even witnessed a physical confrontation between the imperious Fox and temperate Jelesnik. After Fox sold the KDYL stations in 1953, Jelesnik continued for decades his much appreciated public musical performances and leadership in annual celebrations. And, he hosted KSL televisions "Talent Showcase," featuring budding youthful performers, for more than 40 years.[114]

KDYL's talent bench was deep for many years. KDYL employees included Tom Shirley, who came from Hollywood and who appeared in Charlie Chaplin's film *City Lights*. Shirley eventually moved to Chicago's WBBM. Dave Simmons, a KDYL salesperson, continued in sales with the John Blair Company, a national station representative firm in New York. Fox was one of Blair's first customers and they remained friends well after both retired from broadcasting. Several people were hired to copy the national news, which came to KDYL and other stations in international code. Tony Kontgas was a talented telegrapher, as was Ray Buck, who decoded the news that was then read over KDYL by the announcers. There were yet no actual news reporters for the station. Buck, who had been in the Merchant Marines, reportedly could copy and send code better than anybody in the business, anywhere. A wireless

114   Eugene Jelesnik was involved in CBS radio and in W2XAB CBS television experimentation in the early 1930s. The entertainer, popularly known as "The Gypsy Violinist," had gainful bookings over the years at popular New York City venues and, at age 24 in 1938, was booked with his Continental Ensemble into what became a very successful nine-month run at the elegant Hotel Utah in Salt Lake City. He returned to New York and performed at the 1939 World's Fair in the Turkish pavilion. By 1940, he had his own NBC TV slot called "Gypsy Moods." He did stateside and overseas USO shows during WWII. In one three-month period in 1944 on tour with the USO he performed in fifty-seven hospitals in forty-five U.S. cities in 23 states. In 1945 Jelesnik returned to Salt Lake where he resided until his death in 1999. For more about Jelesnik, see Gerald M. McDonough, An Improbable Journey, Shadow Mountain, Salt Lake City, 1997.

purist, he continued to use only code on his amateur station in Hemet, near Palm Springs in southern California. Buck and Snell in San Jose remained friends from the early KDYL days and weekly corresponded only by code for years, until Snell died in 1990.[115]

In 1935, Lasky moved to San Francisco to manage KTAB and later KSFO, a station owned by Wesley Dumm, a mortgage banker. That relationship with Dumm continued for 20 "happy and very productive years" and included the start of KPIX, San Francisco's first television station in 1948. Unlike Fox, Lasky cultivated no sycophants, and no retinue of people followed him wherever he went. Lasky often took raw talent, shaped it and sent it on to bigger and better endeavors with his sincere best wishes:[116]

> I've always prized people around me who were achievers --that had active talent-- and were ambitious, you call it drive. In San Francisco over the years I had occasion to know and hire some people with that quality. More than a few went on to big time as performers, such as Ralph Edwards, Phyllis Diller, Art Link letter and others as executives. Such people delight me. You found that quality in George Snell, a serious minded intellectual person; you found it in Ben Larson, an effervescent outgoing personality; and others such as Baldwin, Farr and [Alvin] Pack. They were self-starters who never stopped working at it. Yes, I've always admired people who regarded life's opportunity as a personal goal to be mastered.

The tireless entrepreneur

In 1933, Fox, true to character, continued to seek offshoots in business, unapologetically appropriating someone else's idea. For example, on the ground floor below the KDYL studio and offices, Fox launched a company to sell a product called "Crazy Crystals:[117]

---

115   Tim Larson interview with Tony Kontgas, May 5, 1988, at his Price, Utah, home. Tim Larson interview with Ray Buck, September 6, 1988, at his home in southern CA.

116   Lasky interview with Tim Larson, 46.

117   Fox biography, [circa 1970] p. 8; and Tim Larson conversation with Fox when he was in a Salt Lake City nursing home after being hit by a car for the second time. [circa 1980].

It was a laxative, boxed in a rather ordinary box, and it sold for $1.00 and $1.50 a package. I found out that they had a sort of franchise proposition in which they sold territories, where a man had to buy so much merchandise, and they were reputed of making two to three million dollars net a year. Their product was taken from the wells of Texas and then dried out and became a powder form, it looked like diamonds.

Two friends – one known only by his last name Bowers and Leo L. Capson joined Fox to produce a product similar to Crazy Crystals. Bowers was in the construction business and Capson in real estate. They called their product, also a laxative, "Miracle Diamonds." They formed the Miracle Diamonds Corporation of Utah, in which Bowers and Capson manufactured the product and Fox promoted it and sold distributorships. Indeed, many Utah entrepreneurs have always fancied the business potential of selling products such as "Miracle Diamonds."

Salt for "Miracle Diamonds" was harvested from the Great Salt Lake, dried, packaged and sent to distributors. The distributors paid $.40 each for packages selling retail for $1.00, and $.65 for those retailing for $1.50. The distributors engaged drug stores to carry the product in their exclusive territories. One distributor contracted with Fox on September 25, 1933, for exclusive rights to the "Miracle Diamonds" distributorship of Northern California. He gave Fox 100 shares of Beneficial Loan Company stock for the first six months of the "Miracle Diamonds" distributorship. It paid a $37.50 dividend and Fox immediately sold the stock. By October 11, 1933, John J. Oxley, the northern California distributor had placed "Miracle Diamonds" in more than 100 retail outlets, with 40 or 50 more predicted within the following month. Oxley also invested heavily in advertising, for which Fox agreed to reimburse him. Crazy Crystals, their competitor, purchased time on 156 daytime programs on KPO in San Francisco. Oxley matched that with ad buys on KTAB.

Everything seemed sensational. All contingencies had been accounted for, except one. The U.S. Post Office called both "Miracle Diamonds" and

"Crazy Crystal" principals to Denver to discuss their respective advertising claims. Both products were exhorted to clean out the body's system and to avoid diseases that might be caused from a reaction to improper elimination. The Post Office inspectors said that both products would have to be called "laxatives" if the mail channels were to be used to distribute them.

Fox probably could have complied except he soon discovered an additional problem peculiar to "Miracle Diamonds." It shrunk in the package as it dried out. Customers complained they were being cheated when they opened the package and it was half empty. Fox ceased selling "Miracle Diamonds" and got out of the "laxative" business. He paid back his investors and distributors and lost huge sums of money.

By late October 1933, Fox had a plan to recoup his losses. He turned the "Miracle Diamonds Corporation", now totally owned by him and separate from IBC, to manufacturing a new product. Fox contracted for original radio scripts about famous diamonds and produced twenty-six 15-minute radio shows, which mostly were written in Hollywood by Alice Ward. Olive Gould, whom Fox hired in his programming department and who later became his programming manager and personal secretary, arranged for the writing, acting and production of *Diamond Dramas* for Fox in Hollywood. These were polished shows, not locally produced or amateurish productions.

With great fanfare about how "well-known screenwriters" wrote the shows and how Hollywood's best acting and directorial talent produced them, Fox sold the programs to 100 radio stations around the country. With the syndicated episodes, Fox sent promotional materials to help the stations sell the shows to local jewelers. They were an easy sell for Fox and *Diamond Dramas* were so successful that Fox recouped his financial losses.

Diamond Dramas went on hiatus in 1945 but was resurrected as "an inspiring and tested series of quarter-hour transcriptions, tailor-made for jewelers." By this time, some of the original "stars" of the programs had actually become "outstanding" celebrities in radio beyond KDYL. They included Jay Jostyn, who became "Mr. District Attorney" on radio; Hanley

Stafford, who became famous as Baby Snook's beleaguered "Daddy"; Barbara Luddy, star of the "First Nighter" dramatic program; and Gale Gordon, star of *In His Steps* and other radio and film productions. Gordon would go on to play Lucille Ball's boss on the various radio and television series starring the famous comedian. Fox used "All Star Radio Productions" – a slight deviation from "All Star Productions," which was his film distribution company that he founded in 1921 to distribute *Diamond Dramas*. Fox said the reissue enjoyed great financial success. Recordings of these *Diamond Drama* programs are housed in the Marriott Library Special Collections at The University of Utah.

Transitions and change in owners

In 1953, Fox sold the KDYL AM and FM radio and TV stations to Time, Inc. (for an 80% share) and to Larson (for a 20% share) at a price of $2.1 million. After being gone for nearly 25 years, Larson came back to KDYL to be part owner and to manage the station. More about this transaction and its impact are discussed in Section III, which chronicles Utah's first wave of television stations.

Time, Inc. sold KDYL AM to Columbia Pictures in 1959, and the KDYL call sign was changed to KCPX, which became the dominant Top-40 station competing for the teen audience with KNAK. KCPX eventually siphoned Lynn Lehman from KNAK to do mornings at the station. KNAK hosts, Gary "Wooly" Waldron and "Skinny" Johnny Mitchell, preceded Lehmann to KCPX. Waldron was the afternoon disc jockey and program director, and Mitchell was the night jock. Along with newscaster Joe Lee and others, Waldron and Mitchell captured the teen market during the 1960s and especially in the 1970s. This also was the breakout era for the Beatles, the Beach Boys and the Rolling Stones. The audience evolved and KCPX's dominance abated, giving way to FM's appropriation from AM of the music audience beginning in the early 1980s. Lehmann remembers when KCPX fired him on December 5, 1980, three days before John Lennon was murdered.[118]

---

118 Various sources include the Jackson Dell Weaver interview with Gary Wooly Waldren accessed at https://www.intownmedia.com/no-fear-intro-video?fbclid=IwAR0AlZ7WVRBW6aqM 2QQYD TO4iZCubi6zHWlwuzwZuR4ACIV49v3mZ71VJI; Barry Mishkind, SLC Section of They Broadcast Archives, accessed at https://www.oldradio.com/archives/stations/slc-hist.htm; YNOP.

Columbia Pictures ended its 24-year KCPX ownership in 1983, selling the station to what became the Price Broadcasting Group. John Price changed the call sign to KBUG (1983), and then KMEX (1988), and then KUTR (1989), and back to KCPX and to KCNR (1992), and to KFNZ (1996). The Price Broadcasting Group also owned stations in Charleston, South Carolina; Wichita, Kansas; Spokane, Washington; Modesto, California; Reno, Nevada and Wheeling, West Virginia. Price at the time was a successful contractor in Salt Lake City and real estate mogul, and with his wife, they became widely known as major benefactors for The University of Utah. Price later became U.S. ambassador to Mauritius and the Seychelles, located off the coast of Southeast Africa, during the George W. Bush administration.

Radio stations flipped ownership frequently during this period, which gives historians of broadcast radio pause to double check the ownership and call letters of these pioneering stations. Citadel bought KFNZ in 1996, merging with Cumulus in 2011 and later sold the station to Kona Coast Radio in 2017. Kona Coast Radio changed the call sign to KNIT, but KNIT at 1320 kilocycles went dark that year before coming back on the air two years later as a Christian format affiliate of "Your Network of Praise." Over the years under several owners the station hosted various formats including adult-contemporary, oldies, news/talk and all-sports. But, KCPX AM never reclaimed its unequaled 1970s success, which was earned with Top-40 jocks including Lehman, Waldron and Mitchell.

Fox's IBC would establish KDYL-TV, Salt Lake City's first television station, with regular broadcasts beginning on April 19, 1948, on its W6XIS experimental television station. Fox anticipated using ample returns from his KDYL radio operation, to cover KDYL television's startup expenditures. But, Fox did not realize that KDYL-TV would require huge sums of money to startup and would siphon advertising revenue from its cash cow counterpart of radio. Within five years, Fox would sell the venerable KDYL AM station along with the FM band counterpart, which was launched in 1947, along

org accessed at http://www.ynop.org/stationlist.html; KNIT Wiki accessed at https://en.wikipedia.org/wiki/KNIT_(AM); radio-locator accessed at https://radio-locator.com/info/KNIT-AM and Wikiwand accessed at https://www.wikiwand.com/en/KNIT_(AM)#/KDYL

with the television stations to stop the enormous bleeding of his personal fortune. Starting a radio station now seemed considerably far easier and more financially tolerable than the incredible amounts of resources that launching a new television station would incur.

More about KDYL -TV is chronicled in Section III of the book.

CHAPTER 6

KLO: OGDEN

In 1923, the Redfields and the Peerys of Ogden teamed up to build a radio station. Carl Redfield and his brother, who owned the Redfield Electric Company at Five Points on Ogden's north side, also had the Utah, Idaho and Wyoming distributorship for receivers manufactured by the Tusca Radio Corporation. Harman Peery and his brother owned what they described as "Ogden's Leading Amusements," which included the Ogden Theater, where "Quality Photoplays" could be seen; the Egyptian Theater, dubbed "The Show Palace of the West;" and, the White City Gardens, a dancing establishment called "Ogden's Pleasure Park Beautiful." Harman Peery also reportedly was known and feared as Ogden's tempestuous mayor.

In the winter of 1923, the Redfields convinced amateur radio operator W. Glen Garner to take demonstration Tusca radio receivers to the three-state area covered in their distributorship. Because the Tusca name was not well known, Garner was not very successful in selling the receivers. The Redfield's soon discontinued the Tusca line but continued in the radio parts business.

In June 1924, Peery and Redfield obtained a government license for a radio station in Ogden, and began work on KFUR, which eventually would become Utah's third radio broadcasting station that would be sustained beyond the 1920s. Peery and Redfield asked Garner to design and help construct the station. The Redfield Electric Company, which supplied many of the parts for the new radio station, financed the venture. The Peerys wanted the station so they could broadcast from their White City Gardens dance hall and advertise their two theaters. Garner constructed KFUR, which later became KLO, in the Peerys' Ogden Theater, at 420 25th Street in Ogden's central business district. He put the transmitting antenna on its roof.

Garner consulted with Kaar and Cope, friends whom earlier had shared his passion for amateur radio. Garner, like Kaar and Cope, became interested in wireless at a young age and received his first amateur license (7EW) in Evanston, Wyoming, before World War I. He obtained his first official Utah amateur license, (6OZ) in 1920 and later received a Special Land Station License (6ZAM) and then W7SU. Garner reportedly held an amateur license for 69 years, from 1920 until his death in 1989. If so, he would have been Utah's most senior licensed radio amateur when he died.

Garner installed an input audio amplifier for KFUR that was designed and patented by Cope, who was at KSL. Cope designed similar amplifiers for Paramount Pictures in the 1930s, after the studio produced sound movies in Hollywood. Cope charged his friend Garner $100 ($1,400 in today's value) to use his innovative circuit in building the Ogden station (KFUR).

The station went on the air in Ogden on January 28, 1925, with Garner in charge as announcer and operator. For weeks after opening KFUR, Garner worked at the station on Wednesday, Thursday and Saturday nights from ten to midnight.[119]

The Peery brothers reportedly were elated with KFUR after it went on the air, with news that the station's signal was heard throughout the west and in Hawaii. Telegrams received from a wide area attested to the fine reception. Soon after KFUR was completed, the Peerys bought out the Redfields on a turnkey contract that was negotiated before construction began. Much of KFUR's early programming originated from the Peery brothers' amusement businesses. Wesley Mullens performed on the Wurlitzer organ from the Egyptian Theater, records and remotes were handled from KFUR's Ogden Theater studio, and special features and orchestral performances were presented live from White City Gardens.

KFUR's tenuous early years

KFUR was not the only Ogden radio station to take shape at this time.

---

119   Ogden Standard Examiner, January 29, 1925, 8.

On November 25, 1924, before KFUR opened, the Browning family formed the Browning Bros. Radio Co. and proposed KFWA. The Brownings were descendants of the John Mose Browning family of gun manufacturing fame and wanted to use radio to advertise their sporting goods business. Laurence J. Haight, a friend of Garner, was contracted to construct the station for the Brownings at their Kiesel Avenue store.

Haight, well known in Ogden for his radio knowledge, was an amateur operator for the American Radio Relay League. On the same day the Brownings formed their radio company, Haight was applauded in the *Ogden Standard-Examiner* for ending trouble for radio fans by tracing a radio interference problem to an electrical leak at a Utah Power and Light electrical station. Haight also was the prime mover behind the formation of the Ogden Radio Club in December 1924. He and Garner were appointed head of the club's technical committee on interference. At the first social gathering of the Ogden Radio Club on December 23, officers Dr. F. W. Baker, E. J. Sorenson and H. C. Marchant put on a radio program to enliven the Christmas party. Wives and friends were said to have enjoyed a club member's stunt of using a loudspeaker to interrupt music with bogus news stories and other humorous items.[120]

Haight put the KFWA antenna at the rear of the Browning Bros. Sporting Goods Store, and the station went on the air on March 30, 1925. Utah now had four radio broadcasting stations, with KFWA going live only two months after KFUR. Robert Nevine was company manager for the 500-watt KFWA station, and Mailander, the well-known KDYL announcer from Salt Lake City, was KFWA's first announcer.

Within a year, Garner also went to KFWA as an announcer. In order to provide live music, Garner convinced the Baldwin Piano Company to furnish a piano for the station, in turn for promoting the Baldwin name on the air. KFWA later subscribed to a wire service and, among other things, Garner used the service to reconstruct baseball World Series games nearly live play-by-play over KFWA. Although the reconstruction of baseball games, complete

---

120   Ogden Standard Examiner, December 23, 1924, 12.

with sound effects, became popular in later years with Wally Sandack at KSL, Garner and KFUR may have been the first in Utah to program in this format.

In1926, Garner was invited by the Western Branch of the National Association of Broadcasters (NAB) to go to San Francisco for a radio exhibit and demonstration. NAB was founded in 1922 in Chicago. The gathering featured a curious mix of attendees, including Glade who represented KSL, and Aimee Semple McPherson of the Four Square Church of Los Angeles. Despite what Garner had heard about McPherson's radical, unconventional religious broadcasts, he found her "to be a charming and beautiful woman. She was well educated and not at all like the press featured her in articles about McPherson Temple in Los Angeles and its notorious director and broadcaster of religious services."[121] Garner left broadcasting and went on to earn his degrees in the medical and public health fields. Later, he became director of Ogden's municipal division of laboratories and environmental health.

In the late 1920s, the Browning Brothers closed their sporting goods store and shut down KFWA in Ogden. The station was moved to Idaho Falls and acquired the KSEI call sign. Meanwhile, the Peerys continued to operate KFUR. It was on the air from noon to 2 p.m., six days a week, and every Tuesday, Thursday and Saturday evening from nine to midnight. Although KFUR was on the air during this time for approximately 900 hours a year, it sold no advertising. The station was privately financed by the Peerys, and it continued to promote programs originating from their White City Gardens, Egyptian Theater and Ogden Theater properties.

With the passage of the Radio Act of 1927, KFUR faced becoming extinct. The Act required every station in the country to show how its continuance would be in the public interest, convenience or necessity. Because of interference, especially in rural areas, the Federal Radio Commission intended to eliminate many radio broadcasting stations nationwide. Thus, within 60 days of the passage of the Act, every licensed station was required to justify its continued existence by reapplying for a new license.

---

121   W. Glen Garner, unpublished autobiography, [circa] 1986, 42.

The Peerys did several things to ensure KFUR could continue but, primarily, they emphasized KFUR's uniqueness as the only privately supported station in the area providing dependable daytime service for the goodwill of the people of Ogden. In his reapplication, Harman Peery emphasized that an increase in power also would be in the public interest of the people in the KFUR coverage area:[122]

> There are but three broadcast stations including this one in the State of Utah, and due to the fact that our nearest other entertainment by radio is over 600 miles airline distant, and this is too far for reliable reception during summer months, and also due to freak conditions in this intermountain country making it hard to receive outside stations.

In its efforts to retain its license and stay on the air, KFUR was aided by one FRC commissioner in particular – Harold A. LaFount. Five FRC commissioners, one from each of the newly formed five districts in the U.S., were appointed on March 1, 1927, and the Senate confirmed three on March 4. but then the 69th Congress adjourned. Commissioner John F. Dillon from California died on October 8 and was replaced by LaFount. Readers will recall that Dillon in October 1920 scolded his boss for approving H. C. Wilson's request to broadcast on KZN using a higher wavelength than the 200 meters allowed regular amateurs. LaFount stayed on the FRC until its replacement by the FCC in 1934 but was not appointed to the FCC.

From November 24, 1927 to March 29, 1928, there were only four commissioners approved by the U.S. Senate, including LaFount. Utah readers will be intrigued to know that LaFount's daughter, Lenore, married George Romney, parents of Willard (Mitt) Romney, the 2002 Salt Lake Winter Olympic chair, former governor of Massachusetts, a 2008 and 2012 presidential candidate, and a U.S. senator representing Utah, who was elected in 2018.

Each FRC commissioner was required to live in the district they represented. LaFount represented the 5th Radio District, in which Utah and

---

122   Federal Radio Commission, Washington, D. C., "Application for Radio Station License, Peery Building Company," April 1, 1927, 3.

ten other western states and the territories of Hawaii and Alaska were located. He was from northern Utah and showed special attention to the three Utah stations, especially KFUR, even to the point of having had an "interest" in the KFUR construction permit. On December 7, 1927, LaFount wrote to the Peerys:[123]

> At the time I left Salt Lake I advised you that any and all interests I had in the Construction Permit of KFUR, I assigned with your consent to [Salt Lake City] Mayor C. [Clarence] Neslen. This I did absolutely without any financial consideration and it was at that time my understanding that the Mayor would proceed along the lines that I had outlined. I told him of the people who contemplated joining me in the undertaking. ... I am extremely anxious to know whether or not Mr. Neslen is actually at work making the improvements as provided in the Construction Permit.

Under a contract entered into in January 1928, amateur Ralph Flygare and Claude Coray were employed by the Peery Building Company to operate KFUR. Flygare and Coray were given complete control of the station and were "permitted to use such parts of the present equipment of Station KFUR as they may wish in building new apparatus and new equipment. In case of cancellation of this agreement, all new equipment installed by the operators shall become property of the operators."[124]

On March 22, 1928, Claude L. Coray, representing Peery Building Co., Inc., informally requested permission from the FRC to move KFUR to a location on the eighth floor of the Hotel Bigelow. The hotel was located at the corner of 25th Street and Washington Avenue in Ogden, about 200 feet directly across the street from the existing KFUR studios in the Ogden Theater. Ralph Flygare filed a formal application for the move on April 19 and, at the same time, asked for an increase in power.

---

123   Harold A. LaFount, Federal Radio Commission, Letter to Peery Building Company, December 7, 1927.
124   Elmer W. Pratt, Federal Radio Commission Assistant General Counsel, "Memorandum to Commissioner Harold LaFount," February 7, 1929.

With LaFount's help, KFUR survived the FRC's nationwide station closings. On June 15, the date the FRC implemented frequency changes nationwide, KFUR was allowed to continue operations using 50 watts of power at 1330kc, and by November was broadcasting on 1370kc from the Hotel Bigelow with 500 watts of power.

The call letter switch to KLO and staff changes

In 1928, at about the same time that KFUR moved to the Hotel Bigelow, its call letters were locally and unofficially changed to KLO. In official correspondence with the FRC, KFUR continued to be used, but on station letterhead and program schedules and in local public promotions, the K-L-O signature was used to identify the station. The 'L-O' in KLO likely came from Bigelow. Archie Bigelow, an Ogden banker, owned the hotel. When the stock market crashed in 1929 and Bigelow's bank failed, the name of the hotel was changed to the Ben Lomond Hotel because it was considered imprudent to have a hotel named after a failed bank. Ben Lomond is the name for a peak in the northern portion of the Wasatch Mountains. Conveniently, the KLO call letters remained meaningful and were left intact.

In 1928, KFUR (later KLO) was on the air about 10 hours a day, six days a week. An additional hour on Sunday was aired from the Elks Lodge. Daily programming included recorded music and such shows as *Dorothy Gray Housewife Talks* and *Frank White's Cooking School*. Regular features also included a children's program from the Ogden Public Schools and studio programs presented by paid union musicians, with names like "Kings-of-Syncopation" and "Jud-Brown-and-the Joy-Boys."

Later in 1928, Earl Glade approached the Peerys with a proposal to tie KFUR to KSL for certain periods of the broadcast day. As such, KFUR would carry some NBC programming and, for the first time, would provide advertising time to Ogden businesses other than those owned by the Peerys. KSL would also provide needed business and technical expertise to KFUR.

For the Peerys there was one significant problem with Glade's proposal to link KFUR to KSL. It was that the original KFUR contract with Flygare and Coray was still in effect. That contract gave Flygare and Coray all the new station equipment if the operating agreement was canceled. On December 31, 1928, when a 30-day notice canceling their agreement was given, Flygare and Coray immediately filed to take ownership of KFUR and applied for a construction permit for them to be licensed as station operators. They also requested a change of call letters to KOU, which would have been an even more meaningful call sign for a station in Ogden, Utah. The FRC denied their application, however, and the station license remained with the Peery Building Company.

Flygare and Coray subsequently were replaced at KFUR, and Glade formed the Interstate Broadcasting Corporation (IBC) as parent to KFUR. He then became Interstate's president and managing director. Cope, then KSL's chief engineer became technical director, and his brother Frank was made station manager. Cope designed a new transmitter and later installed it at a site four miles southwest of Ogden, approximately one mile west of the municipal airport.

Upon officially taking over KLO (still KFUR in FRC records) in January 1929, Glade printed new letterhead, promoting Ogden as "Utah's Railroad and Industrial Center", and KLO as "The Voice of the Great New West." In addition, he issued Interstate Broadcasting Corporation capital stock in the amount of $100,000, of which $75,000 represented the value of the KLO broadcast license. In putting value on the license and issuing stock against it to raise capital, Glade followed Fox's lead at KDYL several years earlier.

On February 7, 1929, the Peery Building Company executed a conveyance transferring all of its "right, title and interest" in the KFUR equipment to Glade and Cope. Under the original contract, even though the KFUR equipment seemingly had reverted to Flygare and Coray, no record could be found that they exercised any claims against Peery, Glade, Cope or KSL, so it went to the Interstate Broadcasting Company uncontested.

It appears Flygare, especially, did not want KSL or the Church of Jesus

Christ of Latter Day Saints to be exposed to criticism and, thus, recorded no public complaint about Interstate's acquisition of equipment that by previous agreement was supposed to go to him and Coray. As a result of remaining silent, Flygare and Coray essentially became minor footnotes in Utah broadcasting rather than the important players they might have been. When the author interviewed a Ralph Flygare family member in the 1980s by telephone, the respondent confirmed that Flygare was not happy with the KLO sale but also did not want to offend the LDS Church, which was the owner of KSL.

On April 11, 1929, the FRC officially approved the call-letter change from KFUR to KLO, and finally the practice of using those call letters was proper. The KFUR call sign was no more.[125] A curious side note: Although Glade did not actually represent himself to the FRC as KFUR's "attorney," he had signed his request for call-letter changes with, "By Earl J. Glade on behalf of the Peery Building Company," and that was the typical way lawyers at that time signed for clients in correspondence before the FRC.

Glade assumes control of KLO

On July 22, Glade and Cope also assigned their respective interests in KLO equipment to the IBC. Simultaneously, the Peery Building Company, by now carrying only a 10% interest in KLO, filed an application to assign the license to the IBC, because Glade and Cope had invested a large sum of money for the construction and equipping of KLO and now effectively owned the station. FRC approval came in 1930. Glade continued to manage KSL while he was a near-majority owner who operated KLO, with the Peerys as minority owners. Glade now had the challenge of making KLO a profitable operation without competing against KSL.

When Glade assumed control of KLO, it still was programmed mostly with entertainment originating from the Peerys' amusement holdings. For instance, station manager, Gene Halladay, played nightly organ concerts from

---

125   Acting Chief, Radio Division, Federal Radio Commission, "Letter to Peery Building Company, Broadcasting Station KFUR," April 11, 1929.

Peery's Egyptian Theater. In January 1931, Glade decided to give KLO a more cosmopolitan sound, so he hired University of Utah student Alvin G. Pack as an announcer. Pack, a recently returned LDS missionary to England, was the brother of Gene Pack, KSL's chief engineer and was the son of Frederick Pack, a University of Utah geology professor. Later, Alvin would become uncle to Gene Pack Jr., longtime KUER-FM classical music on-air host. Glade originally hired Alvin Pack to be the KLO announcer for the Keith Holbrook Big Band, which originated from the Empire Room of the Hotel Utah in Salt Lake City. Four nights a week, Wednesday through Saturdays, nine to midnight, Pack announced from the Hotel Utah for KLO. Pack said that Glade liked his announcing voice because it was sophisticated, but not "highfalutin' or sententious."

After a month, Glade asked Pack to be a full-time announcer at KLO in Ogden. For the next five months, Pack went to University of Utah classes in the morning and then hopped the Bamberger Electric train to Ogden at 1 p.m., did a shift from 2:30 p.m. to midnight on KLO, and then returned to Salt Lake City by 2 a.m. He went to KLO five days a week to do his shift and was glad to have a job during the heart of the Great Depression.

Records were the main fare on KLO, and Pack playfully serenaded his young bride, Lena Marie, in Salt Lake City by interspersing love tunes tacitly dedicated to her. In 1931, KLO had no official network affiliation, and station announcers didn't usually add production value to their local programs. Pack tried to change that. He said he had heard network announcers when he worked at Coney Island in New York, so he emulated them and packaged music by themes and artists. To mark the segments of his shows he labeled them, such as "Musical Medley", "Music in the Evening" or "Afternoon with Guy Lombardo." In addition, Pack wrote copy and introduced the concepts of continuity, program development and promotion at KLO.

On March 8, 1931, a Sunday night, KLO station manager Gene Halladay called Pack and asked him to cover a half-hour time segment that had not been filled. At 9 p.m. in the absence of any regularly scheduled programming, Pack created a travelog about his European travels. He interspersed musical selections like *When Irish Eyes Are Smiling*, *Rule Britannia*, and *Bonny on the Moor*, with banter about their locales. The program was an immediate success and became a regular weekly program on KLO. Pack enlisted Lena Marie to help write and produce the *Pack Travelogue*, and on April 5, 1931, she joined Alvin on the air for the first time. According to Lena Marie, Glade called after that program and said, "Mrs. Pack, your voice is as clear as a bell. I want you to continue broadcasting."[126]

After the second program on April 12, the Packs received their first fan letter – from a listener in Alaska. In May 1931, Glade brought Alvin Pack from KLO to KSL to be an announcer, and, about the same time, Lena Marie began a cooking show on KSL. Thus, this began a lasting friendship with "Mr. Glade," as the Packs always called him, and a thirty-year radio career for this husband-and-wife team. Alvin, in 1945, assumed the KALL station manager position when that station went on the air, which is discussed later in the book.

By 1934, the largest shares of IBC were 41% owned by Glade and his Radio Broadcasters, Inc., 19% owned by the Columbia Trust Company and Attorney H. L. Milliner of Salt Lake, and 10% by Louis Peery. The IBC officers included President Glade, Vice president and Attorney Samuel C. Powell, Secretary Oliver G. Ellis, and Auditor Dan H. Vincent. KLO's staff included Gene Halladay, manager and program director, F.W. Stanbrough, production manager, and Eugene G. Pack, chief engineer who was borrowed from KSL.

Although KLO was selling commercial time, it generated little income and continued operating, mostly supported by the Peerys and their "other" amusement businesses, and very likely by Glade personally. By March, 1934, only 18% of KLO's programs were commercially sponsored and, although the station broadcasted 12 hours a day and re-broadcasted many network programs via KSL, Glade could not attract Ogden advertisers and was ready to give up his efforts at the station. In Testimony before the FCC on February 2, 1935, in Washington D.C., Glade expressed his frustration:[127]

---

126   Alvin and Lena Marie Pack, Interviews conducted by Tim Larson, September 4, 1986, through February 10, 1987.
127   Testimony of Earl J. Glade, Hearing before the FCC regarding applications for Utah Broadcasting Stations, Docket No. 2612, February 2, 1935 in Washington, D.C., p. 455.

All I wanted ... was to try to arouse the people of Ogden to the value
of that institution [KLO] and I had done more than my part in that
regard. I had made over 700 trips to Ogden, there and back, in an
endeavor to help that situation, and KSL had big brothered it all
down the line. I ran remote controls and did everything that could
be done. We have often run, with the permission of the Columbia
System [CBS], as many as ten national programs over KLO, to see if
we could not enliven the interest of the people of Ogden; but I have
never seen such apathy in my life. KSL is doing a lot of work for that
city [Ogden] right now.

It was evident that Glade's relationship with KLO had lost its shine and
promise. By 1934, Glade reluctantly had allowed much of IBC capital stock
to be acquired by the *Standard Examiner's* A. L. Glasmann. Through Harry
Anderson, an intermediary, Glasmann quietly took control of the IBC and
KLO. Glade soon completely gave up his financial interest in KLO and went
back to his primary full time job managing KSL. Glasmann subsequently
infused $100,000 into making KLO a commercially successful operation,
and the station progressed through a series of power increases and frequency
changes under the guidance of its new chief engineer, W. D'Orr Cozzens.

The arrival of Abe Glasmann

Glasmann was the editor and publisher and one-sixth owner of the Ogden
Standard Examiner newspaper in 1934. Members of his family held most of
the other IBC shares. A potent civic figure with much influence, Glasmann
was also a major financial force in the Eldredge Glasmann Investment
Company, the Alhambra Theatrical Company, the Ute Theater Company,
the A.L. & B.V. Glasmann Development Company, and Glasmann Farms, all
real estate holdings. The Glasmann family also was involved with Paramount
Pictures in owning the Paramor Theater Company.

Glasmann was thrust into the newspaper business when his father,
William, died unexpectedly in 1916. The elder Glasmann had owned the
newspaper for 23 years, at the time of his death. Although he grew up working

at his father's newspaper, Glasmann intended to pursue an engineering career.
His impression of the newspaper business was that "it was a lot of work for a
little money." World War I came and Glasmann was left to run the newspaper
when his three brothers were called to military service. In 1920, Glasmann
consolidated The *Ogden Examiner* and his Ogden *Standard* into a single paper
with daily afternoon and Sunday morning circulation. In 1927, the Glasmann
Radio Company was formed. It was a radio parts company and the first family
enterprise associated with radio.[128]

Glasmann did not enter radio broadcasting, however, until 1934, when he
became controlling stockholder of IBC and assumed ownership of KLO from
Glade and the others. KLO was Glasmann's first broadcast holding, but he
and his family later became involved in stations in Terre Haute, Evansville and
Fort Wayne, Indiana; in Pocatello and Boise, Idaho; and in Honolulu, Denver
and Salt Lake City. The Honolulu and Salt Lake City stations, respectively,
later essentially became the properties of sons-in-law Cecil Heftel and George
Hatch, both of whom got their start in broadcasting at Ogden's KLO.

Glasmann soon put his deep imprint on KLO's operations. In 1935,
Glasmann hired Paul R. Heitmeyer to be KLO vice president and manager.
Heitmeyer had worked at newspapers in Oregon and Washington from
1922 to 1931, and at radio stations in Portland and Hollywood from 1931
to 1935. Other people employed by Glasmann at KLO in the 1930s after he
took ownership of the IBC, included program traffic manager Ethel G. Clark,
advertising manager Merrill J. Bunnell, secretary Helen Francis, bookkeeper
LeMaus Wyatt, production managers Arthur M. Wright and Nick Barry,
announcers and copywriters William Steele, Howard Flynn and Ray Fadel, and
engineer W. D' Orr Cozzens. Technicians Wayne T. Booth, Darwin Hunsaker
and Leonard Byington also were employed at KLO in the 1940s. George Hatch
replaced Heitmeyer as station manager, and, in 1945, when Hatch opened
KALL in Salt Lake City, George B. Morgan, former advertising manager of the
Standard Examiner became KLO's station manager.[129]

---

128   Utah: A Centennial History, 1948, p. 396.
129   Information about the stable of KLO employees was garnered from FCC records and
hearings, Glasmann company records and newspaper, KLO license renewals and other pertinent
documents.)

By the late 1920s, KLO was carrying NBC programs relayed to Ogden from KSL, and when KSL switched to the CBS network in the early 1930s, KLO followed suit. KLO's first formal network affiliation separate from KSL came with the Mutual Broadcasting System in 1941 and then ABC in 1958. In 1937 KLO also was affiliated with the NBC Blue Network. KLO continued to be located in the Ben Lomond Hotel, where Glasmann kept an apartment with his wife, Eidress. Sometimes Glasmann wandered into the KLO studios late at night to observe happenings. Morgan White, a KLO disc jockey and later known as Denver's KIMI Pogey Poge, said that it was not uncommon to look up from the board at midnight to see Glasmann observing station operations through the window of the announcer's booth.[130]

Glasmann was a powerful Utah business leader, a man of stature and, according to his daughter Wilda Gene Hatch, he had a keen sense of humor. But he also could be hard-nosed about tough decisions when it came to his business enterprises. Glasmann's daughters, Joyce and Wilda Gene, married men who came to develop those same qualities. Joyce married Cecil Heftel, and Gene married George Hatch. Both men cut their broadcasting teeth at KLO and became important in Utah, Intermountain and national broadcasting circles in the decades after World War II.

KLO's postwar era

In the late 1950s, Kimball Ward, Sr., a former police officer, was the KLO manager. With KLO co-owner Cecil Heftel, he expanded the station's promotional efforts and collected a stable of announcers and DJs that significantly grew the station's audience. Included were Keith Farr, Morrie Reichley, Len Allen, Kim Ward Jr., Verl Housley, Wayne Moss, Larry Hunter, Ron Hall and "Big Pete" Petersen.

Keith Farr's extensive radio collection is housed in the Special Collections at The University of Utah Marriott Library. A brief professional biography listed with the collection reveals Farr worked as an announcer for KLO

---

130   Tim Larson interview with former KLO announcer, Morgan White, about Glasmann, [circa 1986].

between 1959 and 1961. Among other KLO duties, he hosted the "Sandman Serenade," a program that aired from midnight to six a.m., and was heard throughout the central and western United States and into parts of Canada. Farr recalled KLO's success during his tenure at the station:[131]

> [It was] the first time that KLO did something with the station, and the mail that I got, my god, "Unbelievable!" ... Kim [Ward] Jr. said, "Do you realize the mail you're getting with your audience from midnight to dawn probably **co**vers more than our KLO audience in the daytime?" ... And the mail came in. ... from Los Angeles and .... all over. On KLO one night around one o'clock in the morning, I get this call. He says, "Hi! This KLO?" ... "Would you play a song for us?" I said, "Yeah, sure! ... Where are you? Ogden? Salt Lake? Provo?" He says, "Hell no!, Halifax, Nova Scotia. ... That's up from New York. ... I could hear KLO in the background ... They sent me a reel-to-reel air-check and a nice letter with everybody's signatures. I thought, "My god! [KLO reaches a faraway audience].

After his time at KLO, Farr joined KVOG-TV in Salt Lake City in 1961, and then KIFI-TV, Idaho Falls, Idaho in 1963 and finally KWIN/KCVR, Stockton, California between 1968 and 1990. Farr now resides in Lodi, California and continues researching and documenting the early period of AM radio broadcasting history.

Cecil Heftel, Glasmann's son-in-law, involved at KLO in the 1950s, moved to Denver to operate KIMN radio, taking KLO's announcer Pogo Poge (Morgan White) with him. Like at KLO Pogo Poge would do most anything to get people to listen to KIMN. When he was inducted into the Colorado Music Hall of Fame, it was said, "He got his name after hopping from Denver to Boulder on a pogo stick. He sat atop a flagpole for days and once played the Kingston Trio's *Tom Dooley* for 18 hours straight. The most famous stunt he masterminded put him in the hospital: He spent nearly two weeks in a snake pit with more than 100 snakes and was bitten by a water moccasin."[132]

---

131   Keith Farr interview by Tim Larson and Gregory Thompson in Lodi, California, December 1, 2008.

132   See KIMN Radio at https://cmhof.org/inductees/kimn-radio/; Tim Larson interview with

KLO's ownership and license stayed in the Glasmann and/or Hatch family from 1934 to 1970, and various others owned the station from 1970 to 1990, when John Webb assumed control of the station. Webb died at age 67 in 2014, and his son Matt formed the Capital Broadcasting Company, which continues to own KLO. In 2000, KLO switched from nostalgic music to an all-talk format to attract a younger listener.

KLO was the third of Utah's pioneer stations and the last one to be established in the 1920s. Major changes in regulations were afoot, which slowed the momentum of Utah's radio stations for a short while until the 1930s and 1940s, when seven new pioneer stations eventually would join the first three in the statewide market. The following brief chapter reviews the Federal Radio Commission's Quota System and the regulatory changes brought about by the Communication Act of 1934 allowing for new 100-watt Utah broadcasting stations.

former KLO announcer, Morgan White, about Glasmann, [circa 1986].

CHAPTER 7

THE QUOTA SYSTEM AND
100-WATT STATION APPLICATIONS

After the passage of the Radio Act of 1927, the number of Utah radio stations was officially frozen at three by the Davis Amendment. This provision, drafted by Tennessee's Representative Edwin L. Davis, dictated that essentially all the people of the U.S. were entitled to equality of radio broadcasting services. To achieve this, a system to provide a fair and equitable "quota" of services within zones across the U.S. was adopted, and a "unit-value" for every radio station in the U.S. was calculated according to class, power, frequency, coverage area and population. It also was determined which stations could be used for simultaneous operation without objectionable interference. The FRC determined that 400 radio "units" fairly represented the entire U.S., and, because there were five zones, each zone equitably would be allocated 80 "units," to be divided among the states in each zone according to population.

As mentioned earlier, Utah was put in the 5th Zone, with eleven western states and the territories of Hawaii and Alaska. The 80 "units" given to the Fifth Zone were divided according to population, with California receiving 38.53 units, Washington receiving 10.16, Colorado receiving 6.74, and so on. Utah, the sixth largest state in Zone 5, was assigned 3.27 units.

Under this quota plan in 1927, a 1000-watt station operating full time on a regional channel, would be considered one "unit." KSL, operating full time at 5,000 watts in 1928, thus, took up more than two units of Utah's quota. Meanwhile, KDYL, operating full time at 1,000 watts, took another two units, and KLO took still another two. As a result, 6.62 units were already charged to Utah because of the three existing stations. This was 102% over quota for the state and contributed to the 16% overage for Zone 5. As such, the FRC was reluctant to entertain any new 5th Zone radio license applications, especially from Utah, for seven years until at least 1934.

The quota system carried over to the Communications Act of 1934. A new quota plan was devised, under which the state of Utah was due 1.54 nighttime and 2.78 daytime broadcasting units. Because Utah already exceeded both its nighttime and daytime quotas, it would have continued to be impossible for new applicants to obtain a license if not for the window of opportunity provided to them under Section 307(b) of the new 1934 law. Under this section, applications were encouraged in states where markets could support additional stations, even if zone and state "unit" values had been exceeded.

In Section 307(b) of the 1934 Federal Communications Act, the Commission was authorized to:

> Grant applications for additional licenses for stations not exceeding one hundred-watts of power if the Commission finds that such stations will serve the public convenience, interest, and necessity, and that their operation will not interfere with the fair and efficient radio service of stations licensed under the provisions of this section.

New activity was immediately afoot. After June 19, 1934, eight new applications were filed for construction permits to build 100-watt stations in northern Utah. Because these applications would affect the "units" charged to Utah's quota, the newly formed Federal Communications Commission delegated all of them to hearings. These hearings would determine if an applicant was qualified to hold a broadcasting license to serve the "Public Interest Convenience and Necessity" (PICAN). In the hearings, the FCC evaluated each applicant's U.S. citizenship, character, financial, technical, and several other qualifications to operate a radio broadcasting station. Other criteria included: (1) local residency of the owner; (2) integration of ownership and management and active participation in day-to-day station operations; (3) active participation in civic affairs and recognition of community needs; (4) background and interest diversity, and (5) past broadcast experience.

After considering personal qualifications, the FCC turned to an applicant's proposed programming. Proposed programming, with an emphasis on localism was favorably weighted, enhanced by the proposed use of local talent. Program diversity also was highly favored. Encouraged were the following types of programs seen as serving PICAN: programs for children, religious programs, educational and public affairs programs, editorializing by licensees, political broadcast, agricultural programs, news programs, weather and market reports, sports programs, service to minority groups, and entertainment programming.

On January 30, 1935, the FCC opened hearings to evaluate the eight 100-watt radio station applications in northern Utah. A brief description of each of the eight applications is presented below followed by a discussion of the FCC's decisions regarding each application.

Utah Radio Educational Society, Salt Lake City application, May 25, 1934

The Utah Radio Educational Society (URES), a "mutual association" composed of 100 members, was organized for the expressed purpose of operating a 1,000-watt radio station at 1450kc in Salt Lake City. URES applied on May 25, 1934, even before the 1934 Act officially went into effect. This unincorporated group of people stated lofty, if not heavenly inspired, goals for the station in their Articles of Association:

> The objects and purposes for which this Society is formed are:
> To protect and defend the rights of the common people in radio
> matters. To promote and elevate the standards of radio broadcasting
> programs. To promulgate education by radio for the welfare and
> benefit of the whole people. To exert by radio broadcasting a
> wholesome influence upon the youth of the land. To instill and
> inculcate American ideals, patriotism, love of country and respect for
> its tradition, history, institutions and its laws, and to help preserve
> radio facilities for such purposes. To cooperate with all worthwhile
> undertakings in the preservation of the principles and ideals of the
> Declaration of Independence and the Constitution of the United

States. To maintain, disseminate, send out, and broadcast by means
of radio apparatus.[133]

A list of URES members was not given to the FCC, and the two people appearing before the FCC on behalf of URES (Orman W. Ewing and Walter P. Monson, Jr.) testified that they knew only about a dozen of the estimated 100 members of the association. Ewing practiced land law, and Monson was a field representative of the Federal Housing Administration and formerly had been in the real estate business. Neither of these men had any radio broadcasting experience. No financial statements were provided for URES, and there was no money in the treasury of the society. Funds in excess of $15,000, needed for constructing and operating the station, were proposed to come from an assessment on the URES members and from the Utah Federation of Labor. The applicant projected that the station signal would provide service in a 200-mile radius of Salt Lake City. FCC engineers determined that the station would, at best, serve only a 24-mile radius.

Munn Q. Cannon, Logan application

No hearing went forth for this applicant (Munn Q. Cannon). He did not appear in support of his Logan application.[134]

Great Western Broadcasting Association, Logan and Provo applications,
July 6, 1934

Great Western Broadcasting Association (GWBA), applied for two stations, one in Logan and the other in Provo. GWBA proposed that the Logan station would be used by the LDS Church for religious programming, the Utah Agricultural College (later USU) for educational programming, and by community groups for musical programming. GWBA proposed that the Provo station would serve Utah Valley merchants, and that BYU would be a significant source of quality programming. The FCC found that the granting

---

133   Federal Communications Commission, Examiner's Report No. I-126," Docket No. 2612, Box No. 568, Record Group 173, National Archives, Washington, D.C.
134   Federal Communications Commission, "Examiner's Report No. I-126," Docket Nos. 2565 and 2600, Box No. 568, Record Group 173, National Archives, Washington, D.C.

of either license would not cause interference with any other area stations.

The GWBA applications, however, were more complex than initially thought, and the name of the principal owner of GWBA was a surprise. The FCC discovered that Sidney S. Fox surreptitiously applied for these two new stations under the corporate name of Great Western Broadcasting (GWBA). GWBA was incorporated under the laws of the state of Delaware with 100 shares of stock issued to a single person, H. R. Duvall.

As the FCC hearings evolved, the testimony revealed that Great Western Broadcasting Association was an invention of the Intermountain Broadcasting Company (KDYL) of Salt Lake City and Fox, its president. Fox and his Washington attorney, Paul M. Segal, had incorporated GWBA as a shadow company to apply for the Logan and Provo stations.[135]

Duvall turned out to be a woman employee in Segal's Washington, D.C. law office. An "associate," she was called. She did not appear at the hearings and Fox represented her by proxy, even though no legal documents were provided that gave him that authority. No background information was provided about Duvall, and no other stockholders were listed for GWBA. Little information was given concerning GWBA's proposed financing, although Fox certainly was in a financial position at that time to easily cover any expenses. The verbal agreement between Fox and Duvall had her giving all her Great Western Broadcasting stock to Fox after the two licenses were granted.

Apparently, Fox's purpose in applying was to obtain these licenses to stifle competition to KDYL. Although local programming was proposed, it likely was Fox's intention to use the Provo and Logan stations to extend KDYL and NBC coverage to those communities. That is, to simply repeat KDYL's programming rather than originate local programming. When asked why he wanted licenses for two new stations, Fox replied, in a plain pragmatic tone, "I am applying for the applications for Provo and Logan for the reason that it is good business, and the opportunity could be made available to support

---

135   Federal Communications Commission, "Examiner's Report No. I-126," Docket Nos. 2563 and 2564, Box No. 568, Record Group 173, National Archives, Washington, D.C.

a station in both cities, and in the interest of public convenience, necessity and interests." When asked how the Provo and Logan programing would be different from that on KDYL, Fox replied:

> Well, the only difference that there may be --we are not making any definite plans on that. We have not committed ourselves as to that. We, of course, as you know, are operating a network station (KDYL), and I would assume that our program and the arrangements would be of a constructive character, that is consistent with any successful operation. I mean by that, operating the station both from a public standpoint, and a commercial standpoint, and to successfully operate for the public interest, it has got to be successful.[136]

FCC Hearing Examiner Tyler Berry replied to Fox's responses with, "I don't know that that means a great deal to me, but we will let it go at that." Throughout the hearing, Fox appeared to answer FCC questions about his proposed applications with less than candid or clearly understandable thoughts.

Paul Q. and Louis H. Callister (who were brothers), Salt Lake City and Provo applications, respectively, August 1, 1934

Paul Callister, Salt Lake City: Paul applied to operate a 100-watt station in Salt Lake City, while his brother applied for a Provo station. Both grew up in Salt Lake City. Paul became president of three different Utah oil and gas related companies and, with cash and stock assets exceeding $170,000 and a 60-acre farm, was well positioned financially to construct and operate his proposed radio station. He had no broadcasting experience but planned to manage the station with the assistance of another brother, Reed, a lawyer with broadcasting experience by virtue of his involvement in two California radio stations but who had no intentions of moving to Utah.

---

136   Federal Communications Commission, Testimony of Sidney S. Fox: Hearing before the Federal Communications Commission, Washington, D.C., January 30, 1935, 203.

Callister's proposed programming appeared to be well balanced, and he emphasized local service, with no KSL or KDYL duplication. No network affiliation was contemplated either. He set advertising rates at $17 per hour, in contrast to those at KSL and KDYL, which were running from $60 to $90 per hour. He said his rates were set low to allow access to local advertisers who had been priced out of KSL and KDYL. There was one significant problem in Callister's application. He was applying to operate on 1370kc, and another applicant was applying for the same frequency in Logan, only 70 miles away. Two stations that close together, operating on the same frequency, would without a doubt have interfered with each other where their signals overlapped, and comparative hearings would have been required to determine the best applicant.

Meanwhile, his brother Louis Callister failed to appear to discuss his application for a Provo station. His hearing did not go forth.[137]

Utah Broadcasting Company, Salt Lake City application

The Utah Broadcasting Company (UBC) comprised a partnership of Jack L. Powers, Frank C. Carman, David G. Smith and Grant R. Wrathall. Even before UBC incorporated on January 11, 1935, its principals had applied for a 100-watt station in Salt Lake City. The UBC principals, all young enterprising men, proposed constructing the station using personal assets.

Powers, 23, worked at the Salt Lake Hardware Company and his father operated a dairy ranch near Park City on 500 acres of land. Powers could contribute as much as $6,000 cash toward station construction. Carman, 24, was single, with no outstanding financial obligations. He was in the radio service business and had $800 in equipment and a $1,500 piano that he could put into the KUTA application. As a licensed engineer, he earned about $150 per month. Smith, 25 years old, owned livestock, real estate and some stocks. He was single and had assets in excess of $50,000 to support his obligations to the station. Wrathall, 28, was a University of Utah electrical engineering

---

137   Federal Communications Commission, "Examiner's Report No. I-126," Docket No. 2566, Box No. 568, Record Group 173, National Archives, Washington, D.C.

graduate, employed as a consulting radio engineer in Washington, D.C. His financial contribution to UBC primarily would be in the form of in-kind engineering services. He also had $4,000 in land, buildings and livestock that could be used as security for a loan.

Although not a principal, Dan B. Shields, an attorney who later was involved in other Utah radio applications, told the FCC that he was willing to assist in financing the station. In the final analysis, it appeared that Smith had $18,000 in liquid assets and was the primary source of the money for UBC principals to build their station.

The applicants contacted 157 businesses to ascertain their needs. Of the 157 businesses they contacted, 71% said they would support a new local radio station. Many business people complained that favorable hours were not available on KSL and KDYL, and that the prices they charged were beyond their means. Carman proposed to use recordings and transcriptions for the first six months on-the-air but promised he would replace these sources with local programming as time went on and he attracted local advertisers.

Cache Valley Broadcasting Service Company, Logan application, September 20, 1935

Cache Valley Broadcasting Service Company (CVB) applied for a Logan station and was the second applicant for a station on 1370kc. CVB principals included J. S. and J. M. Reeder, and L. R. Jensen, from Salt Lake City. They entered into a contract with Seymore L. Billings of the Billings Lumber Company, to secure financing for their proposed station. The contract provided that upon the granting of the application, Billings would get title to all of the station's equipment and one-fourth interest in the capital stock of CVB, to cover his loan to the corporation. CVB proposed programming from many of the same sources as the other Logan applicants, primarily involving the college and the agricultural community.

Impact of the hearings

The applicants for these new stations uniformly contended that KDYL and KSL were not adequately serving all of the northern Utah communities. As such, they claimed that one or more new radio stations were needed to serve local interests. In the FCC hearings, it became incumbent upon Fox and Glade to show that their existing stations provided access to local talent and local advertisers. Fox and Glade, representing KDYL and KSL respectively, protested the granting of any new radio station licenses in northern Utah.

When confronted with public interest issues at the FCC hearings, however, Fox and Glade immediately found themselves defending their own stations rather than protesting the entry of new stations. The FCC essentially challenged Fox and Glade to show that KDYL and KSL adequately served the people of northern Utah, thus obviating the need for one or more new stations. Tacit in the FCC's challenge was that a new station would be assigned in northern Utah if Fox and Glade could not show convincingly that KDYL and KSL adequately provided a significant local service to the entire area.

Fox and Glade testified that KDYL and KSL, respectively, in fact, provided excellent local service, especially to local advertisers. Of the 550 local firms in Salt Lake doing business in 1934, KDYL was said to serve 352 and KSL, 300. KDYL claimed a sales force of "from three to six" who solicited local advertisers, and a total employee count of 30 persons. KSL employed 41 full-time persons and up to 600 part-time staffers over a given year. About 2,000 locals each year were allowed access to KSL as free talent.

Great Western Broadcasting Association (GWBA) represented an interesting paradox for Fox in his appearance before the FCC. As owner of KDYL, an existing station, Fox ironically was protesting the applications for two new stations for which he was the applicant. Glade, too, presented a befuddling paradox in his appearance before the FCC. In fact, the most persuasive evidence to counter the argument that new stations in northern Utah were not needed came from Glade himself.

When the hearing turned to Glade's testimony, the FCC called his attention to letters he had written in 1932 about KLO, the Ogden station, requesting authority to move the KLO transmitter to a site in Salt Lake City. Glade contended in those letters that there was a need for a new local radio station and that the public interest would be served by granting KLO a license to serve local Salt Lake City merchants and organizations. In one letter, dated July 13, 1932, Glade wrote:[138]

> While national chain programs are possibly more desired here in the great isolated inter-mountain empire than anywhere else in America, and it is urgently important that both of the other stations (KDYL and KSL) carry all of them that they consistently can. KLO, being a local station, can do a tremendous local service by giving special opportunity for local expression, which is also cordially appreciated. In the proposed new location, this opportunity will be greatly extended and thousands more of our people served in addition to our present following.

On July 28, 1932, Glade added to his earlier letter:[139]

> I believe we can then immediately get the station [KLO] on a network for an hour or two a day to carry the surplus, which KSL cannot take. You realize how that will help 'pep up' our KLO programs. KLO has the active support in this proposal of KSL.

Glade's testimony before the FCC in 1934, protesting new stations, seemed vacuous in light of these letters, written only two years before, which exhorted the need for KLO to provide a local service to supplement the national service provided by KSL.

On May 1, 1936, after extensive hearings, held over a nine-month period, the FCC concluded that there was a need in the Salt Lake City area for a radio station devoted to local programming and to serve the needs of local

---

138 Federal Communications Commission, Testimony of Earl J. Glade, Hearing before the Federal Communications Commission, January 31, 1934, page 398.
139 Federal Communications Commission, Testimony of Earl J. Glade, Hearing before the Federal Communications Commission, January 31, 1934, page 400.

advertisers. At the same time, the FCC denied all but one of the applications discussed above. There were various and differing reasons for the denials.

FCC rulings on the applications

Utah Radio Educational Society, Salt Lake City application: Denied

The Utah Radio Educational Society (URES) application was denied on the grounds that the names of its members were not revealed, and its legal, financial and other qualifications could not be determined as a result. It also was denied on the grounds that the state of Utah already was 103% over quota and that granting URES's application for a 100-watt station – before the Communications Act was promulgated-- would be in violation of FCC Rules and Regulations. Because URES applied for a 1000-watt station, granting it a license would be in violation of Section 307(b) of the Communications Act of 1934, in that only 100-watt stations were approved in excess of quotas.

Paul Q. Callister, Salt Lake City application: Denied

Paul Q. Callister's application also was denied. Found to be legally, technically and financially well qualified to operate the 100-watt station, he had no radio experience. To counter his inexperience, Callister proposed to form a partnership with Reed, the California lawyer who had experience in radio, considering that he owned 40% of a San Diego radio station. Because his brother did not intend to move to Utah and that another brother was an applicant for a station in Provo contributed to the denial. In addition, need was shown for one local broadcast station in the area, and the grant of another 100-watt station applicant would better service the locality. Callister's application, thus, was deemed not to be in the public interest.

Great Western Broadcasting Association, Logan and Provo applications: Denied

Fox's GWBA two applications were also denied. In going before the FCC, Fox assumed that no matter what he said, the FCC would look favorably on his nine successful years in broadcasting at KDYL, his legendary financial wizardry, and his well prepared technical plan. KDYL's talented chief engineer John Baldwin prepared the technical aspects of GWBA's applications. Initially, Fox assumed correctly. Despite all the vagaries in his testimony and the mystery surrounding GWBA's applications, the hearing examiner recommended approval of Fox's Provo application on October 29, 1935. In the end, however, the recommendation was reversed, and the FCC denied both of GWBA's applications as not being in the public interest, because Duvall – identified by the FCC as a "he" but actually a "she" – the designated applicant did not possess the legal qualifications necessary to hold the license. Furthermore, no citizen qualification was furnished, financial qualification was not established, the nature of the program service to be rendered was not disclosed, and all the information called for by the questions in the application was not provided.

Cache Valley Broadcasting Service Company, Logan application: Denied

The application by Cache Valley Broadcasting Service, Inc. (CVB), for a Logan station on 1370kc, also was denied because the applicant's proposed financing plan was ruled faulty. The person loaning money to CVB was Seymour L. Billings, the grandfather of Peter Billings, a prominent Utah Democrat in the early 1990s. He was not a CVB partner in the corporation identified as making the application, yet he would have been given all the station's assets and control of the license if the Cache Valley Broadcasting principals were unable to repay their loan from him. This was against FCC rules. In addition, the granting of the license, the FCC ruled, would cause objectionable interference with an existing station, and the applicant did not sufficiently disclose the nature and character of the program service intended to be rendered. A reconstituted Cache Valley Broadcasting, Inc., with most of the same principals, later submitted another application for a Logan station that was approved. That station, KVNU, went on the air in Logan on November 20, 1938, and is discussed in a later chapter.

Munn Q. Cannon Logan and Louis H. Callister Provo applications: Denied

Two other applicants, Munn Q. Cannon for a Logan station and Louis
H. Callister for a Provo station asked that their applications be dismissed
without prejudice, meaning they could resubmit their applications at another
time. Several of the other applicants at this time objected to dismissal without
prejudice, because neither Cannon nor Callister had appeared at any of the
hearings or presented any evidence in support of their applications. The FCC
subsequently dismissed both applications with prejudice, meaning they were
dismissed permanently from reapplying.

Utah Broadcasting Company, Salt Lake City application: Granted

With all other Utah applications denied, the FCC had to decide if the
Utah Broadcasting Company (UBC) was legally, financially, technically and
otherwise qualified to operate a Salt Lake City station. The FCC determined
there was a need for the service by (a) the population of the area, (b) the
importance of the area as a trading center, and (c) the demand of local business
concerns for lower advertising rates and more desirable hours than presently
were available on the two other stations in the market. The FCC also looked
at UBC's proposed management structure and found UBC's owners all to be
residents and citizens of Salt Lake City, with their business interests centered
there. And all the UBC principals appeared to be familiar with the needs of
the people in the proposed area of service. Thus, the FCC deemed that the
background and experience of this group seemed to "fit them admirably for
the operation and management of a station."[140]

UBC's KUTA is treated first in the chapters that follow even though it
was not the first pioneer station of the seven to go on the air. As discussed
above, the founders of KUTA submitted their FCC application in 1934. Its
construction permit was issued in 1936, but the station's launch was delayed,
and it did not go on the air until 1938, due to various nuanced objections from
a competitor. Two other stations launched operations earlier: KEUB in Price

140   Federal Communications Commission Reports, 3 F.C.C.,
246.): The denials and single approval are reported In: "Decisions, Reports, and Orders of the
Federal Communications Commission of the United States, July1, 1936-Febuary 28, 1937."

(1936) and KSUB in Cedar City (1937).

One could ascertain from the above that the eight applicants varied in their broadcasting knowledge and experience. One of the applicants clearly recognized the financial potential inherent in radio station ownership, knew how to play the system and how to pretend to demonstrate particular qualities the FCC valued, while also thwarting competition. Other applicants claimed their proposed station would serve a public good but also recognized a business opportunity that implied stature and standing and maybe even one that provided independence and wealth. A couple of the applicants involved young men who struggled through the Great Depression and engaged their older successful relatives in their efforts to obtain a license. Two applicants didn't even appear at the hearings in defense of their applications, maybe choosing not to risk personal resources or deflect attention from their core businesses. All of the applicants faced opposition from the KDYL and KSL principals who wanted to suppress competition. As seen, only one of the applicants was granted a license, the favorable outcome the result of an extraordinarily well prepared application that addressed all the FCC's requirements.

The contribution of these eight applicants, though almost universally denied at the time, should not be undervalued. These applicants provided a template for future applicants, a guide to navigate the complex application process involving government regulations, a community focused operating agreement, management involvement, proposed programming, technical competency, superb character and, of great importance, financial viability.

The founding of the seven pioneer radio broadcasting stations, engaged in the chapters that follow, depended on the models proffered by the applicants that preceded them.

CHAPTER 8

KUTA: SALT LAKE CITY

On September 11, 1936, more than two years after it filed its FCC application, and three months after the Davis Amendment and the zone quota system on the number of radio stations were repealed, the Utah Broadcasting Company (UBC) received permission to construct a new station in Salt Lake City. UBC officers were Frank C. Carman, president and general manager; Jack L. Powers, advertising manager; David G. Smith, chief announcer, and Grant R. Wrathall, engineer.

The UBC principals were well connected in the community of radio pioneers in Utah. Carman and Wrathall obtained their degrees in electrical engineering from the University of Utah, and both specialized in radio engineering and were licensed radio operators. Carman had been an amateur operator for 14 years, starting when he was 12. Wrathall had worked at KFUT radio on the University of Utah campus, the station earlier built by Ira Kaar.

On October 1, 1936, the Great Western Broadcasting Association and the Intermountain Broadcasting Company, actually the one-in-the-same corporate entity owned by KDYL's Sidney S. Fox, filed an appeal to the FCC's decision, which allowed the UBC to construct another station in Salt Lake City. Fox's appeal essentially was a nuisance document, meant to slow the inevitable construction of a competing Salt Lake City station. As Carman recollected, it was the first of many appeals that Fox filed:[141]

> I got my permit, but Sid Fox protested it [on the grounds that] we'd
> put him out of business, that there wasn't enough business for three
> stations [in Salt Lake]. We had several hearings at the FCC, and we

---

141   Frank C. Carman, Interview by Tim Larson, 27 June 1986, Tape No. 484, transcript, 11, Everett L. Cooley Oral History Project, Marriott Library, University of Utah, Salt Lake City, Utah.

kept winning them, but then he applied to the Appellate Court in
Washington. He delayed us a good two years.

On December 6, 1937, after more than a year of appeals, the court
overruled Fox and upheld the FCC's decision to grant Carman and the UBC a
construction permit. Carman constructed the station, and KUTA went on the
air on August 1, 1938, with studios in Salt Lake's Belvedere Hotel at 29 South
State Street near where City Creek mall stands today. KUTA opened after
four long, frustrating and expensive years from the time Carman first filed an
application in August 1934.

Frank Carman's entry into radio

Carman was born on May 21, 1909, to Dr. George and Nina Richardson
Carman. Carman's father was a prominent Salt Lake City dentist and the
family lived on 600 South Street, just a few houses west of Mount Olivet
Cemetery and east of 1300 East Street, near the University of Utah campus.
Carman attended Douglas Elementary School and Roosevelt Junior High
where he helped organize the first orchestra.

In 1921, at age 12, Carman became an amateur radio operator with station
W6CRS, a spark-type station using code. Carman said his interest in radio was
stimulated by "Ike Kaar and Everett Seeley, somewhat older Salt Lake boys who
had the radio bug."[142] Herbert Hoover, then Secretary of Commerce, signed
Carman's first amateur license six years before the Federal Radio Commission
of 1927 and 13 years before the Federal Communications Commission of 1934
were established.

An indication of Carman's early passion for amateur radio was his
collection of "DX-ing" cards collected between 1922 and 1926. "DX-
ing" referred to the detection and verification of distant amateur stations.
Beginning at age 14, in 1923, Carman would tune in signals from all over the
U.S. and many foreign countries on W6CRS, his amateur station. Upon tuning
in a distant transmitter, or a "DX," he would write to that station, requesting

---

142   Salt Lake Tribune, September 12, 1954.

verification of what he heard. Upon receiving verifications, he would carefully tack the returned station verification cards on the wood-paneled wall of his W6CRS transmitting room, located adjacent to the garage behind his parent's 600 South Street home.

In 1988, I retrieved more than 200 of Carman's DX-ing verification cards from the walls of that room. Carman's DXing cards, verifying his contact with other amateur stations worldwide in the early 1920s, had remained tacked to the wall of his old W6CRS transmitting room for 66 years, behind rakes and shovels and through several ownership changes in his family's original property. In 1989, a few months before Carman died, I took the DX-ing cards I found at Carman's boyhood home to show him at his retirement home in Lincoln City, Oregon. As he carefully examined the cards, now 80, Carman's eyes welled up in tears. He clearly was pleased with the discovery. The DXing cards are now held in the Marriott Library Special Collections at The University of Utah.

In 1926, when Carman graduated from East High School, he had already become an accomplished pianist. He attended the University of Utah, taking classes in music and business. These dual interests left him wondering what he should do after graduating from the University of Utah:[143]

> I asked a friend on the faculty, B. Rowland Lewis, which I should be: pianist or engineer. Professor Lewis indicated that there was ample room in the world for good engineers, not so much demand for good pianists. He was trying to tell me that in terms of success, there was a vast difference between talent and genius in the arts.

Carman chose engineering and radio broadcasting, and that brings the story to 1938 and the FCC's final approval of KUTA's license application. Carman located the KUTA transmitter on six acres of land at 1324 South Third West, a mile away from the proposed Belvedere studios on State Street. He rented the site for $20 per month from the Morrison Brothers, who were auto mechanics. Carman feared that the Morrisons would not allow him to

143   Salt Lake Tribune, "Business Portrait," September 12, 1954.

put radio towers on their property, so he told them that he was going to start a chicken farm. Carman put the transmitter in the bedroom of the farmhouse and the tower in the field alongside.

It was a joke for a long time. "Some chicken farm," said Carman. KUTA studios first were in the Belvedere Hotel at 29 S. State St., moved to (Motor Ave.), better known as Social Hall Avenue, by 1964 and then to North Salt Lake, at 1550 West and 2200 North Street by 1969. KUTA/KLUB remained there for more than 40 years, essentially on the shore of the Great Salt Lake, until Carman sold the station to Sun Mountain Broadcasting in 1985.

The early years of KUTA operations

One of Carman's first hires at KUTA in 1938 was Arch L. Madsen as program director. Madsen and his bride, Peggy, the former Margaret Higgenbotham, whose family ran Salt Lake's Radio Supply, Inc., lived in the farmhouse at the Morrison property antenna and transmitter site for a short time. Madsen came to KUTA from Cedar City, where he had been managing KSUB for Leland Perry, a station discussed in a later chapter in the book. When KUTA went on the air, Madsen, Carman, Wayne Rogers and Harvey Jensen were the station operators. They kept the station on the air from seven a.m. to midnight, each taking alternating shifts of about two hours each, throughout the day. Other employees and operators soon came to include Lyle Wahlquist, Wendell Bell, Virgil Howell and Gus Vogeler. Madsen left KUTA within a year to go to Provo to put KOVO on the air for contractor Cliff Tolboe, another station discussed later in the book.

Carman initially used mostly phonograph records and the NBC Blue network to fill KUTA's schedule because there were no local advertisers to support local programming. Glade, KSL's manager, came to Carman in the autumn of 1938 with a "Ford and Cadillac" time sales proposition. Glade proposed to use KSL's three sales representatives –Bill Featherstone, Ed Broman and Frank McClatchy – to sell KUTA time. As Glade explained to Carman, if an advertiser wanted a "Cadillac" station, they would be put on KSL. If the advertiser wanted a "Ford" station, they would be sold time on

KUTA. In the beginning, the three KSL salesmen sold KUTA time to local advertisers who were priced out of KSL and KDYL or couldn't find available time on those stations.

This sales arrangement lasted a few months, until Glade hired Gordon Owen from San Francisco to be KSL's sales manager. The three KSL sales reps then withdrew from KUTA at the direction of Radio Broadcasters Inc.'s (KSL) new president, J. Reuben Clark, and his new assistant, Ivor Sharp. Nevertheless, Glade and his KSL salesmen gave KUTA "a pretty good start," according to Carman.

On March 29, 1941, in accordance with the Havana Treaty, the FCC adjusted the frequencies of radio stations across the U.S. and other nearby countries in the Americas and the Caribbean – Canada, Mexico, Cuba, the Dominican Republic, and Haiti – to avoid interference, among other things. KSL was moved from 1130kc to 1160kc, and KUTA, which had operated at 1500kc for several years, was scheduled to move to 1490kc on the dial, or thereabouts, in compliance with the Havana Treaty. But before the switch, KUTA received FCC approval to construct a 5,000-watt station to operate at 570kc. The FCC instructed Carman to proceed at that frequency and to ignore its earlier assignment.

Carman had never built a 5,000-watt transmitter so he started accumulating parts and equipment. He went to Sioux City, Iowa, for an unusually structured, hard to climb Wind-Charger tower and gathered equipment piece-by-piece from several other sources. It was late in 1941 by the time he had all the necessary parts in his possession.

Meanwhile, the U.S. had entered WWII in December 1941, and an application from the Walker Bank Group was pending before the FCC for another Salt Lake City station. It was for a new station on 610-kHz. The Walker Bank applicants had significant financial resources, and they made a deal with RCA to obtain the finest equipment. They also were negotiating to take the NBC Blue Network rights away from KUTA. Approval of this new station would have been devastating for KUTA, which could have gone out of business.

Fortunately for Carman's KUTA, in 1942, the U. S. War Productions Board ruled that no scarce resources could be used to construct a radio broadcasting station. Included in the scarce category was the equipment needed from RCA for the Walker Bank station. As such, Walker was not able to obtain equipment to construct its station and the FCC vacated the application. Because Carman had accumulated most of the parts for his new 5,000-watt transmitter before the war started and was building it, he was allowed to proceed. Carman immediately took steps to get the 610-kHz frequency out of Salt Lake City. He prompted Reed Bullen, another major radio figure who is discussed later in the book, and Bullen's father, who had joined the Reeders at KVNU in Logan, to apply for the frequency. KVNU received it and competition for KUTA in Salt Lake City was avoided for several more years.

Carman developed local talent and a good local sales staff in the meantime. Employees at KUTA included Vern Bruggeman, Marshall Small, Nelson Hall, Florien Wineriter, Warren Fletcher, Dick Eskelson, Hal Zogg, Al Thomas and Frank McIntyre. Eskelson did nightly broadcasts from the Jerry Jones Rainbow Rendezvous on 500 South Street in Salt Lake. Bill Sears, touted as the most talented sports broadcaster to ever come to Utah, was also attracted to KUTA. "There was no television, and radio was king": The NBC Blue network became the ABC network and KUTA featured network programs such as the Don McNeill Breakfast Club, the Bing Crosby Show and many others, which helped make the station popular.[144]

KUTA becomes KLUB

In the mid-1950s, Carman moved KUTA to storefront studios on Salt Lake's Social Hall Avenue and changed the call sign to KLUB. From the street, through the large studio window, clocks could be seen showing the time in various capitals around the world. Carman began hiring a talented group of personalities that became known as the "Fabulous Five": Ray Briem, Marshall Small, Paul Droubay, Bill Terry, Ron McCoy, Ron Bailey and Paul Coburn, in

---

144   Vern Bruggeman interview with Tim Larson, August 25, 1989, at his home in Salt Lake City.

various combinations of five performers who were identified as the "Fabulous Five." In the late 1950s, Paul Coburn and other members of the "Fabulous Five" claimed to have discovered the Kingston Trio and introduced their song *Tom Dooley* on KUTA. This reportedly put the Kingston Trio on the way to a hit song across the nation, and, as a result, the "Fabulous Five" on KLUB became known as the "hit makers." Other people who came to KLUB during the 1950s, including Hal Collipriest, Ginny Barlow, Lee Craig Felt and Richard Dixon, also contributed to KLUB's success.[145]

During this period, variations of the KLUB call letters were used frequently in station promotions, and the station became known as "KLUB 57," shortened from its 570-kHz frequency. The morning program was called *The Breakfast KLUB* and the evening show was called the *Night KLUB*. Drive-times became known as the *Commuters KLUB*, and such phrases as the *Friendly KLUB* and *Join the KLUB* were frequently heard on the station. The use of "KLUB" became so important a brand for the station that Carman, fearing somebody would steal it, had the call letters and the word "KLUB" registered as a trademark. The state of Utah gave Carman exclusive rights to such phrases as Radio Station KLUB, KLUB 570, and KLUB Broadcasting Company. The state of Utah also gave him exclusive rights anywhere the KLUB signal reached in the surrounding states of Idaho, Montana, Wyoming, Colorado and Nevada. It is not clear how these rights would be preserved if violated, but, on February 18, 1956, the "KLUB" trademark was registered to Carman by the state of Utah.

Nonetheless, Carman's use of the name KLUB caused concern to at least one government agency soon after the station moved to Social Hall Avenue. On the front of the building was a marquee with large-sized letters advertising "KLUB 570 – Home of the Fabulous Five." It may be apocryphal, but a story has Carman being approached by officers from the Utah State Liquor Commission, investigating alcohol sales and entertainment in a "club" (or KLUB) without a license.

---

145   Paul Coburn interview with Tim Larson, 21 November 1988, Tape No. 903, Everett L. Cooley Oral History Project, Marriott Library, University of Utah, Salt Lake City, Utah; Ray Briem interview with Tim Larson,, September 5, 1988, at the ABC Network Offices in Southern California; Marshall Small interview with Tim Larson,, August 5, 1988, in Salt Lake City.

Although Carman had financial partners, his business partner was Katherine, his wife. She was the daughter of Salt Lake contractor John L. Griffith who, among other construction projects, built the original University of Utah football stadium. The Griffith Company name appears today, even many decades later, on manhole covers in Salt Lake City. Katherine was the main force behind the construction of the Beta Phi Alpha sorority house near the University of Utah campus during the heart of the Great Depression in the 1930s. She obtained the financing, bought the property and saw the building through to completion as president of the sorority (which later was absorbed into the Delta Zeta sorority). She married Carman on July 4, 1937, and became an off-site but, nonetheless, active partner in KUTA when it went on the air in 1938. KUTA employees knew that both Carmans carried the title of boss.

Madsen relates an incident as KUTA program director in the late 1930s, when he neglected his duties and ran into Mrs. Carman's stern rebuke:

> I worked at least twelve hours a day seven days a week for over a year without one minute off. Hard time. One exception was one Christmas Day when my wife's sister's husband's mother died. It was in Ogden and, believe it or not, they had the funeral on Christmas Day in Ogden. What happened? I was in the KUTA studios on the subfloor rooms of the Belvedere Apartment Hotel, south side, at 3:00 o'clock in the morning. I went over that morning, Christmas morning, at 3:00 because, you see, on holidays you change all the advertising copy for the day after Christmas from 'Christmas Greetings,' and 'Best wishes and Merry Christmas' …to regular advertising. So I had to change all that copy for the day after Christmas. I prepared all the program logs, changed and typed all the new copy. … I typed all the new programming logs and copy. I had it all done. Nine o'clock Peg comes with her family, the car horn sounds! I've got to go to this funeral. Earlier I told Frank Carman, "I've got to go to this funeral." He said, 'That's fine. Just get your work done." The car honked and honked. I said to [a fellow operator], who was the announcer on duty at that hour, that I was going to leave

and would he please pick [up the daily log sheets] and put them in the book. ... It was Christmas morning and he wasn't quite sober. ... He said, "Sure." I came back about 4:00 o'clock in the afternoon to be greeted by Frank Carman's wife. She really took me to pieces. I was a no good lousy, lazy inefficient worker, et cetera. I replied, "What's wrong? I had all the work done. ... What's happened?" About a half hour after I left, [my fellow announcer] passed out on the control board. The Carmans didn't discover it for two or three hours. The station break commercials and the station identification were missed during this time. When they [the Carmans] were unable to get a response to their telephone calls, they came to the station and found [him] still dead drunk in the control room. Memory --what a precious gift! Such experiences were all part of my education in the school of "hard knocks."[146]

Katherine Carman continued as a major force at the station. In later years, it was known by the KUTA DJs that certain songs, like those categorized as rock 'n' roll, were never played on the air. If played, an errant DJ was assured of a call from her, threatening severance. Katherine also was the bookkeeper for KUTA and for the other holdings of the Carman Broadcasting Group in other states. She mastered business methods at the University of Utah and likely earlier from, among others, her contractor father. Her temperament was tough or gentle as appropriate, and she was an essential member of the Carman broadcast team for nearly 50 years.

The Carmans made KUTA highly profitable during the war years. "We got our investment back every fifteen days for four years.[147] Carman and the other principals of the UBC took some of that profit and formed the Rocky Mountain Broadcasting System, which owned KLIX in Pocatello, KIFI in Idaho Falls, KGEM in Boise, and KOPR in Butte, Montana. KUTA became the hub for the ABC Network in the Rocky Mountain Region, feeding programs to stations in Nevada, Idaho, Montana and Wyoming.

---

146   Arch L. Madsen, Interview by Tim Larson, 13 August 1986, Tape No. 542, transcript, 64, Everett L. Cooley Oral History Project, Marriott Library, University of Utah, Salt Lake City, Utah.
147   Frank C. Carman, Interview by Tim Larson, 24.

George Hatch, in the 1980s, wanted Carman to sell him KLUB radio, or, more accurately, the frequency. Hatch had always wanted the 570kc frequency occupied by KLUB, and he suggested a $6.5 million figure to Carman for both KLUB and KISN. That deal and another from the Gannett newspaper group fell through, but Ballard Smith, then president of the San Diego Padres and a member by marriage at the time of the Ray Kroc family of McDonald's Corporation fame, reportedly offered Carman $4.8 million cash and $300,000 on a five-year, non-compete contract.

Carman accepted and finalized the KLUB sale on August 5, 1985. With that, he retired on a partial basis to Lincoln City, Oregon. In August 1987, he purchased KNPT AM and KVQT FM in Newport, Oregon, near his retirement home. He stayed active at the station but later hired David Miller from Utah to manage the station. As had been the case at KLUB for several decades, Carman's grand piano – the $1,500 one that he had when he applied for KUTA in 1934 – was put in the KNPT studios for his frequent use. He often could be heard perfectly playing *Autumn Leaves*. with its cascading runs, and *Stardust*, his favorite song.[148]

Yaquina Bay Communications, Inc., with David Miller as president and general manager, acquired KNPT/KVTQ on January 1, 1996, and that group owns the combo to the present.[149]

Carman's W6CRS was an active amateur station for sixty-eight years, up to the time he died on September 19, 1989. Carman was buried in Salt Lake's Mount Olivet Cemetery, not 100 yards from his boyhood home on 600 South and the room adjacent to the garage in which his first amateur station was located and his DX cards were found.

Later, in Section III Carman's involvement in the founding of the television broadcasting station, KUTV-TV, is chronicled in a chapter.

---

148   David Miller interview with Tim Larson, September 25, 1989, at KNPT AM and KVQT FM in Newport, Oregon.
149   https://archive.sltrib.com/story.php?ref=/business/ci_13263965.

CHAPTER 9

KEUB: PRICE, UTAH

Sam G. Weiss was prompted to apply for a radio station in Price, Utah, after he was impressed with a fly-by-night "wildcat" radio company that came to Price in the summer of 1935. Two brothers had a truck-mounted broadcasting station they took to small towns around the West and operated for community enjoyment. The mobile broadcasters set up their portable station in a local hotel, solicited advertising, put on programs using local talent, and stayed about two weeks. According to Weiss, the community received the itinerant broadcasters very well, and people were pleased with the programs they put on air. These same brothers later also set up their station in Cedar City and prompted Leland Perry to apply for a radio station in that city, the subject of a later chapter in the book.

E.M. Williams, music instructor at the Carbon County High School, was especially pleased with the itinerant broadcasting station. His high school band performed on the portable station and the response was quite satisfactory:

> At the time we played with our high school band, it seemed that everyone in the local country here was interested in hearing our band at its best and, of course, the machine was new here to us. While we were playing it was just almost a steady stream of phone calls [that] came in to us helping us to fix our band, and telling us what was coming over --cloudy, or too soft-- and we could hardly get our band to go through for the phone calls. ... People were really interested in the band concert. Especially ... in all of the students that took part in it.[150]

---

150   E. M. Williams, In re: Sam G. Weiss, d/b as Eastern Utah Broadcasting Company, Deposition testimony taken pursuant to order of the Federal Communications Commission before George G. Armstrong, a Notary Public, residing in Salt Lake City, Utah, September 18, 1935. FCC File No. B5-P-648, Docket No. 3150, Box 693, Record Group 173, National Archives, Washington, D.C.

Before the itinerant broadcasting brothers came to Price, Weiss had been thinking about applying for a radio station in other places. He investigated putting a station in Wolf Point, Montana, or Alamosa, Colorado. He also considered buying a 1,000-watt station in Twin Falls, Idaho, which had been on the air for seven years. He then looked at several Utah cities before choosing Price:[151]

> To begin with, I have lived in the small communities of Eastern Utah all my life, and we find out on occasions that we have certain social and other activity we would like to have the community know about, and we could not make that available to them, so the idea of radio has been in my mind for a long time. I thought at one time that Vernal would be a good spot, and also, possibly, Roosevelt. ... But the economic situation would not justify it. I was acquainted with the entire Eastern Utah, and it occurred to me, from going there and coming back in the course of my regular travels, that Price is favorable, both economically and socially, and is more or less isolated from the rest of the State. ... It is surrounded by mountains. Although it is a part of the State, they have different social and economic condition[s] there. The people there are not all of one nationality; they are different that way from the rest of the State. Economically, Price is unique; it is the large coal-producing center in the county --the only coal-producing center. It is the main industry outside of livestock. ... About sixty per cent of Carbon County's population would be in Price and Helper, in and around the mining camps. I find that conditions there were such that the public mind is civic-minded, and there is considerable activity going on around Price and Helper and Carbon County in general, and they have no way and had no way of making all of their activities available for those who lived in and around Price and in Carbon County.

Like the other Utah radio applicants at this time, Weiss applied for the

---

151   Sam G. Weiss, d/b as Eastern Utah Broadcasting Company, Deposition testimony taken pursuant to order of the Federal Communications Commission before George G. Armstrong, a Notary Public, residing in Salt Lake City, Utah, September 18, 1935. FCC File No. B5-P-648, Docket No. 3150, Box 693, Record Group 173, National Archives, Washington, D.C.

KEUB (<u>E</u>astern <u>U</u>tah <u>B</u>roadcasting) license under the provisions of Section 307(b) of the new Communications Act of 1934. As explained previously, under Section 307(b), the Federal Communications Commission (FCC) was authorized to exceed a state's quota if the public interest would be served in granting a license for a station not exceeding 100 watts of power.

Weiss was a resident of Salt Lake City, although he frequently attended to property his mother owned in Carbon County, and he was well known in Price by virtue of the Uintah Basin pelt, hide and wool-trading business he and his dad had conducted in the area for many years. He was the sole owner of the Eastern Utah Broadcasting Company, and said he would move to Price to manage the station if he was successful in getting a license. His application was supported by many prominent Price business and civic leaders, including Joseph W. Potter and Elmie Bernardi of Eastern Utah Electric, a radio sales and repair business; bank president A. W. McKinnon, who later became a KEUB partner; and, Price Mayor, B. W. Dalton.

Community support gathers for a radio station

These Price citizens and civic leaders wholeheartedly supported Weiss's contention that radio reception in the area was poor and that the public interest would be served with a local station. Joseph Potter was a notable supporter. He did his own survey of radio reception in the Carbon County area and found that KSL from Salt Lake City was the only daytime signal that could be received in Price. However, it was intermittent during the day and faded at night when outside clear-channel stations from California and Denver reached Price. KSL wasn't a local station, but it was at least more proximate than the other more distant stations.

Potter, on September 18, 1935, testified about his survey findings to the FCC:[152]

---

152   Joseph W. Potter, In re: Sam G. Weiss, d/b as Eastern Utah Broadcasting Company, Deposition testimony taken pursuant to order of the Federal Communications Commission before George G. Armstrong, a Notary Public, residing in Salt Lake City, Utah, September 18, 1935. FCC File No. B5-P-648, Docket No. 3150, Box 693, Record Group 173, National Archives, Washington, D.C.

> [KSL] is only periodically ... satisfactory, and it isn't what the modern
> radio public has a right to expect in broadcasting. ... We are now
> coming to a stage ... of high-fidelity receivers, and with the noise
> we have here it is impossible to get those results. ... It [takes] a good
> modern machine with all the conveniences of noise support and
> automatic volume control to hold any of the stations. [For instance],
> ... in our car [and home radios], you have to operate a receiver at full
> volume to get reception, and whenever you operate a radio apparatus
> at full power your distortion level ... rises up, and your quality is
> cut down [from what] can be expected [from] the modern radio
> broadcast.

In further support of Weiss' application, Potter pointed to the age and
quality of radio receivers owned by Carbon County residents. Most radios
in Price were purchased five or six years before or immediately after the
Radio Act of 1927 was passed, when many listeners believed they finally
would be able to hear a wide range of distant radio stations without annoying
interference. This proved not to be the case. Radio sets, even the more costly
ones such as the Majestic brand, still did not provide any daytime listening
service and only marginally acceptable nighttime reception. As such, there
were few new radios in Price, in light of the fact that decent reception could
not be possible with or without a modern radio. Until there was a local station,
few people in the Price area saw a need to purchase a new radio. Potter
indicated, however, that recent speculation of a possible local station had
triggered inquiries and radio purchases to start again.

Weiss wanted to meet the needs of the local community by providing a
radio service to the city of Price and to the ten mining communities within a
15-mile radius. Those who were not finding any acceptable radio service, day
or night, lived in the communities near the mines where they worked. The
electrical power lines and machinery used in the mines also contributed to the
quality of the radio signals being degraded, near the mines.

Weiss believed that a local station also could provide an outlet for different
voices and controversial points of view, as well as local and national news.

Coal production was falling off, miners were threatening a strike, and crime was increasing. Weiss speculated that the United Mine Workers, for instance, could talk from one point –the radio station– to their labor union members in the many different camps surrounding Price, with the hopes of greater understanding among all parties.

Weiss proposed various programs and posited that the "interest, convenience and necessity" of the whole Price River Valley, including Carbon and parts of Emery and Sevier Counties, would be served with a local station. He also reported great interest from merchants who wanted to advertise. The only advertising media available in 1935 were the *Sun Advocate* weekly newspaper, a loudspeaker truck and the telephone. Weiss also proposed to broadcast market reports for the benefit of the agricultural and livestock interests in the area.

The only market reports came a day late to Price in daily newspapers brought in from Salt Lake City and other towns. Weiss and others reported that they had experiences with "agri-buyers" who knew the people of Price received their market reports a day late and who came to Price to purchase from ranchers at the more favorable prices from the prior day:[153]

> From personal experience I know that a man on the range [around Price] does not have the contacts that the slick city buyer has when he has available the telegraph; he can receive definite information from his home buying office as to the market outlook and rush out miles from town and make [unfavorable] deals [with the uninformed ranchers who don't have up-to-date market information].

In addition, many ranchers in the outlying areas of Carbon County were without electricity and listened to battery-powered radios. To receive radio signals took a lot power, and Weiss may have erroneously posited that less power would be required to tune into a local radio signal, and battery power would be preserved, resulting in less expense for Carbon County residents.

---

153   Sam G. Weiss, d/b as Eastern Utah Broadcasting Company.

Weiss also wanted to provide an outlet for local talent and the musical groups in the community, especially the thirteen bands, one of which had recently won first place at the 1933 World's Fair in Chicago. Educators would be granted free time as they desired, and Weiss said the station would provide a moral uplift for people by permitting all the different churches --LDS, Catholic, and Community-- to use the facility.

A particular need, according to Weiss and others, was to help the 52% of the Carbon County population who were foreign. About half of the immigrant population was Italian and a significant part was Greek. A story told over-and-over at the time Weiss applied for the station was that the Italians and Greeks were brought in as miners and merchants to replace the Chinese workers, who had been rounded up in Scofield, Utah, where they lived, and sent away in a railroad boxcar. The boxcar was set loose to run down the Soldier Summit Hill until it jumped the track, killing all the Chinese inside. Thus, was the circulating, albeit apocryphal, explanation for how the Italians and Greeks came to Price. As the story goes, the Italians and Greeks were needed to work in the mines after the Chinese disappeared, a result of the 1882 Chinese Exclusion Act, the only national law ever enacted that specifically excluded one nationality from immigration. It made no difference that there were no reliable sources to support this story. In any case, in 1935, a radio station was believed to be a vehicle by which the Italian and other ethnics who replaced the Chinese in the mines could be "Americanized," and their social status improved. The source for this was J. Bracken Lee, former mayor of Price and Utah governor, who told me about this mythical story, circulating at the time in the Price area.[154]

B.W. Dalton, the mayor of Price, said that the governments of the six cities and towns in Carbon County could also use a radio station to share information with the citizens of their communities. Dalton was totally in favor of a local radio station and was convinced the merchants and general public would support it. He was, however, in a peculiar position because Weiss's Price application was not the only one being considered by the FCC in October

---

154   J. Bracken Lee told of this Chinese story that was circulating to Tim Larson. J. Bracken Lee, Interview with Tim Larson, January 19, 1993, Salt Lake City, Utah.

1935. Price citizen James H. Braffett also applied for a 100-watt station on the same 1420 kilocycles frequency, and his application was set for a later FCC hearing. Dalton was a lawyer employed by the Church of Jesus Christ of Latter-day Saints and politically a Republican. He could not be seen as too partisan at Weiss' hearing because, in the event that Braffett, also a lawyer but who identified as a Democrat, was successful over Weiss, various interests --whether they were the city of Price, the LDS Church's or that of Dalton-- could be alienated from radio. Braffett also was owner of a hotel near the train depot in Carbon County.

It appears that Braffett did not complete all aspects of his application in a timely manner. Braffett's lawyer, Orman W. Ewing, who at the time also was representing applicants for other stations in Utah, assured the FCC that Braffett's application was filed in a timely manner, and that it would be part of the upcoming FCC hearing. Nevertheless, it was not part of the October 28, 1935, FCC hearing in Washington, D.C., and it is assumed that it was ruled in default, leaving the way for Weiss to receive FCC approval without any objections.

It is unclear what exactly happened to the Braffett application because there is no record of it ever going to an FCC hearing. When the FCC determined that the "public interest, convenience and necessity" (PICAN) would be served by granting Weiss' application, and that he was legally, financially, technically and otherwise qualified to meet the radio needs of Price, Braffett likely withdrew his application. In any case, due to quota requirements, the FCC likely would not have entertained another Price station even at another frequency. There appeared to be little controversy or conflict between Braffett and Weiss over their applications. It appears both wanted what was best for Price.

Weiss was forty-one years old when he applied for the Price station in 1935. Growing up, he went to the Salt Lake City public schools and was in his junior year in chemical engineering at the University of Utah when he enlisted in 1916, to serve in the military during WWI. After the war, Weiss worked for about six months as a chemist at the International Smelting and Refining

Company in Tooele, Utah, and for about a year at the Utah Potash Company in Monroe, Utah.

As mentioned earlier, during the 15 years prior to applying for a Price radio station, Weiss and his father were self-employed in the hide and pelt business in the Uintah Basin of northern Utah. In his application, Weiss listed his employment as a salesperson for the hide and pelt business, and, although residing in Salt Lake City, he spent most of his time traveling on family and other business in Utah, Idaho, Montana, Colorado, and parts of Oregon, Washington, and North and South Dakota. Weiss also maintained a residence in Roosevelt, Utah, where he had been a director of the Roosevelt State Bank since 1929.

KEUB wins FCC approval

Weiss' application was heard before an FCC examiner on October 28, 1935, and a construction permit was granted on December 20. He was granted approval to construct a 100-watt station at 1420kc and hired Frank Carman to engineer it. As noted earlier, Carman received a bachelor of arts in business in 1930 and a master's degree in electrical engineering from the University of Utah at the height of the depression in 1933. With his fellow graduate and close friend, Grant Wrathall, and others, he applied for KUTA in Salt Lake City on August 22, 1934. While waiting four years to obtain the Salt Lake City license over Sidney Fox's protests, Carman went to Price and put KEUB on the air for Weiss and the Eastern Utah Broadcasting Company. Carman built the station and received one-third interest for his efforts. When his Salt Lake City application was finally approved in 1938, Carman sold his share of KEUB and used the money to construct KUTA.

Weiss launched KEUB on October 30, 1936, using the equipment Carman had constructed. When KEUB went on the air, Weiss was manager, and he employed Carman as chief engineer, Jack Richards as program director, and Owen Ford as an operator. Opening week operating hours were listed as weekdays from 7:30 a.m. to 10 p.m. and Sundays from 9 a.m. to 10 p.m. This schedule was not honored very long, if at all. Within two years, KEUB usually signed on weekdays at 7 a.m. and was off air at 7 p.m., although with special programs, such as election night coverage in November, the station operated until midnight. On Sundays, operating hours were from just before noon to 5 p.m.

In a typical 12-hour weekday, only 1.5 hours of programming was sponsored. The remaining 10.5 hours each day were logged as sustained (non-sponsored) programming. In early 1938, just over a year after KEUB went on the air, sponsors included only Western Auto Company, Carbon Fruit Markets, Helper Furniture, Price Lumber Company, and Gamble stores. In 1939, Standard Optical, Max's Market, Carbon Drug Company, Price Trading Company, Lewis Optical Company, American Packing Company, Carbon Emery Bank, Diamond Market, and Johnson's Service Station were added to KEUB's stable of advertisers. All the weekday advertisers were local businesses. There were no national or regional advertisers on KEUB in those early years.

On Sundays beginning in 1937, only the Jehovah Witnesses' Watch Tower and the Seventh Day Adventists were logged as sponsors of two 15-minute programming segments. Also in 1937, KEUB received free space in the local newspaper, the *Sun Advocate*, with an approximate value of $30 per month for which the newspaper received two announcements daily except Sunday, which were valued by the station at $27.50 per month, or $330 per year.

In the beginning, KEUB carried Transradio News releases and transcribed programs from NBC. Other programming included KSL rebroadcasts of CBS programming, and recordings of great artists of the time were a staple, including Louis Armstrong, Tommy Dorsey, Duke Ellington, and Glen Miller, among others.

The opening weeks of KEUB were accompanied by the showing of the movie *The Big Broadcast* at the Strand Theater in Price. Featuring radio comedy stars Jack Benny, George Burns and Gracie Allen, Martha Raye, and bandleader Benny Goodman, it was a comedy about a radio broadcasting company. The "various complications that the principal characters ran into gave it a twang and happy ending."[155]

Program Director Jack Richards, who reportedly was disenfranchised by his wealthy New York family for marrying his father's secretary, moved to Price in 1936. Before coming to KEUB, he had acquired 10 years of general business experience and a year of radio experience as commercial manager and an announcer at KGFL radio in Roswell, New Mexico. At KEUB he also soon took on the added responsibilities of commercial manager and chief announcer. Richard's wife, K. Rita Richards, had two years' experience as a stenographer, cashier and bookkeeper. She would later become secretary of Eastern Utah Broadcasting and handle all books, accounts and commercial copy.

Owen J. Ford had come to KEUB after a year's experience as a press operator at the Fort Douglas radiotelephone station in Salt Lake. He stayed at KEUB as an operator-announcer for a year and then spent two years as an operator and pressman for Fox at KDYL in Salt Lake City. Ford returned to KEUB in 1939 as chief engineer and operator. Described as a thoroughly competent operator and engineer, with a fine announcing voice, Ford stayed at KEUB during World War II and beyond.

John Gould, an on-air announcer, was at the station in 1938, and Carl Wolfram, who started as an operator-announcer at KSUB in Cedar City in 1937, came to KEUB in 1940. He was described as popular, a fine announcing personality, and having a thorough knowledge of the transmitter.

Corporate control of KEUB is transferred and call letters changed to KOAL

Weiss controlled 94% of KEUB and the unincorporated Eastern Utah Broadcasting Company. His parents and some others owned the remaining percentage. On April 25, 1938, Weiss applied to the FCC to transfer KEUB from Eastern Utah Broadcasting Company and Weiss to the newly founded Eastern Utah Broadcasting Company, Inc. The FCC approved the transfer on October 25, and Weiss remained the major stockholder with shares valued at

---

155   Sun Advocate, November 19, 1936, 36.

$5,542, while Jack Richards became corporation secretary and Mary Weiss, Sam's mother, became the only other board member.

This corporation operated KEUB for the next few months, until Weiss, as board president, called a special meeting on March 22, 1939, to enact an application asking the FCC for consent to transfer control of the corporation. A week later Weiss signed an agreement giving Jack Richards and A.W. McKinnon, president of the Carbon Emery Bank of Price, the option to purchase 5,542 shares, all of Weiss shares or 94% ownership, of capital stock of the Eastern Utah Broadcasting Company, Inc. for $6,500. McKinnon, whose net financial worth was given as $53,800, subsequently purchased 4,500 shares, and Jack Richards, whose net worth was given as $4,435, bought the remaining 1,042 shares by raising money in the community.

On May 1, 1939, Carman appraised the station and property at $7,142, and the FCC approved the transfer of the license to Richards and McKinnon on July 26. Salt Lake City lawyer, Dan B. Shields, who later became involved in a Logan, Utah, station, with Reed Bullen, supervised the transfer and was assisted by local lawyers F. W. Kedler and T. N. Jensen.

KEUB/Eastern Utah Broadcasting's financial position significantly improved with the transfer to Richards and McKinnon. One important factor was that expenses were reduced because no replacement was necessary for Weiss. Previous to the transfer, he was listed as station manager and drew a hefty salary while contributing very little to day-to-day operations. Jack and Rita Richards had been the de facto managers and operators of the station since just after it went on the air in 1936.

Richards became president, treasurer and a director of Eastern Utah Broadcasting Company, Inc., McKinnon became vice president and a director, Rita Richards became secretary, and David G. Smith, the partner with Carman in Salt Lake City's KUTA, also became a director. Richards soon acquired additional KEUB stock and by May 1941, controlled 29% of the corporation. McKinnon had 21% and Smith had 27%, with several local stockholders holding no more than 10% each. By 1946, Jack and Rita Richards controlled

64% of KEUB stock after buying out Smith. McKinnon controlled 27%, with minority stockholders holding the other 9%.

The Richards lived in an apartment at the radio station and worked with a small staff consisting primarily of Owen Ford and Carl Wolfram. Richards eventually acquired all the stock in the station:[156]

> Jack didn't have the money, so he sold little shares to every business in town. The corporate records show many owners having shares, and he had a buy-out agreement on all of them. So then, over the next five or six years, he bought back from the [Price] merchants all of the stock in the corporation.

By the early 1950s, the Richards had acquired most of the outstanding stock of Eastern Utah Broadcasting, Inc. and, except for a few shares, were the sole owners of what was now known as KOAL. Improvements to the station included insulation to soundproof the studios against the noise of passing trains on the tracks located immediately across U.S. Highway 50 from the KEUB building. And the call letters were changed to KOAL, to better represent the most important industry in "coal" country.

Richards was KOAL's program director, and one person he never denied access to KOAL was J. Bracken Lee, the popular politician who deftly used radio as mayor of Price from January 1936 to December 1947, to reach the grassroots citizens. As a mayoral candidate, he promised to abolish the property tax and, upon being elected by a margin of two votes, did just that.[157]

Lee became great friends with the Richards and had a regular Saturday morning radio show. Rita Richards relates one instance where Lee used radio as a bully pulpit for his views:[158]

---

156   Thomas B. Anderson, Interview by Tim Larson, Tape No. 770, Transcript page 2, May 3, 1988. Everett L. Cooley Oral History Program, Marriott Library, University of Utah, Salt Lake City, Utah.
157   J. Bracken Lee, interview with Tim Larson.
158   George B. Russell, J. Bracken Lee: The Taxpayer's Champion (New York: Robert Speller & Sons, Publishers, Inc., 1961) 25.

When the Salt Lake department stores installed gas and oil furnaces,
Bracken took to the radio to tell the public about it, pointing out
how our Carbon county economy depended on coal. He suggested
that some letter and telephone protests explaining that factor, with a
hint that charge accounts might be transferred elsewhere, should get
results. They did.

The Richards said of Lee:[159]

We feel that J. Bracken Lee is the finest and most sincere public
servant in the country. He always works for all the people, regardless
of their political beliefs. In fact, he is the man we would like to see in
the White House.

KEUB/KOAL programming

Returning back to November 1937, Richards contracted for news with
Transradio Press (TP), whose national and international spot news was sent
regularly in code via short-wave radio and decoded and read over the air. At
the same time, KEUB entered into an agreement with World Broadcasting
System, Inc. for its "Sustaining Program Service." Programs consisting mostly
of music were produced on electrical transcriptions (ETs) --large 16-inch
records-- and mailed to the station. ETs from World represented about 2 1/2
hours of programming per day on KEUB, at a cost of $117 per month.

Beginning in September 1940, regional programming was provided by
the Intermountain Network (IMN), consisting of KEUB in Price, KOVO in
Provo and KLO in Ogden. These three stations were interconnected on a leg of
the Mutual Broadcasting System lines, and the stations frequently exchanged
commercial and sustaining (non-commercial) programs and cooperated in
securing regional advertising. Sustaining programs were exchanged at no
costs, but the originating station received 15% on commercial programs sold
on the other stations.

---

159   Russell, J. Bracken Lee: The Taxpayer's Champion.

There were no contracts for the IMN interconnections and programs were informally exchanged. IMN actually didn't even officially come into being until March 1941. Also, in September 1940, KEUB contracted with the Mutual Broadcasting System (MBS) for national programs. Mutual paid KEUB about $30 per hour for programming KEUB carried during the prime hours from 6 to 10 p.m. and lesser amounts for daytime and fringe time programs. A typical daily program schedule in the early 1940s consisted of 15 hours per day, divided as follows: 10.5 total hours from Mutual, consisting of 6.5 hours of music, two hours of drama, 1.5 hours of news, and one-half hour of educational programming. In addition, 1.25 total hours came from the Intermountain network, consisting of 45 minutes of news, 15 minutes of music and 15 minutes of educational programming. The station provided 2.75 hours of local programming, consisting mostly of music.

Thus, only a small percentage of the broadcast day was filled with local programming, even though such was the major reason cited by Weiss in his original application. KOAL reported it had trouble finding good local talent to put on the air. In 1949, in reply to an FCC inquiry about local programs being aired only 1.2% of the total time in a typical week, Richards wrote:[160]

> May I say that for the past thirteen years, ever since this station
> went on the air, we have been most anxious to broadcast local
> talent. The plain answer to our problem is that this live talent is
> lacking in this locality. What we have been able to obtain has been
> such that listeners have not complained about its quality, with very
> few exceptions. ... May I assure the Commission that we are doing
> everything within our power to give the listeners in this area the
> very best of varied program service, which we can devise. We have
> had no complaints whatsoever in this regard and this is particularly
> significant in view of our isolated position as far as other stations
> are concerned, with reception of these being very poor at almost all
> times.

---

160   Jack Richards, Letter to Mr. T. J. Slowie, Secretary, Federal Communications Commission, Washington, D.C., September 7, 1949, in response to Slowie's letter of August 31, 1949. File No. BR-901, Box 693, Record Group 173, National Archives, Washington, D.C.

It is important to note that the people of Price in 1949 didn't want
a predominance of local programming, preferring instead, national
programming from the Mutual Network. Richards provided the FCC with
numerous letters from listeners, indicating that KOAL was providing a great
public service to the Price area. Interestingly, however, of the many and varied
local services to business and industry proposed by Weiss in his original
application in 1935, only one service actually came to be desired by the citizens
of Carbon County. KOAL provided a great service to the diversely located
coalmines of the community. In the 1948 KOAL application for license
renewal, Richards wrote:[161]

> We would like to inform the Commission about our service to the
> Coal Mines of this community. Three times daily, including Sundays,
> we announce what mines are working or what mines are idle. This
> service, supplemented by any desired announcements about sudden
> changes of working schedules at the mines, has become so important
> to the miners that they rely upon KOAL almost entirely for this
> information. In addition, whenever a work stoppage occurs, such
> as the United Mine Workers strike last spring, no miner in this area
> returns to work until KOAL has broadcast the message to do so over
> the signatures of the heads of the local union to which he belongs.
> KOAL prides itself on this unusual service and we are proud to say
> that our record of accurate announcements has never been impaired.

To conclude the KOAL and Jack Richards story: In 1958, Tom Anderson
was a high school junior in Price. His mother was raising him, but she died
that year. That left Anderson with no parents, as his dad had died earlier. One
of Anderson's high school teachers suggested that he go out to KOAL and
apply for a job. Jack and Rita Richards gave him a job at KOAL and sort of
just "took-him-in." They had no children of their own. Anderson graduated
from high school in 1959 and went to Salt Lake City to work for the Wycoff
Trucking Company and to attend the University of Utah. After graduation, he
worked at the trucking company for another year and then decided to go back

---

161   Jack Richards, KOAL FCC License Renewal Application, Exhibit C, Section IV, Part I, Par. 7,
November 22, 1948.

to Price. Jack Richards had been in poor health, and the station was financially down. Anderson came back as station manager and salesperson in 1965.[162]

In 1972, Rita Richards died, and Jack spent little time at the station after that. In 1981, when Anderson was 41, Richards legally adopted him. This made official the father-son relationship they had maintained since 1958. Richards died in 1986 in Fullerton, California, and Anderson assumed control of KOAL in that year. Anderson, 71, died September 27, 2012, in St. George, Utah. His wife (Virginia) assumed Eastern Utah Broadcasting ownership when her husband died. She died on December 12, 2015, and the Anderson siblings, Paul Anderson, Kelly Lane and Christina Oliekanj, are the current Eastern Utah Broadcasting principals and owners of KOAL/KARB/KRPX.[163]

---

162   Thomas B. Anderson, interview with Larson, Tape No 770, transcript, 4, May 3, 1988.
Everett L. Cooley Oral History Project, Marriott Library, University of Utah, Salt Lake City, Utah.
163   Paul Anderson email to Tim Larson, December 16, 2021.

CHAPTER 10

KSUB: CEDAR CITY

The first airplane most people in Cedar City ever saw landed on September 27, 1920, at about 11 a.m., just north of town. The crowd was excited and noisy. The first public demonstration of radio broadcasting in Cedar City occurred on November 9, 1923. People gathered at the J. C. Penney store and listened over earphones to a San Francisco station. It was the first radio broadcast most had ever heard. Unlike with the arrival of the plane three years earlier, the crowd was quiet.

In the early 1920s, Cedar City was developing as an agricultural, mining, and commercial center serving southwestern Utah and parts of Nevada and Arizona. With the opening of the Hotel El Escalante on March 29, 1924, Cedar City also began developing as a tourist center. There were four parks near Cedar City: Bryce and Zion National Parks, Grand Canyon's North Rim and Cedar Breaks National Monument, to which tourists flocked by the thousands each year. Cedar City became the destination for many tourists, and the Hotel Escalante was the staging area for bus and automobile visits to all four parks.

Randall Jones, a local citizen, photographer and artists, who had spent most of his life exploring the environs of southern Utah, convinced the Union Pacific Railroad that it could develop a thriving tourism business if it built lodges and accommodations in the parks. Through its subsidiary, the Utah Park Company, the Union Pacific purchased the Hotel Escalante and maintained lodges and hotel accommodations in the parks. Union Pacific organized tours that brought people from points east to Cedar City by rail, and then bussed them to the national parks. Union Pacific became dominant in Cedar City and had a virtual monopoly on tourism in 1934.

But with all its industry, people and resources in the early 1930s, Cedar

City did not have a radio broadcasting station of its own, but an event in the autumn of 1934 would change that. Two brothers who were traveling the state conducting radio demonstrations set up a bootleg radio station in Cedar City. They were the same brothers who had dazzled Sam Weise and the people of Price with their radio broadcasts from that city. On Monday, October 15, 1934, the program of a Lions Club meeting was broadcast over the brothers' "temporary" Cedar City radio station:[164]

> [The broadcast consisted] of a cello solo by Harold Johnson, a vocal solo by Leland Perry and a pianologue by Beth Leigh, and three talks. The talks were given by Mayor Charles R. Hunter who told of the aims of the Lions International; Leland Perry, president of the Cedar City Lions Club, who discussed briefly the aims of the local club; and Wilson N. Lunt, president of the Cedar City Chamber of Commerce, who told of plans for that organization.

On November 30, 1935, a year after each had performed on the itinerant broadcasting station, Leland M. Perry (the vocal soloist) and Harold Johnson (the cello soloist) applied for a 100-watt station on 1310kc in Cedar City. No new broadcasting stations had gone on the air in Utah since KLO in 1925, and Perry and Johnson had little information to guide them in completing their application. They knew only that the newly formed Federal Communication Commission (FCC) required that a radio station be operated in the public interest, convenience and necessity (PICAN), whatever that meant.

To conserve money, Perry and Johnson prepared their own application and didn't use a Washington, D.C. attorney. They provided information in four broad areas: character, engineering, finances and programming. To show their personal qualifications and integrity, Johnson and Perry pointed to their reputations and standings in the community.

Perry grew up in Cedar City. As a young man he operated amateur station W6AHD for many years and had considerable musical talents, especially in organizing and conducting singing groups and choirs. For five years he had

---

164   Iron County Record, October 18, 1934, 1.

been city manager for Cedar City and handled all city engineering problems concerned with the construction and maintenance of roads and the water and sewer systems. He also had been a building inspector.

In 1935 when he and Johnson applied for KSUB, Perry was 29 and was employed as a civil engineer for the federal government in the Federal Emergency Administration. He was a traveling engineer and was responsible for Wyoming, Colorado and Utah. In 1936, he became involved in a federal project in Heber City, Utah, and moved to Provo, while he pursued the Cedar City radio application.

Johnson, Perry's partner in the radio broadcasting station application, was 39 years old when he applied, and, although born and raised in Utah, had been in Cedar City only four years, having operated mercantile businesses in Iowa City, Iowa, and Provo, Utah. He was half owner of the Moderne Style Shoppe, a retail business with stores in Cedar City and in St. George. He followed Perry as president of the Lions Club and was extremely well liked and known for his "even temperament, friendly disposition, honesty and sincerity." He was known as a superb cello player and played gratis for nearly every civic, educational and religious group in the city.

The next information that Perry and Johnson provided to the FCC in their application dealt with their proposed financing for the station. Perry's financial contribution to the partnership was about $3,000, coming mostly from loans totaling $7,500, for which his parents put up Cedar City real estate as collateral. Perry's assets totaled $4,010. In addition, his annual salary from the federal government was listed as $3,200, which could provide some on-going operating funds for the station. Johnson's share of the costs for constructing the station also was $3,000. His assets totaled $7,600, including a cello valued at $5,000. His cello reportedly was made in Brescia, Italy, in 1584 by the famous luthiers Giovanni Paolo Maginni and Gaspara da Salo. It was considered a major asset that could be used as collateral to raise money for the station, if needed.

Johnson and Perry estimated that construction costs would be about

$6,000 and that monthly operating expenses would be $900. Expenses
were balanced against monthly advertising revenues projected to be $1,400.
Johnson and Perry received assurances from numerous Cedar City merchants
that they would advertise on the station, and two Salt Lake advertising
agencies expressed interest. One of the most encouraging financial aspects
of the application was Union Pacific's agreement to lease Perry and Johnson
space for the station's studio on the third floor of the Hotel Escalante. With
its significant tourist trade, the Union Pacific was persuaded that an in-house
radio station might be attractive to its guests. These quarters were estimated to
be worth about $3,500 annually to Johnson and Perry when compared to the
cost of other space.

The third area of concern in their FCC application was programming.
Perry and Johnson were definitely civic minded and, although they wanted
to make a profit, they also were concerned with providing a quality radio
service:[165]

> Comparatively few of the inhabitants of Cedar City enjoy daytime
> radio reception at present. ... The proposed radio station will serve the
> public interest and convenience by providing daytime radio reception
> in Cedar City. It will bring entertainment and instruction into many
> homes unable to afford expensive radio receivers, and will permit the
> merchants to use radio as an advertising medium, a facility not now
> available.

To satisfy the FCC that their 100-watt station would serve the public
interest and was needed in the community, Johnson and Perry hired Cedar
City resident Ms. Lucille Swapp to canvas the city with a questionnaire about
radio reception. During the period from January 20 to February 10, 1936, she
contacted 354 people with radio sets and found that only 5% of them were able
to play their radio during the daytime and get fairly good reception. Another
11% reported that they played their radio occasionally during the daytime
with partial success, leaving 84% of the people with daytime service that was

---

165   Federal Communications Commission, In the Matter of Harold Johnson and Leland M.
Perry, d/b as Johnson and Perry, Application for Construction Permit, File No. B5-P-841, Docket
No. 3843, Supplementary material to Exhibits A and F, October 26, 1935.

"entirely unsatisfactory or impossible." Salt Lake's KSL was the most listened to station in Cedar City, followed by a California and a Denver station, all mostly at night.[166]

To further support their claim that local radio reception was poor, Johnson and Perry obtained testimony from Claude E. Boden, a Cedar City electrical engineer and radio technician: "To [my] own knowledge and according to [my] best belief, radio reception conditions in the said Cedar City and vicinity are considerably below the average for similarly situated areas."[167]

Boden was the closest thing to a radio expert in Cedar City at this time, and his support was helpful. He held a commercial radio operator's license and ran amateur radio station WLVV for the U. S. Army Signal Corps in Cedar City. He also operated a radio repair shop and had the opportunity to ascertain the quality of radio reception when he visited homes in the city.

Perry and Johnson also provided the FCC with letters of support for their application from educational, business, religious and government leaders. Typical was the following from Mayor Charles R. Hunter:[168]

> I as Mayor of Cedar City make a special appeal to you [the FCC] to grant the permit asked for by Mr. Perry and Johnson as it will mean so much to our city in advertising its products and will also help to raise the standards of the music and culture of the small communities adjoining and adjacent to our city.

As an aside, Hunter was the father of Charles F. (Forest) Hunter who eventually started his radio career at KSUB and later constructed Cedar City's KBRE AM and FM in 1971, the first local competition to KSUB in Cedar City. Jon C. Hunter, the mayor's grandson, later became general manager, chief

---

166   Lucille Swapp, "Results of Telephone Survey of Cedar City Residents Regarding Radio Reception," February 10, 1936.

167   Federal Communications Commission, Claude E. Boden, In the Matter of Harold Johnson and Leland M. Perry, d/b as Johnson and Perry, Application for Construction Permit, File No. B5-P-841, Docket No. 3843, Supplementary material to Exhibit E, May 21, 1936.

168   Mayor Chas. R. Hunter, Cedar City, Utah, "Letter to the Federal Communications Commission," October 30, 1935.

engineer and news director of KBRE.

Although Johnson and Perry in their application boasted that KSUB would make an effective facility for "timely" advertising, an obvious jab at the local weekly paper, they also went to the owner of the *Iron County Record* to get his support for their application and to assure him that they would cooperate in making sure his newspaper would not be economically injured by their proposed radio station:[169]

> We would attempt to work out an arrangement, which would not disturb the newspaper in any degree. With [the newspaper's] willingness we would try to work a combination arrangement so that their interest would not be affected. ... They would not have very many accounts that we would be concerned with. That is, they do not have very many accounts now, and there are some of the larger ones that they have there that would buy a duplication of our service.

Johnson and Perry proposed programming to and from nearly every organization and venue in the area.[170]

> We expect that this station will present a new device for the presentation of programs developed by high class musical and artistic talent [from] our schools and churches in this locality as well as serving the agricultural interests by the dissemination of timely information. We expect ... to be of service to the police ... the highway patrol and law enforcement generally, [and to broadcast] ... news ... market and weather reports for the beneficial information of the residences of the vicinity, [and] to conduct auditions and amateur contests to train and develop local talent, [and] to broadcast every worthwhile local event without cost. Yes, we expect that the churches will use the facilities of the proposed station not only for broadcasting

169   Federal Communications Commission, Washington, D.C., Testimony of Leland Perry, In the Matter of Harold Johnson and Leland M. Perry, d/b as Johnson and Perry, Application for Construction Permit, File No. B5-P-841, Docket No. 3843, June 25, 1936
170   Federal Communications Commission, Washington, D.C. Deposition of Harold Johnson taken in Cedar City, Utah, In the Matter of Harold Johnson and Leland M. Perry, d/b as Johnson and Perry, Application for Construction Permit, File No. B5-P-841, Docket No. 3843, July 15, 1936.

of programs by its members in various church organizations, but also in broadcasting of quarterly conferences of the church.

Johnson and Perry must have assumed that the FCC understood what a reference to " the church" meant in their application for a station in Utah.

KSUB receives its license

Johnson and Perry's last area of concern in the FCC application was their engineering proposal. It actually was fairly simple. Under Section 307 (b) of the Communications Act of 1934, they proposed a 100-watt station, with unlimited time of operation at 1310kc. A hearing on Johnson and Perry's application was set for June 25, 1936, at the FCC in Washington, D.C. Perry was the more knowledgeable partner of the two and, without consulting legal counsel, prepared to go to Washington and personally present the application. This did not seem unreasonable; until he was informed in May that KEUB in Price and another Utah station wanted to be respondents in KSUB's upcoming FCC hearing. That is, KEUB and another station in Logan supposedly had some pertinent information that they wanted to present at the FCC hearing on KSUB's application. Perry telephoned Weiss, owner of KEUB, and Weiss said he had no opposition to the KSUB application in any way.[171]

Nevertheless, to avoid delays, Perry engaged the services of Washington, D.C. attorney H. H. Shinnick to help him present the KSUB application to the FCC. Shinnick had earlier contacted Perry suggesting that it was to KSUB's advantage to have a D.C. lawyer tender the application. Perry disregarded Shinnick's original suggestion but, in light of rumored KEUB and other opposition, reconsidered and hired him for $300 to appear on behalf of KSUB at the FCC hearing.

An extraordinary thing happened next. At the 1936 FCC hearing on June 25, Shinnick appeared representing the applicant, KSUB, as well as the respondents, KEUB and KSVN, a Logan station. (There was no KSVN in

---

171   Leland Perry, Letter to John B. Reynolds, Acting Secretary, Federal Communications Commission, Washington, D.C., June 6, 1936.

Logan. Possibly, it was KVNU that sought a construction permit.) The FCC hearing opened with Shinnick testifying as follows:[172]

> Mr. Examiner I desire to state that I represent each of the respondents and that each of them have instructed me to enter an appearance this morning for them for the purpose of stating that they have no objection to the granting of the application of Harold Johnson and Leland M. Perry doing business as Johnson and Perry for a radio station operating on 1310 Kilocycles with 100-watts power, unlimited time, that it is the sole purpose of filing an answer by each of the respondents and their appearance in this case.

Shinnick then went on to represent Perry and KSUB at the hearing. Fifty years after the FCC hearing, Perry, with some humor, still marveled at how Shinnick essentially created a client out of KSUB by making his other Utah clients innocuous respondents at the KSUB hearing in 1936. As stated above, the sole purpose for Shinnick's appearance on behalf of his other clients at the FCC hearing in 1936 was to state that these client stations had no objections to the KSUB application.[173]

On October 27, 1936, Johnson and Perry's application was granted and the FCC issued them a construction permit. While engineer W. D'Orr Cozzens built the transmitter and other technical equipment, Perry's father and brother, Theo, constructed the transmitter building and ground system. The ground system for their AM station involved a spoke-like system of buried wires stretching out from the base of the transmitting tower. Perry's father found an innovative way to bury the wires. An AM radio station's entire tower and spoke-like grounding system are used to propagate a signal using ground, sky and direct waves to reach listeners. Perry recalls:[174]

---

172   Federal Communications Commission, Washington, D.C., H. H. Shinnick, In the Matter of Harold Johnson and Leland M. Perry, d/b as Johnson and Perry, Application for Construction Permit, File No. B5-P-841, Docket No. 3843, June 25, 1936.

173   Leland Perry, interview with Tim Larson, Provo, Utah, June 24, 1986

174   Leland Perry, Transcript of a speech given on the occasion of KSUB's inaugural broadcast using 1,000 watts of power," Cedar City, Utah, March 21, 1980, 2.

Dad's ingenuity came into evidence when he constructed a tool made
from an old plow by which the approximately three miles of copper
wire in the ground was plowed into place with a team of horses at a
considerable reduction in cost under the usual method of digging
trenches by hand.

Delivery of some equipment was delayed by a strike in the East, but
on June 3, 1937, it was announced that the equipment had arrived and that
workers were busy constructing a studio, installing equipment in space on the
third-floor of the Hotel Escalante, and raising the tower. The opening date
for KSUB was set for June 15. Johnson and Perry bought their radio tower
from a New Jersey company and had it shipped in sections to Cedar City.
They hired a local pump and windmill man to erect the 165-foot flagpole-type
tower. The erectors used a construction technique that involved pushing the
tower up from the bottom while stabilizing it with guy wires. A section would
be lifted and then another would be put under it. As sections were added to
the bottom, workers steadied the tower with the guy wires while allowing the
tower to be raised. But, when the tower was pushed up about 100 feet, an
optical illusion caused a disaster, as Perry recalled in 1986:[175]

> I was watching [the erector] and he was staring up there at [the
> tower]. ... You do that long enough [and] you get the idea that the
> thing is coming right over on top [of you] for sure. Well, suddenly
> that must have really gotten to him, I guess. ... He jumped up off the
> ground and let the [guy wire] go, and the thing started to jib and
> collapsed. Fell to the ground, smashed, made an awful mess of the
> tower.

Perry's dad rigged a device from railroad ties, log chains and hydraulic
truck jacks to straighten the tower, and the June 15 opening date was
postponed for only two days, to June 17. On Sunday morning, June 14, Perry
contracted with E. M. Colvin, a bridge builder in Hurricane, Utah, to try again
to raise the tower. Everything went well this time to a height of 120-feet. Then
one of the guy wires broke loose and the tower again collapsed, this time so

---

175   Leland Perry, interview with Tim Larson, 9.

highly damaged it could not be straightened. A subsequent examination revealed that there was a defect in a guy wire connector.

The New Jersey company that made the tower agreed to replace it but not in time for the June 17 opening date. Perry contacted U.S. Representative Abe Murdock, whose home was in Beaver, Utah, as well as U.S. Senator Elbert D. Thomas, who successfully intervened on behalf of KSUB with the FCC. They helped obtain permission for KSUB to go on the air using a temporary antenna, consisting of a long wire supported by two-by-fours nailed together. Opening day for KSUB was reset for July 3, 1937.

Interestingly, forty years later, almost to the day that the KSUB-AM tower fell, the KSUB-FM tower fell and was destroyed as it was being lowered in place by a helicopter at a site known as Tip-Top-Claim on Iron Mountain. As happened in 1936, guy wires got tangled and the tower came crashing to the ground. As one KSUB employee put it, "It seems like there's someone standing over us putting the hex on this project."[176]

KSUB finally starts operations

In reality, a hex seemed to have been placed on KSUB from the very beginning. In their 1935 application, Johnson and Perry said they proposed to personally manage KSUB and felt qualified to do so. In reality, neither man became intricately involved in day-to-day operations. Johnson was made station director, but he knew nothing about broadcast programming. And, Perry traveled extensively in his federal civil engineering job and was soon relocated to the San Francisco office of the Public Works Administration. The partners thus employed a staff of people to operate KSUB for them.

Robert R. Burton was hired as station manager. Burton had been interested in radio since 1922 during his days at Ogden High School. He studied electrical engineering and reportedly built one of Ogden's first vacuum tube receivers. He finished his education at Weber College and went on an LDS three-year mission to Germany. He returned to be secretary-treasurer

---

176   Color Country Spectrum, September 14, 1976, 1.

of the Mid-Mountain Fur Farms, one of the largest silver fox ranches in the West. In 1930, he received his amateur and commercial operator licenses and became part of the technical staff at KLO before coming to KSUB. Inez Corry was hired as Burton's secretary in early June 1936, and visited KLO in Ogden to learn about duties at a radio station.

Perry persuaded "Archie" –since then, it has always been "Arch"— Madsen to become KSUB's chief engineer. From Cedar City, Perry had regularly communicated by code with Madsen in Salt Lake City. Like Ira Kaar had earlier done, Madsen had experience as a radio amateur with the Army Amateur Radio System of the U.S. Signal Corps. He had been the chief radio operator for the U.S. Forest Service in Missoula, Montana, and a transmitter technician at KSL. Just prior to joining KSUB, Madsen was employed by Radio Supply, Inc., a wholesale radio distributor business in Salt Lake City, owned by the Higgenbotham family. Madsen would soon marry Margaret (Peggy), a Higgenbotham daughter.

A friend of Madsen's, Cutler (Cut) L. Miller, was hired as chief announcer at KSUB. Although hired as an announcer, Miller also had technical expertise. He had completed three years of an electrical engineering degree at the University of Utah and had five years of experience as the key station operator in the Army Amateur Radio System. Like Madsen, Miller had regularly communicated with Perry by code on his amateur set.

Jones, the local citizen and artist mentioned earlier, closed the KSUB switch on July 3, 1937, and it went on the air. KSUB formally was opened with a celebration at the school auditorium, with keynote speaker Governor Henry H. Blood, master of ceremonies and KSUB lawyer Scott M. Matheson --the father of a future Utah Governor. Secretary of State E. E. Monson and State Fish and Game Commissioner Newell B. Cook also spoke. Various local musical groups and individuals entertained at the school and afterward at an open house held at the KSUB studios in the Hotel Escalante. Musician Beth Leigh, and Roy L. Halverson, music professor at Branch Agricultural College which would become Southern Utah University, entertained that first night on KSUB and often thereafter. Jim Urie, another business friend, was master of ceremonies back at the KSUB studios, and the celebration went on well past midnight and into the 1937 Fourth of July holiday. Johnson and Perry received compliments and praise for all their efforts and perseverance.

In the beginning, Burton was station manager and Madsen and Miller were the announcers, technicians, reporters, code receivers and everything else at KSUB, as Madsen said many years later:[177]

> The station, of course, was losing money. We [Madsen and Miller] had to do all the programming. We had no network. We had records, [electrical] transcriptions and the news. ... We really got the [KSUB] job because both of us could copy the Morse code. Transradio Press [using code] was the only way we could [get the news], with no money to buy the news from the United Press or Associated Press. Besides, at that time, [UP and AP] weren't so hot about serving radio. ... The way it operated, there were two of us to be operating on the air sixteen hours a day, seven days a week, in eight-hour shifts. We'd get the headline news from Transradio ... but we had no time to review it [before going on the air.] ... I'm sure it must have been one of the most atrocious station operations ever! Cut Miller and I had never had any experience announcing. I had come from Lake View, a rural community east of Utah Lake. I was full of all kinds of rural accents ... and everything. ...They had to tolerate our announcing or turn off. KSUB was the only signal they could get in the daytime.

Arch Madsen becomes station manager

It was not long before it became apparent that Burton was not a good choice for KSUB station manager. By all accounts, he was a fine man, but he reportedly didn't know the "faintest" about broadcasting. From the first day it opened, the staff knew KSUB was headed for disaster and, after three months, Burton was removed, and on October 1, 1937, Madsen was made the station manager: "Well, ... I became nauseated! I knew that I'd have to sell. Sales --I knew that was [now] my major responsibility, and I was really... a zero and I

---

177   Arch L. Madsen, interview with Tim Larson, 49 and 56.

knew it. That's the way I felt."[178]

Madsen later reported he thought that there was "nothing good" in him in 1937 when he became KSUB manager at age 24. Madsen went on to achieve great success in broadcasting locally, nationally and internationally, but his enormous achievements belie the tremendous, overpowering inferiority complex he said he had in those early years, resulting from his experience with polio as a young child:[179]

> The physical disability gave me a fantastic inferiority complex. I can't describe it. Your peers aren't exactly kind. I don't know if you've been around a bunch of kids [like that], but sometimes they are merciless. ... Very cruel. Out of that environment I had to build my own world.

Madsen had retreated inward, immersing himself in reading and in odd jobs to help his family. But, in 1928, a major change came in his life when he received a 1922, two-tube Crosley radio. It had a primitive loudspeaker made of paper connected to a regular earphone. He recalled many years later, "Oh, a glorious day I shall never forget! I had a great treasure and all my own. ... One day I accidentally [changed] the tuning range of that radio up to the ... ham-radio band. To my amazement, out comes a voice ...'This is WDPJ, Provo Utah." Madsen said he listened and retrieved the operator's last name: Miller. He said he called every Miller in the book and found one with an amateur radio station: "What a joyful event. ... it was Cutler R. Miller. ... He became my dear friend, perhaps the dearest friend I've ever had. He stepped in at a time when I desperately needed him."[180]

Madsen received his amateur license in 1930, and his station was given the call letters W6APM. Madsen graduated from high school in 1932, at age 19, and as it was during the Great Depression, there were few jobs available. But soon after President Roosevelt assumed office, he set up the Civilian Conservation Corps (CCC) for unemployed youth. Miller and Madsen applied at Fort Douglas, hoping to get into the CCC as radio operators. But they had

---

178   Arch L. Madsen, interview with Tim Larson, 50.
179   Arch L. Madsen, interview with Tim Larson, 27.
180   Madsen, interview with Tim Larson,, 31

to undergo a physical examination at Fort Douglas, and that was problematic
for Madsen:[181]

> I had only 30-percent legs. As we checked in, we had to strip and
> stand in a line. I'll never forget it as long as I live. A medical colonel
> ... let out a roar, "How in the hell did you get in here? ... The Army
> doesn't need half-men. ... Get the hell out of here." I went back to
> Provo with my friend [Miller] who kept my spirits up by saying, 'We'll
> fix this in a hurry."

That night Miller and Madsen communicated on the Army amateur
channel with their soon-to-be boss, Capt. Robert B. Woolverton, in Presidio,
California, who in turn talked to his superior, General Malin Craig, later U.S.
Army chief of staff. A message was relayed back, instructing the medical
officer at Fort Douglas to give Madsen a physical without regards to his legs.
Madsen passed, and he and Miller were inducted into the CCC and soon were
on their way to an eighteen-month tour of duty in Fort Missoula, Montana.
They set up station WBUL, and it served as a relay for the military between
San Francisco and Washington, D.C. Madsen said in 1986, "We were part of
the military. ... We were a full-fledged, integral part of the United States Army
Signal Corps. ... At the time I joined the CCC my code speed was inadequate.
Cut [Miller] promised [them] that he would make me proficient. My speed
[got] up to about forty words per minute."[182]

With humor in his tone, Madsen recalls that late in 1934, KSL said that if
he decided to interrupt his schooling, He could have the next job that opened
up in the engineering department. "Well, I did, and they didn't," he added. He
took a job with Radio Supply, Inc. in Salt Lake, in the spring of 1935, and after
two years, he accepted Perry's invitation to become chief engineer at KSUB and
later became station manager.

Madsen still had lingering feelings of inadequacy when Perry tapped him
to be KSUB station manager in the early winter of 1937. He had gone into

---

181   Madsen, interview with Tim Larson,, 36
182   Madsen, interview with Tim Larson, 38.

radio engineering so he would not have to be in front of the public:[183]

> So this assignment to be [KSUB] manager and salesman was almost
> a terminal shock to me. ... I thought the sun and moon and stars
> were all wrapped up in the technical ... and all of a sudden I'm in a
> field totally foreign to me. ... Everything is so nebulous in selling. ...
> [I think] I'm looking at a condenser and all of a sudden it turns into a
> tube socket. ... It's hard to put your hand on anything [in sales].

This was a turning point in Madsen's life, however. He married Peggy Higgenbotham on March 30, 1938. She joined him in Cedar City, and he had a new dimension of responsibility and motivation. As he recalled, "[She] gave me the courage and determination to succeed, even if I didn't know anything about selling or managing. She is the finest, best wife any man could ever wish to have. My greatest blessing!"[184]

Challenging first year

KSUB was not financially successful in its first year. Even the best advertisers on KSUB spent only $15 to $20 per month. Madsen, Miller, and operator Carl Wolfram kept the station on the air and provided as much local programming as they could by giving free airtime to community projects, the schools, the churches and the library. KSUB also aired programs of local interest including the semiannual LDS General Conference. In addition, KSUB provided 10,000 words of news daily from the International News Service, all copied from code by Miller and Madsen. "Hundreds of southern Utah people [were] given radio experience, through the privilege of appearing on various programs."[185]

In the meantime, in September 1937, Perry had been transferred to San Francisco to a desk job that allowed him no travel. At Christmas, he took a two-week leave to visit KSUB and found that he needed to be closer to Cedar City to supervise the station. In February 1938, he received a transfer back to

---

183   Madsen, interview with Tim Larson, 51.
184   Madsen, interview with Tim Larson, 52.
185   Iron County Record, June, 30 1938, 1.

Provo, albeit at a significant demotion and pay cut. Perry recalled many years later:[186]

> And this was now [after] about nine months of operation. We weren't doing so well. My partner Harold had no experience at all in radio, so he couldn't make any contribution there. But he was quite a showman and a very proud individual, and so we had to do things in first-class style. But I kept arguing [with Johnson] that we had no business maintaining the studio ... and that ... we ought to, if necessary, build a little bit on to our transmitter shack out [by the college] and operate everything from [there]. Well, we talked about it and decided maybe we had to retrench or we were going to go under.

In July, Perry went from Provo to Cedar City to celebrate KSUB's first anniversary and to talk further with Johnson. Perry and his wife, McNone, and their three children camped for the Fourth of July on some property they owned up in Cedar Canyon, about 11 miles from town. On Sunday, July 3, 1938, at six p.m., KSUB celebrated its first anniversary of operation with a program from the LDS Church First Ward Chapel. Musical talent from the area, talks from civic officials, and prizes for KSUB's essay contest winners were part of the festivities. An open house was also held at KSUB's newly improved Hotel Escalante studios.

As part of the anniversary celebration, it was announced that a presentation of *The Dark Hour* play was scheduled for preview on KSUB, with Madsen directing the production. The immortal lines of Euripides suggested the name of the play: "How oft the darkest hour of ill breaks brightest into dawn." Ironically, a truly dark hour for the financial well being of KSUB did beset on the morning of Tuesday, July 5, 1938. Perry's partner, Harold Johnson, and KSUB announcer Carl Wolfram went hunting in Cedar Valley that morning. They parked their car at about 5:30 a.m. and went in different directions, agreeing to meet later. Johnson didn't return and Wolfram couldn't locate him after a search. Wolfram returned to Cedar City and brought back Sheriff Hal Christensen and Cutler Miller from the station, among others.

---

186   Leland Perry, interview with Tim Larson, 14.

Miller found Johnson at 11:30 a.m., dead from an accidental gunshot wound to the heart, sustained while crawling through a fence. Perry was up at his camp in Cedar Canyon waiting for Johnson's arrival, to talk about the troubled KSUB:[187]

> [Harold] Johnson said, "I'll be up [to your camp on Tuesday] morning, and we'll make some definite plans [for the station]. ... But I'm going rabbit hunting first. ... Carl Wolfram and I are going out [and] I'll be up about ten." [I said], "Let the rabbits alone. This is July. You don't hunt rabbits until it snows." Twelve o'clock came [on Tuesday] ... and no Harold. Arch Madsen and his wife, Peggy, and Cutler Miller came up the road to our [camp], and from the look on their faces I knew something was wrong. ... Arch got out of the car ... and said, "Harold is dead."

When Perry and Johnson originally discussed their proposed radio partnership over a soda in the Cedar City Drug Store, back in 1934, they agreed to share all expenses and profits of the station. When asked at the FCC hearings about the pertinent terms of their oral partnership agreement, Perry said: "Both parties are responsible for the act of the partnership, either or both. ... Each is responsible for the full debts of the partnership.[188] With Johnson's death, Perry, thus, was responsible for all the expenses, debts, liens and loans of KSUB: "[Johnson] had pledged some assets that he had. He had ... what he thought was a very expensive cello ... and a few other things. But when we got looking around, there wasn't anything that we could get a hold of. So here I was stuck with the whole mess of what we had."[189]

On July 21, 1938, Madsen resigned from KSUB and left Cedar City to work at Carman's new KUTA in Salt Lake. Miller became KSUB station manager, but he, too, left after a time. Eventually he went to work for Raytheon. Sadly, Madsen's empathetic, gentle and loyal best friend, Cut Miller, was later

---

187   Perry, 17.
188   Federal Communications Commission, Washington, D.C., Testimony of Leland Perry, In the Matter of Harold Johnson and Leland M. Perry, d/b as Johnson and Perry, Application for Construction Permit, File No. B5-P-841, Docket No. 3843, June 25, 1936, 3.
189   Perry, 16.

killed in a Phoenix airplane crash. In the five months after Johnson's death, Perry drove from Provo to Cedar City every weekend to try to straighten things out at KSUB. He'd arrive on Friday at 10 p.m. and work through Sunday morning and then drive back to Provo.

In order to stabilize the business, KSUB was incorporated as the Southern Utah Broadcasting Company (SUBC), and several Cedar City citizens were put on the board of directors, with Perry as president. Except for Perry, none of the board members had any financial stake in KSUB, but he wanted their business advice. This board was ineffectual, however, because Perry wasn't in Cedar City much of the time and couldn't adequately consult the board members. Eventually, Perry asked attorney Durham Morris to attend to KSUB business and to pay the bills and negotiate debt payments. Morris was given a block of SUBC stock for his work, but Perry still owned most of the shares. Morris by all accounts did a good job and took a tremendous burden from Perry by negotiating with KSUB program service providers.

Rapid turnover in station managers

Carl Wolfram managed KSUB after Madsen and Miller left, but he soon left for KEUB in Price. In 1939, Sherman T. Wright became KSUB station manager. Wright had been an amateur since the 1920s with code station W6AXA, call letters he would keep for 60 years. After high school in 1928, Wright went to work for the Utah Electric Radio Company (ULECTRA) in the Sugarhouse neighborhood of Salt Lake City. He was put out of work, when on the day after the stock market crashed in 1929, ULECTRA closed its doors.

Wright wanted to get into broadcasting, so he went to KSL to seek employment. Eugene Pack, KSL's chief engineer, told him he needed to have an operator's license. Wright went to Lumis Radio College in Washington, D.C., and hoped his schooling would lead to a job. But it was Christmas 1929, and the economic outlook was more than bleak —it was nearly hopeless. Fifty-nine years later, Wright recalled:[190]

---

190   Sherman T. Wright, interview with Tim Larson, July 11, 1988, 19.

Times were tough, and you'd go out on the street and a fellow was
there selling apples for a nickel or a dime apiece and trying to keep
warm around a little stove. ... It was really rough. ... Once a day we
would go to a little hole in the wall [in Washington, D.C.] and get us
a plate of beans, with a little piece of meat on it. ... In those days ...
we would eat a half a loaf of bread and a bottle of ketchup with our
dinner.

Wright received his operator's license and returned to Utah in March
1930, to work for his dad in the brick masonry business. He soon applied
for and found a job with Stan Soule who owned KGIQ (later KTFI) in Twin
Falls, Idaho. Wright was happy to have a job when so many others had no
work or money, and he saved enough to be married to his girlfriend from Salt
Lake City. They were married on the air at KGIQ on August 28, 1931. It was
reportedly the first-ever radio marriage in Idaho. Wright stayed with KGIQ
another seven years, until Soule died and the new owners wanted to start over
with different people.

In 1939, Wright was enticed to Cedar City by Perry to manage KSUB.
He stayed for two years and, in April 1941, a few months before Pearl Harbor,
moved to Grand Island, Nebraska, as the FCC's assistant monitoring officer.
Everybody knew that the U.S. would soon go to war, and the FCC put Wright
in charge of monitoring the airwaves for subversive uses of radio in the
Midwest.

Ironically, Wright got the monitoring job when FCC officials came to
KSUB to investigate some questionable uses of radio to communicate between
Cedar City and Provo. It seems that Perry, instead of calling Wright on the
phone from Provo, would use his amateur radio set to regularly talk to him
for free. Often they would include discussions about KSUB business, even
though it was illegal to discuss such business on amateur frequencies. FCC
officials, who had monitoring equipment located near the State Capitol in Salt
Lake City, evidently intercepted communications between Perry and Wright
and decided to personally investigate. As it turned out, the FCC officers and
Wright became quick friends, and they told him about the available FCC job in

Grand Island.

A KSUB announcer and operator, took over as manager when Wright left KSUB in 1941. He did not stay very long, however, because he reportedly was on the wrong side of a secret plan to oust Perry from KSUB and to seize his parent's property and make KSUB a Cedar City Community station. Perry was informed of the plan and traveled to Cedar City from Los Angeles to talk to friends and his station employees. After a few days, the new manager resigned and left the station, and takeover discussions became inconsequential.

Hurschell Urie, KSUB's chief engineer, followed as station manager. Urie had been hired by Madsen and worked his first shift alone as transmitter engineer on July 4, 1938, the day of KSUB's first anniversary celebration, one day before Johnson died in the hunting accident.

In 1941, following the Pearl Harbor bombing, there was an exodus of men from KSUB and nearly every other radio station in Utah. Men enlisted in the military and stations were left without experienced people. So Urie hired two women to announce and to keep logs on KSUB during the war. These were reportedly the first women announcers in the West. Although women were on the air at many stations, they usually were actors, interviewers or homemakers and not full-fledged announcers. One of the women was the wife of an Army cadet, training in Cedar City. Urie was the only licensed First Class operator at KSUB for the first three years of the war: "During that [whole] period of time, I had three days off, including holidays and Sundays. ... So you can understand that there was pressure there. I would go home and take a nap in the afternoon or evening with the radio on, and, if it stopped ... it would wake me up. ... I conditioned myself to be able to do that."[191]

He had four part-time, inexperienced employees from the Branch Agricultural College and had not had a vacation in three years. Equipment was worn and needed to be replaced, and KSUB's hours of operation were irregular. KSUB sign-on was at nine a.m., and, with two hours off in the

---

191   Hurschell Urie, interview with Tim Larson, July 5, 1988, 9. Interview was conducted exactly 50 years to the date from when Harold Johnson died.

afternoon, was on the air until 10:15 p.m. Sunday hours were fewer with sign-on at 11:30 a.m. and sign-off at 6 p.m.

Because rooms at the Hotel Escalante were a priority for military cadets in training, the entire KSUB operation was moved into three cramped and otherwise unsatisfactory rooms at the transmitter site. There was a small studio at the Lunt Hotel in downtown, but it was ill equipped, noisy, dark and poorly ventilated. KSUB received some programs from the Intermountain Network through KLO in Ogden, but reportedly they were always unsatisfactory and usually unintelligible. Revenue from advertising averaged about $700 per month, and commercial spots were being sold for whatever KSUB could get. Some advertisers paid only eleven cents a spot. There were no policies in place concerned with sales, promotion, programming or any other part of the operation except, possibly, engineering.[192]

KSL takes over KSUB

During the war years, Perry began discussing with Earl Glade the possibility of KSL buying KSUB. Nothing came of these discussions, because Glade's offer required Perry to abandon his investment, retain all his past debt and to transfer the KSUB license to Glade personally, essentially at no costs to Glade. Perry's parent's property, put up as collateral for KSUB, also would have been sacrificed in the transfer.

KSL, without Glade's involvement, later revisited purchasing KSUB. Madsen, after managing KOVO (a station discussed later in the book) in Provo from July 1939, to April 1944, went to KSL as assistant to Ivor Sharp, KSL's general manager. Madsen was able to spark the KSL board of directors' interest in KSUB on the basis that it would extend the coverage and influence of KSL in southern Utah.

In August 1944, KSL bought KSUB by purchasing a 50.2% share in Southern Utah Broadcasting Company (SUBC), its corporate owner. Perry retained a 39% interest and remained vice president and an SUBC director.

---

192   "Resume of Activities -KSUB", author unknown, circa July, 1945.

Before KSL bought the station, others wanting to buy it approached Perry, and, although the purchase prices offered were higher, he nevertheless sold to KSL, strictly for reasons of personal value and belief:[193]

> Maybe I am crazy and maybe I have been short sighted, but I did not want to sell it to someone outside the [LDS] church. I have been very cranky about that because right from the beginning ... I made a resolution first that I would never permit ... tobacco advertising or beer advertising. ... [Even] if we close the station down, I will not advertise beer and tobacco. ... I could have saved myself ten years of hard work if I would have just broken down on that, just that one thing. One beer company's ads would have put us in the black. ... One contract with a beer developer would have taken off all the [financial] pressure.

Even after KSL assumed controlling interest, Urie remained KSUB's resident manager, under the supervision of KSL's Lennox Murdoch. Murdoch had been at KSL for 12 years, first as an announcer and then as a continuity editor, production manager, commercial manager and sales manager. Murdoch spent the better part of a year in Cedar City with Urie, helping him manage the station and generating sales revenue.

Urie and Murdoch took steps to get a better KSL signal to Cedar City for rebroadcast, and negotiations with CBS were underway for network service to KSUB. Buildings and property were improved and uninterrupted hours of operation from 7 a.m. to 10 p.m. were established. By February 15, 1945, KSUB was back in the Hotel Escalante in newly constructed studios and offices. The Utah Parks Company welcomed KSUB back to the Hotel Escalante after a brief absence during the war years. This time KSUB was on the first floor, instead of the third. A full-time announcer, Melvin Rowley, and a full time secretary and traffic person were hired, and most of the part time people were let go. These adjustments in personnel helped the station to achieve a more efficient operation. KSUB did, in fact, experience an 80% increase in revenue in the first year of KSL's ownership.

---

193   Perry, 20.

In August 1945, Urie gladly went back to full time technical work at
KSUB and got out of management. Roscoe Grover took over as KSUB's station
manager in August 1945, when Urie stepped down. Grover was a Utah native,
born on July 21, 1901, and raised in Nephi, Utah. Grover double-majored in
speech and theater at the University of Utah and worked nights at KSL. He
married Arlene Harris in 1934, who, in the early 1920s had attended BYU
High School and was in a physics class with Philo T. Farnsworth. After she
graduated from college in 1929, she visited Farnsworth in his San Francisco
experimental television laboratory and learned from him about his new
invention called television.[194]

Roscoe Grover as KSUB resident manager

In August 1945, Roscoe Grover was appointed resident manager of KSUB
and, like Urie had been, was supervised by KSL's Murdoch, who directed
Grover to develop and produce local programs and to encourage local
participation by educational, religious, civic and agricultural groups. Grover
was challenged to "help local organizations in the community build acceptable
radio programs in an effort to increase listener interest in KSUB." With 12
years of announcing, producing and teaching experience, Grover was well
qualified as KSUB's manager to achieve what Murdoch asked of him.[195]

In October 1946, after producing programs of local public interest and
managing KSUB as he was charged to do, Grover was relieved of all program
production duties, except for special announcing assignments. This was done
so he could concentrate on "sales and public relations exclusively." Grover
was removed from the *Farm Program,* the *College Hour* and other programs
he produced, to eliminate what Murdoch called, ... "complaints relative
to [program] preparation, production quality and finesse." Production
responsibility was turned over to Assistant Manager Dick Ashard, so Grover
could focus on sales and public relations in Cedar City and the surrounding
cities of St. George, Beaver, Milford and Panguitch. Murdoch wrote, "Mr.
Grover should start selling in those towns. ... It is going to require the services

<hr>

194   Arlene Harris Grover, interview with Tim Larson,, Salt Lake City, Utah, August 29, 1989, 14.
195   Federal Communications Commission, Washington, D.C. Application for FCC approval of
increase in KSUB power from 100 to 250 watts at 590kc, October 30, 1944, 36-A and 39.

of a salesman to spend at least one day each week [in these surrounding cities]. ... The balance of [Grover's] time will be spent in Cedar City selling and servicing accounts."[196]

The creative and talented Grover was taken from the programming responsibilities, for which he was hired, and directed by Murdoch to sell advertising in the towns surrounding Cedar City. As such, Grover was assigned an impossible task, because the low power KSUB signal did not provide good reception in the surrounding towns. Grover became unhappy, understandably. He was not particularly good at or inclined toward sales, and that now was his foremost responsibility as KSUB station manager.

The situation for Grover improved considerably, however, in 1948, when Arthur Higbee became KSUB manager and eased Grover back into program production and on-the-air work. Grover excelled at that and enjoyed being talent. Soon, he became known as "Uncle Roscoe" through a KSUB children's program he did on Saturdays. He communicated very well with children over the air and delighted them in person in the community with his paintings and other artwork.[197]

KSUB wasn't able to put a quality signal into the communities surrounding Cedar City until 1950, when the FCC approved a power increase to 1,000-watts on 590kc. At the dedication service for the new 1000-watt KSUB, Perry was the honored guest speaker. He recalled how in 1937 Madsen and Miller had prepared the original 1,000-watt application for the FCC. He was elated that several applications and 13 years later, it had finally come about under KSL ownership: "The Lord has indeed been good to me. KSUB is now in good hands. My faith is in KSUB and it is my hope and prayer that this station may render a great public service and continue to be The Voice of Southern Utah."[198]

---

196   Lennox Murdoch, "Office Communications: A review and analysis of station operations at KSUB," to Ivor Sharp, Executive Vice President, Radio Service Corporation, October 30, 1946.
197   Arthur L. Higbee, interview with Tim Larson,, Logan, Utah, Tape No. 530, transcript, 5, August 25, 1986. Everett L. Cooley Oral History Project, Marriott Library, University of Utah, Salt Lake City, Utah.
198   Leland Perry, Transcript of a speech given on the occasion of KSUB's inaugural broadcast using 1,000 watts of power, Cedar City, March 21, 1950, 6.

Grover had been at KSUB for a total of five years when KSL transferred him back to Salt Lake City to play Uncle Roscoe on KSL television's *Playtime Party*, a children's program. He also did a program on KSL radio called *Reading with Roscoe*. Arlene, his wife, recalled the circumstances in a 1989 interview:

> Oh, yes. I don't know how many hundred thousand children he had on his program over the years. ... [The] Hotel Utah was his sponsor. He designed a children's menu for them. No child ever [came to the Hotel Utah] without being accompanied by an adult ... so they thought it was very good business [to have a children's menu]. For years he was never home for dinner. He was always at the Hotel Utah going around and making drawings for the children on their menus or whatever.[199]

Grover's television program was on KSL until the mid-1950s when network cartoons began to capture children's interest. After television, Uncle Roscoe continued teaching art to schoolteachers through the Utah State University Extension Service and, even after a 20-year absence from television, remained a favorite of children in Utah's public schools

As stated earlier, Higbee became manager of KSUB in 1948. Higbee, who grew up in Cedar City, had an immediate passion for KSUB when he first heard it in 1937 at age 15. He hounded Madsen and Miller to let him help out at the station, free of course:[200]

> [Madsen and Miller] were the two that were really running the station when I kind of elbowed my way into it. They were young fellows. You know, one of them had to work if the other one was off to go [out] that night. They liked to go out together, so I said, 'Well, hey, let me come and do the announcing tonight.' So they gave me an opportunity. They hooked up the control room system to where I could practice on it and learn to operate it without actually

---

199   Arlene Harris Grover, interview with Tim Larson, 14.
200   Arthur L. Higbee, interview with Tim Larson, 5.

broadcasting on the air. They put it on a dummy-antenna type thing and after they felt like I had a little ability, they said, "Okay. We'll be gone. You this and this and this, and we'll be back to sign the station off the air." Then they would sneak away for a little while.

Perry had given Higbee his first paying job at KSUB in 1942, as an announcer and bookkeeper. In 1944, Higbee joined the Army Air Corps and, after nearly two years, came back to KSUB as program director. In 1946, Higbee moved to Logan to attend the Utah State Agricultural College, now Utah State University, and worked for Reed Bullen at KVNU. When he finished college in 1948, Higbee went back to Cedar City and KSUB, and soon became station manager, a position he held for nearly ten years.

KSUB and the new era of television

In June 1955, the FCC amended its rules to allow television stations to operate on as low as 100 watts of power. This action was taken to encourage the construction of television stations in smaller communities. In 1956, Higbee, speaking for the Southern Utah Broadcasting Company (SUBC) board of directors, outlined a proposal to provide television service to southern Utah residents. The proposal involved getting people to invest in a Cedar City low-power television station by purchasing stock in SUBC instead of subscribing to wired (cable) television. Higbee wrote in 1956:

> We suggest that instead of paying the large connections fee, plus monthly service payments to the [cable] antenna system, that you invest the same amount of money in capital stock of Southern Utah Broadcasting Company to help establish a FREE television station for the enjoyment of everyone who lives in this area. Such a FREE television station would provide the service to everyone who owns a TV set, regardless of where you live, and whether you're rich or poor. Such action is typical of Southern Utah people when they wish to obtain schools, churches, Colleges, and other establishments of benefit to the area.[201]

---

201   Arthur Higbee, "Southern Utah Broadcasting Company Proposal to Provide Free Television

This television proposal wasn't immediately acted upon and was put aside when there was a change in KSUB ownership. In January 1957, Radio Service Corporation of Utah (KSL) sold its stock in Southern Utah Broadcasting and KSUB to four Cedar City residents. KSUB stock shares totaling 6,722 were transferred to Cedar City residents Durham Morris, Lorin C. Miles, Lanell N. Hunt and Arthur Jones, for a total of $33,773, a figure considered somewhat below market value for the station. In October, these new owners then sold KSUB (Southern Utah Broadcasting Company) to Beehive Telecasting, a company based in Provo. Beehive remodeled and reconstructed the transmitter building west of the city, in order to house both KSUB radio and the resurrected KLOR-TV proposal. KSUB maintained a sales office and a small studio in the Park Building in Cedar City, and major programming changes took place, including a switch to the NBC network in February.

In 1957, when KSUB changed ownership, Higbee left the station and went to KDYL radio in Salt Lake City, and then to KTVT television where he worked with Roy Gibson, Jack White, Jack Goodman and others on the local 11 p.m. television news. When Higbee left KSUB in 1957, the president of Beehive, Samuel Nissley, appointed Lewis Sayers as KSUB station manager, to promote color television in southern Utah. Sayers had experience in broadcasting but reportedly used high-pressure sales tactics to sell Beehive color television stock, and his approach was not well received. As such, he was not successful in bringing color television either to Provo or south, to Cedar City.

In October 1959, the imminent collapse of the Beehive Telecasting Company nearly destroyed KSUB, and Howard Johnson of Granite District Radio Broadcasting in Salt Lake stepped in and saved it from oblivion. Johnson assumed control of Southern Utah Broadcasting and, once again, KSUB became financially viable by changing back to the CBS network and scrapping its television efforts.

Donald E. Cartwright succeeded Sayers as station manager. He was first appointed by Beehive but continued as station manager when Howard Johnson

---

Service to Southern Utah Residents," January 1956.

assumed ownership of KSUB. Cartwright sustained KSUB as an important voice for southern Utah in sports, education, the arts and news. First employed at KSUB under Higbee in 1951, Cartwright was involved in KSUB's early 1950s coverage of the atomic bomb tests in the Nevada desert, west of Cedar City. KSUB rented an airplane to cover the very first atomic blast:[202]

> By putting some of our shortwave equipment on board the plane, we were able to ... fly out over mountains west of St. George, west of Cedar City towards the test sight where they could get a direct view of that above-ground shot, and they could contact us by shortwave radio ...[with] their descriptions. ... Myself and Dick Gunn who were the engineer-announcers at the transmitter ... would go out the back door ... and look toward the test sight, and of course, you could see the explosion in the early morning hours ... the mushroom cloud. ... I remember [for later atomic blasts that] we had an opportunity to send our station manager [Arthur Higbee] and news directors [Frank Bareca and Robert Heyborne] down to the site, and watch some of the coverage there.

Decades later, the nuclear fallout was blamed for causing high rates of cancer and death among the people of southern Utah. Cartwright died of cancer, but, in his last years of life, didn't seem to blame the government, or directly associate his disease to fall-out from the atomic bomb tests:[203]

> Well, we were pretty well involved in that from the word go. There had been some controversy regarding how much [the government] let the public know and how much they didn't. I have always had the feeling that they were trying to be at that time honest with us. They were making an effort to let us know what was going on. Unfortunately there were many things that they ... couldn't let us know. ... I was pretty closely involved, [but I still don't know the whole story].

---

202   Donald E. Cartwright, interview with Tim Larson, March 23, 1988, Parowan, Utah. Everett L. Cooley Oral History Project, No. 756, Marriott Library, University of Utah, Salt Lake City, Utah.
203   Cartwright, interview with Tim Larson.

In 1950, on the occasion of KSUB's inaugural broadcast using 1,000 watts of power, Perry provided an anecdotal history of KSUB that briefly summarized times he remembered most vividly during his early years at the station. This telescopic history gives insight into his behavior and thinking at the time and provides a point of closure for KSUB and his story:[204]

> KSUB was on the air and Southern Utah had its radio station. Our troubles had just begun. ... Much could be said about the problems that were met and solved [at KSUB]. ... But vivid in my memory are recollections of sessions in Salt Lake and Ogden with Scott Matheson [KSUB's lawyer and father of Utah's governor in the 70s, and grandfather of one of Utah's former U.S. Representatives] pacing the floor and dictating legal matters while I transcribed on the typewriter; of seemingly endless hours of conference with Durham Morris [KSUB's business manager], some in a cold automobile in the early morning hours at Lund [northwest of Cedar City on the Union Pacific route] when I stopped off between trains; of conferences with creditors in an attempt to work out our financial difficulties; of garnishments and threats of suits which would have taken my parent's property [used as collateral for the original KSUB construction loan]; of volumes of reports and material submitted to the Federal Communications Commission; of negotiations for the sale of stock and for the sale of a portion of the station [to KSL] in order to bring in new capital and stabilize the business; but, eventually we worked out our difficulties.

Born August 23, 1901, Perry lived in Provo, Utah, at the time of his death on December 16, 1999, at age 98. He was working on a history of the LDS Mexican Mission at the time. He was called to the Mexican Mission at age 24 and served from December 1925 to December 1927.

But why did Perry hang onto KSUB for so long in the face of the hex that the station seemingly was under from the very beginning? The primary reason is revealed in his speech above. That is, if the station failed, lenders would

---

204   Leland Perry, transcript of a speech, March 21, 1950, 4.

have foreclosed on his parent's property. Perry borrowed $7,500 ($142,500 in today's value) from his parents in 1937, to construct KSUB. His parents had borrowed the money from a lender, using as collateral prime property they owned in Cedar City. Perry's biggest shame would not have been to lose KSUB but to have his parent lose their property if he defaulted on his loan payments. In a 1990 interview, Perry explained why: "You see, I had gotten to the point where I wasn't so much concerned about KSUB as I was about my dad's property on Main Street. I was anxious to get out from under that. ... I had reached a point where I didn't care very much whether the station succeeded or not." [205] When Perry paid his parents, they, in turn, would pay their lender. And if Perry didn't make his payment, it would be hard for his parents to make theirs.

Somehow payments were managed, and Perry's parents were able to hold on to their real estate. On February 13, 1950, a new chattel mortgage was received from his parents, John H. and Nomey M. Perry, for the sum of $3,210. After the capital stock of Southern Utah Broadcasting was increased to $100,000 in 1951, Perry's parents finally were paid off and their property was free and clear after being encumbered for 15 years. There was no more important historical moment at KSUB for Perry than this one. His parent's property was securely back under their ownership, and he had no more KSUB financial worries.

On the occasion of KSUB's 25th anniversary celebration on July 3, 1962, Howard Johnson's Southern Utah Broadcasting Company reaffirmed KSUB's commitment to Southern Utah.[206]

> Today, as in the past, the basic premise for the being of Radio
> KSUB, is our service to the citizens of the tri-state area. Not only
> do we provide an unexcelled advertising media, but we do so with a
> programming concept which is based on filling needs. Our facilities
> are always available to public and community service activities,
> our network and local news facilities meet your 'need-to-know.'

205   Leland Perry, interview with Tim Larson, Provo, Utah, March 16, 1990.
206   Broadcast on Radio KSUB on the occasion of KSUB's 25th Anniversary, "Voice of the Rainbow Canyons - Serving the Entire Tri-State Area, July 3, 1962.

Entertainment and information programs call upon the best of network talent, local talent, and our extensive source of recorded entertainment.

Indeed, KSUB's story may be one of the best among Utah's first 10 radio stations for epitomizing what were the most challenging circumstances for any pioneers coming into the Utah high desert when they arrived.

CHAPTER 11

KVNU, LOGAN

KVNU in Logan, Utah, was that city's first radio station offering a broadcasting service to endure over time, but it also was not Logan's very first radio station. KVNU went on the air in December 1938, but Logan's KFXD preceded it 13 years earlier. On August 18, 1925, J. F. Dillon, supervisor of radio licenses in San Francisco, approved an application from L. H. Strong Motor Company of Logan for a 10-watt station to operate on a frequency of about 1460 kilocycles. Ada Strong signed the application on behalf of the motor company. L. H. Strong was the Studebaker-Packard automobile dealer in Logan, and he owned the building in which KFXD operated. Although the KFXD license was granted to the company, the station owners as listed in the 1925 application were H. L. Peterson, Winston B. Jones and Spencer Hall.

Laurel S. (Larry) Cole, although not listed as an original applicant or owner, helped build KFXD on a tabletop with Jones, Peterson and Hall. Cole had recruited Peterson and Jones to become interested in amateur radio while they were in high school. Cole and Jones even obtained their amateur licenses at the same time in 1923, and they had sequential call letters. Cole had amateur station 6CKI, and Jones had 6CKJ. Meanwhile, financial help for KFXD came from Peterson's father who was a high school teacher in Logan for many years, as well as Jones' father, who was a doctor, having come from Alabama to practice in Logan, and the Cole family, which had been in the lumber business for several generations.

The L. H. Strong Motor Company kept the KFXD license for only four months and, on December 29, 1925, transferred it to the Service Radio Company, a "company" loosely formed by its KFXD operators. Spencer Hall and Cole held second grade commercial licenses and became the principal operators for the station in its first months. Sidney R. Stock, an Agricultural

College of Utah (later Utah State University) mechanical arts instructor, constructed an innovative carbon microphone for KFDX using engine gasket material to create a vibrating diaphragm.

Beginning in 1926 and for the next year or so, Cole filled out and signed the KFXD license renewal applications, even though he and Jones were in Salt Lake City attending the University of Utah. In November 1927, KFXD was sold and the license was transferred to Jerome, Idaho. Cole finished at the University of Utah in physics and mathematics, and Jones completed a pre-med program. Jones never went on to medical school but, instead, came back to Logan in 1929 and, with Cole, opened a radio sales and repair business called the Radio Service Shop. This was a derivation of Service Radio Shop, the name given the early KFXD license holder. Cole and Jones sold Stewart-Warner radios and built huge 100-foot long antennas for people to receive distant radio signals on the sets they sold. One time they took a battery powered receiver up on top of Mt. Logan, east of the city, and easily received radio stations from San Francisco and other West Coast signals. The Radio Service Shop was located on Main Street, next door to the Jensen Candy Store, a well-known confectionary shop in Logan.

After a couple of lean years in the Radio Service Shop, the business was dissolved. Cole went to California and worked at a radio store in Pasadena, and Jones moved to Maryland and for years operated a radio parts distributing company. In 1939, Cole came back to Logan and subsequently developed a radio electronics program at Utah State University to train radio operators for the military. After the war, Cole took a sabbatical and went to Stanford for a year, "earning the degree of Engineer." He later helped develop the electrical engineering program at Utah State University, becoming head of the department of Electrical Engineering in 1951. He served as acting or associate dean of the College of Engineering during the period 1959 to 1969. Cole stepped down as Department Head in 1970 and retired in 1972, with Professor Emeritus status, for his work at Utah State University over a thirty-three-year period.[207]

---

207   Larry S. Cole, Interview by Tim Larson, December 4, 1990, Logan, Utah.

After KFXD went dark in 1928, there was no local radio station in Logan until 1938, when KVNU began operation after a three-year application period, which tested everyone's patience. Seymour Levi "Hap" Billings, Jr., president of the Union Investment Company and Union Trust Company of Salt Lake, became the first president of Cache Valley Broadcasting Company (CVB) when it was formed on August 8, 1935, becoming the parent of KVNU.

Like other Utah applicants, after the passage of the Communications Act of 1934, CVB applied for a 100-watt radio station in Logan under Section 307(b) of the Communications Act of 1934 that allowed low power stations to be constructed in the "public interest, convenience and necessity" (PICAN). The original stockholders of Cache Valley Broadcasting, besides Billings, were J. A. and J. M. Reeder, Wm. P. Conner, Leo R. Jensen, and lawyer Dan B. Shields. The Reeders and Jensen each came to control 25% of CVB, Billings controlled 24%, and his Union Trust Company employee, Conner, owned 1%. Shield's share was tied in with Billings' 24% CVB ownership.

Eventually, Reeder became vice-president and director of CVB and commercial manager for KVNU. Reeder, who held a first-class operator's license and was in the radio supply business, built the station and became its chief operator and engineer. Jensen, who also became a KVNU director, had radio experience as an operator, programmer and manager at several radio stations before coming to KVNU. Conner, who was called by his middle name, Park, was in the mortgage loan business and was employed by Billings at the Union Trust Company. He also was an experienced and accomplished musician and held auditions and trained and developed local talent for KVNU when it went on the air.

Hap Billings, KVNU's principal founder, came with his family from Kansas at the turn of the century. His father, Seymour, owned the Utah Coal and Lumber Company in Park City and provided lumber for the mining industry. The Billings also owned lumber businesses in Salt Lake and in Holladay. When his father died, Billings assumed responsibility for the lumber outlets but, when mining floundered in Park City, closed Utah Coal and Lumber and, after a period of time, sold the Salt Lake Valley retail outlets and focused on the wholesale lumber business. In the Great Depression, there was a decreased need for lumber in construction, so Billings, with the help of his brother-in-law, Dan B. Shields, and others, entered the investment and trust business.[208] After World War II, Billing's Union Trust Company became a full-fledged bank. Billings continued in the banking business until he retired to California in the 1950s, and the Eccles of First Security Bank purchased Union Trust.

Billings was never involved on a daily basis at KVNU but was a major stockholder and director in the Cache Valley Broadcasting Company for nearly a decade, beginning in 1935. As president of CVB, Billings had a net worth of $75,000, and he personally guaranteed the payment of the notes totaling $6,000 held by the corporation. He also agreed to purchase $9,000 in CVB stock that had not been issued, should it have ever become necessary to finance the station's construction. The KVNU license application clearly would not have passed FCC scrutiny without his financial commitment.

On June 25, 1936, almost a year after the Cache Valley Broadcasting Company applied for a station, an FCC hearing was held and an examiner recommended that the KVNU construction permit be granted. Predictably, KDYL's Fox and his Great Western Broadcasting Association, Inc., almost immediately filed exceptions against the FCC's recommendation to grant the KVNU construction permit. Oral arguments on Fox's exceptions were held before the FCC on December 17, and it was found that Fox did not raise any questions that were not already being considered. Fox succeeded in manipulating FCC procedures to slow the approval of stations that might compete against his KDYL. He filed nuisance objections to keep KVNU from going on the air and, at the same time, had objections pending on Carman's KUTA application.

KVNU had additional problems than those manufactured by Fox, however. On February 23, 1938, the FCC granted CVB's application for KVNU

---

208   Peter W. Billings Sr., interview with Tim Larson, March 5, 1993, Salt Lake City, Utah.

but required they file another application specifying the exact transmitter location and the antenna system to be used. After FCC approval of KVNU's transmitter location, a final construction permit was issued on June 21, 1938, and CVB officially began construction five days later.

Finally, after three years of handling nuisance objections and solving FCC technical problems, KVNU sent the following telegram to the FCC at 4:40 p.m. on December 17, 1938:

> EQUIPMENT AND FREQUENCY TESTS COMPLETED AND ALL REQUIREMENTS MET STOP ALL REQUIRED APPLICATIONS FORMS PROPERLY EXECUTED ARE IN MAIL STOP THIS IS NOTICE THAT WE WILL BEGIN PROGRAM TESTS TUESDAY DECEMBER TWENTIETH.

KVNU launches programming

The first KVNU broadcast on December 20, 1938, was a test program by remote from Nibley Hall on the Brigham Young College campus –a college and high school in Logan founded by Brigham Young on August 6, 1877, just 23 days before he died.[209] It later became the site of Logan High School. Jack Luther was manager of the station when it started, and he appeared on the first program. Station employee Reed Bullen, who later became KVNU manager and owner, also appeared on that first broadcast, not as an employee but as president of the Logan Junior Chamber of Commerce.

But the KVNU license to officially broadcast wasn't issued even after these test broadcasts were conducted. It seems that some addresses were altered in the modified applications submitted by CVB, and the FCC was again concerned with the location of both the KVNU studios and its transmitter.

J. A. Reeder, CVB vice president, answered the FCC's concerns with the following simple explanation:[210]

---

209   Brigham Young College: See https://www.google.com/search?client=firefox-b-1-d&q=Brigham+Young+College+campus+in+Logan
210   Letter to Mr. T.J. Slowie, Federal Communications Commission, Washington, D.C., from

Regarding discrepancy in location address of main studios previously
mentioned as 43 South Main Street was due to the fact that [the]
stairway entrance through 43 South Main was closed and our
entrance was changed to 41 South Main Street. The studios are in
exactly the same location as stated in our application. In regards
to the transmitter site 1/2 mile north of Logan was an error in
transcription. It is located 1 mile north of Logan.

The explanation apparently satisfied the Washington bureaucrats.
Following Reeder's letter, the FCC issued KVNU a temporary license on
January 24, 1939, pending resolution of still other problems concerned
with the tower height. It seems that the height of the tower, 191 feet, was
satisfactory if certain technical stuff-n-stuff --like shunt excited radiators--
were used but unsatisfactory if other technical stuff-n-stuff --like tower
insulation vertical leads-- were not employed correctly. By April 1939, Reed
Bullen was made station manager and, having experienced several month-
to-month conditional renewals, wrote to the FCC reassuring that KVNU's
application was correct regarding its tower height:[211]

In talking with our chief engineer, he advises me that the application
as sent in is correct and in order, that is, that the height of the vertical
lead and the overall height are each 191 feet. He further advises me
that this is correct inasmuch as we are employing a shunt-excited
radiator.

In 1938 and 1939, during the time these seemingly picayune FCC
problems were being dealt with, the original principals in Cache Valley
Broadcasting Company were joined by several other stockholders. The
communal ownership was evident. By October 1939, Billings (28% CVB
owner), J. M. Reeder (12%), Shields (4%) and Conner (2%) were joined by
Henry F. Laub (17%), manager and owner of Cache Valley Electric Company
in Logan; J. Eastman and Adrian W. Hatch (7%), the latter, a manager
and owner of Hatch Insurance Agency, Inc. in Logan; C.G. Merrill (7%) of

J.A. Reeder, Vice President of Cache Valley Broadcasting Company, dated December 27, 1938.
211   Reed Bullen, Letter to Federal Communications Commission, Attention: T. J. Slowie,
Secretary, April 24, 1939.

Richmond, Utah, a KVNU operator; John S. McCune (5%), manager and part owner of McCune Stores Inc. (Ben Franklin Stores) in Logan; and Otto Mehr (1%), manager of the Logan Garment Company and manufacturer of Knot Goods.

In addition, Herschel Bullen (5% CVB owner), manager of First Federal Savings and Loan Association and a Logan real estate dealer, joined his son Reed (8%) and the others as a stockholder. Two-percent of the stock was held in the CVB treasury. Original CVB investor Leo R. Jensen no longer controlled any CVB stock and was not an officer by October 12, 1939, when a renewal application was made for KVNU's first full term license. Billings was CVB president, Laub was vice president, and Reed Bullen was secretary-treasurer-manager of the corporation.

On November 20, 1939, the FCC issued CVB its first longer term license, one for nine months instead of month-to-month as had been the case during 1939. KVNU's broadcast day was from 7 a.m. to 10 p.m., and programming consisted of 59% music --with program names like "Sunrise Serenade," "King Cole Swing Trio," "Matinee Melodies" and "Pinky Tomlin and His Orchestra;" 22% news, --with eight 15-minute newscasts per day from "U.P. World Coverage News," 30 minutes of "A Look at the Local Side of News," 40 minutes of farm and sports coverage and five minutes of "Pathfinder News Commentary; and, 15% drama and variety, with shows like "Dr. Sellers True Story" and the "Conoco Variety Show."

As WWII approached, the CVB stockholders tended to their respective non-broadcasting businesses, while Reed Bullen managed KVNU. After the U.S. entered WWII, like other radio stations in Utah and across the nation, Bullen found KVNU without any operators:[212]

> I lost all my help. I had to have licensed engineers to operate, and all
> my people had left for the service. I didn't have a licensed engineer,
> and I didn't have a license myself. ... For a period of time, about
> 6 months, everything that was said on KVNU, I said. Everything

---

212   Reed Bullen, interview with Tim Larson, 16.

that was sold, I sold --over the telephone. Everything that was written, I wrote. Everything that played on the air, I played. From morning to night. And I kept my station going. Finally, I went to the commanding officer at the Navy School [located on the Utah State University campus] and told him my plight and asked him to release some help that could come down to the station just to keep me on the air so I could keep my license. He gave me three people. ... They came down and relieved me and saved my station for me.

Bullen was on the verge of burnout. Anticipating the end of the war and the expansion of radio, however, Cache Valley Broadcasting principals bought KID Broadcasting Company in Idaho Falls, and Bullen went there from July 1 to December 31, 1944. Also, at this time, Herschel Bullen successfully applied for a construction permit in Elko, Nevada, while Dan B. Shields applied for a station in Provo. In early 1945, Bullen came back to KVNU from KID and, according to him, was faced with Laub's unfriendly intentions to sell his KVNU interests.

'A parting of minds'

There was a parting of minds and Laub announced his intention to sell his shares to outside investors, which was not acceptable to the Bullens. Laub purchased Billing's stock and that of all the other KVNU stockholders, except the shares owned by Hatch, the Bullens and Shields. Hatch subsequently sided with Laub and allowed him to vote his interests, and Shields sided with the Bullens. Laub offered Shields several times the value of his CVB shares:[213]

> It was a battle for control. [In the end] my father and I were able to pick up enough stock to buy everything. There was a group that wanted to get control and they were able to buy everybody's stock except Dan Shields. The group that was fighting me went down to Dan Shields and offered him 17 times the value of the stock --book value. But he said, 'No, I'm sticking with Reed Bullen.'

---

213   Reed Bullen, interview with Tim Larson, 10.

With Shield's help, the Bullens fought back Laub's plans to sell to outside investors. The fact still remained, however, that Laub wanted to sell his CVB stock. A deal was struck by which H .F. Laub acquired 50.2% of the CVB stock and, in turn, agreed to sell it to the Bullens.[214]

It was to Laub's benefit to agree to sell to the Bullens rather than to outside interests. KVNU stock was priced at $.50 a share and Laub's shares would have been worth only $7,497 to an outside investor. When on March 3, 1945, Laub agreed to sell his controlling interest to CVB insiders, it was worth substantially more:[215]

> It is understood that in consideration of $20,000.00, Henry Laub, acting for himself and as agent for Adrian W. Hatch, Claire M. Laub Huchel, John H. Laub and Emma K. Laub, has delivered to Herschel Bullen, acting for himself and others, 14,994 share of capital stock of the Cache Valley Broadcasting Company.

After this transaction, Laub apparently wanted assurances that the CVB principals would not speak poorly of him to the FCC because of his somewhat threatening posture concerning his CVB stock sale. In the style of a "Know-All-Men-By-These-Presents" document, Herschel Bullen and Laub signed an understanding:[216]

> It is further understood that Henry Laub and agents obtained all the above [Cache Valley Broadcasting Company] stock in an honorable and business ... like manner and that no fraud or illegitimate pressure[s] were used in the obtaining by purchase any part or portion of the 14,994 shares of stock represented in this transaction and transferred to Herschel Bullen and others on this date.

---

214   Federal Communications Commission, "Consent to Transfer Control of Corporation Holding Construction Permit or License," September 23, 1946, 50. Approved December 17, 1946. Record Group 173, 58-A-4, Box 93, National Archives, Washington, D.C.

215   Federal Communications Commission, "Consent to Transfer Control of Corporation Holding Construction Permit or License," dated September 23, 1946.

216   Federal Communications Commission, "Consent to Transfer Control of Corporation Holding Construction Permit or License," dated September 23, 1946.

On December 17, 1946, the FCC gave its final consent to transfer control of CVB and the KVNU license to the Bullen family. In the transfer, Herschel Bullen became the largest stockholder with a 45% share of Cache Valley Broadcasting Company. Reed Bullen owned 32%, and his sister and brothers, Helen Bullen, Thurlow H. Bullen and Herschel Keith Bullen, each had about 6% ownership. The Bullens secured a loan of $17,000 from the First National Bank of Logan, and both pledged all of their KVNU stock as security. This was an intriguing transaction because most of the value of the station was in the license, which the licensee, the CVB and Bullens, didn't actually own. The license was owned by the "public" and could be transferred only by FCC approval and not by loan default.

Herschel and Reed Bullen legacy

Herschel Bullen had been trained in writing and banking. He became a fancy penman, or calligrapher, and entered journalism when he founded the *Logan Republican* newspaper in the early 1900s. The Logan newspapers at that time were strictly political, and Bullen started his paper to compete with the Journal (now the *Herald Journal*), the newspaper in Logan that spoke for the Democratic Party:[217]

> My father was always fighting in the newspaper business. I hated fighting. He was fighting someone all the time. ... He fought the Democratic Party, the big Democrats. They would even make each other tell how many bonds they bought for the war effort [during World War I] and things like that. They fought worse than we fight today.

When Herschel Bullen entered the radio business in 1938, it was money from his banking and real estate ventures, not his newspaper business that financed the station. Unlike the financial backing of KSL by the *Salt Lake Tribune* interests and of KLO by the *Ogden Standard-Examiner* interests, KVNU was not directly aligned with a newspaper when it started in 1938. All three stations in 1938, however, also were substantially supported by their

---

217   Reed Bullen, interview with Tim Larson, 9.

respective owner's involvement in banks, investment companies and real estate.

By 1946, KVNU was completely a Bullen family owned operation, except for Dan B. Shields' 7% share. The Bullen family voted Shields as president of CVB, while Herschel Bullen became vice president and Reed Bullen remained secretary and treasurer, as he had been since 1939. Shields was a close family friend and was not involved in the operation of the station, nor did it seem he was concerned with his KVNU investment:[218]

> He [Shields] had $3,000 worth of stock. He had $1,000 worth of stock, but I [Reed Bullen] gave him $3,000 for it. I didn't give it [to his family] until after he died. ... He was the United States District Attorney [for Utah]. He was a top Democrat in the state. He was a member of the Utah State Senate and the head of the party. He was the titular head of the party for all the years he was there because of having been U.S. District Attorney. ... [His willingness to sell us his shares is what] kept the business for me and my family [when Laub wanted to sell to outside interests]. ... Dan was a tremendous man.

As indicated, Shields was a brother-in-law to Hap Billings. Both men were staunch Democrats, and it is not known why Shields was so adamant in selling to the Bullens, who were loyal Republicans. Shields was mostly a self-taught attorney. He and Albert Thomas, who was a professor at The University of Utah, were the leaders of the Democratic Party in the early 1930s. In 1932, they thought that with Franklin Roosevelt coming to office, there was a good chance that a Democratic senator would be elected from Utah. Shields and Thomas were good friends and they decided that only one of them should seek a senate seat. It was agreed that Thomas would run for the senate and, when elected, would get Shields appointed as a U.S. district judge. The district judge at that time had been appointed by President Woodrow Wilson in 1915 and was thought ready to retire. However, the old district judge didn't accommodate Shields and Thomas and stayed on the bench until into his nineties. Instead, Shields was appointed as the U. S. district attorney for Utah, a position he held

---

218   Reed Bullen, interview with Tim Larson, 10.

for many years.

Reed Bullen, Herschel's first son, was born November 17, 1906, and began work early at the *Logan Republican*:[219]

> I was raised in [the *Logan Republican*]. I've been dunked in the ink barrel more times than any kid alive. I was the boss's son and every time ... I did something that was a little questionable, they'd dunk me in the ink barrel. ... But I did everything I could do. I had a [paper] route and delivered newspapers to the business section of Logan. ... Actually, I ran everything except the linotype. I ... set some type by hand using the old method. ... And I wrote two or three sports articles for his paper that were printed. This was all a good start for me. ... The paper was a tri-weekly. I was just in my teens. ... I celebrated the Armistice Day [November 11, 1918] in Logan. I remember vividly what happened. When they announced the Armistice, the newspaper built a man with his arms up [in a surrender position] and they put it in a trailer pulled by an old Ford and ran it up and down Main St. ... It was the Kaiser giving up.

The younger Bullen went from his father's newspaper business to Utah State University, where he graduated in 1929. Although he never got a job as a result of his father's political connections, he lost at least one as a result of his father's stridently Republican newspaper:[220]

> I once got a job taking the census. It was a government created job. ... I [began] the next morning and was walking down the street just east of my home over North. A car drove up and the occupant [asked what I was doing]. ... I told him who I was and the man says, "You're a Republican aren't you?" I said, "I guess I'm a Republican, my father is." They said, "That's right, we know that." They fired me right on the spot because I was a Republican. ... That stuck in my mind all my life. I got into the radio business and was a Republican

---

219   Reed Bullen, interview with Tim Larson, February 1, 1993. 2.
220   Reed Bullen, interview with Tim Larson, 12.

all during the Roosevelt administration. People wouldn't give me business because I was a Republican [when the state was completely controlled by Democrats]. They [the Democrats] were tougher on us as Republicans than we ever were on the Democrats once we got control [of the state].

For six summers during and after college, Bullen drove tourists around the parks in southern Utah, working out of the Hotel Escalante depot for the Union Pacific. It was only five years later that Leland Perry brought KSUB to the third floor of the hotel, as mentioned in an earlier chapter. Perry and Bullen were not acquainted at that time, but Bullen was one of the people who helped make Cedar City and the environs a popular and financially successful tourist destination area and an attractive location for Perry to launch his station.

After graduating from Utah State University and serving six years as a bus driver and transportation agent in the national parks, Bullen enrolled at Stanford Law School and successfully completed a year, but he hated school at all levels, including the study of law. His father wanted him to be a lawyer or a doctor, and Reed tried to please him. But Bullen dropped out of law school and went to California with his friend Perry Stewart, to work in a gambling establishment owned by Stewart's brother-in-law, in Santa Monica. When gambling was voted out of California, Bullen returned with Stewart to Logan and obtained a Chrysler-Plymouth automobile dealership. Seth Blair, who already had a Chrysler dealership on First North Street in Logan, objected to Bullen and Stewart's competition, and they subsequently lost their distributorship.

The younger Bullen eventually bought out his father and the other family members and became sole owner of KVNU. One of Bullen's sons, Jonathan, joined him at KVNU and eventually became manager. In 1970, Reed and Jonathan Bullen obtained the franchise for cable television in the city of Logan. Originally, George Hatch of KUTV proposed a Logan cable television partnership with the Bullens. Hatch proposed to put up the money and build the system and become a 50/50 owner with the Bullens.

At the same time, however, the Church of Jesus Christ of Latter-day Saints, the de facto owners of KSL, wanting to get into cable, approached the Bullens and they chose that offer over Hatch's proposal. In the late 1970s, the Bullens bought out the LDS Church's cable shares, and Jonathan Bullen took ownership of the cable system, while Reed Bullen kept KVNU. Jonathan later sold the cable system to Sonic Cable and resumed handling the KVNU operations. Jonathon went on to own the building in which both the cable system and KVNU operated in Logan.

The Bullens and their Cache Valley Group owned and operated KVNU for 50 years. Reed was the general manager for the majority of those years, followed by his son, Jonathan, who served as general manager until the Bullen family sold the station to the Sun Valley Radio Group in 1996, which remains KVNU's present owner.

CHAPTER 12

KOVO, PROVO

In 1938, two competing applications were filed with the FCC to construct the first radio station in Provo. One of the applicants was the Provo Broadcasting Company, whose principals included attorney Dan B. Shields (mentioned in previous chapters), among others. Shields was a legal consultant for KOAL in Price and KUTA in Salt Lake City, and a director of KVNU in Logan. The other applicant in Provo filed under the name of "Citizens Voice and Air Show." Its principal was Clifton A. Tolboe, a Provo building contractor. Because the applications were mutually exclusive, the granting of one by the FCC would preclude the granting of the other, necessitating an FCC comparative hearing.

When Shields applied for a radio station in Provo, he had practiced law for 34 years, since 1904. He had been a member of the Utah Legislature in both chambers and had served as state attorney general. In 1933, Shields was appointed the U.S. attorney for the District of Utah, a position he held for more than 20 years. He boasted of having been only the second Kiwanis member, west of Chicago.

Competing against Shields for the Provo radio station license was Clifton Tolboe. He was born in Salt Lake City on January 2, 1899. His father, Christian A. Tolboe entered the contracting business in 1900, moved to Provo in 1908 and founded the Tolboe Construction Company in 1909. The younger Tolboe graduated from the Brigham Young University High School and served in the military during World War I. In 1925, Tolboe joined his father in the construction business, and they formed the Tolboe and Tolboe Construction Company. During the Great Depression, the company had a job building a bridge on the Colorado River, but they were not paid for their work and subsequently went broke. Clifton sold his house in Provo in 1932 and invested

in a company that sent him to Detroit and then to Indianapolis. In 1934, when
the company was going to transfer him to San Francisco, Tolboe quit and came
back to Provo:[221]

> So I came home and my dad was having a big struggle. He was
> building a Mutual Home up in Provo Canyon for the MIA girls,
> and just on a little small salary. So I told him, "Well Dad, we got to
> get back in the business some way, so let's go and see the bonding
> company and see what they will do." So, we went up to see them.
> They said, "Sure, we'll go with you. We're just as destitute for work as
> you are." So [in 1936] we bid three schools out in Duchesne County,
> one at Roosevelt, Myton, and Duchesne. We made $100,000 on those
> three schools; it was just a godsend for us. ... So that started us back in
> the construction business.

The FCC held hearings on September 28 and October 8, 1938, to weigh
the comparative merits of the services proposed by Shields and Tolboe in their
mutually exclusive applications and to determine which applicant for a Provo
station would best serve the public interest. The FCC found both Shields
and Tolboe to be legally, technically, financially and otherwise qualified to
construct and operate their proposed stations. Each had filed for a station
at 1210kHz, with power of 100-watts night and 250 watts daytime. Each had
more than adequate financing, ranging from $10,000 to $13,000, to construct
their proposed station, and each had excellent programming proposals, with
entertainment, news, sports, and a significant amount of free time for civic and
religious groups, as mainstays.

With the two applicants seemingly equally qualified and in good standing
in the community, the FCC had to identify some unique meritorious criteria
in order to choose between Shields' Provo Broadcasting Company and Tolboe's
"Citizens Voice and Air Show." The FCC found two distinguishing technical
factors on which it based its final decision.

In his application, Tolboe proposed to maintain remote lines for the

221   Clifton A. Tolboe, interview with Tim Larson, May 6, 1988, Tape No. 772, transcript, 2.
Everett L. Cooley Oral History Project, Marriott Library, University of Utah, Salt Lake City, Utah.

purpose of broadcasting happenings of interest from six cities in the vicinity of Provo. Meanwhile, Shields' group made no such proposal. In addition, Tolboe proposed to broadcast 136 hours a week, while Shields proposed to be on the air 96 hours. Hence, based on maintaining the remote lines and on its proposed longer hours of operation, and, possibly, on Shields involvement in several other Utah radio stations (KOAL, KUTA, and KVNU), the FCC granted the license to Tolboe's "Citizen Voice and Air Show" company.

Tolboe sets up for KOVO launch

After Tolboe got the construction permit for KOVO, he partnered with consulting engineer Grant Wrathall, who had three years earlier been one of the original KUTA applicants with Frank Carman. In the partnership, Tolboe was responsible for getting the building ready for KOVO, and Wrathall and his brother-in-law Howard Johnson, later KNAK's founder (discussed in the next chapter), were responsible for acquiring and installing all the technical equipment. For his part, Tolboe rented space above the Hedquist Drugstore on Center Street in Provo, widened the stairway access, and gutted the second floor. He constructed studios and a control room in preparation for the technical equipment that Wrathall was going to install.

Tolboe then went looking for a KOVO station manager. As such, he talked to Arch L. Madsen who, though quite young, had several years of radio experience, as outlined earlier in the book. Madsen had worked as a civilian operator for the U.S. Army, in charge of radio station WUBL in Missoula, Montana, from May 1933 to September 1934. From February 1935 to September 1935, he worked at KSL as a transmitter technician and, from June 1937 to July 1938, was manager and chief engineer for Leland Perry's KSUB in Cedar City. For a year after that, he was commercial manager for Frank Carman's KUTA in Salt Lake City. Even with this impressive experience, however, Tolboe wasn't persuaded that the young Madsen was the right person. KSL's Earl J. Glade convinced him otherwise.

As Tolboe explained it:[222]

---

222   Clifton A. Tolboe, interview with Tim Larson, 4.

I just thought that [twenty-four] was too young for a kid ... to run
a radio station. So that night ... Earl Glade called me on the phone,
and he says, "Cliff, I'm coming down to see you." ... He came down
in behalf of Arch Madsen. He says, "[Madsen's] the brightest young
man I've ever run across in the radio business. ... And if you give him
a chance, I'll promise you I'll come down ... once a week if there's any
trouble." So I debated with myself. I thought, "Well, I can't," but I
decided to take that gamble."

In July 1939, based on Glade's recommendation and offer of assistance as
needed, Tolboe hired Madsen as KOVO's first station manager. In September,
Madsen subsequently hired others, who then comprised the KOVO staff when
the station went on the air. These included Bill Westover and S. Garn Carter
in sales, production manager David Walker, announcers George Killian, Jack
Davies and Shirl Black, technicians Gerald W. Peterson and Harold Goates,
and staff stenographer Violet Clark. After the station opened, Beth Bird took
over as stenographer in April 1940 and was joined by Helen L. Knight in
November. Willard E. Done and Parley P. Rasmussen, both holders of First
Class FCC licenses, joined chief operator Gerald Peterson as technicians in
1940. In addition, Madsen hired commercial director James L. Lawrence
and announcer and copywriter Joe Lee in February 1941, and news editor
announcer J. Wayne Kearl in March of that year.

With the staff hired, and based on Wrathall's projections of when the
technical equipment would be installed, Tolboe and Madsen set September 21,
1939, as the date for KOVO to go on the air. An enormous amount of publicity
was prepared. Area businesses even took out a full-page spread in the *Provo
Herald* to congratulate KOVO on its inaugural night. Included in these were
Huish Electric, P. L. Larson Plumbing and Heating, Cherry Hill Dairy, Peck
Electric, Mountain Fuel Supply, Utah Valley Glass and Paint, Tri-State Lumber
Company and Lewis Ladies Store.[223]

With the offices and studios in place, with staff hired, and with all the
publicity prepared, there still was one significant problem associated with

---

223   Provo Herald, September 20, 1939, Sec. 2, 2.

the scheduled opening of the station on September 21: KOVO didn't have
a construction permit to make modifications on its antenna system, and, as
result, Wrathall and Johnson didn't have KOVO technically ready to go on the
air. On September 16, 1939, five days before KOVO's formal launch, Tolboe
sent the following urgent telegram to the FCC:[224]

> KOVO TRANSMITTER EXCEPT ANTENNA COMPLETED
> STOP ELABORATE PUBLICITY CAMPAIGN RELEASED
> ANNOUNCING OPENING SEPTEMBER 21 STOP
> CONSTRUCTION PERMIT HAS FAILED TO ARRIVE STOP
> PLEASE EXPEDITE ACTION REFERRED TO IN YOUR
> LETTER OF AUGUST 15 1939 STOP PLEASE WIRE COLLECT
> PERMISSION TO COMPETE ANTENNA SYSTEM TO MAKE
> POSSIBLE EQUPMENT [sic] TEST MORNING SEPT 19 CITIZENS
> VOICE AND AIR SHOW.

The FCC sent the permit but that did not completely solve the problem.
Madsen further explained what happened in the days leading up to KOVO's
opening:[225]

> We set an opening date and started heavy advertising. Unfortunately,
> Wrathall and his brother-in-law, an engineer, really goofed. Even
> up 'till ten days before, he promised everything was in order. The
> transmitter, he claimed was all completed. It was just a matter of
> running a checkout for the FCC. The console equipment was coming
> all built and tested. It was just a matter of putting it in place, so we
> continued our opening publicity. Three days before we were to go on
> the air, the console arrived in kit form. I went numb! I did not know
> what to do. ... I felt we must meet our announced opening date. I
> worked straight through three days without sleeping! The engineer
> had lied to me. The transmitter, he said, was all set to go, all tested.
> We went on the air as scheduled with haywire studio and remote
> equipment. We had planned a big program at College Hall on the

---

224   Western Union Telegram from Clifton A Talboe (sic) to J. S. (sic) Slowie, secretary, Federal
Communications Commission, September 16, 1939, Provo, Utah.
225   Arch L. Madsen, interview with Tim Larson, 66.

BYU campus. ... No one could hear us! We were broadcasting --oh, yes-- we were broadcasting on the same frequency as the Sacramento police. ... We had gone on the air with the biggest technical mess imaginable! Temporary hay wired equipment in the studio while we worked for days to fix the console. That was my beginning in Provo.

The fact that KOVO did launch on schedule, Thursday evening, September 21, 1939, at 7:30, is a minor miracle of sorts, despite having less than an adequate signal. Utah Governor Henry Blood, KSL's Earl J. Glade, and the mayors of a number of Utah county communities were on the stage of College Hall on the Brigham Young University campus for the inaugural broadcast of Provo's first radio station. Prior to the first program at BYU, an air-check was made at 5 p.m. from KOVO's studios at 108 West Center Street, and that officially was when the station went on the air, albeit, with a whimper.

Tolboe soon assumed total ownership of KOVO and came to give Madsen complete power and authority and responsibility with respect to selecting and producing programs and the sale of commercial time. But, Madsen had no legal contract or agreement with Tolboe. His employment was based on trust and an oral agreement, sealed only with a mutual understanding of the tasks. Thus, a lasting friendship between Tolboe and Madsen took hold:[226]

> Well, as we went along, Arch would call me [Tolboe] in and ask me a question, and I [would say], "Arch, you're running this station, not me. If you make a mistake, so what, you'll never make it a second time. So you run the station the way you want to run it. Don't ask me how to run it." So at that time Arch started to manage it the way he wanted to run it. And I'll say that he's been the greatest friend I've ever had in my life. He is still to this day.

KOVO's programming

KOVO provided various programs of local, national and international character as it developed. Local musical programs were prepared using a

---

226   Tolboe, interview with Tim Larson.4.

transcription service provided by the National Broadcasting Company's (NBC) Thesaurus Service that included 2,000 musical selections. KOVO was not affiliated with NBC, but this was a programming service provided through the mail and was not a network service delivered live over telephone lines. KOVO news personnel also prepared local and regional news for the station. In addition, KOVO subscribed to the United Press Radio News Service and Transradio, to carry 15-minutes of "Round-the-World-News" several times each day. Madsen also contracted with the British Broadcasting System to rebroadcast, on a non-commercial basis, news programs originating in the BBC studios in London.

As promised in the original application, other programs originated from the remote sites in communities around Provo and from the Brigham Young University campus. Tolboe became close to the BYU administration and to its President, Franklin S. Harris (1921-1945). Almost from its beginning, KOVO carried BYU sports and, in recognition of this, in January of 1954, BYU President Ernest J. Wilkinson (1951-1971) gave Tolboe a plaque thanking KOVO for 15 years of BYU sports broadcasting. Another connection with BYU was through J. L. Pardoe and the Speech and Language Department. Over the years, Tolboe encouraged Pardoe to send his best students to KOVO and to Madsen for training.

For Tolboe, his primary source of income was from his construction business. Certainly, he saw KOVO as a business, but he likened it more to a hobby dedicated to public service, and he didn't count on the station for personal income.[227] KOVO lost about $660 in 1940, after one year of operation. Then it began to generate income after that and, in 1943 produced a $4,237 profit. However, this "large" profit concerned Tolboe:[228]

> The trouble was the war hit and the government put a regulation on
> what you could make in the station. It was so low that [Arch and I
> would] go to every [NAB] convention. We'd charge that off [to reduce
> KOVO profits]. I went to all the conventions in the East with Arch.

---

227   Utah: A Centennial History, New York: Lewis Historical Publishing Company, 1949, Vol. III, 345.
228   Clifton A. Tolboe, interview with Tim Larson, 4.

If KOVO was first a public interest hobby and second a business for Tolboe, it was the opposite for Madsen. Although giving attention to public interest, Madsen clearly operated KOVO to maximize profits. From the beginning he focused on expanding KOVO's source of revenue, beyond local advertisers, to regional and national advertisers. While still working at KSUB in Cedar City, Madsen had attended a General Motors sales seminar in Salt Lake City, and that launched his selling career in broadcasting. At the three-day seminar, Madsen learned successful selling techniques and gained tremendous confidence in his selling abilities. After taking the job as station manager at KOVO, Madsen was so confident in his sales abilities that he went to New York and tried to pitch KOVO to a national account executive at the J. Walter Thompson Advertising Agency:[229]

> I made my little pitch. I had prepared, studied hard trying to use what I had learned in the Chevrolet zone meeting. ... When I finished, she said, 'That's very interesting, but you know, there are more people within two blocks of my office than in [KOVO's] entire coverage area. ... It's too tiny for us to think about. What you need to do is figure out some way to get a bigger tie-in.'"

The Intermountain Network (IMN)

Upon returning to Utah, Madsen took seriously the suggestion about a tie-in. He contacted owner Jack Richards at KOAL radio in Price and manager Paul Heitmeyer at KLO in Ogden, and proposed that they form a three-station network with KOVO, to distribute commercial programming to the population centers of Utah. Richards and Heitmeyer were agreeable, and thus began an early version of the Intermountain Network (IMN). In 1940, no written agreement existed covering services provided by the three IMN stations. As earlier stated, each station simply agreed to make every effort to sell advertising for the other stations on the network. And, when commercial time was sold, the originating IMN station was to be paid a 15% commission on the sales.

---

229 Madsen, interview with Tim Larson, 72.

Although established in 1940, IMN had no way to distribute programming in real-time to all three stations. The telephone company said it would be too costly to connect stations in Provo, Price and Ogden. But, with the help of Congressman J. W. Robinson of Provo, Tolboe and Madsen were able to persuade AT&T and Mountain States Telephone to install, in the middle of winter, lines from Ogden to Salt Lake City and Provo, and then through Spanish Fork Canyon to Price. The three stations were affiliated with the Mutual Broadcasting System, and the network lines used for the Intermountain Network were the same as those used to bring the individual member stations the regular Mutual Network service. This was the embryonic beginning of the Intermountain Network. George Hatch later expanded IMN into a regional network involving radio stations in six states (the discussion of IMN is resumed in a later chapter).

Arthur Gaeth's rise as radio personality

KOVO carried Mutual Network programming for about half of its broadcast day. Included were musical programs, national news, and popular personalities such as commentator Fulton Lewis Jr. By 1944, KOVO also was carrying Mutual entertainment shows such as Lawrence Welk, Superman, and Tom Mix, as well as other influential commentators such as Gabriel Heatter, Lowell Thomas, Morton Downey and Arthur Gaeth.

Although Gaeth became a very popular network commentator, he started his career at KOVO in Provo. In 1940, he was associated with BYU and was knowledgeable about Europe, after having served an LDS mission in the former Czechoslovakia. Gaeth wanted to be on KSL, but the station seemingly didn't want him, so he came to Madsen at KOVO. After some coaching by Professor Pardoe for a speech problem, Gaeth went on the air every day at noon on KOVO, for 15 minutes, doing commentary about the war and happenings in Europe. Madsen gave Gaeth $3 a broadcast, and he was sponsored by a group of Utah Valley furniture stores called Dixon-Taylor Russell.

After attracting an audience, Gaeth was then lured away from KOVO by
KSL. He was on the air at that station until his commentary was judged not
balanced. Madsen related his recollection of events:[230]

> [Gaeth] got in trouble [at KSL]. He was reportedly accused of
> being left wing. I found him to be fair. He tried to give a balanced
> commentary, which was a very difficult task. ... I don't know the
> extent of it, but he did tangle with the ownership of KSL that accused
> him of --slanting his commentary. ... KSL took him off the air and we
> [KOVO] quickly put him back on the Intermountain Network.

Back on the IMN for a time, Gaeth again was hired away, this time by
the Don Lee Network, with stations in California, Oregon and Washington.
Don Lee was a successful California automobile dealer turned network owner.
Then ABC took Gaeth away from Don Lee and put him on radio coast to
coast, sponsored by the Electrical Workers Union. After the War, Gaeth was
selected as a network pool reporter to cover the Nuremberg war trials and
received national awards for his excellent reporting.

In the early 1950s, the fear of communism began to consume America
and, when Gaeth's sponsor, the Electrical Workers Union, was allegedly
infiltrated with Communist sympathizers, he became a victim of the Red Scare
and was accused of being a "fellow traveler." Very timid radio executives,
who feared being investigated, as their movie industry counterparts had
experienced in front of Congressional committees such as the House Un-
American Activities Committee (HUAC), or by anti-communist zealots in
Congress such as Senator Joseph McCarthy, took him off the air. After being
blacklisted, Gaeth went to Denver as vice president of a savings and loan
company, and eventually got back on radio working for a Denver station. He
worked on air for many years in that city but never got back on the IMN.

Madsen leaves KOVO, and eventually returns

In 1944, Madsen left KOVO and went to KSL to be the assistant to

---

230   Arch Madsen, Interview by Tim Larson, September 9, 1986, Tape No. U-542, 204.

manager Ivor Sharp. As noted earlier, Sharp was J. Reuben Clark's son-in law. Clark held high office in the LDS Church, while also president of the Radio Service Corporation of Utah, KSL's parent company. Many individuals, including Madsen, believed that because Sharp knew nothing about broadcasting, his appointment by Clark to replace Earl Glade was a pure act of nepotism.

When KSL purchased an interest in KID radio in Idaho Falls, Madsen took advantage of an opportunity to manage the station. He commuted back and forth for about a nine-month period, but eventually tired of being away from his family, as well of flying in DC-3s in all kinds of weather, and working 18-hour days. So, still unhappy with the climate and leadership at KSL, Madsen left in 1946 to work for the IMN, which, by this time, was expanding into a regional network under George Hatch, including states surrounding Utah. When Madsen left KSL for the IMN job, KSL management told him he could never come back. Given the circumstances at the time, Madsen thought that was "fine."

When Madsen left KOVO in 1944, Tolboe became general manager of the station. As such, in 1946, he appeared at an FCC comparative hearing to testify in support of Lester R. Taylor, one of two applicants for a new station in Provo. The ubiquitous Shields was the other applicant. Shields' consulting engineer was the equally ubiquitous Wrathall, who had been Tolboe's consultant eight years earlier. Taylor was 53 years old and a partner in the Taylor Bros. Department Store in Provo. His sons, Lester P. and Edward joined him in the Mid-Utah Broadcasting Company to apply. Although appearing on behalf of Taylor, Tolboe testified that he would aid whichever applicant was successful. Shields' application was denied, and the FCC issued a construction permit to Taylor in September 1947, to build KNEU.[231]

In July 1947, brothers Frank A. and Harold E. Van Wagenen applied for a third station in Provo, under the name of the Central Utah Broadcasting

---

231   Federal Communications Commission, Washington, D.C., Testimony of Clifton A. Tolboe, In re Applications of Dan B. Shields, D/B as Utah Valley Broadcasting Company, and Lester R. Taylor TR/ as Mid-Utah Broadcasting Company, Provo, Utah, Docket Nos. 7571 and 7572, July 25, 1946, 200. National Archives, Washington, D.C., Record Group 173, Box 20.

Company. Their father, Alma Van Wagenen, founded Utah Valley's first automobile dealership in 1909, for Buick, having been in the carriage business since 1898. He had served as mayor of Provo and, at the time his sons applied for a Provo station, was president of Van Wagenen Investment Company, founded in 1921.

Prior to going into the U.S. Navy in 1944, Frank Van Wagenen managed the Van Wagenen Investment Company and was responsible for all the advertising and marketing of fruit crops from farms owned by the company. Harold had worked for Utah Power and Light, the Coca Cola Bottling Company and Geneva Steel. Because there was no competing application to Central Utah Broadcasting Company's application, a construction permit was quickly granted, and KCSU went on the air in November 1947, two years before KNEU did, even though that application was filed long before the one for KCSU.

When KNEU and KCSU were proposed shortly after the war, Tolboe testified that he was not concerned with the competition they would have with KOVO. Yet, by 1948, he had become concerned enough to call Madsen at IMN, to ask him to once again return to manage KOVO. With KCSU on the air and KNEU about to open, Tolboe needed somebody who could keep KOVO competitive. Madsen accepted Tolboe's offer and resumed where he left off, trying to attract national and regional advertisers to KOVO.

At that time, the large national retail chains, like Sears, only advertised in newspapers. They had "printers' ink in their veins," according to Madsen. He courted the local Sears manager with little success, until he tempted him with free advertising time. Madsen offered Sears $600 a month of free air time on KOVO for a period of three months. But, there was a condition: In return, Sears had to feature exclusive items in its radio advertising – items that were not advertised at the same time in the newspaper. Sears also had to keep track of the sale of the products that were exclusively advertised on KOVO. Madsen related that the campaign was a huge success, and, when the results were shown to Sears's executives in Chicago, the local Sears manager was given permission to make radio buys in Provo as he saw fit. One can only imagine what Madsen would have accomplished in the age of social media, given his savvy of tracking engagement through radio. This really was a smart strategy. It also shows that what people think is new in marketing and promotion actually has an historical counterpart or parallel in early radio.

A similar situation happened with other regional and national clients. Tolboe related that:[232]

> [Arch] and I went to San Francisco and called on a couple of clients down there. We called on Folgers and tried to get them to go radio. They said, "We've never spent a dime on radio. We don't know whether that's good sense or not." So Arch gave them a pep talk ... and they gave [him] a contract for six months. They've never been off [radio] since. ... And today they are one of the biggest producers of coffee. I don't think Arch has ever had a cup of coffee in his life. ... [Yet he] brought that client in.

During this time, Madsen also became the Utah state membership chair for the Broadcast Advertising Bureau (BAB), a national association established to promote both radio and television as viable advertising media. As a result of his success in attracting national advertisers, like Sears and Folgers, to radio, and in signing up Utah stations as members of BAB, Madsen was made a board member and later was offered a job at BAB in New York. In 1953, he left KOVO and Center Street. in Provo for BAB and Madison Avenue in New York.

Tolboe looks to expand his broadcasting holdings

In 1953, even before Madsen left KOVO for New York City, Tolboe was investigating the feasibility of starting a television station in Provo. The FCC's four-year freeze on television licenses had been lifted, and, in its Table of Assignments released on April 14, 1952, the Commission had assigned Channels 11, 22 and 28 to Provo. Tolboe and KLO's Abe Glasmann had been friends and IMN business associates for over a decade, and they began discussing a television partnership to apply for Channel 11. But Tolboe

---

232   Tolboe, interview with Tim Larson, 7.

decided he didn't want to get into a broadcasting partnership:[233]

> I was more interested in the construction business because I made
> more money that way than in the broadcasting end. Abe was fair
> with me. ... I always had good relations with him and I never had
> occasion to question him. ... He was a sharp dealer. ... [But] I've been
> very successful with the construction business, and there was no use
> getting mixed up in something [like television] as part owner.

On May 25, 1953, however, Tolboe did apply for a television station on his
own, without Glasmann as a partner. Another application was filed on June 4,
by the Van Wagenen Brothers, doing business as Central Utah Broadcasting,
Inc., operators of KCSU radio, and Tolboe's competitor in Provo. Tolboe
explained his rationale:[234]

> [So] I applied for television. I figured that if I had a TV station in
> Provo, maybe it would work and maybe it wouldn't. ... [But] the more
> I studied it, the more I could see it wouldn't work because, in the
> meantime, [Glasmann] bought Frank Carman out [of KUTV] and I
> thought, "Well, that took the only network that was available at the
> time, so I just dropped it." ... The other fellow was granted the station
> in Provo ... but he went broke almost before he started. ... It's the
> [station] that BYU took over. ... It became the Channel 11, [KBYU].

An interesting development occurred in 1957, several years after Tolboe
applied but then decided not to pursue a television station in Provo. Samuel B.
Nissley's Beehive Telecasting Corporation applied for Channel 11 in that city.
At about the same time, as mentioned earlier, he also applied for a television
station in Cedar City. Beehive never successfully established television in either
Provo or Cedar City. Channel 11 in Provo, originally a commercial station, was
made a non-commercial channel, and, in 1965, the Church of Jesus Christ of
Latter-day Saints obtained a license and eventually put the public broadcasting
affiliate KBYU on that channel.

---

233   Tolboe, interview with Tim Larson, 14.
234   Tolboe, interview with Tim Larson, 14.

In 1954, after Madsen left for New York City, Tolboe made L. H. Curtis general and commercial manager of KOVO, and he operated it without much change for the next two years. In 1956, Ashly Robison and Glenn Shaw offered to buy KOVO for $130,000, and, in October, Tolboe accepted. Robison was an entrepreneur from Sacramento, California, and Shaw was the commercial manager at KDYL in Salt Lake City. They met in the 1940s when Robison was promoting television in Sacramento and Shaw was managing a radio station in Oakland.

Shaw began in Utah broadcasting in the early 1930s at KLO in Ogden. While working at an ice cream company, he would read "Farm Flashes" on Glade's KLO. In 1933, Glade hired Shaw as an announcer on KSL. Like many KSL employees of the 1930s, Shaw first worked for Glade's Radio Broadcasters, Inc. (RBI), and only later for KSL, after Glade was no longer manager of the station. In 1943, Shaw went to Oakland, California, to be station manager of KLX, the *Oakland Tribune* owned station in that city. After ten years in that position, he was called into the office of Russell Noland, his boss, and son of Joseph R. Noland, publisher of the *Tribune*, and fired for trivial reasons.

In 1954, after being out of broadcasting for a year or so, Shaw took a job with Ashley Robison in Sacramento, California, to help him promote UHF television in northern California. They were unsuccessful at it because few people had television receivers, and fewer yet had receivers that could pick up UHF television channels. Shaw soon came back to Salt Lake City to be vice president and station manager of KDYL-AM, under General Manager G. Bennett Larson and Time-Life, Inc.

In the meantime, Robison struck a deal with Tolboe to buy KOVO and persuaded Shaw to join him. Robison owned all the station assets by himself, and held 75% of another company, KOVO, Inc., holder only of the KOVO operating license. Shaw owned the other 25% of KOVO, Inc. When they assumed ownership of KOVO on October 1, 1956, Robison became president, Shaw became executive vice president and general manager, and L. H. Curtis became commercial manager. Robison never moved to Provo and wasn't involved in day-to-day operations. Other employees included program director Don Spainhower, promotion manager Russ Grange, and chief engineer, Leland K. Davies.

Shaw eventually came to own a 50% share of the entire assets of the station, but he and Robison reportedly never really had a compatible or harmonious business partnership. Nevertheless, they owned and operated KOVO for 18 years, until in 1974, Shaw left and the station was put up for sale. In March 1976, KOVO was sold to First Media Corporation, a subsidiary of the Marriott Corporation. There was a court battle, and, as a result, Robison and Shaw did not finally make a settlement on KOVO until the early 1980s.[235]

Madsen's resilient career

Madsen's career, after leaving KOVO in 1954, had some dips, but he eventually landed on top. When television became competitive with radio, the Broadcast Advertising Bureau's name was changed from BAB to RAB, or the Radio Advertising Bureau, and Madsen continued with that association until 1956, when he left for a job with *Sponsor* magazine. Within a year, he took a job at WLS in Chicago and, after only a short time, was fired for reasons that were complex and political, even though, according to Madsen, he was doing the job asked of him.

After being out of work for several months, Madsen became financially strapped and psychologically demoralized:[236]

> It's a terribly demoralizing experience [to be out of work]. After a while you begin to think you have no capabilities or worth that you'll never get an opportunity to do what you'd like to do.

Ward Quaal, president of Chicago's WGN, came to Madsen's rescue in 1958 and recommended him to Lester W. Lindow, executive director of the

---

235   Glenn C. Shaw, interview with Tim Larson, February 28, 1996, Provo, Utah.
236   Madsen, interview with Tim Larson September 9, 1986. 112.

Association of Maximum Service Telecasters (AMST) in Washington, D.C. AMST was an association of independent television stations nationwide that became involved in the struggle for spectrum space, and the best allocation of television channels for both government and private users. He traveled extensively for three years lobbying and making presentations on behalf of AMST.

In January 1961, Madsen was asked by Church of Jesus Christ of Latter Day Saints President David O. McKay to come back to Salt Lake City as president of KSL. After meeting with Tolboe in the Alta Club and getting his counsel, Madsen accepted McKay's offer. When Bonneville International Corporation (BIC) was established three years later as the holding company for the LDS Church's radio and television properties, Madsen became its first president. As BIC President, Madsen significantly expanded and increased the value of the LDS Church's electronic media properties nationwide. After BIC purchased an international shortwave station, Madsen also became immensely influential on the world-broadcasting scene, with membership on the boards of several international broadcasting organizations. In venues around the world, Madsen spoke with conviction and confidence about democracy, free speech and free markets.

In 1986, Madsen was replaced as BIC President and made President Emeritus of BIC, followed by a short time as manager of Temple Square. After retirement, he was appointed by President Reagan to the Board of International Broadcasting, and he refocused his attention on such organizations as Radio Free Europe/Radio Liberty and the Cuban aimed Radio Marti U.S. international stations. Madsen was inducted into the Utah Broadcasters Association Hall of Fame and a recipient of the Peabody Award, the Distinguished Service Award from the National Association of Broadcasters, and the "Giant in Our City" award from the Salt Lake Area Chamber of Commerce. Madsen died on April 7, 1997.

And, what about Tolboe? His Harlan and Tolboe Construction Company built many industrial and school buildings throughout the state, including the Marriott Library on The University of Utah campus. After he retired, he and his wife, Eunice, divided their time between residences in Salt Lake City and Palm Springs, California. Clifton A. Tolboe died February 16, 1990.

KOVO was the last of the pioneer radio broadcasting stations to go on the air in the late 1930s. WWII intervened and no Utah new radio applications were tendered until KNAK and KALL in the mid-1940s, which are covered in the next two chapters.

CHAPTER 13

KNAK: SALT LAKE CITY

On February 6, 1940, before the U.S. entered World War II, Howard D. Johnson, his wife Lucille, and members of her family officially incorporated Granite District Radio Broadcasting (GDRB). Johnson earlier had filed for an FCC license to construct KNAK AM, Salt Lake City's fourth radio station at 1400kc. Lawrence A. Miner, Lucille Johnson's father and a lawyer, originally became president of GDRB, and Lucille became vice president. Miner died in 1941, and Johnson became president of the corporation. Due to WWII restrictions on scarce resources, the FCC dismissed Johnson's KNAK application without prejudice in August 1942, but on March 27, 1944, he resubmitted it. A construction permit was conditionally granted for KNAK on September 12, pending approval by the War Production Board for the use of critical wartime materials and labor to construct the station.

Born September 4, 1910, in Richfield, Utah, Johnson, at age 11 in 1921, built his first radio receiver and listened to the Kansas City Nighthawks on KDKA out of Pittsburgh, a year before KSL and KDYL would go on the air in Salt Lake City. He attended the Brigham Young Academy in Provo, and went to schools in Roosevelt, Parowan and Salt Lake City, finally graduating from the LDS High School in Salt Lake. He went on an LDS Church mission to the East Central States but came back after six months, with a diabetes condition. Howard married Lucille Miner on August 23, 1933, the same day he took the test for his FCC First Class Operators License. He went to BYU and then to Utah State University, graduating in 1936, with a degree in electro-physics and a minor in mathematics. While at USU, he operated a radio repair business to pay expenses.

Later in 1936 Johnson took a job as a meteorologist with the U.S. Department of Commerce in Salt Lake City. For the next five years, among other things, he analyzed atmospheric conditions for the U.S. Weather Service, using radio sound. During WWII while at the Weather Service, Johnson tried several times to get into radio work in the Armed Forces. He even was offered two commissions but could not get a release from his government work with the weather service. However, on the basis of his electronics training and knowledge of radio, Johnson was sent to Washington, D.C. for a time to work on a device called the ceilometer, an instrument used to measure cloud heights (i.e., ceilings). The device used radio sound to measure weather conditions, without having to send instruments aloft in balloons, as was previously done. While in Washington, D. C., he also did some work with the McNary and Wrathall Engineering Company. Grant Wrathall, with whom he had worked engineering KOVO in Provo, was his brother-in-law. Johnson was sent to Seattle to continue work for the weather service, doing radio sound experimentation. The work was classified because Johnson was working on a device to monitor the sky for balloons containing bombs sent to the U. S. by the Japanese, which rode along the winds of the jet stream.

In 1944, Johnson moved back to Salt Lake City from Seattle to build KNAK. Because of the War Production Board's limit of $250 on the use of new equipment and critical labor, Johnson built the KNAK equipment using used or surplus components. When the government inspected KNAK prior to its going on-the-air, it found that Johnson had spent a total of only $55 for new equipment to construct KNAK, and that was for copper wire needed for the AM tower grounding system.

For labor to construct the tower, Johnson used friends and relatives, including Postmaster I. A. Smoot, who also was a stockholder in Granite District Radio Broadcasting. The group of novices constructed the tower by starting with the top section and adding lower sections to it, pushing the tower up from the bottom using a gin, much like Leland Perry did with his KSUB tower, but with more immediate success. John M. Baldwin, KDYL's chief engineer, conducted the antenna measurements for the KNAK tower after it was constructed and found them to be true. The tower, constructed in 1944, stood in use for more than 40 years.

In early 1945, there was no electrical power available to run KNAK, so Johnson rented a generator for the station's premiere broadcast. scheduled for February 11, 1945. Also, there was no telephone service, so Johnson employed an indirect scheme involving the use of the police communication system. Because he had acquired all the necessary components for the station and built it by hand, Johnson was granted FCC and War Production Board permission to put KNAK on the air, five years after his original application and just months before the war ended on September 2. KNAK became the only Utah radio broadcasting station to go on the air during World War II:[237]

> **NEW S.L. RADIO SLATES PREMIERE FOR SUNDAY**
> Featuring three hours of continuous entertainment in its first broadcast, KNAK a new Salt Lake City radio station, will present its premiere program Sunday [2/11/45] at 7 p.m. The opening broadcast will include an address by Mayor Earl J. Glade. Allen LeRoy will act as master of ceremonies on the station, which will include recordings from a new library of transcriptions. The station located at 1400 kilocycles on the radio dial, will operate from 7 a.m. to 10 p.m. daily beginning Monday. The 250 watt station will deliver a clear signal throughout Salt Lake valley.

The announcement included other details:[238]

> Howard R. Johnson is president of the company and builder of the transmitter, situated at 1016 S. 6th West St. He made application for the franchise to operate a fourth station in Salt Lake five years ago. Other officers are L.M. Johnson, vice president, and Francis W. Schaelling secretary treasurer, R.K. Christensen, who has had extensive radio experience in WDC, has been appointed program director. Stockholders include C. Nello, Westover, Otto Fisher, Mrs. L.A. Miner and Paul Q. Callister.

---

237 Salt Lake Telegram, February 10, 1945, 9.
238 Ibid.

But the premiere did not go as planned. February 11 arrived, but the KNAK transmitter did not respond, so the inaugural broadcast was scratched. KNAK apologized three days later for the delay:[239]

> APOLOGIES TO 100,000 GUESTS
> Apologies for technical difficulties.
> Sorry to have disappointed you Sunday evening, --because of technical difficulties— we could not present our Premiere Program as advertised. But KNAK is now [2/14/45] on the air --daily 7 a.m. to 10 p.m.-- with the finest in music and latest in news.

In March, a month after it went on the air, KNAK's transmitting power was increased from 250 to 500 watts, giving it a wider coverage area, and its frequency was changed from 1400 to 1280kc, which has remained as the operating frequency to the present, albeit with a different call sign.

At KNAK in 1945, among the first staff members were Lee Walker, Larry Sutton, Tommy Greenhowe, Cliff Owen and Commercial Manager Vern Bruggeman. Bruggeman came over from KUTA and remembered the facilities in the first few months at KNAK:[240]

> An old house ... they just went into [it] and wired things up with literally bailing wire. ... I made more decisions about that station than Howard did. ... I moved them from an old house down on about Seventh West to the Continental Bank Building [downtown] ... the annex actually ... because it was a little more appropriate for them. ... Not the greatest in the world but it was better than what they had.

KNAK's post-war years and programming

KNAK did not have a network affiliation when it premiered. Four other Utah stations had already captured the four major radio networks: NBC, CBS, ABC and Mutual:[241]

---

239   Salt Lake Telegram, February 14, 1945, 7.
240   Vern Bruggeman, interview with Tim Larson, August 25, 1989, Salt Lake City, Utah.
241   Deseret News, September 13, 1945, 18.

[But] KNAK joined a new broadcasting network, the "Associated
Broadcasting Corporation" [ABC] for its inaugural program on
September 16, 1945. The new network was headquartered in Grand
Rapids, Michigan, with program origination from Hollywood,
Chicago, New York and Washington, D.C. Governor Herbert B. Maw
and Mayor Earl J. Glade participated locally from KNAK studios
located at 219 Continental Bank Bldg.

This was a time of confusing acronyms, which merits a brief description.
The Associated Broadcasting Corporation (ABC) made its coast-to-coast
debut from its WWDC affiliate in Washington, D.C, one of its 22 affiliates,
including KNAK in Salt Lake City. ABC had a legal conflict with the American
Broadcasting Company, which had begun network operations in 1943. Both
identified as "ABC." Associated changed its name in December 1945, to the
Associated Broadcasting System (ABS), to avoid confusion but even then, the
ABS experience was a short-lived one.[242]

On January 11, 1946. Richard Connor, vice-president of operations for
the Associated Broadcasting System visited KNAK. His visit reportedly was
to conduct routine ABS business, but he and Johnson likely also attended to
some KNAK business. On February 1, 1946, a year to the month after the
station opened, Richard F. Connor acquired an interest in Granite District
Broadcasting Company and KNAK, and assumed the general manager
position. Connor fortuitously left Associated Broadcasting System employment
before it ended operations on April 28, 1946, just three months after he left
ABS for KNAK.

Connor entered the radio business at station KMIC (KRKD) in
Inglewood, California, and later worked at KMTR in Hollywood and KMPC in
Beverly Hills, California. In 1937, Connor had opened the R.F. Connor Radio
Advertising Agency. In addition to his agency work, he did a program called
"Affairs of State" for the Don Lee Network. When the U.S. entered World
War II in December 1941, Connor directed the Pacific Coast Emergency
Plan of Combined Networks and Independent Stations for the Western

---

242   ABS. See https://www.oldradio.com/archives/prog/nets.htm

Defense Command. In December 1942, he moved to Washington, D.C., and became Chief of Station Relations for the Radio Division of the U. S. Office of War Information. Beginning in March 1943, Connor was at the Mutual Broadcasting System in New York as director of station relations, and then at the Associated Broadcasting System in Grand Rapids, Michigan, for a time.[243]

In March 1947, King Harmon left KUTA and joined KNAK as an announcer and had a few shares of GDRB. He became sports editor and was touted as a human sports encyclopedia. He interviewed many famous sports personalities and reportedly took great delight in stumping the sports fans with his "Sports Question" on his early evening sports review.

By 1948, the now-independent KNAK "specialized" in music, as emceed by its station's personalities. There was Ray Noll, or "Cousin Ray," who had a two and one-half hour daily western music program. Noll came to KNAK from southern California where he was heard on the Mutual Don Lee network. Al Collins, or "Jazzbo," a jazz stylist and impresario had a two-hour daily stint each afternoon. He came over to KNAK from KALL (which is discussed in the next chapter). Bruce Vanderhood, a big jolly fellow, was the morning "waker-upper." He entertained his listeners with zany antics and was touted as the "world's biggest disc jockey." Eldon Walton, from Salt Lake City, entertained "night owl" listeners with everything from symphony to Spike Jones. He came to KNAK as an announcer immediately after he was discharged from the military in November 1945.[244]

Local programming and news evolved over the following year. Tom Ivory, KNAK's news editor, posted worldwide and local happenings and lent a hand to special events and sports activities. Other programs included the Swingettes live every Saturday night at the rustic Old Mill; Dewey's Café over KNAK from 11 to 11:15 weekdays; amateur contests every Sunday 9:45 p.m. at the Clover Club; morning news from 7:45 to 8 a.m. each morning, 9:45 each evening, and on-the-hour 10 to 12 p.m. every Saturday night; news flashes in conjunction with the *Deseret News*; swap sales; and Pioneer League Salt Lake Bees baseball;

---

243   Deseret News, January 28, 1946, 16.
244   Salt Lake Tribune, November 14, 1948, 72.

and much transcribed music.

The Johnsons controlled about 34% of the common stock of Granite District Radio Broadcasting. And, after opening KNAK, Howard managed it for about a year. He then became more involved in engineering other radio stations. Besides KNAK, Johnson was the engineer and, sometimes, part owner of some 20 stations in the Intermountain West, several of them in Utah.

KNAK's golden era of rock 'n' roll

In the 1950s, KNAK was promoted as "Salt Lake's 24-Hour Independent Station." KNAK fostered a group of popular disk jockeys who were playing the most listened to music of the day, including rock 'n' roll. In 1957, people awoke six days a week to Will Wright playing the Top-30 records on his "Wright Side of the Day" show; "Waxin Wayne" Logan was next in mid-morning; Mel Remy on "The Mel Remy Show" played popular records and interviewed artists on his mid-day show; and, Bill Hesterman, with "Hestermania," came on at 6 p.m. each evening. Hesterman also entertained at KNAK's weekly *Record Hops*. Joe Lee, who started at KOVO, was KNAK's 24-hour-a-day, it seemed, newsman and announcer. He did live news five minutes before every hour, six days a week and, otherwise, supervised KNAK's news broadcasts each hour around the clock. [245]

KNAK was a powerhouse rock 'n' roll station. In the 1960s and 1970s, disc jockeys such as Lynn Lehmann, Gary "Wooly" Waldron, Skinny Johnny Mitchell, Sleepy Gene Davis, Ray Graham, Chad O. Stevens, Big Daddy Hesterman, Michael G. Kavanagh, Johnny Rider and Jordon reigned. Several of these jocks went over to KCPX and eventually usurped KNAK for the crown.[246]

The 1950s and 1960s were golden times for KNAK. During this time, besides featuring popular artists on radio, KNAK was involved with bringing the hottest musical groups to Utah for concert appearances. KNAK reportedly

---

245   Joe Lee, interview with Tim Larson, August 20, 1988; L. John Miner, interview with Linda Davies, February 2, 1989.
246   "Whatever happened to KNAK and KCPX?". See https://archive.sltrib.com/article.php?id=2909527&itype=CMSID

introduced The Beach Boys to Utah, live at the Lagoon Amusement Park. KNAK then introduced Utahans live to the Rolling Stones, Eric Berg and the Animals, Paul Revere and the Raiders, and the Dave Clark Five from England. In 1963, KNAK even chartered an airplane and took 50 fans to Las Vegas to see another English group, The Beatles, when they appeared at the Las Vegas Convention Center.

One interesting anecdote occurred in an evening in 1964. Howard Johnson's daughter, Shirley, used her dad's Ford Thunderbird to go to the library to study, or at least that was what she said was why she needed the car. Instead, she joined friends at a Salt Lake City drive-in for music, food and fun. Shirley was at KNAK the next day to observe a Beach Boy interview prior to their concert. Chinwag at the station revealed Shirley's deception the night before. She was grounded and Daddy literally took the T-Bird away. It was later discovered that the incident with Shirley inspired The Beach Boys' *Fun, Fun, Fun* song. She didn't know it at the time but Brian Wilson and cousin Mike Love, founder of The Beach Boys, took in the chatter about her at the station – library deceit, sans the T-Bird and all -- and on the way to the airport on their way out of town, they wrote the lyrics to *Fun, Fun, Fun*:

> *Well, she got her daddy's car*
> *And she cruised through the hamburger stand, now*
> *Seems she forgot all about the library*
> *Like she told her old man, now*
> *And with the radio blasting*
> *Goes cruising just as fast as she can now*
> [Chorus]
> *(Fun, fun, fun, 'till her daddy takes the T-bird away)*

Shirley Johnson England later relates her take on the story.[247]

> A little while later that song came out. And [I] said [at the time], 'Hey, that could be my song," And it wasn't until a few years later when

---

247   Danielle MacKimm, "ABC4.com, 'Fun, fun, fun': SLC woman inspired famous Beach Boys song," April 8, 2002. See https://www.abc4.com/news/digital-exclusives/fun-fun-fun-slc-woman-inspired-famous-beach-boy-song=.

I was attending a concert and the Beach Boys were there at the
University of Utah for the 4th of July. I opened up the program and
there was the whole story of [Brian and Mike] driving to the airport
and how the song was really written for me. I looked at that and
turned to my daughter, saying, "Oh my gosh!" … I guess it's true!'
That's how I heard about it.

KNAK's sale and ownership changes

In 1952, after serving in the military and owning two different radio
stations in northern California, L. John Miner, who was Lucille Johnson's
brother, joined KNAK as office manager. Later, after acquiring GDRB stock,
he became treasurer of the corporation. When GDRB acquired KBLI radio
and KTLE-TV in Idaho, Miner oversaw those operations and maintained
his employment at KNAK. Much later Miner divested of his GDRB stock
and purchased KDXU in St. George. Utah, and later brought stereo radio to
southern Utah with KDXU-FM.

In 1950, the Utah State Federation of Labor secured a two-year option
to buy KNAK for $200,000. This option lapsed, but a decade later, in March
1962, another group seriously negotiated with Johnson and Granite District
Broadcasting to buy KNAK. Two California corporations, Essex Productions,
Inc. and Dena Pictures, Inc., with radio interests in Seattle, Portland and
Spokane, formed a joint venture and proposed to buy KNAK for $450,000. The
backing was connected to some of the best-known celebrities of the time. The
president of Essex was singer Frank Sinatra, and the assistant vice president
was filmmaker Howard Koch. The president of Dena Pictures was entertainer
Danny Kaye. His wife, Sylvia Fine Kaye, was secretary-treasurer.[248]

Numerous local Salt Lake City business operators and citizens protested
the proposed sale of KNAK to Essex and Dena or, as they called it, a sale to
"outside individuals." The protestors wrote to the FCC asking the Commission

---

248   Federal Communications Commission, Washington, D.C., Application for Consent to
Assignment of Radio Broadcast Station License, Granite District Radio Broadcasting Company
to Essex Productions, Inc. and Dena Pictures, Inc., a joint venture, d/b as Seattle, Portland and
Spokane Radio, January 25, 1962.

to intervene to stop the sale. One letter-writer even wanted the opportunity to put together a local group to buy the station. The major complaint of most protestors, however, was not that they hadn't been given an opportunity to buy the station, but that "it has been rumored that the prospective purchasers are business men who have gambling interest in the State of Nevada."[249]

A letter from Bernice S. Hawkins, a resident of Salt Lake City, seemed to summarize the general feeling of most protestors:[250]

> It has been brought to my attention by our local papers that an outside concern is trying to buy a local radio station [KNAK]. I am very much against this outside concern coming into our community and probably bringing a type of element that rumors claim is not conducive to our way of life. We have been very happy with the local owners of KNAK and the high-type programs, advertising, etc., that is carried on their station and I would like it to stay this way. ... Please consider your decision seriously before letting this concern buy this station."

The protest sentiments were satisfied but little is known that it was the protest that changed minds. Johnson wanted to use the capital realized from the sale of KNAK to the Sinatra-Kaye group, to build and improve the other broadcast holdings of Granite District Broadcasting. He went to Las Vegas and met with Sinatra and the other Essex principals, and Kaye came to Salt Lake City to meet with the Granite District principals. It is not known what part the local protestors played, but the FCC let it be known to Johnson that it would not approve a transfer of KNAK to a group in which Frank Sinatra was involved, because of his alleged mob and racketeering affiliations. On January 28, 1963, after a year of negotiating, Johnson took KNAK off the market and requested that the FCC dismiss the application of the Sinatra-Kaye joint venture to buy the station. The FCC did so without comment.

---

249   Ray L. Richards, Letter to the Office of the Secretary, Federal Communications Commission, Washington, D.C., and May, 11, 1962.
250   Bernice S. Hawkins, Letter to the Secretary of the Federal Communications Commission, Washington, 25, D.C., May 10, 1962.

In 1962, at the same time that the Sinatra-Kaye negotiations for KNAK were being conducted, Johnson and Granite District Broadcasting ran head-on into their perennial nemesis, George Hatch. Once again, Hatch and Glasmann had more economic and political power in a situation requiring as much. Granite District held 79% of the capital voting stock of KBLI, Inc., licensee of KBLI radio in Blackfoot, and KTLE television in Pocatello, Idaho. KTLE TV, Channel 6, was an NBC affiliate, but when Hatch acquired the NBC affiliation for KUTV, Channel 2, in Salt Lake City, he convinced the network to drop Johnson's KTLE, and affiliate instead with his television station in Montana. Hatch had leverage, because not only did he have the television station in Montana, but also, as discussed later, he owned, with Bob Magness of Montana, the microwave and cable systems to deliver NBC programming to the other population centers of the state.

Johnson retained ownership of KNAK until March 1975, when he sold his interest in Granite District Broadcasting to Arthur P. Williams, after controlling the corporation for 35 years. Williams also had other broadcasting interests, including KSHO-TV in Las Vegas. Williams, from Santa Barbara, California, was married to the heir of the Signal Oil Company fortune, and that likely was a financial source. When she died, their son, Samuel Williams, became the owner of KNAK, taking over the presidency of Granite District Broadcasting from his father. The call letters were changed to KWMS and the format was switched from contemporary to all-news within a year. In 1979, KDXU's L. John Miner, former Granite District shareholder, acquired KDLT in Delta, Utah, and changed that station's call letters to KNAK, after Williams and KWMS released them.

Although Johnson owned KNAK for more than three decades, and had a 55% interest in Uintah Radio and Television, Co., licensee of KVEL, in Vernal, Utah, and came to hold a 78% interest in Southern Utah Broadcasting Company, licensee of KSUB in Cedar City, Utah, his full-time employment was not actually at any of these stations. Rather, he engineered radio stations and, from 1952 until 1970, was employed at The University of Utah as an electrical engineer and a coordinator of Army contracts. Among other things, he was involved with a project that used television to monitor the radioactive cells at the Dugway Proving Grounds, including the monitoring of the remote-controlled railroad that was operated in the cell area. During this time, he also was involved in the administration of the Junior Science Symposium supported by Duke University, the University of Utah and the U.S. Army.

As an artifact of his work with high radiation fields, Johnson made his radio colleagues and government officials aware of the effect of radiation, such as that coming from a nuclear blast, would have on the emergency broadcast system in the Intermountain area. In addition, Johnson was instrumental in getting Utah Governor Clyde's approval for state funded FM and TV translators to bring broadcast signals to rural Utah. Johnson retired from the University of Utah in 1970 and, again, directed his attention to building radio stations, this time to construction for FM broadcasting. He engineered KVEL-FM in Vernal and KSUB-FM in City Cedar City, Utah, in the mid-1970s. Finally, in 1981, with his sons, Johnson opened the last of his stations, KLVR in Heber City, Utah.

Unsurprisingly and deservedly so, Johnson was elected to the Utah Broadcasters Hall of Fame in January 1982, and was a member of the Broadcast Pioneers, and vice-chairman of the Emergency Broadcasting Service for the state of Utah. He also was a senior engineer for the Society of Broadcast Engineers, based in Washington, D.C. Johnson died at his home in East Millcreek on August 5, 1989, at 78. Lucille Johnson died on February 2, 1991, reportedly killed as a result of an intruder at her Salt Lake City suburban home.

CHAPTER 14

KALL: SALT LAKE CITY

KALL radio had its roots in KLO and the descendants of the William Glasmann family. As noted in an earlier chapter, William's son A. L. Glasmann of the Standard Corporation (*Oden Standard Examiner*) in the 1930s acquired KLO, one of Utah's three 1920s enduring pioneer radio broadcasting stations. In 1940, with his son-in-law George Hatch, Glasmann expanded KLO's influence throughout the Intermountain Region by expanding the Intermountain Network (IMN), to disseminate regional news. In 1945, Hatch/Glasmann and Abrelia Clarissa Hinckley put KALL radio on the air in Salt Lake City. KALL soon became the IMN flagship station, with KLO also being an important station in the network.

The story of KALL radio is nuanced and cannot be fully appreciated without a brief history of the William Glasmann family and its involvement and contributions to Utah print and electronic media, dating to the 1880s. William Glasmann moved to Utah from Iowa in the 1880s. Known as "The Bald Eagle of the Wasatch," William Glasmann manufactured leather harnesses and operated the Glasmann Ranch and roadside inn at the south end of the Great Salt Lake near Black Rock. The bison he raised on the ranch were said to have stampeded to Antelope Island in 1892, across a sandbar formed by a violent windstorm. The animal descendants of the bison reportedly still live there today. Glasmann went north to Ogden in 1892 to become an editor for Frank J. Cannon's *The Standard Newspaper* and later took control of the newspaper. Glasmann, a Republican, except in 1912 when he supported Bull Moose candidate Theodore Roosevelt, served three terms as mayor of Ogden and as speaker of the Utah House.

William and his wife, Evelyn, had five children. Their oldest child was Ethel, followed by four sons, Roscoe (Ross), Abraham (Abe), William (Bill) and Blaine. When Glasmann died unexpectedly in 1916, his wife took over management of the newspaper, and son Abe succeeded his father as editor. On April 1, 1920, two Ogden newspapers joined to form the *Standard-Examiner*. In the decades after World War I, Ross and Bill managed other Glasmann family investments, including its movie theater interests, while Blaine managed the classified advertising department at the *Standard-Examiner*. Ethel Glasmann Clark was program director at KLO at the time of her death in 1943. Ross and Bill died 20 days apart in 1964.[251]

In 1934, Abe Glasmann completed the purchase of KLO from Earl J. Glade and other minority owners. The history of KLO was related in a previous chapter, so the story now moves to the Glasmann family and the Standard Corporation's other post-WWII electronic media investments beginning with KALL in 1945.

The origins of KALL

KALL radio was the first of many entrepreneurial telecommunications businesses that The Standard Corporation invested in during the three decades after World War II. Others included radio stations in Montana, Idaho and Hawaii; television stations in Utah and Hawaii; cable and microwave systems in several Western states; and a closed-circuit television equipment manufacturing plant with offices in cities around the world.

The history of these media enterprises parallels the story of the entrepreneurial efforts of George Clinton Hatch. Born in Pennsylvania, and educated in California, Hatch came to Utah in 1945, with Wilda Gene,

---

251   This information was synthesized from Joseph F. Breeze and Wilda Gene Hatch, "A Pioneer in Communications: The History of the Ogden Standard-Examiner and the "Electronic Advancements of The Standard Corporation," April, 27, 1972. The story of The Standard Corporation prepared for the members and friends of The Newcomen Society of North America, which honored the Ogden Standard-Examiner at a dinner held in Ogden, Utah, on April 27, 1972, when Mrs. Wilda Gene Hatch, President, and Mr. Joseph F. Breeze, Executive Vice President, were the guest of honor and speakers.

his wife of five years who was the daughter of Abe Glasmann. Gene, as she was called, succeeded her grandmother, Evelyn, as president of The Standard Corporation, which included newspaper, radio and later TV broadcast holdings. George Hatch would become vice president of the Standard Corporation.

Besides business partners, the Hatches, while greatly involved in the community, over decades were ardent supporters of Utah's wild lands. They helped to create the Antelope Island State Park (1969), to elevate Capital Reef (1971) and Arches (1971), from national monuments to national parks, and to expand the Glen Canyon National Recreation Area (1972), among other Utah civic-minded commitments.

A political activist, free speech advocate and environmental steward, Hatch was described by his family as a fervent supporter of Utah higher education. To wit: his 14-year membership (1969-1983) on the Utah State Board of Regents, where he served three years as chair.

A media visionary, Hatch was hard driving and unceasingly attentive to corporate matters. He parlayed his KLO and KALL beginnings into a communication empire that spanned several decades and included financial investments that exhibited extraordinary talent and focus. John W. (Jack) Gallivan, *Salt Lake Tribune* publisher (1960-1984) and Kearns Tribune Corporation president and CEO (1960-1997), described Hatch, often a media partner, as "one of the most intense business personalities he ever met." Hatch, however, didn't micromanage day-to-day operations in his media holdings. Homer Peterson, longtime KALL manager and executive vice president (1957-1990) endorsed Hatch's administrative style and said Hatch attended to "his corporate things and whatever he [was] involved in up there," and for the most part left station operations to him. Only on occasion, he humorously relates, Hatch "drove me up the wall" with his involvement. Jeffery, a Hatch son and KUTV-TV president and general manager (1989-1996), said although his dad in business matters had a "sharp pencil," he was "very future oriented and very hard driving in terms of working toward the things he wanted to achieve." Hatch had a ubiquitous presence for decades in Utah and Intermountain West radio, television and cable, but his daughter, Diane Orr, agreed with the consensus that her dad was a "behind the scenes person."

KALL radio was one of a very few stations in the U.S. to obtain a construction permit during WWII, when the federal War Production Board controlled strategic materials needed to construct a radio station. In 1944, the FCC held a hearing on the application submitted by Hatch and Abrelia Hinckley for KALL radio in Salt Lake. At the hearing, an FCC engineer recommended denying the application because of an interference problem, but FCC Chairman James Fly put aside the engineer's objection. FCC Commissioner Rosel Hyde, who later was very helpful to KSL in its television application, then objected to KALL's application because he said it was against FCC policy to grant approval of an application that required the use of strategic materials during the war. Hyde argued that if KALL's application was granted, others, whose applications were denied, should then be reconsidered. Chairman Fly also put aside Hyde's objections and called for a vote by all the Commissioners on the KALL application. It was approved.

Not very long after this vote, on November 6, 1944, James Fly resigned from the FCC, and Paul Porter became chairman. Hyde then went to Porter to again raise his objections to KALL's application. Porter seemingly told Hyde not to worry, that the War Production Board (WPB) would very likely deny Hatch and Hinckley's application for strategic materials, and that it would subsequently be sent back to the FCC for reconsideration. As Porter predicted, the WPB staff recommended against the grant of a construction permit for KALL.

In the meantime, however, in response to a call from the White House on behalf of the KALL applicants, Chairman Julius A. Krug of the War Production Board overruled his staff's recommendation and approved the use of the materials and equipment needed to construct the station. The KALL applicants overcame one final hurdle when they satisfied some objections of the Civil Aeronautics Authority concerned with the placement of towers and such.[252]

Robert Hinckley was a silent partner applicant for KALL, along with his wife, Abrelia, and Hatch. Hinckley was well placed in the Roosevelt administration and was particularly close to Truman because of the support given him as Roosevelt's vice-presidential running mate in 1944. Hinckley had known Truman since 1935 as one of Missouri's U.S. senators. The White House intervened on behalf of the Hatch/Hinckley KALL application as a favor to Hinckley, despite the policy that rationed strategic materials during wartime.

An understanding of how Hinckley came to be a friend of presidents is helpful. Hinckley was born on June 8, 1891, in Fillmore, Utah, and grew up in Provo. He attended the Brigham Young Academy, beginning at age five, and his kindergarten teacher was Ida Smoot Dusenberry, the sister of Republican Senator Reed Smoot. In 1915, Hinckley married Abrelia Seely, daughter of John H. Seely, and a cattle and sheep rancher in Mt. Pleasant, Utah. Hinckley became a high school teacher and, with his brother in law, Leonard Seely, established the Seely-Hinckley Automobile Company. The family would be engaged in the auto business in Utah for the next 70 years, even as Hinckley moved to Washington, D.C. and worked for the Roosevelt and Truman administrations in the decades to come.[253]

In 1918, at the age of 27, Hinckley, a Democrat, was elected to the Utah legislature from Sanpete County.[254]

> I moved into the Hotel Utah, where legislators were given a
> special rate. Throughout that session I was known as the "baby"
> of the legislature because of my youth, and I soon drew attention
> to my liberal views when I voted against the anti-cigarette
> bill, which became law in the next legislative session but was

252   Ernest L. Wilkinson, Letter to Ivor Sharp, KSL Radio, August 31, 1946.
253   Wiki: Robert Hinckley: https://en.wikipedia.org/wiki/Robert_H._Hinckley.
254   Charles Redd Monographs in Western History, No. 7, "I'd Rather be Born Lucky Than Rich:" The Autobiography of Robert H Hinckley, by Robert H. Hinckley and JoAnn Jacobsen Wells, Provo, Utah: Brigham Young University Press, 1977, 28.

subsequently repealed because of its unpopularity.

Early in the Great Depression Hinckley and others formed the "Friedenkers" group. It was a collection of "free thinkers" who met once a month to discuss what was wrong with the country. Abe Glasmann, Gene Hatch's father and publisher of the *Ogden Standard-Examiner*, was a member of the group. Although the group continued, its name was dropped after some wags wittingly changed it to the "Free Drinkers."

Hinckley's networking skills were superior. In 1933, Utah Governor Henry Blood asked Hinckley to head the federal Civil Conservation Corps (CCC) in Utah, the emergency conservation organization. In 1934, with his CCC work, Hinckley caught the attention of Harry Hopkins, President Roosevelt's assistant. Hinckley went to Washington, D.C. in 1934, to be Hopkin's assistant administrator of the Federal Emergency Relief Administration (FERA).

On May 6, 1935, the Works Progress Administration (WPA) was established and Hinckley was put in charge of Region Five, the eleven Western States. WPA workers constructed the Salt Lake and Ogden Airports. In fact, the airport in Ogden was known as the Robert H. Hinckley Field in 1942 and remained such until Harman Peery, a Republican and co-founder of KLO radio, as Ogden mayor, renamed it the Ogden-Hinckley Airport, which it remains today.

In 1938, Roosevelt created the Civil Aeronautics Authority (CAA) to regulate civil aviation. Hinckley was appointed to the CAA, and served with Edward Noble of Life-Saver candy fame. In 1943, Noble bought the NBC Blue Radio Network, and changed the name to the American Broadcasting Company (ABC). During this time, Hinckley sometimes informally dined with Hopkins and Roosevelt and reportedly enjoyed a warm friendship with the President.

Over a 15-year period, Hinckley served both Roosevelt and Truman in a dozen important government positions, and, accordingly, he received help from both presidents' administrations. The KALL construction permit was granted on April 12, 1945, and the station was constructed during the war. Incidentally, Roosevelt died on that same day and Truman became president.

The Hinckleys sold their 50% share in KALL to the Salt Lake Tribune Publishing Company in 1946, when John Fitzpatrick, publisher of the *Tribune*, sold the newspaper's interest in KSL, acquired in 1925, and joined the Hatch/Glasmann family to own the station. Hinckley successfully had fostered the KALL applicant's efforts to build a radio station during wartime and then went on to other matters.

On January 23, 1946, three months after KALL went on the air, Hinckley joined Noble as vice president in charge of Washington operations for ABC and as a member of its board of directors. Nine days later, Hinckley joined Noble to help him found the ABC Television Network.

As an aside, KALL wasn't the only Utah broadcasting station that benefited from political influence in high places, however. In a later chapter, the story of KSL's television application will be told in greater detail. The point for this discussion is that KSL applied for a television permit, while another Salt Lake company also was about to apply. KSL's political friends in high places convinced the FCC to consider twelve applications in a single day instead of its normal three. As such, KSL's FCC application, which was thirteenth on the list to be considered, was approved in two days, preempting any competing applicants such as Howard Johnson's Granite District Broadcasting for Channel 5 in Salt Lake.

KALL builds its operations

KALL 910, which became Utah's 10th pioneer AM radio broadcasting station, was issued an official FCC license on January 21, 1946, although with FCC approval it had been on the air since the previous September.

Before KALL actually went on the air, Hatch, the general manager, hired Alvin G. Pack to be its first station manager. Prior to coming to KALL, Pack had been employed at KDYL under Fox and was known to have good management and creative abilities.

Hatch assigned Pack the task of buying equipment, hiring staff, developing programming and establishing overall station policy. For promotional reasons, Pack attempted to get the station on the air before the end of the war, but was thwarted because equipment was scarce and staff was difficult to find and train during the war. But on September 30, 1945, immediately after the war ended, KALL went on the air. Ruth Hansen Hale, sister to Pack's wife Lena Marie, gave the initial sign-on announcement.

The initial KALL employees included:

> George C. Hatch, general manager
> Alvin Pack, station manager
> Thomas H. Anderson, sales manager
> Albert R. Collins (Al "Jazzbeaux" Collins), program director
> Robert Warner, promotion director
> Stanley Benson, chief engineer

To compete against KDYL and KSL, Pack employed a three-pronged programming strategy: news, music and sports. For news, Pack brought Jack Goodman over from the *Salt Lake Tribune* and made him news director. Goodman only recently had come from New York and a newspaper background. Originally, he was the only one in news, so he also was the news writer and editor. Actually, Goodman worked at both KALL and the *Tribune*, as there were some overlapping assignments.

Although Goodman eventually married the niece of Utah industrialist, Joseph Rosenblatt, he humorously related that the main reason he came to Salt Lake was because his garage rent in New York was too high. Because of the war, house rents were frozen in New York, but garages weren't subject to the price freeze. While keeping Goodman's house rent stable, his New York landlord continuously raised the garage rent, forcing Goodman to move out, he said.[255]

Pack launched the musical leg of his programming strategy by hiring Al "Jazzbeaux" Collins as Program Director. Pack relates:[256]

> He [Jazzbeaux Collins] was about five feet six inches tall and almost [that] broad. But talk --this fellow had a flow of language; you could never stump him. His self-effacement --he didn't lack in that, but his ability to put himself into a situation was almost perfect. He had pizzazz, he had presence, everything.

Collins was one of the nation's first DJs playing jazz music on radio and it happened to be in SLC. He creatively made jazz music accessible by conducting Man-on-the-Street interviews that became popular with KALL listeners. He described a favorite stunt that sprung from Pack's Man on the Street instigation:[257]

> [Regarding] the Man on the Street Show, from the second floor they hung a microphone down and onto the sidewalk. And I [Jazzbeaux] would take it and start broadcasting from there. But I noticed that every time I started a broadcast with that microphone, everybody would run away [knowing I was going to air Jazz music,] and go on the other side of the street. So, one day I ... took a blanket out of my car and put it down on the sidewalk, and I stretched out like I was either dead or unconscious. Pretty soon there were about twenty people standing around, and Nephi Sorenson, who was the engineer, gave me the sign, and I jumped up and I had a ready-made audience, and they never left after

---

255   Jack Goodman, interview with Roy Gibson and Tim Larson, August 29, 1996.
256   Alvin G. and Lena Marie Pack interview with Tim Larson, Everett L. Cooley Oral History Project, Tape No. U-612 through U-619; U-679 through U-682, September 4, October 6, December 3, 4, 10, 1986; January 27, February 3, 10, 1987. 249
257   "All Too Rare: The Rise and Fall of Jazz DJs on Utah Am Radio, 1945-1965." Utah Historical Quarterly, Vol. 77, No. 4, 2009 by Utah State History. https://issuu.com/utah10/docs/uhq_volume77_2009_number4/s/10239085

that. I used to do it every day. Then it got to be a gag … You didn't
see guys doing that in Salt Lake at that time.

Collins began his career at KALL but later went to New York and then
to San Francisco. He lived near San Francisco and commuted to work
at a radio station in New York. In semi-retirement, Jazzbeaux, as he was
familiarly known, continued to do a jazz program at a public radio station
in the San Francisco market. Unfortunately, Collins' memorabilia and
material were destroyed in the 2008 Universal Studios fire, as were those of
hundreds of other musicians.[258]

KALL finds its niche in news, sports

In 1945, two other stations in Salt Lake City, KSL and KDYL, carried
daytime network programming, consisting mostly of soap operas and
game shows sponsored by national advertisers. Pack counter-programmed
on KALL with Jazzbeaux and other music DJs sponsored by local and
regional advertisers.

Pack then advertised nationwide for another newsman. From two
hundred applicants, he hired Paul Sullivan:[259]

> He came into that office like he had just ridden on a rodeo bull. …
> He was disheveled … his hair had a cowlick in the back … and all
> he said was, "Howdy." He looked like a scatterbrain, but [Collins
> said], … "That guy's got plenty of brains to scatter." … That did
> it … when I listened to that voice, now turned magnificent at the
> microphone, I agreed. He had plenty of brains to scatter, plus a
> savvy of current events, how to interpret them, and a voice that
> betrayed those first impressions. So we hired him on the spot.

Sullivan supposedly planned this inauspicious first meeting with
KALL with some self-protection. He felt he needed an escape, in case

---

258   Al "Jazzzbeaux" Collins, interview with Tim Larson and Gregory Thompson, Sausalito, CA,
(circa 1990).
259   Alvin G. and Lena Marie Pack, interview with Tim Larson, 248.

he didn't like the Salt Lake "corn field" he thought he was entering. To his own surprise, Sullivan became a star newsman at KALL and on the Intermountain Network.

In 1946, Daniel (Danny) Rainger, a recent discharge from the U.S. Air Force, was hired as a continuity writer at KALL for a few months until he was wooed by Fox to KDYL, for $20 more a month. He had a brilliant Salt Lake radio and television career. Rainger is also discussed in a later chapter about KDYL-TV. Gordon Crowe, another recent discharge from the military, became a KALL announcer at this time. Crowe later formed the Cooper and Crowe Advertising Agency. Mel Standage worked at KALL early on, as did Art Tucker who later went to Richfield, Utah, radio.

After a year on the air, Pack and Goodman arranged to cover the off-year election returns on KALL. On election night, crowds of people traditionally gathered at the Tribune Building window to get election returns. In addition, Pack projected election results from the fourth floor of the Tribune Building to a big screen on the Kearns Building across Main Street in downtown Salt Lake City. Loudspeakers were positioned on the outside of the building and the returns were covered on KALL in conjunction with the newspaper. The Tribune's cooperation in this effort with a radio station was unprecedented at the time and particularly important, because both major Salt Lake newspapers (the *Deseret News* being the other) saw radio stations as competitors.

For the sports leg of his programming strategy, Pack went to Theron Parmelee, a University of Utah Athletic Council member, to ask for the broadcast rights to University of Utah football and basketball. Pack's earlier requests for broadcast rights when he was at KDYL had been turned down, but KALL was now the flagship station for the Intermountain Network and, unlike KDYL, could reach the major population centers of Utah and significant parts of five surrounding states. Pack secured the rights, and Mal Wyman became the voice of University of Utah sports on KALL and was the first of a progression of popular KALL sportscasters over the years, including Bill Marcroft and Bill Riley, among others.

Possibly the most significant event in solidifying KALL's University of Utah sports image, however, happened in February 1947. The U of U basketball team was invited to the NIT tournament in New York's Madison Square Garden. It was thought to be too expensive to send Mal Wyman and a whole crew to New York, especially when the Utes were huge underdogs and not expected to go far in the tournament. Jack Paige, a Mutual Network vice president in New York, with no direct connection to Utah, was asked to hire a New York play-by-play sportscaster for KALL, for what was expected to be only a couple of games. Paige called a few of the New York sportscasters he knew – Teddy Hughsing, Harry Wismer and Red Barber — and they all had commitments. He finally persuaded WOR's Stan Lomack to do the games, under the condition that Paige would do the color. As it turned out, Lomack and Paige called game-after-game as the Utes moved through the brackets up to the championship game against Kentucky. It has been estimated that 9 out of 10 radios in the Intermountain region were tuned to KALL that night in 1947 for the championship game. The excitement catapulted KALL into a status with significant meaning for Utah listeners. Pack explained:[260]

> Utah won ... in the last minute, and KALL became the radio hero. ... Boy, we could walk up and down the streets and have people practically bow. ... Remember, this was 1947, with the centennial in Utah of the coming of the pioneers, 1847, and so this was a whale of a kickoff for Utah.

Paige had this to say:[261]

> Great team – Arnie Ferrin, Wat Misaka [nicknamed "Kilo-Wat"]. Little Wat Misaka ... fought the six-foot [plus] Dave Beard, put on an exhibition that will never be forgotten. ... [Utah] went on to win and become the NIT champions. As far as [the Utah

---

260   Alvin G. and Lena Marie Pack, interview with Tim Larson, 301.
261   Jack Paige, interview with Tim Larson, August 26, 1986. 78.

audience] was concerned, we [Lomack and Paige] had almost
done it single-handed. I never got so many wires and telephone
calls in my life, and George Hatch was ecstatic, of course."

Because it was the centennial celebration of the pioneers entering
the Salt Lake Valley, the Salt Lake City Chamber of Commerce used the
Utes' NIT success to organize a banquet to honor Utah athletes in all
sports. Wyman was involved, and Paige was invited to Salt Lake City to
be the announcer for a program called "Century of Champions." On
April 2, 1947, KALL, with Paige announcing from the LaFayette Ballroom
of the Hotel Utah, fed the Mutual and IMN Networks with a 15-minute
program, honoring Utah's athletes in several sports. Boxing champion Jack
Dempsey, cyclist Frank Thatcher, Olympic runner Alma Richards, skier
Alf Engen, world land-speed record holder Ab Jenkins, and, of course, All-
American basketball player Arnie Ferrin, were honored. Paige interviewed
Ute basketball coach Vadal Peterson along with Vern Gardner and Ferrin,
who was named most valuable player, and the show was a huge success.

Besides the sports connection, the most effective tool for KALL's
success likely was marketing promotion. Pack, with 15 years of experience
producing and selling programs with his wife, Lena Marie, and in
merchandising for Boyles Furniture and ZCMI, Utah's historic department
store, had found that contests and give-away promotions consistently
attracted audiences and sold products, especially when combined with
live audience shows and appearances by popular personalities. Third-
party promotion and endorsements in radio would set the stage later in
television, blockbuster films and the internet's social media platforms.

One KALL contest utilized the ubiquitous "Kilroy-Was-Here" theme.
KALL listeners followed clues to locate KALL's Kilroy, who travelled
between the business establishments representing KALL advertisers. After
six weeks without a contest winner, Kilroy was spotted walking across
Main Street on a high-wire attached to the J. C. Penney's Building in
downtown Salt Lake City and finally was identified. Thousands of people
reportedly were on hand for the carefully orchestrated event. Another

promotion, a spelling bee, sponsored by Dupler Furs was held live each Monday at 9 p.m., from Charlie Pincus' Utah Theater. As a movie ended, the lights would go up and KALL's popular "Jazzbeaux" personality would come on stage to host a half-hour spelling bee. Each week, people would spell relatively easy words to win $10, and more difficult words to win a fur coat. Such promotions were many and frequent and paid off handsomely for KALL.

KALL's role as media ambassador for city

KALL progressively acquired a reputation for being a station whose owners Hatch/Glasmann and the Kearns-Tribune Corporation were heart-deep in the Salt Lake City community. KALL was a great ambassador for the city and for all of Utah. In its first two years of operation, KALL received praise from more than 50 service organizations, in thanks for the contributions it made to the community. One KALL series, *The World of Tomorrow*, was particularly popular. Pack spoke at civic gatherings, informing people about the inventions of tomorrow, including touch-tone and mobile telephones, digital recordings, microwave ovens and wristwatch televisions. These talks were presented all over Utah and many western states, on behalf of KALL. After hearing Pack speak, Madsen, who was then manager of KOVO, in Provo, and an IMN vice-president wrote, "Congratulations for the marvelous talk before the Ad Club. You taught more truth in a few sentences than I've heard before. May more and more people have the opportunity of hearing you."[262]

As KALL's network image expanded, and the station became commercially successful, coverage of regional events became more prevalent, making it a major broadcast outlet for millions in the Intermountain West. For instance, KALL went to Jackson Hole, Wyoming, in 1949 to cover the dedication of Menor's Ferry, a Rockefeller project on the Snake River. The event was recorded live on "electrical transcriptions" (ETs or large records.), and they were taken to KALL for immediate airing. The use of a mobile telephone and the live recordings enhanced KALL's

---

262   Alvin G. and Lena Marie Pack, interview withTim Larson, 248.

local image in contrast to the national image of KSL and KDYL, with their network programming.

Meanwhile, in September 1949, after the NIT tournament, Hatch, then 30, went to New York to persuade Paige to leave the Mutual Network and work for him at KALL. Hatch took Paige to the Press Box, a pub that New York journalists frequented:[263]

> George ... was a two-fisted drinker. ... He had two to my one, and he didn't seem to show at all. ... The more he drank, the more lucid he became. ... and then he began to sell and when George Hatch starts to sell, there's no salesman in the world like him. And by the time he'd finished a half-hour later, in this harangue that he gave me, I was fully convinced that my destiny lie in Salt Lake City. ... The next day I picked up Radio Daily, and here was the announcement of my being hired by KALL and the Intermountain Network, and it was absolutely one of the finest things that I've ever had in my life. And I looked at it in wonderment, and during the day he [Hatch] had planted stories in every publication --Variety, Billboard, everything else --the same story. ... I don't think I've ever been so delighted.

Hatch gave Paige a $2,000 bonus for signing with KALL and IMN. With that he purchased a Chrysler New Yorker and headed to Salt Lake. On the way he stopped in Denver to spend time with his friend Gene O'Fallon of KFEL. This was the same O'Fallon that Sid Fox got advice from in the 1920s. Glasmann, Hatch and Cecil Heftel, another Glasmann son-in-law, later purchased KFEL. Heftel became station manager and changed the call letters to KIMN. In the years to follow, he made the station a great success by using the experience he earlier acquired at KLO in Ogden.

Paige stayed at the Capitol Hotel his first night in Salt Lake City and went to the Keith Building the next morning, only to discover that KALL

---

263   Jack Paige, interview withTim Larson, 119-120.

had moved to the Utah Theater at 136 South Main. Paige began working at KALL the next day, November 1, 1949, where he met, as he recalled, "the delightful Jack Goodman and the others." He added:[264]

> At that time radio station KALL was managed by a chap named Alvin Pack. The sales manager was ... Tom Anderson, and it was the most carefree radio station that I think I have ever been in. We had some great salesmen. One in particular was Sam Baird, ... he was a wonderful guy ... and Bill Danes. ... They were the nucleus of the whole [sales] setup. Of course, George Hatch was in the office, and he ran the whole thing. ... In charge of our control room was Nephi Sorenson ... a steadfast friend of mine. We had a lot of other characters around there. Gordon Owen did one of the programs that we had at 8:15 in the morning. [He] called himself the old philosopher, and he did fifteen minutes of absolute [enjoyment] ... When he went on vacation for two weeks, it fell to my lot to do his program every morning for two weeks, and it was the laughing stock of the entire place.

W. D' Orr Cozzens was KALL's chief engineer when Paige arrived. Cozzens built KLO in the 1930s and then constructed KALL for Hatch and the others in 1945. Cozzens and Wyman became friends of Paige, but they initially had a confrontation involving the AFTRA union. Cozzens and Wyman, with their lawyer, Wally Sandack, tried to make KALL a union shop. Sandack, before becoming a lawyer, was a KSL announcer. Hatch gave Paige the job of making sure a union shop didn't happen. After discussions concluded, a vote was taken and the KALL employees rejected AFTRA by a vote of 13 to 2. If KALL had been successfully unionized in 1950, KSL, KDYL and KUTA would certainly have followed. Wally Sandack, although a very successful labor lawyer in other venues, never accomplished unionizing any Utah radio station.[265]

Just as they did for the NIT, Wyman did play-by-play and Paige did

---

264   Jack Paige, p. 132
265   Wally Sandack, interview with Tim Larson, July 13, 1988.

color for the U of U basketball games in 1949. In 1950, Paige and his wife, Francis, resurrected for KALL, a show similar to one they earlier did in Washington, D.C. This husband and wife team debuted in March 1950 and was "fairly successful." Paige, some 38 years later, recalled the show:[266]

> Well, Francis and I were not getting along very well at all, and there were many times we went on the show, we'd been arguing before … and then when the music would end, we would come on sweet and smiling with each other and do an hour show from ten to eleven every morning with a show called "Mr. & Mrs. Melody."… We had a very loyal bunch of listeners.

Initially, Hatch had given KALL manager Alvin Pack nearly free reign to make employee and programming decisions and to run the station as he saw fit. But as KALL matured, Hatch as president gradually took control of station operations, and Pack became a figurehead. In June 1950, Alvin Pack resigned from his manager/executive vice-presidential position at KALL and the Intermountain Network, and Thomas Anderson was promoted to KALL general manager in 1951.

After leaving KALL, Alvin and wife, Lena Marie Pack, used their years of experience and name recognition to start their own advertising agency business. It was called Pack Advisors and their slogan was "Advertising for Sales." They had advertising accounts and provided recording and production services of various kinds. True to their LDS focus, they never engaged cigarette or alcohol advertisers. They operated that endeavor for two years and then Alvin returned to KDYL when Time, Inc. bought those stations from Fox in 1953.

Although first and foremost a salesman and promoter, Pack held strong opinions about radio and its ability to make humankind more accountable to a higher being. For Pack, radio programming was not an end in itself; it was a means to an end. To him, radio was an electronic extension of one's thoughts, and the effects of those thoughts on others

---

266   Paige, interview with Tim Larson, 136

needed careful consideration. In his personal journal, Pack expressed his observations about what he described as "raunchy radio:"[267]

> I'm somewhat sickened by the great industry that I helped to spawn. ... Why do we allow such perversions? What are we thinking? ... Are we proving the truth of the Alexander Pope epic?
>
> > Vice is a monster of such frightful mien
> > That to be feared needs but to be seen
> > Yet, seen too often, once familiar with her face,
> > First we pity, then endure, and then embrace.
> > This must not be ... for the sake of future generations.

As an aside, Pack and the Featherstones of Boyle Furniture Company later designed the KALL-Man, which sat atop the Utah Theater and Keith Building, where KALL originally was located. The KALL-MAN later was put atop the KALL Building on South Temple, where it remained until Clear Channel took over KALL in early 2003. I could not discover what happened to the KALL-Man --was it stored or destroyed?

The KALL call sign became synonymous with the community, University of Utah sports and the Intermountain region, and that image was nurtured and continued for decades. While KSL and KDYL aired network programming, KALL magnetized an audience and endeared itself to the community with its local involvement, its locally originated programming and especially its identification with the University of Utah.

KALL's staff strengthens its market position

After Pack left KALL, Paige became Uncle Jack for a show, sponsored by Waldorf Biscuit, called, *The Stump-Us Game*. The show, which originated from the KALL studios, was distributed over the IMN network. People sent in postcards naming songs they hoped could "stump" Uncle Jack. It became a popular program on eleven stations of the

---

267   Alvin G. and Lena Marie Pack interview by Tim Larson, 283.

Intermountain Network.

Soon after the show went on, Hatch sent Paige to Montana and Wyoming to sign up IMN affiliates:[268]

> Well, [we] got into ... a pretty bad blizzard. ... So at 4:00 in the morning, I finally arrived [by airplane] at Billings in the middle of a snowstorm. ...I walked into the old airport and standing there at the door was a man named Franz Robi ... who [immediately] took me to the Windmill Cafe which is jumpin' [at 4:30 A.M.]. I walked in the door and the bartender said, "Here's Uncle Jack!" Well, everybody in Billings evidently listens to "Stump Us."... At nine o'clock in the morning --all these guys who had been up all night-- we had a meeting, which lasted until five in the afternoon. When I got through I had twelve [IMN] affiliates in Montana ... and I picked up eleven more on my next stop in Wyoming. And the first thing you know we had ninety-one radio stations spread all over the country. Of course, it took me about six or seven years to do that. But my indoctrination was in Montana in the Windmill Cafe at 4:30 in the morning in a blizzard as the head of the *Stump-Us Game.*

Paige was later made Intermountain Network (IMN) executive vice president and devoted full time to that job, although his office still was at KALL. Lynn Meyer, president, sold IMN nationally, while Peterson sold it regionally and Paige "held it together." His job focused on station relations, by keeping all the IMN affiliates happy. In 1958, KALL and IMN dropped the Mutual Network and picked up ABC. IMN then placed regional news bureaus in Denver, Cheyenne, Helena, and Boise and, of course, Salt Lake City. IMN sales offices were also located in Denver and Salt Lake. By 1978, IMN had become the largest regional network in the U.S., with 97 affiliates. In 1978 after 30 years at KALL and IMN, Paige, at 75, retired "unwillingly" to St. George and his hobby, which was bridge.

---

268   Paige, interview with Tim Larson, 156-157.

Returning to KALL's developments in 1951, as stated, Tom Anderson who was brought by Pack to KALL from KDYL in a sales capacity in 1945, assumed the general manager position when Pack resigned as station manager. Anderson managed the station until Homer Peterson assumed that position in 1956. Peterson, at age 32 in 1952, quit his job of ten years with the White King Soap Company to go to work at KALL in sales. In a 1985 interview, he said:[269]

> I was about the fifth man on the totem pole in sales ... it was very difficult. ... At any rate, I got all the choice accounts that had never been on the air, and I must say it was very disheartening. But I wanted to prove that either I could sell it or I couldn't sell it. So I worked away at it for three months ... and by December I'd made some headway. ... but I decided I didn't like radio. So the middle part of December -- and it's always a good time to do it at Christmas time, I told George, ..."It's been nice." He [Hatch] said, no. We've got other plans for you.

The "other plans" included regional account sales for IMN, as well as some local accounts on KALL. Peterson self-effacingly said he had "some success" with IMN and he enjoyed traveling, calling on regional accounts and selling for IMN affiliates. In 1956, Hatch came to Peterson and told him he had been chosen to be station manager at KALL. Peterson said, "I don't want the job. I like what I'm doing. You don't know what the hell I'm doing. I'm my own boss. I come and go, and you're not sure whether I'm doing anything or not."[270]

Hatch was not easily deterred. Within a short time, Peterson became KALL's manager and inherited the stewardship of all the Hatch stations --those in Great Falls, Butte and Boise as well as KALL. Peterson employed an open-door management style. He said he treated everybody equally, with the exception that people he really liked, he called "son-of-a-bitch." He may have affectionately called people names, but Peterson's

---

269   Homer Peterson, interview with Tim Larson, April 17, 1985, 2.
270   Peterson, interview with Tim Larson, 2.

selling style incorporated the philosophy that the best way to get what he wanted was to give as many people as he could what <u>they</u> wanted. An example of this was when Peterson was trying to get the cable television franchise in Elko, Nevada. One holdout to the agreement was a council member who was also a dairy farmer. The farmer changed his mind and voted in favor of the franchise when Peterson convinced his good friend at the Meadow Gold Dairy Company to begin purchasing the farmer's milk. Peterson easily won over people with his candid personal style, as he explained:[271]

> We've all had to work for a living in our organization, and my job is just a little different than someone else's. We're all working for the same thing, and I'm not one to be called boss … my door is always open to anyone that wants to come in. And I like to visit with everybody in the shop, and I like everyone in my place to visit with me.

Peterson "tended the store" and, in his self-described 35-year "reign of terror" at KALL, was usually the first to arrive at work in the morning and the last to leave at night. He expected the best of people and oversaw the results of every employee's work, including the janitors. He knew how to stroke creative egos and built a close-knit KALL family of workers.

Bruce Bell joined Peterson at KALL in 1962 as a copywriter and stayed for 13 years, with a two-year hiatus in 1966 to take a job that included health insurance in order to meet a family need. He returned in 1968 as program director of KALL's FM partner station, KQMU, later becoming assistant manager for both stations. Bell was hired back by Bruce Miller who became station manager of both stations and played a big role in the growth of KALL. Bell provided support for KALL/KUTV's sports broadcaster Bill Howard, who went on to do play-by-play for the Utah Stars basketball team.[272] Bill Marcroft came to KALL when Howard

---

271   Peterson, p. 2.
272   Bruce Bell conversations by Tim Larson over 30 years and an email in November 2021.

left for the ABA league. Marcroft became the "Voice of the Utes" and for 35 years covered the University of Utah games for KALL and KUTV as a sports broadcaster.[273] Bell, a modest, smart, creative and thoughtful individual, after leaving the station, partnered with Skip Branch at Branch and Bell Advertising and later formed Bruce Bell and Associates, an advertising and marketing consulting firm.

Bennie Williams joined Peterson and Bell at KALL in 1963 in sales, and later became sales manager, program director and then general manager of both KALL and KQMU. He was a self-described up-front guy who resolutely involved KALL in the community and at the University of Utah in his 25-year tenure at the station. He promoted the Junior Chamber of Commerce and was greatly involved with the big local event of the 1960s: the Santa Parade and the decorating of Main Street in downtown Salt Lake City. Williams was sometimes chided for his trade-outs of unsold advertising time, which sometimes denied commissions to his salespeople. After retirement, Williams founded the Business Company of America and was a consultant and an incessant listener of motivational audiotapes while driving.[274]

Also, in 1963, Peterson added Billings to his management responsibilities after he spent three months organizing and developing sales for the Hatch station in that Montana city. In 1966, the Communications Investment Corporation (CIC) Board of Directors elected Peterson to the position of executive vice president of owned and operated stations, which totaled 12. Also, in the 1960s, Peterson spent considerable efforts in Idaho, Montana, Wyoming and Colorado, as well as Utah, seeking cable franchises for Hatch. In 1974, IMN President Lynn Meyer retired and Peterson inherited that position. Thus, he held simultaneously three major titles: executive vice president of CIC, the

---

273   Bill Marcroft interview with Tim Larson, March 22 and October 2, 1990; May 3, 1991; March 3, 1992. Marcroft's Moments: See https://continuum.utah.edu/web-exclusives/marcrofts-moments/
274   Bennie Williams interview by Tim Larson, August 21, 1986; Bennie Williams: https://www.legacy.com/us/obituaries/saltlaketribune/name/bennie-williams-obituary?pid=20463074 and https://www.cityweekly.net/BuzzBlog/archives/2009/04/29/tom-barberi

holding company for all of Hatch's broadcast interests, president of IMN, a sub-corporation of CIC, and KALL station manager.

There were various stories about well-known KALL employees. But a behind-the-scenes employee, Mary L. Nelson, joined KALL in 1964. Well liked by the KALL family, she prepared programming logs and undertook other off-air responsibilities at the station for 36 years, semi-retiring on July 31, 2000. She saw the station move to new digs three times and helped transition the station to new owners several times over decades at the station. "I survived all [that]," she said, "I've been very lucky."[275]

Meanwhile, Will Lucas, promotion director at KALL and Peterson's friend, was a great but self-destructive KALL talent. Lucus was always coming up with KALL promotions in and beyond state borders: his small but sincere Christmas Tree across the street from the Tribune's tree in downtown Salt Lake City; his constant teasing of Reed Benson and the Birch Society; and his lampoon of the Impeach Earl Warren billboard in St. George drew national attention. He invented the morning Ski Report on KALL; and when legalization of alcohol was on the ballot, he ran a counter campaign for the control of ice cream, à la the state's liquor stores. He also helped Bennie set and make a success of a pumpkin party at Shakey's Pizza, a huge annual event for many years.[276]

One of Lucas' more protracted promotions or stunts involved the Defense of Marriage Act (DOMA), making it so same sex couples could receive the same Federal benefit as other couples. In the mid-1970s, manic writers warned that if same-sex marriages were allowed, the next step would be to allow men to marry horses, pigs, goats and ducks. This tapped Lucas' curiosity, so he arranged his marriage to a duck in a grand publicity stunt officiated by a nondenominational preacher in the grand ballroom at the Hilton Hotel. It was a black-tie affair where dinner along with Cold Duck champagne was served. Paul Rolly, longtime reporter for the *Salt*

275   Deseret News, September 1, 2000.
https://www.deseret.com/2000/9/1/19526550/veteran-kall-staffer-is-retiring-151-sort-of
276   Bruce Bell, email to Tim Larson, November 1, 2021. Homer Peterson, interview with Tim Larson, August 21, 1986.

Lake Tribune, covered the stunt. His editor told him the story warranted very little newspaper copy, but pictures were wanted if the marriage was consummated.[277]

KALL's next generation of on-air talent

KALL accrued an exceptional stable of on-air creative radio talent over the years. Many employees and personalities regrettably may be overlooked, but arguably, the most notable surrounded Tom Barberi and his morning-drive radio show. Barberi, KALL's iconic morning personality for 34 years, started at KALL under Peterson and Williams on July 5, 1971. Barberi related:[278]

> I'll never forget it. The radio station manager picked me up at the airport, then took me up by the Capitol to see the valley. I expected a desert, but I saw this green valley with snow-capped peaks, the air was crystal clear, it was about 80 degrees—just a beautiful place. Then he drove me downtown to the KALL studio on South Temple, and I noticed there were no cars on the streets, none. I asked him, "Where is everybody?" He said, "It's Sunday, they're in church." I said, "All of 'em?" That was my introduction to Salt Lake City.

Barberi, dubbed the "Voice of Reason," was loved-to-be-hated by religious and political leaders for his on-air provocative repartee and raillery during his long running KALL morning show.[279] Barberi's show included Mike Runge and the DUCK, Hal Hansen, flying morning traffic reports in Hansen's Cessna. Runge became the decades-long University of Utah football game public address announcer, hockey's Golden Eagles general manager, KSTU sports anchor, and a Utah Broadcasters Association Hall of Fame inductee. While flying early mornings for KALL, Hansen was the go-to gifted sound recording expert at his highly respected Edison Street Recording Studio.

---

277   Paul Rolly: https://archive.sltrib.com/article.php?id=56073795&itype=cmsid.
278   CityWeekly: https://www.cityweekly.net/utah/radiohead/Content?oid=2129164.
279   Tom Barberi interview with Glenda Riesen, April 15, 1985.

The news staff at KALL included some of Utah's best-known media professionals. Jim Braden joined KALL in 1974 as a KALL reporter and morning newsman with Barberi. After KALL, he moved to sports at KSL, to morning newsman at KBZN and to the Utah Travel Council for a time. He then became the public information officer (PIO) for the Salt Lake County Commission, and later held the same position for Parks and Recreation and then as press secretary/PIO for the Salt Lake County Mayor.[280]

Ken Verdoia landed a job at KALL in 1974, with help from his old friend, Braden. Verdoia described Braden as a gifted broadcast writer and a wonderful mentor, a friend for 50 years. Barberi, Braden and Verdoia were connected in the early 1970s through shared work experiences in San Jose, California. Verdoia left KALL in 1977 to serve as the news director for Hatch's Intermountain Radio Network operations in Denver. He returned to Salt Lake and accepted a position at KTVX. In 1981, he began his public television career. At KUED, he served as senior producer for public affairs and production director. Over the years, he earned 29 Emmy Awards and other prestigious honors for his storytelling and documentary work.[281]

Phil Riesen, news director for the KALL Intermountain Network, shared KALL's airwaves with Barberi. He moved on after KALL as news anchor for Hatch's KUTV-TV and then to KTVX TV. Riesen also served as an adjunct broadcast journalist instructor in the Department of Communication at the University of Utah. From 2006 to 2010, he was a Democratic member of the Utah House of Representatives. He has kept his hand in announcing and advertising over the years. "One-take" Riesen was a favored recording artist for Hal Hansen at his Edison Street Studios.[282]

---

280   Deseret News: https://www.deseret.com/1992/2/4/18965813/in-your-neighborhood-on-the-agenda

281   Salt Lake Tribune. https://archive.sltrib.com/article.php?id=53115843&itype=CMSID Ken Verdoia's LinkedIn profile: https://www.linkedin.com/in/ken-verdoia-0241ba14/. Ken Verdoia email to Tim Larson, October 21, 2021.

282   Hal Hansen, conversation with Tim Larson (circa 1990s and over 35 years). Mayor Fires Riesen: https://www.deseret.com/2000/2/11/19490409/mayor-fires-media-liaison-br-riesen-sacked-after-only-a-month-on-the-job.

Hans Petersen aired afternoons on KALL after 12 years as the top-rated morning radio personality in Augusta, Georgia, and Rochester, New York, before coming to the station. He left KALL in 1992, but later came back on Salt Lake radio, mornings on KISN AM 570 and KUMT, the Mountain 105.7, with a popular show featuring his own characters, some of which he earlier presented on KALL.[283]

Fred Wix, a jovial person, beginning in the 1970s was at KALL and then KUTV TV, totaling 27 years. He was seen daily at noon on his Gabby Gourmet TV show where he cooked, gabbed, and pioneered the idea of gourmet cooking in daily life.

Some other early KALL employees went on to larger markets and fame. Wyman spent 12 years at KALL and was a great sports name in Salt Lake City, as described earlier. He later purchased several Wyoming radio stations and then went on to Chicago's WSNS television in a long, successful career.[284] Jack Bogut, a KALL morning man, went to Westinghouse's KDKA in Pittsburgh, among other markets. Roger Barkley became famous as part of the Lohman and Barkley team doing a morning show on the west coast. Other KALL personalities included Paul Engeman, Dan Tyler, Don Shafer, Dick Dixon and Phil Nolan.

"Daddy Flo" formally known as Florien Wineriter, started at KUTA in high school in 1943, then announced at KDYL before going to KALL. He later joined the KSL staff. During his 43-year career, he was an announcer, disc jockey and for 25 years was a newscaster before retiring in 1986.[285]

After almost thirty-five years as a "bottom-line" executive for Hatch,

---

283   Peterson Returns (https://www.deseret.com/1992/9/18/19005620/hans-petersen-s-return-may-be-just-what-doctor-ordered-for-am.
284   Mal Wyman: https://www.chicagotribune.com/news/ct-xpm-2013-06-02-ct-met-obit-wyman-20130602-story.html. Deseret News ,June 22, 2007: https://www.deseret.com/2007/6/22/20025853/radio-dial-radiopersonalities-bring-back-memories;
285   Florien Wineriter, an interview by Stan Larson and Lorille Miller, June 8, 1989, Everett L. Cooley Oral History Project, Marriott Library, University of Utah; Conversations with Tim Larson (circa) 1990. Florien Wineriter: https://www.legacy.com/us/obituaries/thespectrum/name/florien-wineriter-obituary?id=12318951

Peterson retired in 1990. His secretary of 20 years, Charlene Dunn, retired soon after. Both served KALL and the Hatch family with great ability and loyalty. Peterson remained a prime organizer of the Utah Open-Heart Open Golf Tournament held annually to benefit the Utah Heart Association. Peterson, who had two open-heart surgeries, recruited the participants for the tournament, helping to make it a financial success.[286]

KALL radio changes ownership

Hatch owned KALL/KLCY in Salt Lake until August 1992, when he sold it to the Apollo Group, owners of KKAT in Salt Lake, under a Local Market Agreement (LMA). The KALL license and station ownership were transferred to Regent Communications in 1995, to Jacor in 1997, to Clear Channel in 1999, to Mercury in 2001 and to Disney/ABC in 2003.[287]

Under an unheard-of-agreement at the time, Clear Channel kept the rights to the KALL call sign and intellectual property (programming and personalities) when it sold KALL to Mercury in 2001. When Disney changed the KALL 910kHz call sign to KWDZ --after Walt Disney-- in 2003, Clear Channel moved the KALL call sign and programming and personalities to its station at 700kHz. As such, the Tom Barberi show and other programming were moved to KALL AM-700 in June 2003. A 2001 *City Weekly* newspaper feature captured the essence of Barberi working in the studio:[288]

> Watching Barberi at work probably isn't what you'd imagine if
> you've listened to the show for any length of time. On the radio,
> it sounds as if the studio is jam-packed with a bustling crew,
> moving things along at a pepped-up morning pace. That scenario
> is half-right: The show does move, but Barberi --KALL's only
> live and local weekday occupant, as the rest of the schedule is
> syndicated-- Sits all alone in the studio. Newsman and comic foil
> Bob Hendricks is isolated behind a soundproof window, poring

---

286   Charlene Dunn, interview withTim Larson (circa 1990).
287   Wikipedia: https://en.wikipedia.org/wiki/KALL.
288   City Weekly, July 5, 2001.

over computer monitors for headlines and updates; producer
[Paige] Bradford is behind another, screening calls and running
the technical end of the show. "If it sounds like we're all together
in one room, then we're doing our job right," she says proudly.

After 15 months on KALL AM 700, on October 5, 2004, Clear Channel
unceremoniously fired Tom Barberi, thereby ending his 34 years under the
KALL call sign.[289] Barberi wittily described the deliverance meeting with his
bosses:[290]

> "It was a little ambush. It was as cold and dispassionate and
> disrespectful as it could be. They called me into the office and
> basically said, "We are going in another direction." I asked, "Does that
> mean I get to sleep in tomorrow?" and they said, 'That's right.'"

Brad Stone, who did sports talk on KALL and later on KFNZ, was fired
from KALL AM-700 with Barberi on October 5. Barberi died on December 24,
2021, after a chronic illness.

The 21st century switches in ownership diminished what was one of Utah's
greatest radio legacies. In 2015, Disney sold KWDZ 910kHz to iHeartMedia,
formerly Clear Channel, owner of KALL call sign at 700kHz. iHeart
surrendered the KWDZ license operating at 910kHz on April 25, 2018, and the
Federal Communications Commission canceled the license on June 26 of that
year. The original 910 AM KALL, founded by the Hatch/Hinckley people in
1945, was silent many years later.[291]

Glasmann, Hatch, the Kearns-Tribune Corporation and Frank Carman
partnered in KUTV television in 1954 and are discussed in a chapter in the
next section that focuses on Utah's first television broadcasting and cable
stations. Hatch also started and was president of Community TV of Utah,

---

289   Deseret News: https://www.deseret.com/2004/10/7/19854496/barberi-loses-job-seeks-a-new-one
290   Salt Lake Tribune: https://archive.sltrib.com/story.php?ref=/utah/ci_2424 *Deseret News: https://www.deseret.com/2003/2/28/19706759/a-utah-radio-first-separate-deals-on-content-frequency
291   KWDZ: https://en.wikipedia.org/wiki/KWDZ.

which eventually merged with Bob Magnus' cable company and became the largest cable television company in the world.[292]

292   To further investigate the Hatch and Glasmann media holdings, consult "The George C. and Gene Hatch Papers 1908-1999," accessible through the University of Utah Marriott Library Special Collections and Archives in Salt Lake City. Included are extensive materials pertaining to the operation of The Ogden Standard Examiner, The Standard Corporation, KUTV, KALL, and other Hatch/Glassman media ventures. George C. and Gene Hatch papers, 1908-1999 - Archives West, http://archiveswest.orbiscascade.org/ark:/80444/xv54879/pdf

Photo Gallery

National Archives, Suitland MD: Marriott Library's
Robert Staab & Gregory Thompson assisted the author's
archival research

National Archives, College Park, MD

KZN inauguration on May 6, 1922: Latter-day Saint President
Heber J. Grant announcing at the station atop the Deseret
News Building

Philo Farnsworth's first
television transmission was
on September 7, 1927

Earl Glade KSL, KLO

Louise Hill Howe and Joe Kearns
KSL Players

"KSL Players" Program began by Earl Glade in the 1930s. Louise Hill
Howe directing KSL Players Francis Urry, Parley Baer and another
performer.

Introduced by Earl Glade, the "Bates Boys" Parley Baer and Francis Urry, comedic characters who had a three-night-a-week run on KSL in the late 1930s and after WWII.

Orchestra Leader Eugene Jelesnik (standing) with Mayor Earl Glade and Salt Lake City Park Commissioner L.C. Romney planning a public musical

Ira Kaar outside the KSUB radio station in Cedar City in 1983

Ira Kaar family home at 243 East 700 South where KDYL first aired on May 10, 1922

Ira Kaar inducted into the Utah Broadcasters Hall of Fame 1983. Mervin Hogan, Kaar, Jack Gallivan, (2nd row) Arch Madsen, Howard Johnson, Kaar's friend, (3rd row) Frank Carman, Thomas Parmley, (4th row) Richard Harris and Alvin Pack

QST Magazine, June 1920: Ira Kaar's
6ZA Special Land Station used to
open KDYL on May 10, 1922, from
Kaar's parent's home

Marvin Andelin, Ira Kaar's amateur
radio teen friend

KDYL's Sidney S. Fox always
nattily attired and with
ever-present cigar

John Baldwin, KDYL's chief engineer (2nd from left)
and other workers atop KDYL-TV's Oquirrh
Mountain transmitter construction site in 1952

KDYL's Sid Fox (left) and John Baldwin (right) with O. B.
Hanson, NBC chief engineer beside an RCA TRK-12 TV
introduced at the 1939 World's Fair in New York City. It
cost $600, more than for a modest car at the time.

Harman Peery KLO Co-Founder

Arch Madsen, KSUB, KOVO, KSL

Abe Glasmann KLO, KALL, KUTV,
Ogden Standard Examiner

Frank Carman KUTA, KUTV TV

Frank Carman's amateur Dxing cards retrieved from his 1920s boyhood home tool shed in 1988

Tom Anderson KOAL, Price

Leland Perry KSUB, Cedar City

Larry S. Cole KFXD, Logan

Reed Bullen KVNU, Logan

lifton Tolboe KOVO, Provo

Howard Johnson KNAK and KSUB

*George Hatch KLO and co-founder
of KALL, KUTV-TV and TCI*

*...bert H. Hinckley behind the scene applicant for
...LL with George Hatch and Abrelia Hinckley.*

*Alvin Pack KALL first manager 1945-1950, and Lena
Marie Pack Hall of Fame Inductees*

...ck Goodman KALL early journalist 1946

*Al "Jazzbeaux" Collins KALL
Jazz disc jockey beginning in 1946*

*Homer Peterson KALL,
IMN 1957-1990.*

*Bruce Bell
KALL 1962-1975*

*Salt Lake Tribune's Jack Gallivan
co-founder KUTV-TV, TCI*

KALL basketball team mid 1970s.

(Front Row) Mike Runge sitting on Hal Hansen, Fred Wix sitting on Ken Verdoia,

(Second Row) Will Lucas, Tom Barberi, Kevin Jones

(Third Row) Bill Howard, George Dyer, Paul Engman

(Back Row) Larry Richardson, Jan Bagley, Jim Braden, Ken Atkin, Harry Gibbons, Clint Hardin (Swanee)

*John F. Fitzpatrick portrait (KSL 1926-
1945 and KALL) with John W. Gallivan
in front*

Bob Magness Co-founder TCI

John Malone TCI, Liberty Media

Philip Lasky, KDYL 1927 to 1935

Morgan White, KLO and "Pogo Poge" at Cecil Heftel's KIMN in Denver (1955- 1965) and Hawaii's KGMB for 15 years after. Heftel was Abe Glasmann's son-in-law.

"Daddy Flo" - Florien Wineriter, KUTA, KDYL, KALL and KSL

Sydney Keffery (Center), Sid Fox's granddaughter with Marriott Library's Gregory Thompson and Nancy Young at Fox's grave site in 1994.

Joan Bournstein, Manny Drucker's daughter holding a photo of her dad, an early KDYL salesman and Sidney Fox friend

Jay William "Bill" Wright, KSL late 1920 & early 1930s; again at KSL 1954-1961

Pat Kirk, KUTV from 1959 to 2000, National Sales Manager in the 1970s and 1980s, in front of photo of husband Brent Kirk, KUTV's first General Manager

Joe Lee, Announcer and broadcast journalist, KOVO, KDYL, KNAK and KCPX

SECTION III

THE PIONEERS OF TELEVISION AND CABLE IN UTAH

CHAPTER 15

KDYL-TV: SALT LAKE CITY

In 1932, John Baldwin, KDYL's new radio engineer, suggested to owner Sid Fox that he should put away some money for television. Fox did not immediately act on Baldwin's suggestion, but he and Baldwin went to the 1939 New York World's Fair, where RCA debuted television. Fox was taken with television's promotional possibilities. Using RCA equipment, he set up an extraordinary television exhibit in Salt Lake's Paris Company in September 1939, similar to what RCA had done at the World's Fair. Among the many hundreds attending the exhibition were Utah Governor Henry Blood and Latter Day Saint President Heber J. Grant, who both reportedly appeared on camera. In years to follow, Fox vigorously promoted television at Utah state fairs and other venues.

KDYL–TV (now KTVT, the ABC Channel 4 affiliate) traces its beginnings after World War II to November 1946 and its W6XIS experimental television license. With W6XIS, John Baldwin had flexibility of operation and was free to conduct television-programming tests that eventually paved the way for commercial KDYL-TV, which became Utah's first television station. Baldwin's lab was in the Old Masonic Temple Building on 2nd South and 2nd East in Salt Lake City. It was later located above the Pioneer Post Office, the present site of the City Creek Mall and formerly the space occupied by the ZCMI Mall.

In 1948, Baldwin put the W6XIS/KDYL television antenna on top of the Walker Bank Building with KDYL AM and FM. Television reach in the Salt Lake Valley was limited at best and the signal only occasionally reached the Provo area. The transmitting antenna needed to be positioned at a higher location so KDYL could assuredly reach Ogden and Provo and all of the Salt Lake Valley. In the spring of 1952, Baldwin conferred with relevant KSL people, but they were not interested in sharing their Oquirrh Mountain Coon

Peak antenna site, which is now known as Farnsworth Peak after Philo T. Farnsworth, a Utah native and the discoverer of electronic television. The Intermountain Broadcasting and Television Company/KDYL TV acquired its own site on Mount Nelson, the highest available point Baldwin could find in the Oquirrhs. He began road construction leading to the site in the spring of 1952, four years after KDYL-TV had gone on the air using its antenna on the Walker Bank Building.

Fox kept asking Baldwin, "Where the hell is that mountain?" Fox did not know where Mount Nelson, later renamed Mt. Vision, was located in the Oquirrhs. To point out the KDYL television site, one night in July 1952, Baldwin put a 1,000- watt searchlight on the transmitter site and shone it brightly toward Salt Lake City. The light caused quite a stir with Salt Lake Valley residents, and many calls were received at the police station from people fearing flying saucers and alien intruders. After the first night, the Salt Lake City newspapers reported that the light source was from KDYL's new mountaintop television site. Baldwin intended to turn off the light after one night, but Fox liked the publicity it generated and directed that the light be left on every night until construction was completed. It was.

KDYL's initial staff

In 1948, KDYL-TV television executives and directors included Fox, president and general manager; Allen L Gunderson, chief engineer; John M. Baldwin, vice president and technical director; Harry Golub, director of sales; and Dan Rainger, the first program manager. All of them held similar staff positions at KDYL AM radio.

Rainger's assent as Salt Lake City's first program manager in television is an interesting story. A native of Newark, New Jersey, he finagled a press pass in 1939 and took freelance football game photos while in high school, selling them to two large Newark papers, *The Star Ledger* and *The Newark Evening News*. After graduating from high school, Rainger had some self-described menial employment and worked as a freelance stringer and photographer. In 1942, he went into the U.S. Air Force and worked his way into a public relations/special services position. He wrote stories and was the sports editor for the camp newspaper in Kearns, Utah, but wanted to get into radio. He reported that he wrote a couple of scripts and impressed the lieutenant in charge and was made a radio writer. He eventually wrote, produced and directed stories about U.S. Air Force personnel in action. And, although not employed by KDYL, while still in uniform, he did some shows that aired on KDYL radio.

Completing military service, Rainger returned to Newark. After a while, his brother, Ralph, a well-known Hollywood songwriter and friend of playwright and prolific screenwriter, Dore Schary, invited him to Hollywood to get some help with a writing career. Having been previously stationed several years in Salt Lake City, Rainger routed his train trip through SLC to see some friends on his way to Hollywood. He contacted friends at KDYL and KALL and was offered a job at both radio stations. Abandoning opportunities for Hollywood employment, which were far from concrete, he took the KALL radio job as a continuity writer for $275 a month, more than he had ever made during the Great Depression. Rainger was at KALL for about two months when Fox, who had known him from his armed services time in Salt Lake City, called and offered him $20 more a month at KDYL radio. Rainger liked Fox, seeing him as a consummate showman. In his early twenties, he saw Fox as "a light" in his young career. So he left KALL for KDYL.

Rainger was visiting family back home in Newark when Sid Fox called him. He related the conversation:

> [Fox] wanted to tell me that he had just gotten a construction permit Okayed, which meant he could build a tower for transmission of TV. TV construction. He said, "We are aiming to go on the air in April … And he said, "You're going to be in television. … You're going to be my program director, my television program director." I said something clever like, "What the hell is television?

Subsequently, Fox sent Rainger to NBC for a "couple days" to learn about TV:

So I went over to NBC New York, and the very first thing they said was, "Okay, we would like you to watch a rehearsal of a show called *Philco Television Playhouse.*" I went down there and … bedlam! There were a hundred and twenty people on the crew and about eighty-five people on stage –actors, guys who built the sets. What the hell is going on here? And there is the director yelling, do this, do that, to the people, and I don't know what is going on. And I am so afraid. THIS is what I was supposed to run in Salt Lake City? Had to learn all this?

Rainger returned to Salt Lake and told Fox, "I can't do this. I want my [radio] job back. … I just couldn't do it." Fox dismissed Rainger's objections and gave him free reign to do his best in a television business that was completely new to everybody then. KDYL-TV was the only television station in Salt Lake City, and there was no template or TV best practices to emulate or to guide him. Rainger did "learn" television programing and was KDYL-TVs program director for the next 31 years

When KDYL-TV began regularly scheduled broadcasts on April 19, 1948, it aired programs to the public starting at 8 p.m. each Monday, Wednesday and Friday. KDYL-TV touted that variety would be the programming keynote, giving the public the best in entertainment, educational features, spot news, sports, special events, and events of national importance. Three nights a week, forty-five minutes a night, the station aired short films introduced by live announcers, including Alan Frank, one of the station's first announcers. Later, Jerry Hill did some sports inserts and Roy Gibson did a Sunday night book review. KDYL-TV had no network affiliation at the time, so locally produced shows and films filled the hours. Dr. Keith Engar at the University of Utah reportedly also helped with some one-act plays on occasion.[293]

By 1952, the stable of KDYL TV executives and directors still included Fox, Baldwin and Rainger and others including: Easton C. Wooley, executive vice president; Fox's stepson, George Provol, commercial manager; and Connie Eckardt, film buyer. Hours of operation were posted as airing from noon to

---

293   KDYL-TV: https://www.earlytelevision.org/kdyl.htmlS.

midnight, but that was greatly overstated.

Cash crisis

Intermountain Broadcasting, and Television (IBT), however, was hemorrhaging cash, as it had uncontrolled financial losses. As of March 31, 1953, Intermountain Broadcasting and Television (IBT) had $720,350 in assets and $415,000 in liabilities including $145,000 in bank notes, $178,000 in television equipment contracts, $34,000 in monthly bills and $35,000 in federal income taxes payable. Using these figures, IBT's debt-to-equity (D/E) ratio was 58%. Companies with a D/E ratio of 33% or more are generally considered highly financially leveraged, often considered a financial disadvantage to investors.[294]

To succeed, a highly leveraged company, like IBT/KDYL, required a dependable and growing cash flow that exceeded its debt service payments and other monthly expenses. It was the opposite for KDYL television, which garnered expenses that far exceeded its revenue, resulting in insufficient cash flow to meet monthly expenses. Fox assumed so much debt to put KDYL television on the air and was so highly leveraged, he would have had to use KDYL AM radio profits, which were unexpectedly diminishing with TV's advent, and personal savings to continue television operations. Borrowing from banks and thus becoming even more highly leveraged was not a reasonable option for Fox in 1953.

Fox's alternative to supporting KDYL television out of radio profits and savings was to sell Intermountain Broadcasting and Television Corporation (IBT/KDYL) to somebody better positioned financially to assume the losses expected over the next several years. In addition, Fox had accrued significant personal debt. All three KDYL stations, AM/FM radio and TV, were up for sale because a stand-alone television station would not attract a buyer at that time.

G. Bennett Larson, then the WPIX-TV vice president and general

---

294   Time, Incorporated, "Acquisition of Intermountain Broadcasting and Television Corporation, 1953. The Papers of Sidney S. Fox (1889-1980), Manuscript Collection (Ms 559), Bx 11, 41 Fds, Special Collections Department, University of Utah Libraries, Salt Lake City, Utah.)

manager in New York City, learned Time, Inc. was looking to purchase a television station:[295]

> I had heard that Sid Fox, who owned KDYL in Salt Lake, might want to sell. So I called Sid up and said, "Look, Sid, I may have a customer for your station if you'll settle on a price. ...I didn't tell him who it was. .... His eyes lit up. ... He was ready [to sell] cause he'd been going to Vegas. ... He was a gambler ... and he owed Walker Bank about a hundred thou. ... Cal Rawlins, his lawyer, met with Time representatives to discuss [a] possible sale, ... and they made a deal to buy Salt Lake. But they bought it on one condition. They needed management. And they didn't want to go out there with some stranger. And a hometown boy, a Mormon, ... just suited them right. And so they wanted me to go out and take over the operation in 1953. ... I quit WPIX, and I went back home with Time, Inc. in my hip pocket and operated the radio and television for Time, Inc. in Salt Lake.

In 1953, Fox, as the majority IBT stockholder, acted as agent for the other stockholders and sold the KDYL radio and TV stations to Time, Inc. for $2.1-million, the equivalent to $21 million in today's value. The KDYL sale and license transfer involved a complicated process whereby Time, Inc., a New York corporation, acquired the stations and then transferred control and the licenses to a subsidiary called TLF Broadcasting Corporation, a Utah corporation. Time, Inc. and G. Bennett Larson owned TLF stock, in the ratio of 80% by Time and 20% by Larson. T-L-F was an acronym for Time, Life and Fortune, the major magazines in Henry Luce's Time, Inc. media empire. KDYL was only Time, Inc.'s second television station purchase.[296]

At the time of the $2.1-million KDYL sale in April 1953, Fox owned 54% of IBT, worth $1,127,700; his sister, Jessie Loeb, owned 21%, worth $362,145;

---

295   G. Bennett Larson, Los Angeles, California, an interview with Tim Larson, July 9, 1984, Everett L. Cooley Oral History Project, Marriott Library University of Utah Salt Lake City, Utah.
296   Time, Incorporated, "Acquisition of Intermountain Broadcasting and Television Corporation, 1953. The Papers of Sidney S. Fox (1889-1980), Manuscript Collection (Ms 559), Bx 11, 41 Fds, Special Collections Department, University of Utah Libraries, Salt Lake City, Utah.

and Fred B. Provol, organizer of IBC in 1926, held only one share (.005%) of stock, worth $105, in his name when KDYL was sold. Hazel Provol, Fred's wife, owned 17%, worth $403,500. Interestingly, at this time, Fred Provol had more shares of Radio Service Corporation of Utah (KSL) stock than KDYL stock. The 8% of IBT stock not controlled by Fox, Hazel Provol and Jessie Loeb was divided almost equally among 13 other stockholders, including Baldwin, Lasky, Rawlings, Drucker, and Jessie's husband, Leo Loeb.[297]

When the sale was completed on June 30, 1953, the 20,000 shares of Intermountain Broadcasting and Television Corporation (IBT) were transferred to TLF, Inc. and to Larson. As earlier noted, after being gone from KDYL for nearly 25 years, Ben Larson, KDYL radio's original Uncle Ben in 1929, came back to be an owner and TLF president, general manager and film buyer. Baldwin, KDYL's engineer for nearly 25 years, became TLF vice president in charge of station operations, Rainger remained as program director, and Allen Gunderson carried over as director of engineering. Douglas Clawson became commercial manager. Other TLF officers appointed in 1953 were Secretary Arthur R. Murphy, Jr. and Treasurer Weston C. Pullen, Jr. Murphy and Pullen were Time, Inc. corporate employees and gave oversight to KDYL operations from New York City. They never actively worked at KDYL. Murphy was a past general manager of *Life* magazine and, in 1953, managed "March of Time." Pullen held the title as assistant to the executive vice-president and treasurer at Time, Inc.

Larson returns to the KDYL family

Ben Larson was an actor, a self-styled comedian and musical phenom – an accomplished performer even while still in high school. KDYL radio's Philip Lasky discovered him in 1926 (as highlighted earlier in the book), and he later took on the Uncle Ben children's show, among other jobs at the radio station.

In 1929, based on his KDYL radio experience, Larson was hired by the NBC radio network, which was established just three years prior. He became

---

297   Time, Incorporated, "Acquisition of Intermountain Broadcasting and Television Corporation, 1953.

skilled at the network advertising-driven radio business and over the next several years did 'terrific" shows for the network. From the beginning, he started with the Fleischmann Yeast Hour Show with Rudy Vallee, and then was signed up for the Chase and Sanborn Show with Eddie Cantor; the Texaco Fire Chief Show with Ed Wynn; and the Gillette sponsored Milton Berle show. He was the producer for the Al Jolson show, and he mentored then budding comic Jimmy Durante, who appeared on the Eddie Cantor Show.

After leaving NBC, Larson produced and directed radio shows for several production companies and advertising agencies. He bought and managed radio station WDC in Washington, D. C., and while at that station, attended the Truman presidential inauguration at the White House on April 12, 1945, the day President Roosevelt died. In 1948, Larson helped put Philadelphia's WCAU-TV on the air and became its vice president and television director. He joined WPIX in 1950, and in 1951 aired the historic hearings of the U.S. Senate committee tasked with investigating organized crime and its impact on interstate commerce and political influence, led by U.S. Senator Estes Kefauver (D-Tennessee). At age 43, in 1953, as Intermountain Broadcasting and Television owner and general manager, Larson was a television programming and production mentor for KDYL-TV's Danny Rainger. He nurtured Rainger on the way to becoming a gifted and talented television professional, who served until his retirement in 1979, despite several ownership changes in the station. Rainger recalls Larson:[298]

> Time Life bought us [in 1953]. Sid was out. … It became very evident that there was a boss over me, where I had never had that feeling before. I was the guy. I had a man named G. Bennett Larson who was the manager of the station. G. Bennett Larson was a tremendous boss. … It was the first time that I had run into a man with so much Madison Avenue experience in advertising and in programming and actually in production. Mr. Larson was one of the old-time network radio producers, who produced such shows as the Eddie Cantor Show and other big network comedy shows of that type. Just being

298   Daniel Rainger, an interview with Ronald Rainger, Everett L. Cooley Oral History Project, No. 222 & 223, January 8 1985. Marriott Library, University of Utah, Salt Lake City.

in the same room with him was very invigorating for someone first
up. I found Ben, Mr. Larson, very interesting, very talented, and we
were sort of on the same wavelength. … It was a whole new side of
the business. I mean, I got the creative side from Ben Larson: how it
was to do network shows and how he built these shows. … I didn't
actually collaborate with Ben on the production of local programs,
but he had some awfully good ideas. … He had his finger on the
growing business, the growing trends of programming, and things of
that type, where I didn't. I was very parochial. He had the big picture
in mind and had the imagination, and in me he had the tools [to]
have the thing worked out by me. So it was a very good collaboration.
As far as creative juices, we got along very, very well. In fact, it was
Ben who later on cautioned me, when I was offered a job with NBC,
"Wide, Wide World", not to take it, but to freelance as I started to
do … "Wide Wide World" [segments]; not to dedicate myself to
NBC New York, because on Madison Avenue and in the advertising
business and the broadcasting business he had found it was a jungle.
He was trying to give me his impression of it: "Get out of it."

Rainger etches his mark as Utah's first television program manager

The KDYL call sign was changed to KTVT-TV, but Rainger's
responsibilities continued as normal. He remained in charge of programming
and production under Larson, producing shows and news hosted by local
talent. He also contributed to an NBC national production. *Wide Wide World*
was a 90-minute documentary series telecast live on *NBC* on Sundays at 4 p.m.
in the Eastern time zone. Each week the show featured live segments from
across the U.S., hosted by Dave Garroway of *Today Show* fame. When NBC
wanted a contribution from the Intermountain West, it tapped KDYL and
Rainger.

In addition to ancillary contributions between 1955 and 1958, Rainger
directed two extraordinary *Wide Wide World* live segments featuring Virginia
Tanner Dance from Salt Lake City, one from the Utah Capitol and another
from the Lagoon Amusement Park. For each show, NBC sent a producer to

plan the segment with Rainger, which included choreography, sets, camera shots, transitions and music. The producer then returned to New York City, leaving Rainger in Salt Lake City to direct the live segment. Everything on the *Wide Wide World* show was live. Rainger was not even allowed to use recorded music for his dance segments. The dancers in Salt Lake City performed coast-to-coast to music played from New York City by a live 38-piece NBC orchestra. It seemed fitting to have dance, which had its own historical pioneer roots in Utah's performing arts scene, as being part of local television history in the making.

As a result of his directing success, NBC hired Rainger, to direct *Wide Wide World* segments at venues around the country, including from the Colorado Springs' Continental Air Command, Ellis Island, Florida and Detroit, among other places. He was adept at using local production crews.

In addition, Rainger over the years directed locally generated news pieces for the live NBC weekday morning *Today Show*, which began nationally on January 14, 1952, hosted by Garroway. One contribution among many was especially notable: An NBC live coast-to-coast *Today* segment involving a hostage-taking prison uprising at the Utah State Prison at the Point of the Mountain on February 7, 1957. Larson produced the coverage and Rainger directed it. The details of the uprising were widely covered in the press:[299]

> Some 500 convicts ended an 11-hour riot at the Utah State Prison today, gave up captured weapons and released all hostages, and ungrudgingly returned control of the battered penitentiary to authorities. ...THE RIOTERS gave up at 5 am. and released 18 men whom they had held since before 8 p.m. Wednesday [February 6], when the outbreak started during a basketball game between a church quintet and a prison squad. However, it took more than three hours before officials, moving slowly and carefully, could get to all guard stations and feel they were again in command.

> By 5 a.m. the following day, the prisoners had given up their weapons,

---

299   Desert Sun, Volume XXX, Number 120, 7 February 1957.

released the 18 well-treated hostages and announced they were surrendering. Rainger and several other news reporters were allowed to enter the prison. NBC had been following the story and alerted KDYL announcer Tom Wayman and Rainger that they wanted to go live nationally with the story of the surrender, at 7 a.m. in the Eastern time zone, just as the news broke in Utah.

Rainger fondly picks up the story in his extensively detailed recollection:

> Got word through my announcer, Tom Wayman, that the main prisoner who was in charge of the hostages … wanted to give up. Now I'm doing something that you can't do anymore: staging the news. And I said, "No way is he going to give up. I got to feed NBC at seven o'clock [this] morning and I'm not going to go out there now [at 5 a.m.] and [tell NBC they gave up]." So Tom and I went into the cellblock where Sonny Randall [the ringleader] was, and we said to him, "Hey, don't be stupid. Don't give up now. Wait until … seven-thirty in the morning. I'll get you on national television and then you will have all the sympathy in the world from all these people. … [If you give up now], who are you talking to? You are talking to three night maintenance guys, you know, in an office building."…. So they decided to do it. And I said, "Here is what you are going to do." Time now went forward, and about … six o'clock in the morning, just before we were supposed to go on, NBC called and said, "How are things going at the prison, Dan." I said, "Well, they're still in there. … Sonny Randal is running the joint." [NBC asked]," Do you think you will have anything for us? We think we can get [to you] around … ten after seven." I said, "Yeah, … I think we can do it." He said, "What do you think you can do?" I said, " Tell you what. I'll set the scene. It'll be daybreak at that time. Pan in on the wall, and the lights. Then we will cut inside and … about two minutes in, I tell you what, I'll cue the surrender. He said, "You'll what?" I said, "I'll cue the surrender, whenever you want. It's all taken care of." "Oh, my God," I could hear him talking to other people, "this son-of-a-bitch is going to cue the surrender out there in Utah." So, anyway, that's what happened. Garroway cut to us at ten after seven. He told me I had seven minutes

and we cued the surrender. Sonny Randall [appeared] saying [among other things], "These are the points that we want to make. We are not well. They don't keep us well out here, you know." So anyway, to make a long story short, the network ran a half-hour, with Dave Garroway coming in now and then. And it was a coup. Not only that, but Dave Garroway wanted our announcer, Tom Wayman, for his [*Today*]] show the following morning. So he flew him back to New York to get him on the show the next morning, and of course that brought attention to us from some of the people in New York City.

Frank Blair, then NBC news anchor for the *Today* show (1953-1975), after viewing the footage where Rainger said, "Cue the surrender!" of the staged act, remarked, "That is probably the strangest telecasts I think I have ever seen."

During his time at KDYL, from 1953 to 1959, Larson developed formats unprecedented at the time. Significant, among other programs, was his introduction of a half-hour local newscast, featuring anchor Roy Gibson, sports with Paul James and weather with Bob Welti. This KDYL newscast topped the Crossley ratings, beating out the KUTV and KSL newscasts, respectively.

Postscript after the 1950s

In 1959, Screen Gems, a subsidiary of Columbia Pictures, Inc., bought KDYL-TV and changed its call sign to KCPX. Screen Gems' KCPX introduced some innovative children's programs in the early 1970s, including Hotel *Balderdash* and *Fireman Frank*, the latter hosted by the eminently talented Ron Ross, who also hosted the *Nightmare Theatre* on KCPX.[300]

Craig Wirth over the decades was an important Channel 4 journalist beginning in the 1970s. Wirth's first time at what later became KTVX-TV was from 1970-1974 as a Reporter, fresh out of high school and KRTV in Great Falls, MT. From 1976 to 1983 he was a Feature Reporter at Salt Lake's KUTV-

---

300   KTVX: https://en.wikipedia.org/wiki/KTVX; Tim Larson conversation with daughter Heather Ross, November 2019.

TV. His second turn at KTVX was from 1998-2002 as a Feature Reporter and Executive Producer for Special Projects. He returned to KTVX in 2013 as a Special Feature Reporter and continues to the present with his weekly *Wirth Watching* Utah Legacy Feature, now in its 30th season spanning his years at the station. In between his KTVX stints, the peripatetic Feature Reporter worked in Milwaukee, New York and Los Angeles at local TV stations and at national TV and cable networks, earning several feature reporting Emmy's along the way. In addition, as a freelance video documentary producer and writer, he produced dozens of documentaries that have aired among other places on PBS stations and National Public Television. Since 1998, Wirth has been an adjunct broadcast journalist and video production instructor in the University of Utah Communication Department, presently holding the title of Adjunct Associate Professor. Wirth, for the last 15 years has been the fulltime Director of Communications for the Episcopal Diocese of Utah, producing communications for the Utah diocese as well as for the U.S. Episcopal Church, which is part of the worldwide Anglican Communion tied to the Church of England.

Two figures notable in KDYL's first phase of operations had moved on to different ventures: Baldwin and Fox. In 1962, Baldwin went to New York City, where he became chief engineer of *Time's* foreign broadcast operations and built stations for *Time* in many foreign countries on several continents. He was a charter member of the Institute of Electronic and Electrical Engineers and a member of the Broadcast Pioneer and Television Pioneer societies. Baldwin retired to Salt Lake in 1970 and was unfailingly accessible to me until his death at age 74 on December 17, 1979. Baldwin once took me to the KCPX television Mt Vision transmitter site atop the Oquirrhs.

In April 1953, after the KDYL sale to Time, Inc. was concluded, Fox went to Los Angeles to attend the National Association of Broadcasters convention and to sell stock in himself and his newly declared management consulting business. His lawyer, Cal Rawlings, sent him a warm and friendly letter:[301]

---

301   Letter from Calvin Rawlings to S.S. Fox, C/O the Statler Hotel, Los Angeles, CA, April 25, 1953.

I am sure you will have occasion to advise those pros in regard
to how they can improve their 'stance.' They have not had the
privilege of being an old-time song and dance man. ... Your old
friends [in broadcasting] will all want the details of the sale and will
take occasion to pay homage to a successful retired Radio and TV
operator who is now embarking as a Consultant on a new adventure.
You should have no difficulty in selling stock in yourself now. Pick up
some substantial subscribers and I will incorporate you when you get
back.

After selling KDYL, Fox remained a KDYL management consultant for two years, essentially doing nothing and earning $50,000 per year. Because of a non-compete clause in the sales agreement, Fox could not engage in any broadcasting businesses in Utah for five years, so he found other business and consulting opportunities. In 1955, he became involved in a business arrangement with Colorado uranium mining leader Arnold Kimmes and Los Angeles furrier Charles Spellman, to take management control of the Royal Nevada Hotel in Las Vegas. The group planned to loan approximately three-quarters of a million dollars to the Royal Nevada Hotel in return for debenture stock --that is, unsecured stock paid for by the borrower in scheduled payments-- convertible to common stock. It is not exactly clear what Fox did at the Royal Nevada, what his level of ownership or control was or whether or not he ever realized a return on his money, but he ceased involvement in the Hotel within five years.

In 1956, three years after Fox sold the KDYL broadcasting stations, he joined Arnold Marquis to form what became Fox-Marquis Productions. The company's purpose was to organize, develop and promote programs for television. Fox owned the radio Diamond Dramas (discussed elsewhere in the book) and Marquis held the performance rights to Will Rogers, Sr.'s life story, among other things. Fox gave Marquis $2,500 for 50% interest in his holdings, and with other costs worked out, the two made plans to produce programs for television. Marquis' son and daughter became involved and some scripts were written, but it doesn't appear as if any actual television programs were sold by the partnership. The two remained friends but went their separate ways by the early 1960s.

Also, in 1956, Fox became sole owner of Miriam's, the women's clothing store that he traded his Hudson Bay Fur Company stock to Fred Provol for in 1948. Fox and Provol had each owned a 45% interest in Miriam's when it was formed in 1946. The store's namesake, stepdaughter Miriam Provol Fox Carson, owned 10%, and it was her interest that Fox bought in 1956 to become sole owner. In 1958, Fox sold Miriam's to non-family interests. In the 1960s, after selling Miriam's, Fox became involved in the trampoline rage of the times. He issued stock and sold trampolines and franchises for trampoline parks. This continued for a few years and, by all accounts, was not satisfactorily profitable.

Fox and his wife, Eva, were said to have kept a house both in Salt Lake and in Los Angeles, beginning in the late 1930s. In reality, they didn't live together very much after Eva moved to California. After Eva died in 1947, Fox married his KDYL secretary Zelda McQuarrie in August 1948. She was 36 years old and he was 59. McQuarrie died unexpectedly in September 1964, at age 52, from a congenital heart defect of which she was unaware. Well before she died, unbeknownst to Fox, Zelda had placed some of her assets into her sister Thelma's name for safekeeping, fearing for her financial well-being in the face of her husband's gambling losses.

As discussed earlier, Fox almost always prevailed in business ventures, especially in the many get-rich-quick deals he undertook. Akin to his broadcasting successes and a penchant for the quick-deal, however, was Fox's gambling addiction. He was a compulsive gambler. Unlike his successes in other schemes, in gambling, Fox was unsurprisingly unsuccessful. Gambling was an out-of-control aspect of his life for over 50 years. To get some idea of the money involved, Fox wrote gambling checks to Las Vegas casinos totaling $500 in 1942, increasing to $6,500 in 1943. From that year on his gambling expenses increased exponentially. In 1948, he wrote 41 checks totaling $22,000 to Las Vegas casinos. In 1952, the year before he sold his KDYL stations, he wrote gambling checks totaling $43,000, equal to over $256,000 in today's value.

On July 7, 1953, Fox received a $749,100 check for his part in the sale of the KDYL stations and paid $271,000 in taxes. Despite the exaggerated estimates by people over the last 50 years about the millions Fox personally reaped from the sale of KDYL, records indicate that when cash and consultancy payments are totaled, and taxes and other expenses are deducted, Fox likely received about $650,000 for himself. In 1954, he invested $353,354 with the J. A. Hogel Investment Brokerage Company in stocks and bonds and, at the same time, wrote 128 gambling checks to Nevada casinos totaling $152,500. In 1955, Fox invested a total of $82,200 and wrote checks totaling $193,000 to Las Vegas casinos, possibly some of that for investing in casino ownership.

Fox's gambling expenses were exceptional but decreased each year after 1955. In 1965, his gambling checks totaled $25,300, and in 1971, when he was 82 years old and out of money, they totaled only $25. Still, ever the gambler until his last days, however, Fox occasionally hopped a bus or would hitch a ride with a friend to Las Vegas to gamble with his only income, a modest Social Security check.[302]

In the last seven years of his life, Fox was helped with living expenses by a group of men who earlier had worked for him or had been helped by him in their careers. Beginning in about 1973, out of respect for his pioneering efforts in Utah broadcasting, these men sent money for Fox's livelihood. The group included former KDYL employees and friends: Baldwin, Lasky, Manny Drucker, Al Jensen, Alan Frank, and KCPX's Rainger, KSL's Madsen, attorney Rawlings, and charter IBC investor and Hudson Bay employee C. D. Creel. This group gave a total of about $2,000 a year to help Fox with expenses in his apartment at the Belvedere Hotel on State Street in Salt Lake City.[303]

His peers honored Fox with two significant awards. He received the Silver Medal Award from the Utah Advertising Federation in 1974 for initiating "new and exciting methods of radio and television advertising throughout his long career." And in 1978, he was inducted with fellow radio pioneer, Earl J. Glade,

302   The Papers of Sidney S. Fox (1889-1980), Manuscript Collection (Ms 559), Bx 7, Special Collections Department, University of Utah Libraries, Salt Lake City, Utah.
303   Letter from Calvin W. Rawlings to S. S. Fox. September 18, 1975.

into the Utah Broadcasters Hall of Fame. He and Glade were the first two to be so honored.

So it was with Fox, the ubiquitous promoter. He boasted about money, which he said never was a matter of great importance to him. He was enormously successful in making it over the years, and his attitude was "easy come, easy go." Fox died March 3, 1980, two months after his 91st birthday. He outlived every immediate family member except his stepson Robert Provol, who lived in Hollywood at the time. A granddaughter, Sydney Keffury, was named after her grandfather, and she lived in San Rafael, California, and later in Las Vegas. She has vivid childhood memories of growing up around her flamboyant "Popsie," as she called Fox.[304]

Other ownership changes inevitably eclipsed the historic circumstances that made KDYL Utah's first television station. In 1975, Screen Gems sold KCPX-TV to the 20th Century Fox Film Corporation, which changed the call sign to KTVX-TV. It held the station under its corporate umbrella, selling to Fox Television Station, Inc., a News Corporation subsidiary, in 2001. Gradually, KTVX gave up its early evenings newscasts, instead deciding to air episodes of *Truth or Consequences* and an 11 p.m. newscast, essentially serving as counterprograming to KUTV and KSL early and late evening newscasts.

Fox Television Stations, Inc., in 2001 almost immediately sold KTVX to Clear Channel Communications, Inc., which in 2007 then sold the station to Newport Television, who, in turn, in 2012 sold KTVX TV to the Nexstar Broadcasting Group, the present owner. Nexstar's initial foray and what became an enduring enterprise, where the company eventually came to own or control 285 U.S. television stations is discussed in a later chapter.

---

304   Sydney Keffury, interview with Tim Larson, at her home near San Francisco (circa 1990), and by phone in Las Vegas (circa 1995).

CHAPTER 16

KSL-TV: SALT LAKE CITY

As early as 1934 when Earl Glade was still managing KSL, the Radio Service Corporation showed interest in television by sending RSC Director John Fitzpatrick to New York City to ask CBS about its television intentions. Fitzpatrick reported back that CBS anticipated no real development for several years. Nevertheless, RSC President Sylvester Q. Cannon challenged KSL management to keep in touch with this phase of radio work in order that [KSL] may be prepared to move along with it from the very beginning."[305] Two years later, KSL received a letter from Philo T. Farnsworth, inventor of electronic television, encouraging KSL to "make a [television] set-up for experimental purposes."[306]

Television was not expected to be an immediate concern or an expected profit center. Even as the war wound down in 1945, there appeared "to be a long way to go before television broadcasting [would] emerge from the present experimental basis to one based on practical business procedures."[307]

Despite this concern, on May 26, 1948, KSL filed a television application with the FCC. KSL's main radio competitor, KDYL, had been on the air with its experimental TV license, W6XIS, and launched KDYL TV on April 19, 1948. a month before the KSL application was filed. The KALL radio principals also had recently filed a television application for one of the two available television licenses. A month later, KSL's Washington attorney, Ernest Wilkinson, urged the FCC to process KSL's application before a third applicant filed that triggered the need for comparative hearings to determine which of three applicants should get the two remaining Salt Lake City television licenses.

---

305 Minutes of the RSC Board of Directors Meeting, June 18, 1935.
306 Minutes of the RSC Board of Directors Meeting, August 17, 1936.
307 Minutes of the RSC Board of Directors Meeting, March 26, 1945.

On June 30, Wilkinson again requested the FCC to grant immediate approval to KSL but, as of July 13, it still had not been processed. Wilkinson then conferred directly with FCC Commissioner Rosel Hyde to determine what caused the delay:[308]

> [Hyde] reported that the difficulty was that [the FCC] had a standing rule that television applications would be processed in the order of their receipt and there were a number of applications [from around the country] filed before [KSL's] which had not yet been processed.

As a point of interest, two FRC or FCC commissioners were especially friendly to Utah broadcasters and to Wilkinson on behalf of KSL. They were FRC Commissioner Harold LaFount (1927-1934) and FCC Commissioner Rosel Hyde (1946-1969). Both were from Utah and graduates of Utah State University in Logan. LaFount left the FRC in 1934 for a successful career in commercial broadcasting, including positions with the Bulova Company, the Atlantic Coast Network, the Broadcasting Service Organization and the National Independent Broadcasters. Hyde, like Wilkinson, graduated from George Washington University Law School and had been on the staff of FRC and FCC. President Truman appointed him FCC Commissioner in 1946. LaFount and Hyde kept Wilkinson apprised of legal happenings affecting broadcasting.[309]

By mid-July in 1948, Wilkinson received more bad news from the FCC about KSL's television application. Within ten days, Howard D. Johnson's Granite City Broadcasting Company, owner of Salt Lake's KNAK radio station, reportedly was going to apply for a television station in Salt Lake City. With Johnson's entry, as indicated earlier, three applicants would be vying for two allocations, and expensive legal proceedings and delays would result. On July 21, Wilkinson conferred with FCC Commissioner George E. Sterling, who said he would try to do everything he could to place KSL's application before the FCC that day, so it would be approved before Granite Cities/KNAK application arrived.

---

308   Ernest L. Wilkinson, Letter to Ivor Sharp, July 13, 1948.
309   Gerald V. Flannery, ed., Commissioners of the FCC, 1927 - 1994, University Press of America, 1994.

Wilkinson also checked with the FCC engineering staff and was informed that there were 12 applications ahead of KSL's and that "because of serious criticism for processing applications out of order, they now strictly adhere to processing in order of receipt."[310] At the rate television applications were being processed at the FCC, approval of KSL's application would be at least four weeks away, with little hope that it would be approved before the Granite City application arrived at the FCC.

However, to Wilkinson's surprise, one week later, on July 29, the FCC approved KSL's application. It was approved before Granite City's application was filed, and KSL thus avoided a comparative hearing. Wilkinson explained that it was not merely a matter of luck by which KSL's license was approved in such a timely manner:[311]

> [FCC Commissioner Rosel Hyde] confessed to me that he had put so much pressure on the engineering staff to get the KSL application up for decision of the Commission that he was just a little afraid some members of the staff might suspect him of being partial. He pointed out, however, that the [KSL application] ... was not considered out of order, but because of the pressure he put on [the staff] to get to it, the Commission last week took action on 12 television applications, whereas customarily three is about the limit for one week.

Immediately after KSL's application was approved, KALL's attorneys contacted Commissioner Hyde to complain about KSL's preferential treatment. Hyde told KALL's attorneys that no preferential treatment had been given, that KSL's application had been pending for two months and that it had been processed in the order of receipt. KALL now faced possible hearings with the Granite City/KNAK applicant for the third Salt Lake television license and told Hyde that "[if] KALL was forced to a hearing, his clients might be critical and might have something to say."[312]

---

310   Ernest L. Wilkinson, Letter to Ivor Sharp, July 21, 1948.
311   Ernest L. Wilkinson, Letter to Ivor Sharp, August 6, 1948.
312   Ernest L. Wilkinson, August 6, 1948.

KSL attorney Wilkinson was incensed at the KALL attorneys' threats and related that KALL radio had received special treatment from the FCC only a few years before: "This attitude [of KALL] is quite reprehensible, especially in view of the fact that KALL [radio] owes its existence to special preference given it during war time allowing it to proceed."[313] Readers will recall an earlier chapter detailing how the KALL radio permits had been granted to Hinckley and Hatch during World War II. Notably, Wilkinson's indignation in 1948 was over the fact that, because Hinckley was close to President Roosevelt and Vice President Truman, the White House had intervened on behalf of the KALL applicants to grant the KALL construction permit, even though it required the use of critical resources during war time. Wilkinson concluded: "There cannot possibly be any attack on the grant to KSL because it was done in a perfectly regular manner and even though matters were speeded up, everything on the docket was speeded up at the same time."[314]

KSL-TV's symbiotic relationship with the LDS Church

As with KSL radio, dating to 1922, KSL television developed and maintained a symbiotic relationship with the Church of Jesus Christ of Latter-day Saints. Earl Glade had taken seriously the teachings, needs and sensitivities of the LDS Church in his programming of KSL, and Ivor Sharp was even more sensitized to the church leadership's needs in his decision-making. After all, his father-in-law was not only his family and professional leader but also his ecclesiastical leader. It is arguable that Clark's election to the position of RSC president was as much to mitigate LDS Church concerns about programming and advertising as it was to put KSL on a better business standing. Clark, in turn, hired Sharp to reorganize KSL and to produce bottom-line business results but also to produce programming and content more acceptable to the leaders and members of the LDS Church.

KSL radio and the LDS Church had significant policy issues in common, especially concerning beer and tobacco advertisements. In October 1938, just before Sharp arrived at the station, there were 52 beer announcements on KSL

313   Wilkinson, August 6, 1948.
314   Wilkinson, August 6, 1948.

radio in that month. By 1942, Sharp saw to it that no beer advertisers were given access to KSL, and, as such, no beer spots were aired for nearly a decade after that. "To many church members served by KSL [these changes] will be approved and of interest."[315]

After KSL opened commercial television operations on June 1, 1949, Sharp maintained the no-beer-ad policy for two years but found that business needs also overrode LDS Church considerations. It involved a lengthy process, but at an RSC Board meeting on October 5, 1951, the ban on beer advertising was reversed and beer accounts were again accepted for commercial sponsorship on all three KSL stations: AM, FM and TV.

The reason for the reversal was due to the fact that beer advertisers were major sponsors on the CBS network. If KSL continued to preempt the beer advertisements, the CBS programs in which beer ads were run would be released through other radio and television stations in KSL's coverage area, and, eventually, CBS would drop its affiliation with KSL. If that happened, KSL's influence in Utah and in the other areas of the Intermountain West served by KSL would be negligible.

This represented a major shift in policy by the LDS Church, the majority KSL stockholder. Under Sharp and Clark, KSL and the LDS Church were closely tied. KSL did not accept beer ads because the church saw such accounts in conflict with its doctrine. In 1951, with resumed acceptance of beer accounts, the church effectively separated its ecclesiastical functions from its temporal or business functions. The decision to accept beer accounts was rationalized to the LDS Church by the RSC Board in the following way:[316]

> [Clark] reported that upon three different occasions this matter [of beer advertisements] had been presented to the majority stockholders and that after careful consideration they had arrived reluctantly at the

---

315   Principal Activities and Accomplishments of Radio Station KSL during the period August 1938 to August 1943, prepared for President J. Reuben Clark, Jr. by Ivor Sharp, August 12, 1943, 9.
316   Radio Service Corporation of Utah, Board of Directors Minutes, October 25, 1951. As reported in "Year End Report...1951 Radio Service Corporation of Utah," Memorandum to President Clark from Ivor Sharp, March 17, 1952, Part 6, 4.

decision to accept Network beer sponsored programs, if approved by the [RSC] Directors. However, they urged that the negative aspects of the commercials be minimized to the extent possible. President Clark stated that the decision of the majority of stockholders had been reached as a result of the recognition that KSL, by virtue of its franchise with the Government [FCC license], was serving in a public utility relationship and, therefore, obliged to serve all of the people and, also because it seemed clear, under existing conditions, that the continued refusal of KSL-AM and KSL-TV to accept accounts under beer sponsorship would reduce the high standing of this Corporation in the radio industry. ... After discussion and upon motion of Earl J. Glade ... the Board voted unanimously to authorize the Management to negotiate such contracts as are necessary to protect and best serve the combined interest of KSL-AM and KSL-TV, including beer business as may be required to this end."

Later in the 1950s, KSL officially put all its activities on behalf of the LDS Church strictly on a business basis to avoid conflict with CBS and the FCC, as well as to ameliorate criticism by LDS Church leaders and members. At that time, an accounting was made of KSL's contributions over the years to the LDS Church, and the results were surprising.

It was found that KSL had been enormously generous with its broadcasting facilities. From 1939 to 1955, KSL radio and KSL-TV provided 1,653 hours of broadcast time to the LDS Church. For the period of 1939 to 1950, cash payments by KSL to the Mormon Tabernacle Choir for expenses and record album sales totaled $97,000. And from 1929 to 1955, RSC dividends totaling almost $300,000 were paid to the LDS Church as majority owner of KSL. In addition, each month, year after year, KSL incurred extra expenses amounting to $600 because of special handling of Tabernacle Choir and LDS Church programs. Besides these payments for services KSL rendered, the LDS Church did very well with its RSC investment in KSL stock. It invested a total of $245,370 in KSL, from which it received dividends and other cash payments of $395,872 in return. An internal memorandum confirmed this:[317]

---

317   Jay W. Wright, "Memorandum to President J. Reuben Clark, Jr." September 30, 1955, 7.

In other words, the Church already has been paid in cash over 160 percent of its total investment. In addition, the value of the original investment had multiplied 210%; the book value of KSL stock as of June 30, 1955, was $410, and thus the Church's financial interest in the station is worth $514,146. This value is on the book basis; the sale value would be much greater.

The above financial data speak only to actual money transactions between KSL and the LDS Church. Not counted are the incalculable hours given free by KSL employees, most of who were affiliated with the LDS Church. For example, in May 1955, "KSL Television had 72 full time employees, 65 of which were members of the LDS Church, and the majority of those were ... active in some capacity in their Ward or Stake."[318]

As an aside, among the church affiliations represented by the seven non-LDS employees at KSL-TV, were Greek Orthodox, Methodist, Episcopalian and one person with no affiliation.

KSL-TV cements its place in Utah television market

By all calculations, Sharp organized an excellent KSL television station, one that became the model for the CBS network and many television stations in much larger markets across the nation. There were some difficult years, however, and it is to Sharp's credit that he sustained KSL's commitment to television, in the face of huge start-up expenses, significant competition, and deep losses in its first two years of operation.

KSL was significantly enhanced when the transcontinental microwave service finally could provide network television service to Salt Lake City, beginning on September 5, 1951. When the microwave was initiated, the Japanese Peace Conference from San Francisco was received via microwave and carried directly on KSL. This was soon followed by a playoff game between the New York Giants and Brooklyn Dodgers to determine the National League

---

318   Employment & Personnel Report, Full-Time Employees KSL-TV, May 1, 1955.

champion for the 1951 World Series. The CBS network thereafter provided about 10 hours per week of live programming via microwave to KSL, at a cost of about $2,600 per month. KSL's revenues increased by 200% in 1951, and it was on its way to profitability.

To increase its coverage and its revenue, KSL proposed to move its transmitting antenna to the mountaintop. A site in the Oquirrh Mountains was surveyed in 1951 and developed in 1952, under the direction of Chief Engineer Vince E. Clayton. The site was west of Salt Lake City on Coon Peak, named after the family that owned it, and later renamed Farnsworth Peak, after Farnsworth, the Utah-born discoverer of electronic television.

Because a private landowner was not willing to give a right-of-way across his property, a used tramway was purchased from the Triumph Mining Company of Ketchum, Idaho, and installed on the west side, or Tooele side, of the mountain to give all-weather access to the KSL transmitter. The tram was used for many years to transport people, materials and equipment, although its use ended in later years because it was deemed unsafe due to vandalism by hunters and others.

On December 5, 1952, the newly constructed KSL TV tower on Coon Peak toppled in winds estimated at 500 miles per hour (see explanation below for why the unusually high velocity likely occurred). The incident, with pictures, was reported in *Life* magazine. The top two-thirds of the structure was made from an old tower, which had been in use for about thirty years, and this was thought to have contributed to the collapse.[319]

Clayton, who prepared the mountain top site explained what he thought happened:[320]

> We had gust velocities in excess of 500 miles an hour. And the way
> this came about was that there was a standing wave relationship
> between the Oquirrh range and ... the Stansbury range ... the next

319   David L. Sargent, Jr. and Hoffman C. Hughes, Letter to K.S.L. Television, December 16, 1952.
320   Vince Clayton, interview withTim Larson, Tape No. U-474, transcript, 8, June 27, 1986, Everett L. Cooley Oral History Project, Marriott Library, University of Utah, Salt Lake City, Utah.

range out there. Then there was a Bernouli increased velocity effect where the winds came up through Big Canyon and came over the top of the mountain. They figured that using those multiplying factors if they all came together when the free space wind was 150 miles an hour that there could have been impulses as high as 500 miles an hour. And the tower wouldn't have stood too much of a chance during that.

As an aside, Chief Engineer John Baldwin of KDYL, was constructing a tower at about the same time in the Oquirrhs and was in a race with KSL to complete KDYL's tower first. Not one to miss a publicity opportunity, Baldwin couldn't resist chiding Clayton in the widely read *RCA Broadcast Review Journal.* As Clayton humorously related: "John had a picture and an article by him on how haste-makes-waste. [Humorously saying], I have never completely forgiven him for it. ... [It was] in all the national publications ... and then Johnny had to follow it up ... saying maybe they were second, but they were best."[321]

In the final analysis, the cause of the collapse was determined to be a combination of things. One thing for certain, the experience was frightening for the engineers present on Coon Peak when the tower blew down:[322]

> The KSL engineers on duty there at the time stated it was the most frightening experience of their lives and they hope that they will never have to go through another ordeal of that nature. Mr. Les Price reported ... that the wind blew hard all night and Friday morning, December 5. In the afternoon it became more gusty and swirling and at times, it would die down to periods of relative calm, then out of a calm it would strike suddenly with a thunderous roar and great force. These boys are not timid but they were frightened and admit it.

---

321   Vince Clayton, interview with Tim Larson, 8.
322   Ivor Sharp, Letter to Professor J. Vern Hales, Mines Building, University of Utah, January 9, 1953.

In 1955, Sharp was ready to step down from his management position at KSL, and Clark and other RSC Board members searched for his replacement. Among others, they conferred with engineer Jay W. Wright, who decades earlier had worked for KSL as a transmitter technician. During World War II, Wright had been involved in contracts with the U.S. government to develop electronic devices to detect the whereabouts of enemy submarines. After the war, Wright helped construct a structure atop the Empire State Building in New York City to secure the television antennas for CBS along with several other networks and stations. Wright initially was hired at KSL as administrative vice president, and Sharp continued for another year, preparing Wright to take over.

In March 1956, Sharp was named vice president in charge of corporate developments, and Wright was named executive Vice President.[323] Sharp seemed to genuinely welcome the change: "This is a welcome relief from the pressure of sales, programs, and operations. My work will be more related to our associations with other radio and television stations."[324]

Wright found change at KSL difficult to achieve. He wanted to take KSL in some new directions, but, because Clark was sick and not available for day-to-day consultation, change came slowly.[325] Even when Steven L. Richards replaced Clark as RSC president, the old ways of doing things had permeated the business process at KSL. Nevertheless, Wright moved KSL forward with the help of people like Joe Kjar, Vince Clayton and Lennox Murdoch. In 1961, after five years heading KSL, Wright was enticed by King Broadcasting to go to Seattle to be vice president of corporate engineering, with responsibilities over the entire radio, television and cable operations. Arch Madsen succeeded him at KSL.

Sharp managed KSL well for nearly 20 years, under difficult

---

323   Broadcasting Magazine, April 9, 1956, p. 66.
324   Ivor Sharp, Letter to Howard R. Driggs, President, American Pioneer Trails Association, April 5, 1956.
325   Jay W. Wright, interview with Tim Larson, February 13, 1992, Seattle, Washington.

circumstances, as he served under J. Reuben Clark, Jr., his all-powerful ecclesiastical, corporate and family leader. His tenure consolidated KSL-TV's operations, which have continued uninterrupted to the present.

CHAPTER 17

KUTV TELEVISION: SALT LAKE CITY

Things were going well with their radio businesses, so on December 24, 1952, the Utah Broadcasting Company (UBC) principals, including Frank C. Carman, David G. Smith, Grant R. Wrathall, and members of the late Jack L. Powers family — Edna O. Powers McCrea and her daughter, Sharon Lee Powers— formed the Utah Broadcasting and Television Corporation (UBTC). Its purpose was to apply for a television station on Channel 2 in Salt Lake City. Each of the four principals held 25% of UBTC's stock, although Carman and Wrathall owned all of the voting stock, with Smith and the Powers' family carrying non-voting stock. D. Ray Owen, Jr. was secretary and a director of UTBC, but not an owner or a stockholder. He was UBTC's local attorney in the law firm of Owen & Ward and was also involved as an officer in some Idaho radio holdings of the UBC.

Just before Carman and UBTC filed their application with the FCC for Channel 2, another group filed for the same Channel 2 allocation. Television Corporation of Utah (TCU), wholly owned by the Salt Lake Tribune Publishing Company, applied just before UBTC submitted its application. Jack Gallivan, secretary-treasurer of the Salt Lake Tribune Publishing Company, was the major force behind TCU's application. Gallivan explained how the two applications were reconciled:[326]

> As I recall, I simply went to Frank [Carman] and said, "Frank, if we get into a hearing before the FCC it's going to cost both of us an awful lot of money. And that is money that we're going to need to offset the early days' operating deficits. If television is as good as we both think it is, fifty percent of the Salt Lake station is enough." And he agreed. And it took just about that long. So, as fast as we could put together a

---

326   John W. Gallivan, interview with Tim Larson, April 4, 1990, Salt Lake City, Utah.

merged application, we did.

To facilitate the partnership, Carman and Wrathall each sold one-half
of their UBTC voting stock to the Salt Lake Tribune Publishing Company,
and Smith and the Powers family did the same with their non-voting stock.
As a result, Utah Broadcasting and Television Corporation and the Salt
Lake Tribune each came to own 50% of UBTC's issued stock. Gallivan then
withdrew TCU's application, and he and Carman filed an amended UTBC
application.

Gallivan and Carman went to Washington, D.C. to appear before the FCC
on their joint application. They stayed at the Hilton Hotel, trying to keep their
presence a secret, because there were rumblings that a third party was also
interested in filing for a Salt Lake television license. That third application
was not filed, but Brent Kirk, who formerly worked for the *Tribune* and *Salt
Lake Telegram* and was then working for the *Washington Post*, found out what
Gallivan and Carman were doing in Washington. Gallivan recalled the story
more than 37 years later:[327]

> To this day I do not know how he [Kirk] found out that I was in
> Washington and why I was there. The Wednesday morning that we
> came down the elevator to go to the FCC to get our merged grant of
> licensing, we were accosted as we walked across the lobby. Brent Kirk
> said, "I want to be general manager [of your new station]." Brent Kirk
> was [KUTV's] general manager the day we went on the air. It didn't
> hurt us at all [that he knew we were applying for the station]. We got a
> great General Manger out of it.

The FCC immediately approved the merged application, almost on
the spot. It, too, was not interested in any lengthy hearings. Each of the
original four UBTC partners contributed $50,000, and the Salt Lake Tribune
contributed $200,000 to construct the station. Approximately $103,000 of
the Carman group's share of financing was provided in the form of television
equipment that they bought prior to filing the joint application. Both Carman

---

327   Gallivan, interview with Tim Larson, 1990.

and Gallivan also contributed their labor in constructing the station. Gallivan remembered the efforts to put Salt Lake's third television station on the air:[328]

> I was involved in management. I would spend about three hours every afternoon over there as we were getting it on the air, working with Frank on a very compatible basis. Starting up any business required decisions every day and they need to be made quickly. To expedite the decisions, I was just there.

Carman was responsible for obtaining and installing all the television studio equipment, as well as the tower and transmitter. He located an available two-hundred-foot tower at the Lake Theatre in Chicago. It could be had at no charge if he took it off the building. Carman went to Chicago for ten days and, working at night, dismantled the tower piece by piece, put it on a truck and delivered it to Salt Lake City. The tower was cut to about 175 feet, to give it more wind resistance and was erected in the Oquirrh Mountains on Coon Peak (later Farnsworth Peak), about 500 feet from KSL's equipment. KUTV used that tower and antenna for 40 years.

Carman also set up a small manufacturing operation and began copying equipment from various television manufacturers. There was no patentable technology involved with the television equipment Carman was copying, so he was not doing anything illegal. Carman copied General Electric's synchronizing generator, RCA's cameras, like Baldwin had done earlier at KDYL, and was trying to copy DuMont's transmitter. The transmitter was more difficult to reverse-engineer, or copy, than the other equipment.

The DuMont Company had a television transmitter installation on Lookout Mountain overlooking Denver, so Carman sent his engineers over there to copy it. After the transmitter was shut down for the evening, Carman's engineers would open it up and make sketches and take all kinds of electrical measurements. From this information, Carman manufactured a television transmitter in his Salt Lake shop:[329]

---

328   Gallivan, interview with Tim Larson, November 16, 1987, Salt Lake City, Utah.
329   Lyle O. Keys, chairman of Teltrust, Inc., Salt Lake City, Utah, Interview by Tim Larson, April 23, 1994.

They were just reverse-engineering [copying] the transmitter.
But there is a certain amount of black-art [extraneous signals] in
transmitters, and building one that doesn't have parasitic oscillations
and other problems is not all that easy. [Black-art] was what was
bugging Carman's transmitter.

Carman unsuccessfully tried again and again to debug his homemade
Channel 2, reverse engineered DuMont transmitter. Several times the *Salt
Lake Tribune* announced an airdate for KUTV, and each time there was a
problem, and the date was missed. Because the *Salt Lake Tribune* took great
pride in this endeavor and was embarrassed by the delays, Gallivan called Lyle
O. Keys, a DuMont salesman and transmitter installer, to ask for his help. It so
happened that Keys was at a Cheyenne, Wyoming, television station swapping
a 25kW transmitter in place of a 5kW one when Gallivan contacted him.
Gallivan asked how long it would take for Keys to find a transmitter for KUTV,
and Keys said he already had one and it would take about a day to transfer it
to Salt Lake City. Gallivan contracted with Keys over the phone to bring the
recently dismantled 5kW DuMont television transmitter from Cheyenne.
Keys put it on a truck to Salt Lake City and had all the associated parts and
electronics air-shipped from New Jersey. Keys then came to Salt Lake City and
in two days of round-the-clock work successfully installed the transmitter and
had it operating without interference.

In a related sidebar, The Kearns-Tribune Corporation, and their KUTV
partners incorporated what became TeleMation Inc., Inc. in the 1960s, to
provide hard-to-get electronic parts for the television industry --closed
circuit TV, cable, industrial and education TV. Keys, the company's talented
president, conceptualized, engineered and marketed many of the company's
proprietary products. TeleMation Inc. later became a division of Bell and
Howell.[330]

---

330   Lyle O. Keys, interview with Tim Larson;
TeleMation, Inc.: https://en.wikipedia.org/wiki/TeleMation_Inc.

KUTV-TV went on the air September 26, 1954. The KUTV call letters were a natural derivation from KUTA, Carman's AM station. KUTV was affiliated with the ABC Network, which provided its only program, Disney's *Mickey Mouse Club*. Early on, KUTV locally programmed around-the-clock feature movies and attracted a very large audience.

Because the Carman group and the Salt Lake Publishing Company each had a 50% share in the station, they each also committed to paying 50% of all the expenses associated with operating it. It was estimated that KUTV would generate $650,000 in advertising revenue per year once it went on the air, and that these profits would be used to pay operating expenses. That figure proved to be very optimistic, and Carman found himself spending the windfall profits that KUTA AM radio generated during the war years and after to pay his share of KUTV television expenses.

Carman and UBTC had grossly underestimated the amount of money it would take to get the television station on the air. Of course, the significant resources of the Salt Lake Publishing Company allowed it to easily pay its share of expenses, but Carman found that he could not generate sufficient revenues from KUTA to pay his share.[331] The Carman group was forced to put its 50% share of KUTV up for sale. As Gallivan remembered: "Actually, Carman gave us notice that he was just unable to match the Tribune in paying operating deficits. George Hatch then approached Carman, representing the Standard [Corporation] principally, but also himself and Gene [his wife] and negotiated a buy-out."[332]

Robert Temple becomes KUTV general manager

In 1956, A. L. (Abe) Glasmann's Standard Corporation and George and Wilda Gene Hatch bought Carman's 50% ownership in KUTV. The Hatches, Glasmann's son-in-law and daughter, acquired a 14% interest in KUTV in the

---

331 Application for a Television Station by Utah Broadcasting and Television Company, Federal Communications, Form 301, 14 March 1953, Exhibit 5C.
332 Gallivan, interview with Tim Larson, November 16, 1987.

Carman buyout. George Hatch became KUTV president, which he remained for 40 years. Abe Glasmann was made vice president, Gallivan was secretary, and George Egan, comptroller of the Kearns-Tribune Corporation, became the treasurer. That constituted the board of directors. Kirk continued as general manager.

Hatch hired Robert H. Temple in 1965 as the KUTV general manager. Temple graduated from the University of Idaho in 1943 and then served in the U.S. Army Medical Corps for three years during WWII. Shortly after the war, he landed his first broadcasting job as a sales person at KREM in Spokane, Washington. He admits he knew little about broadcasting, only "that there were three knobs on a radio set: one to turn it on and off, the other for volume and the third to change the station." However, he rose to become the KREM manager and stayed in Spokane until 1962. He went to KTVI in St. Louis for over two years as national sales manager, and then to Salt Lake City in 1965 as general manager/vice president of KUTV for the next 18 years.

Temple explained how he arrived at KUTV:

> I had a call from Jerry O'Brien who [was] the publisher of the Tribune
> --Jerry and I had known each other in Spokane, Jerry was a Spokane
> boy, a Gonzaga University graduate, … now on the board of trustees,
> has been for many years. And Jerry was then with AP, came down
> [to Salt Lake], became bureau chief, and subsequently was hired by
> Jack Gallivan as assistant to the publisher. I had this call from
> Jerry O'Brien. He asked me if I knew George Hatch. I said, "Only
> by name." He said, "I can't believe that." He said, "He's even been in
> broadcasting longer than you have." You don't mean you haven't met
> him." I said, "No, I just know him by name." "Well," he said, "we
> [Kearns Tribune] own 37-percent of the NBC affiliate [KUTV] here,
> and our station manager died, and I just wondered if you'd be
> interested." I'd made up my mind that I wanted to go back West.

Temple met with Hatch and Glasmann and within four weeks moved to Salt Lake City from St. Louis. Hatch needed a strong KUTV station manager

in 1965 to oversee daily operations. As explained earlier in the chapter about
KALL radio, Hatch was not a hands-on station operator. He focused almost
exclusively on station ownership matters and on corporate growth and
development issues. And, like his counterparts at the time, Hack Woolley at
Channel 4 and Arch Madsen at Channel 5, he hired people and was a promoter
but not a skilled marketer. He was, for the most part, not involved in day-to-
day decision-making or with direct sales to advertising clients.

Temple was given a free hand to engage his three Cs – Communication,
Cooperation and Contribution– with his staff but learned there was an
exception to his efforts. Hatch told him that it was a "small community" he was
managing and didn't want a lot of staff separations. "In fact," Hatch told him,
"We don't want any separations." Hatch was heart-deep in the station's internal
and external communities, and staff hiring and "separations" were under his
consideration and control. A person in the know, however, recounts that on
occasion Temple served as Hatch's "bad cop."

Temple was somewhat ahead of contemporary television operations
and marketing/sales in 1965. He contracted multifaceted audience research
and applied data-driven marketing and sales at KUTV to differentiate its
product. For instance, among other data-driven applications, he introduced
Advertising-to -Sales calculations. An A/S ratio is calculated by dividing
total advertising expenses by sales revenue. The advertising-to-sales ratio is
designed to show whether or not the resources a firm spends on an advertising
campaign helped to generate new sales, and to what extent it generated those
sales. A/S gave a competitive advantage to KUTV's salespeople when they
groomed national, regional and local advertising clients.

Temple recalled how proud he was of the gifted sales talent at KUTV:[333]

> [Al Seethaler] became general sales manager. Pat Kirk as national
> sales manager. Dale Dunn and Al Seethaler were co-local sales
> managers. Pat was the first female national sales manager in a major
> television market in the United States. And we just broke all sorts

---

333   Robert Temple, an interview with Tim Larson, September 8, 1986.

of tradition there. And she gave us an edge because at that time the bulk of the buyers were young females --downtrodden, overworked, abused in every sense of the word [in the business]. And Pat would walk in as national sales manager. And there was an affinity. Wherever there was an even choice, we got it; whenever it was close, [Pat} got it.

Pat Kirk worked at KUTV from 1959 to 2000. She came to Salt Lake with her husband Brent Kirk who became KUTV's general manager in 1956. Pat Kirk joined the KUTV sales staff and worked with National Sales Manager Alan. H. (Skip) Branch from 1966 to 1973. She assumed that position when Branch left KUTV to start his own advertising agency. Mrs. Pat Kirk, as she was distinguished in the Broadcasting Yearbook, was a very successful national sales manager under Bob Temple, as explained above.

George Hatch hired Skip Branch in 1966. He had been the Sales Service Manager for ABC's Western Division in Los Angeles. Branch joined the iconic Harris and Love Advertising Agency in 1999, becoming a partner in 2002. Harris and Love was sold to the Phoenix based Riester Agency in 2005. Branch was a senior partner and ran the Salt Lake office until he retired in 2015.

While at KUTV, Temple also was tapped to serve as a consultant to Honolulu, Hawaii's KGMB, a station owned by Cecil Heftel, who, like Hatch, was a Glasmann son-in-law. The two were at opposite ends of the social spectrum. Hatch was a specialist and, according to Temple, "a consummate glutton for finite detail." Heftel was "a generalist and didn't like detail. He was people oriented; George [was] not." Temple told Abe Glasmann that "if you hadn't put them at one another's throats, you could have wiped up the country," adding, "I'd say they're geniuses."

In addition to expanding marketing and sales efforts at KUTV, Hatch sought to improve the commercial, news and on-air production quality. He brought in Dick Cardwell from Oklahoma City to change the on-air look, making the station's output "more professional and precise." This was enhanced with a stable of new and existing broadcast journalists who joined Doug

Mitchell, KUTV's news anchor, one of the most commanding figures in Utah broadcast journalism history.

Doug Mitchell was the voice of KUTV. He did news, weather and sports when he arrived at the station in the 1950s. Hatch had recruited him from a Boston station to be KUTV's anchor that became a household name, thanks to his rich, deep voice that conveyed the authority of truth and accuracy. Later, Mitchell was joined by other legends, longtime sports anchor Bill Marcroft, and weather forecaster Mark Eubank. Mitchell was known to not use a script but instead memorized the news he reported on air in the 1950s. His anchor career lasted through the 1960s and into the late 1970s when he became the station's public affairs director. Terry Wood and later Patrick Greenlaw assumed the KUTV anchor position, and Mitchell remained in daytime newscasts. KUTV became a ratings powerhouse at that time, often neck-and-neck with KSL's Nourse, Welti and James for the top-rated newscasts in the Salt Lake City market. News Director Rick Spratling and Hatch expended great effort to bring several firsts to Utah news. These included the long-form evening newscast and the conversion from film to videotape, among other important contributions.[334]

While at KUTV and after he retired in 1983, Temple valued community service and gave his time to many local organizations including serving as the president of the United Way of the Greater Salt Lake Area, as well as on the boards of the University of Utah Pioneer Memorial Theatre, the Salt Lake City Chamber of Commerce, the Utah Travel Council and the Kimball Arts Center. He was honored at the Utah Summer Games in 1998 for his advocacy of the broadcasting of high school athletics in Utah.[335]

Ownership changes afoot

From 1956 to 1967, A.L. Glasmann/Standard Corporation/*Ogden Standard Examiner* (51%), the Kearns-Tribune Corporation /*Salt Lake Tribune* (35%), and City Broadcasting/George and Wilda Gene Hatch (14%) owned

---

334   Craig B. Wirth, email to Tim Larson, April 30, 2022.
335   Robert Temple, interview with Tim Larson, September 8, 1986; Deseret News, October 25, 2003.

KUTV.

Jack Gallivan, although he didn't want to, took the Kearns-Tribune
Corporation/*Salt Lake Tribune* out of KUTV-TV ownership entirely in the
late 1960s. The story of this transaction is intriguing. The heirs of U.S. Senator
Thomas Kearns controlled the stock of the Kearns-Tribune Corporation,
owner of the *Salt Lake Tribune*. Two of his grandchildren, John Paul Brophy
– born Gian Carlo Gabellini, and later adopted by Harold Brophy – and Sheila
McCarthey Wood, the daughter of Helen Kearns McCarthey, each owned 22%
of the Kearns-Tribune Corporation stock and wanted to sell their shares. They
didn't believe Kearns-Tribune was paying high enough dividends. Brophy
actually talked his sister into cashing out with him. Brophy explained years
later why he decided to do it." I [told] her, 'Look Sheila, if we do this you can
have $300,000 a year instead of $180,000. ... So we persuaded them to buy us
out. ... We should have offered the stock outside [of the Kearns-Tribune] and
gotten three times the price for it."[336]

Gallivan tried to talk Brophy and Wood out of selling their Kearns-
Tribune stock, but was unsuccessful. So, the Kearns-Tribune bought back 44%
of its stock from Brophy and Wood, using appreciated assets. Included in the
appreciated assets were two Salt Lake buildings and Kearns Corporation's 35%
interest in KUTV. Immediately, Brophy and Wood sold their newly acquired
35% interest in KUTV to Hatch (20%) and Glasmann (80%), making them
100% owners of the station. Brophy talks about what he and his sister did with
the money:[337]

> We retained the two buildings. My sister and I retained the Kearns
> Building and the Tribune Building. ... Anyway, we got a lot of cash
> and put it in the oil and gas business, and we had a great ten years,
> let's put it that way. ... I have had a great time with my money. I have
> had racehorses, yachts. I have been around the world. I have given
> great parties. I have made lots of friends, and people still think that I
> am rich and I am not. ... That is okay, I never look back. ... But I have

336   John P. Brophy, interview by Tim Larson, 4 February 1990, Tape No. 1203, transcript, 49,
Everett L. Cooley Oral History Project, Marriott Library, University of Utah, Salt Lake City, Utah.
337   John P. Brophy, interview with Tim Larson, 50.

that aura about me here [in San Diego]. So I have had a lot of fun
with it, I really have.

From 1967 to 1993, several named Glasmann/Hatch companies
--Standard Corporation, Salt Lake Broadcasting Company, Communications
Investment Corporation --controlled KUTV-TV, licensed to KUTV Inc. or
KUTV Associates. Jeff Hatch, George and Gene's son, was KUTV general
manager from 1989 to 1995. Diane Orr, a Hatch daughter, was news director
during those years. For a year (1993-1994), the Hatch family (60%) partnered
with VS&A (Veronis Suhler & Associates, 40%), with Hatch as president to
cover debt-servicing burdens. By the following year (1994-1995), NBC (88%)
and Hatch (12%) controlled KUTV.

Also, in 1995, CBS/Group W began a complicated musical chairs
ownership exchange with NBC that resulted in CBS (88%) and George Hatch
(12%) in control of KUTV-TV. CBS and NBC exchanged certain television
broadcast stations and assets in Denver, Miami, Philadelphia and Salt Lake
City. CBS, amid exchanges in other cities, acquired, on behalf of the CBS/NBC
joint venture, KUTV-TV in Salt Lake City. The amount of $124 million was
paid for the station, consisting of a combination of cash and the assumption of
the station's debt obligations. Thus, Group W owned KUTV-TV from 1995 to
2000.[338]

For the first time in nearly 40 years, as a result of the exchange in 1995,
Hatch and his family no longer controlled any share of KUTV-TV. As
discussed in the KALL chapter, the highly leveraged Salt Lake Broadcasting
Company, with Hatch as president, had already sold KALL in 1992 to the
Apollo Radio Partners.

In 2000, the CBS Corporation/CBS, Inc. (Viacom Station Group) acquired
full ownership of KUTV-TV, later selling the station in 2007 to Cerberus
Capital Management's Four Points Media Group, which held the television
station until 2011. The station was then sold to the Sinclair Broadcast Group,

---

338   CBS announcement, November 21, 1995; Craig B. Wirth, History of KUTV.

owners of KUTV to the present. Sinclair is discussed elsewhere in this section of the book.

Daughter, Diane Orr, proudly summarized the Hatch media empire: "It showed grace going up and grace coming down."

CHAPTER 18

TELECOMMUNICATIONS, INC.:
STANDARD CORPORATION & KEARNS-TRIBUNE
CORPORATION

This chapter links the past with the future. Cable, or wire, is where it all started, and wire --today, fiber optic wire-- is where it has headed once again. The transformation has been referred to as the "Negroponte flip-flop,'" so named for Nicholas Negroponte, founder and emeritus chair of the MIT Media Lab. In the mid-1990s, he predicted that media previously delivered over the air would be delivered by wire as well as vice versa, or flip-flopped, as it was commonly referenced. As such, Negroponte envisioned that wired telephones would move to wireless delivery and broadcasting would move to wire or cable. Negroponte's predicted flip-flop has become mostly true. We are headed back to the future, initiated in the past by the cable partnership of companies such as the Standard Corporation and the Kearns-Tribune Company of Utah.

The story of the KUTV television partnership has already been told in this book. In this chapter, the Standard Corporation and Kearns-Tribune cable partnership is discussed as a brief history of cable television in Utah, which in turn, chronicles the historical involvement of George Hatch and Jack Gallivan in the founding and evolvement of Tele-Communications, Inc. (TCI), a cable television company that eventually became the nation's largest of its kind.

Soon after they established the KUTV, Inc. partnership, the Standard Corporation and the Kearns-Tribune again partnered to construct microwave and cable facilities to deliver KUTV and the other Salt Lake television signals to communities in the Intermountain West region not served by television. This partnership of two Utah newspaper owners, however, was not the first to bring cable television to the state.

Cable television officially came to Utah on April 1, 1955, not in Salt Lake City, the Wasatch Front or in populated areas of northern Utah, but instead in Moab. The city had cable television before it even had a radio station. Forrest L. Simpson and Fred R. Doppelmayr, entrepreneurs who were owners of a Moab blueprint company, bought out Robert H. Downum, to become the majority shareholders of Moab Broadcasting and Television Corporation (MBTC). They were awarded a cable franchise in Moab and, by March 1956, had "been actively televising programs over their closed-circuit television system for several months."[339]

MTBC provided service to 40 subscribers. It had sold television sets to 34 of those subscribers, and had subscription contracts for 88 more homes, as soon as the connections could be completed. Subscribers paid $150 to hook up and $7.50 per month after that for cable programming. MBTC provided cable programs for a minimum of eight hours a day, consisting of films from the Trans-Community Television Network, Inc.; and programs from ABC and NBC, like *Kraft Theater*, the *Mickey Mouse Club*, *Wyatt Earp*, *Sid Caesar's Hour* and *Ding Dong School*. There also were locally originated news and public service programs for up to three hours a day. MBTC later acquired KURA radio in Moab and operated it for a short time.

On October 1, 1956, a year after Moab received cable, Utah's second cable service began, this time in Vernal. Business owner C.R. "Chuck" Henderson experimented with television signals in Vernal in 1955, and, after a fact-finding trip to Dallas in 1956, formed Basin Broadcasting and TV Company in partnership with Orlan L. Johnson, another Vernal businessman. The first Vernal cable hookup was to the home of Vernal resident Jess Lombard. The original hookup charge was $157.50 with a $4.50 monthly fee for service. However, because of competition from TV translator stations, the installation fee quickly went down to $25 and, finally, to a mere $10, with the monthly fee reduced to $3.50. By the end of the first year of operation, Vernal cable had 150

---

339   Forrest L. Simpson, President, Moab Broadcasting Telecasting Company, Letter to Mary Jane Morris, Secretary, Federal Communications Commission, March 27, 1956.

subscribers and, by 1962, 1,200.[340]

The Vernal cable system was sold to Community Television, Inc. (CTI) in 1962, and it developed synergies with the tri-county television translator system to provide good quality television reception to the greater Vernal community. CTI's principals in Vernal included the Standard Corporation and the Kearns-Tribune Company. This partnership also developed Utah's third and fourth cable systems. The third system was constructed in Ogden in 1964, and the fourth in the more populated areas of Salt Lake County in March 1970.

These cable systems and several others in Utah came to be owned by Tele-Communications, Inc., a company in which George C. Hatch and John W. Gallivan had a significant historical stake. As it expanded, Tele-Communications, Inc. (TCI) would eventually service more than 13 million subscribers nationwide by 1996, but it certainly did not start out in that scale or scope.

The origins of a cable partnership

The TCI story begins in 1955, when Jack Gallivan, assistant to *Salt Lake Tribune* publisher John F. Fitzpatrick took a bus late one Friday afternoon to Elko, Nevada. He traveled some 200 miles west of Salt Lake City, over the Bonneville Salt Flats and past Wendover, Utah, the training site for the crew of the Enola Gay bomber that 10 years earlier had dropped atomic bombs on Japan. They ended up in Elko to investigate the economic feasibility of building a cable television and microwave system to export KUTV and the other Salt Lake City television stations to that community.

Gallivan was the son of a Park City, Utah, silver miner. His father came to Utah in the 1890s from Illinois where his Irish grandfather had settled. Gallivan's mother died when he was five, and his mother's half-sister, Jennie Judge Kearns, the widow of U.S. Senator Thomas Kearns, then adopted him

---

340   Neil Lawrence Warren, Community Efforts to Bring Television to Rural Eastern Utah, Master of Fine Arts Thesis, Department of Speech, University of Utah, August 1968, 139. Interview with C. R. Henderson, President, Basin Broadcasting and TV Co., Vernal, Utah, June 20, 1964.

and his two sisters. Kearns was a Park City silver mining magnate and became owner of the newspaper before he died in October 1918. Until Gallivan graduated from Notre Dame University in 1937, his home was in the Salt Lake City Kearns mansion, which later would become the Utah governor's residence.

In 1937, Gallivan contemplated taking a job with the *Chicago Tribune* but was "ordered" back by Mrs. Kearns to work at the "other Tribune," the *Salt Lake Tribune.* Gallivan explained what happened:[341]

> So, I came back and was horrified when I reported to John Fitzpatrick, thinking he would send me to the *Tribune* ... editor for assignment as a reporter. [After all], I was a writer. What he did was to promptly assign me to the comptroller of the company ... who immediately gave me seven sets of books to keep. I didn't know what a set of books looked like and suddenly I was a bookkeeper.

Gallivan wanted to be a reporter, but Fitzpatrick had other plans for him. Fitzpatrick was preparing Gallivan to succeed him as *Tribune* publisher and manager of the Kearns-Tribune fortune. Fitzpatrick exerted a powerful influence on the civic, cultural and economic advancement of Utah and the Intermountain West, and much of that influence sprang from his newspaper and broadcasting activities as well as his investments. Over the next 23 years, until his death, that was the legacy, which Fitzpatrick would prepare Gallivan to inherit.

Returning to 1955 and Gallivan's trip by bus to Nevada, he found cable TV prospects good in Elko and enthusiastically returned to persuade his boss (Fitzpatrick) to commit $100,000 of Kearns-Tribune money to build the Elko cable system. Fitzpatrick was hesitant, but Gallivan persisted and Fitzpatrick agreed to participate if his friend, Ogden *Standard-Examiner* publisher Abe Glasmann, could be convinced to be a partner. As Gallivan put it, "Of course, Glasmann said yes, and we were off."

---

341   John H. Gallivan, interview with Tim Larson, November 16, 1987, transcript, 10, Everett L. Cooley Oral History Project, Marriott Library, University of Utah, Salt Lake City, Utah.

The Utah partners joined with Bill Gentry of Walnut Creek, California, to install the Elko cable system and its associated microwave facilities. The microwave equipment, built by engineer Fred Klap of Livermore Laboratories in California, was used to relay the Salt Lake City television signals across western Utah and eastern Nevada to Elko. Gentry had 20% ownership in the system, with Kearns-Tribune and the Standard Corporation each owning 40%. The Utah partners took over Gentry's interest in Elko cable by giving him the microwave system. Gentry eventually sold the microwave to cable investor Jack Kent Cook --who later owned the Washington Redskins football team (now the Washington Commanders) -- and Cook eventually sold it back to the Utah partners through Community Television, Inc.

Originally, Gallivan underestimated the cost of building the Elko system by about $10,000 and, because he was embarrassed to ask Fitzpatrick and Glasmann for more money, he went to an Elko bank to secure a personal loan to finish construction. The bank liked Gallivan's plan to bring cable television to Elko and agreed to the loan, as long as Fitzpatrick and Glasmann would co-sign. That defeated Gallivan's purpose of securing a loan to shield himself from going to his boss for more money, so he admitted his error and persuaded the Utah partnership to put up an additional $10,000 to finish the project.

In September 1956, with the showing of the World Series, the Elko system inaugurated its cable service and became an instant success. With a $120 hookup charge and a $7.60 per month subscription fee, the system was making money within 6 months. The Kearns-Tribune and Standard Corporation partnership went on to own successful cable systems in Carson City and Lake Tahoe, Nevada. As an aside, KALL's Homer Peterson was the one who acquired the Carson City franchise for the Utah partnership. As noted earlier, he closed the deal when he swayed the single holdout on the city council to his favor by securing a Meadow Gold Dairy Company contract for the council member's dairy farm.[342]

---

342   Homer Peterson, interview with Tim Larson, August 21, 1986, at the KALL radio station in Salt Lake City.

In 1958, to expand its cable services, the Utah group, represented by Standard Corporation's Hatch and the Kearns' Gallivan, formed a partnership with Bob Magness, who owned cable and microwave facilities in Montana. The partnership that began in Bozeman in 1958, was expanded and formalized on January 2, 1964, when Community Television, Inc. (CTI) was organized to merge the cable interests held by Bob Magness of Bozeman with the Utah group composed of the Standard Corporation of Ogden and the Kearns-Tribune Corporation of Salt Lake City. Minority stockholders of CTI included James E. Forgey of Vernal, Utah, and James Ivers, Jr., Salt Lake City. Ivers was a brother-in-law to Gallivan and a frequent investor with him. Copper Broadcasting of Butte, Montana, a separate operation owned by George and Wilda Gene Hatch, also had an interest in CTI.

Community Television, Inc. (CTI) authorized capital stock of $10,000,000. KUTV, Inc. paid $1,150,000 cash for stock, making it the largest single stockholder in CTI when it was formed. The Standard Corporation, the Kearns-Tribune Corporation and the Salt Lake City Broadcasting Company, owner of KALL, jointly owned KUTV, Inc. The percentage of ownership was fairly complex, but with its KUTV, Inc. common ownership, the Hatch-Gallivan group combined to own about 72% of CTI, and Bob Magness and his wife, Betsy, owned the remaining 28%.

CTI began operations with 10 systems, serving a total of 13,200 subscribers in Bozeman, Butte, Dillon, Helena, Anaconda and Miles City, Montana; Vernal, Utah; Lake Tahoe, California; and, Elko and Carson City, Nevada. After eleven months, CTI had acquired sole ownership of seven more systems, in Riverton, Lander, Thermopolis and Worland, Wyoming; Lewiston, Idaho, and Livingston, Montana; and Lake Tahoe, Nevada. CTI also acquired a 50% interest in eight other systems in Wyoming, Nebraska and Colorado. By December 1964, CTI had a total of 21 operating cable systems serving 31,001 subscribers.

In September 1965, Western Microwave, Inc. was organized to consolidate three microwave systems that had operated under varying degrees of common ownership between the Utah group and Bob Magness. Essentially, the same principals organized Western Microwave, Inc., as CTI. The Utah group, with its intertwined ownership of KUTV and CTI, controlled about 66% of Western Microwave, while Bob and Betsy Magness controlled 34%. Western Microwave, Inc., became the largest privately owned common carrier in the U.S., serving cable systems, television stations and data customers in Utah, Idaho, Montana, Wyoming, Colorado, and North and South Dakota.

CTI and Western Microwave originally maintained offices in both Bozeman and in Salt Lake City, but due to administrative, marketing and travel demands, the Bozeman offices were moved to Denver in 1965. With offers of real estate and other investments, Glasmann of the Standard Corporation tried to entice Bob Magness to move to Salt Lake City instead of Denver. Magness recalled nearly 30 years later:[343]

> [Glasmann] tried extremely hard to get me to move to Salt Lake. Even to having us over and taking us fishing and things like that. He even took me out and showed me ... their places on the Ogden River. [He said], "You can have any (lot) you want at no cost." I'd tell Abe that there was a time that I would have crawled down here for those opportunities, but I learned that you have to take care of them [once you commit]. But Abe would talk you down real close, lay out all the money on a deal then say, "Son you go run them." He was always coming up with something.

But Magness, with wife Betsy's prompting, moved CTI to Denver instead, and new headquarters for the company were opened there. Magness was made CTI president, Hatch was appointed vice president, Paul J. (Jerry) O'Brien, assistant to Gallivan, became secretary and A. L. Glasmann became treasurer. CTI's move to Denver would prove to be fortuitous for its cable distribution operations. With Denver's location on the 105th meridian, it was discovered to have a one-of-a-kind view of global satellites, allowing reach of audiences from Frankfurt to Hong Kong, with a single hop in either direction. Denver's

---

343   Bob Magness, interview with Tim Larson, Denver, Colorado, April 6, 1994.

location was like being at the middle of a curved tunnel with a view of the light at both ends --that is, with a view of both Europe to the east and East Asia to the west at the same time. CTI's relocation to Denver in 1965, combined with the telecommunication industry's deployment of space satellites in the 1970s, positioned the company at the most important U.S. on-ramp to the global information superhighway of the 21st century.[344]

TCI's corporate identity formalized

CTI and Western Microwave continued as separate corporations for the next four years, until, in 1968, the principals decided to consolidate ownership under a single corporation. The name chosen for the new corporation was American Tele-Communications, Inc., but somebody else already took that name, so "American" was dropped and just Tele-Communications, Inc. (TCI) was chosen instead. Magness explained what happened:[345]

> Our people had trouble getting names. We found that there were some microwave systems up in Washington and Oregon that used 'telecommunication' in their name. ... I was delegated to go up and buy those microwave systems, so we bought the name. That's when TCI got formed. ... We became Tele-Communications, Inc., with a hyphen.

As of December 1, 1969, the privately held Tele-Communications, Inc., (TCI) owned 44 cable television systems and had partial interests in 11 additional systems, serving a total of 15 states. Under the umbrella of TCI, CTI was renamed Community Tele-Communications, Inc., or CTCI, and Western Microwave, Inc. was renamed Western Tele-Communications, Inc. or WTCI. Both became wholly owned subsidiaries of Tele-Communications, Inc.[346]

In 1970, TCI's Magness of Denver held 35% of TCI's stock and the

---

344   Thomas Heath, The Washington Post, Washington, D.C., 1994.
345   Bob Magness, interview with Tim Larson, Denver, Colorado, April 6, 1994, 12.
346   Prospectus: Tele-Communications, Inc., underwritten by Dean Witter & Co., Inc., 5 February 1970, 12, 13.

Gallivan-Hatch group of Utah held 63%, with 2% of the stock in the hands of several others. Magness, Gallivan and Hatch had an evolutionary vision for TCI: "The growth of (TCI) lies in its ability to provide the basic antenna service, to greatly enlarge the viewers' choice of programming, and, ultimately, to make it possible for every home and business in the U.S. to have access to a two-way (interactive) visual-data broadband communications system."[347]

This revolutionary vision directed the company's path, but TCI lacked significant resources to evolve to achieve that vision. To raise desperately needed capital for expansion and to reduce debt, Hatch, Gallivan, Magness and the other TCI officers and directors decided to work toward making TCI an industry leader. On February 5, 1970, they made a public offering of common stock in the company. The net earnings from the sale was $6,576,000. Most of this was used to retire debt, with $1.1 million going to replenish TCI's working capital. Unlike what happened when most other private companies went public, none of the original TCI shareholders sold their shares. This assured public investors that Glasmann, Hatch, Gallivan and Magness still had faith in TCI's earning power and that the company would continue under the same management structure and philosophy. TCI officers were Magness, president and CEO; George C. Hatch, senior vice president; John W. Gallivan, second vice president; and, Paul J. (Jerry) O'Brien, secretary. O'Brien was Gallivan's assistant at the Kearns-Tribune Corporation.

As an aside, O'Brien went to the Chicago offices of Dean Witter, Inc. to pick up the $6.5 million check from the public stock offering. Not wanting to carry such a large check home on the plane, O'Brien went to a Chicago bank to open a new account and deposit the huge sum of money. The teller at the bank was a bit overwhelmed by the deposit and, upon completing the transaction, gave O'Brien a set of dinner china, the bank's usual gift for opening a new account. O'Brien brought the $6.5-million deposit slip, the china and a good story back home to the other TCI investors.[348]

---

347   Tele-Communications, Inc., 1969 Annual Report, Denver, Colorado.
348   Jack Gallivan, interview with Tim Larson, April 3, 1990, at the Salt Lake Tribune offices in Salt Lake City.

In 1970, TCI was the nation's fifth largest multiple systems operator (MSO) with 100,000 subscribers, located in 71 cities in 16 western states as well as Pennsylvania and Georgia. But, even with its significant growth, TCI still was a collection of small cable systems, and the corporation was nearly bankrupt.[349] Hatch, Gallivan and Magness who, in the past, operated using banks, personal savings and individual investors to finance closely held community antenna and microwave operations, faced operating in an intensely competitive nationwide broadband cable industry. Also, there was the demand for specialized programming and services and, in general, the industry required entrepreneurial and institutional financing on an enormous scale for its players to be successful.

By 1971, TCI's charter investors realized they had taken the company as far as their intuition, experience and expertise allowed. As such, they searched for a person who could work in complete partnership with the cable-savvy Magness and, while embracing the entrepreneurial spirit of TCI's founders, evolve the company into a major corporation. In 1973, they hired John C. Malone as TCI president and CEO, to succeed Magness. Magness became chairman of the board, and Hatch was made vice chairman. Gallivan became vice president and O'Brien was made secretary. Blaine V. Glasmann, Jr., an attorney in the Ogden firm of Young, Thatcher & Glasmann, and nephew of Abe Glasmann, was put on the TCI board of directors.

When Malone was hired, the Standard Corporation and the Kearns-Tribune Corporation of Utah still owned the majority of TCI stock. And although not from Utah, Malone had a significant effect on the lives of TCI's officers and directors from Utah for many years. As such, some brief biographical information on Malone would be helpful in understanding why he was chosen by Magness, Hatch, Gallivan, Glasmann and O'Brien to take them and TCI into the future.

Malone thought himself as unique and he wanted to make a difference

---

349   Wall Street Journal, September 27, 1993, 1 (A).

with his life. The stuff of the social sciences did not interest him, and as a political conservative in liberal academic settings, he turned to the things of the hard sciences and business, earning a bachelor of science degree in electrical engineering from Yale in 1963, a master of science degree from Johns Hopkins University in 1964, a master of science degree in electrical engineering from New York University in 1965, and a doctorate, in operations research from Johns Hopkins in 1967.[350]

From 1963 to 1968, he also was employed as a financial expert at AT&T's Bell Laboratories. Among other things while at Bell Labs, he wrote a 300-page dissertation on maximizing profits in a regulated company. Malone lived in Weston, Connecticut, and warily saw himself becoming part of the Bell bureaucracy, a group of people who, he thought, would work their whole lives "basically making no impact on anything."[351]

In 1968, to "retool" himself to make a difference in business, he joined the management-consulting firm of McKinsey & Company and was there until 1970. For the next three years, he was employed as a vice president of General Instrument Corporation and as president of one of its subsidiary holdings, Jerrold CATV, a cable television equipment manufacturing company. TCI was an important Jerrold customer and that is reportedly where Magness and Malone met.

In 1972, TCI and Warner Communication each offered Malone the presidency of their respective cable operations. TCI seemingly offered an inferior package in the bidding for Malone. TCI could offer Malone only $60,000, half his present salary. The well-connected and financed Warner Cable logically had the edge in courting Malone. But more important to Malone in his decision than the salary were his personal and corporate passions.

Reportedly, he was attracted to TCI because it offered him what he really wanted, a chance to be unique, to be an individual, to make a difference in

---

350   Reference Book of Corporate Managements 1986, Dun's Marketing Services, a division of Dun and Bradstreet, Inc., Parsippany, N.J., 1985, 3055.
351   Auletta, Ken, "John Malone: Flying Solo," New Yorker, February 1994, 54.

a cable industry occupied by people, except for Magness, that he considered timid and conventional; this, along with an opportunity for a more fulfilling family life in Denver. At TCI, Malone, in partnership with Magness, and uninhibited by eastern corporate bureaucrats, thought he could realize his corporate ambitions while also attempting to honor the commitment to his wife that "she-came-first, the-kids-came-second and career-came-third."[352]

Magness and Malone, though entirely different individuals, symbiotically were one in the entrepreneurial spirit. Magness, the smart, intuitive cable visionary, taught Malone how to do deals, how to fit into and thrive in the TCI culture he had shaped, and how to gain people's trust and respect through loyalty, personal character and sheer will. Malone, the rational systems-engineer-futurist, taught Magness how to play the corporate strategic and creative response game: "a whole lot of moves into the future."

To achieve growth and sustain cable channels and content, TCI needed to generate capital. Money was more than tight. TCI, when Malone was hired, was still on the verge of bankruptcy and before any expansion could occur, it was necessary to stabilize operations and raise capital. So Magness and Malone went back east to rescue TCI and attract large lenders. They were successful --cable television seemed to have an annuity-like cash flow favored by lenders, even in hard times-- and TCI then was in a position to meet the challenges of competition and to engage other innovative strategies to finance growth in both cable operations and programming.

When Malone assumed control of TCI, it was the nation's third largest cable company. He creatively responded and began to expand TCI's holdings exponentially through innovative deal structuring involving minority partnerships, joint ventures, trades and stock swaps.[353] He refocused TCI's strategies on growing its core business through aggressive acquisition of cable television systems and by launching market driven programming and services to existing and new customers, in order to increase revenues, while meeting the FCC's challenge to provide cable programming less reliant on over-the-

---

352   Auletta, "John Malone: Flying Solo."
353   Rocky Mountain News, December 11, 1994, 113 (A).

air television. Malone explained his philosophy in a 1999 interview with the author:[354]

> Each thing that we bought was a brick at a time. It was financed on
> its own. We put enough equity in to do that, plus the financing. And
> I was dealing with quality banks that wouldn't loan you the money
> if their analysis didn't indicate the business plan would work. An
> affirmation. Then I had a set of management guys who could make
> the numbers work. I mean, the most important thing was you don't
> trip. You don't default on anything. You perform, and they did.
> And, so a brick at a time, we started to gain momentum. We started
> with little deals, but we were doing an acquisition a week of cable
> systems. We had it down to a kind of a science. And then toward
> the latter part, I was doing maybe an investment a month. So, a cable
> acquisition a week, an investment a month.

But there were underlying problems working against TCI's traditional structure and culture. With key members of the TCI cohort retiring, the company was hollowed out of its traditional entrepreneurial management on the cable side and began to rely on outside consultants. TCI lost what under Malone was the old style TCI discipline or approach --the bootstrap operation and brick-by-brick planned growth. TCI's tough edge truly was gone. According to Malone, it became more of a "bullshit" marketing kind of thing, rather than a "hard-ass" operation.[355]

TCI's performance predictability diminished, and, by the summer of 1996, Malone started getting calls from old investors, institutional investors that had been with TCI for a long time. Malone again became involved with day-to-day operations and instituted what he labeled "draconian measures" to turn TCI around. He "cleaned house" and did a number of things that raised TCI's cash flow by 42% within a year. After making about 85% of the changes needed to put TCI back on track, on March 1. 1997, Malone brought in Leo Hindery as TCI president to complete the process. Hindery was the Managing Partner of

---

354   John C. Malone, interview with Tim Larson, Denver, Colorado, April 12 1999.
355   Malone, interview with Tim Larson.

InterMedia Partners, a series of media industry investment funds he founded in 1988 and ran until February 1997, when he was named President and CEO of Tele-Communications, Inc. (TCI). In March 1999, TCI merged into AT&T and he became President and CEO of AT&T Broadband.

A merger is tendered

Under Hindery, TCI got back on track financially, but its entrepreneurial culture was still disintegrating. TCI lacked the thread of continuity provided by the old employee cohort now retiring. Magness had died on November 15, 1996, in the midst of Malone's efforts to restore TCI to its early 1990s' stature. And by 1998, almost to a person, the people who built TCI brick-by-brick and deal-by-deal were gone. As such, Malone did not have the "horses," or TCI the organizational infrastructure, to sustain the company as it grew in new services. The gap between the system management and the headquarters levels at TCI was just too wide, and Malone believed that the risk to shareholders of shouldering the entire cost of telephony and broadband implementation was too great. There were too many missing pieces and Malone didn't feel comfortable going outside the industry and outside the company to fill the gaps in order to execute in a determined way critical to keeping the momentum up.

So, in spring 1998, when AT&T came in with a $50 billion TCI merger offer, Malone saw an opportunity to shift the whole telephony and broadband implementation risks onto AT&T while maximizing TCI shareholder value. Malone explained his reasoning:

> If it was still the old thing and everybody was enthusiastic about let's-keep building it, I might have rolled the dice and taken the risk. But with sort of a new batch of people who, basically, I didn't have any long-term experience with, with a massive challenge coming, and with an opportunity, you just couldn't not do it [take] the AT&T offer.[356]

---

356   Malone, interview with Tim Larson.

In the interim, in 1997, before AT&T's offer to buy TCI, the Kearns/
McCarthey family sold Kearns-Tribune to Malone's Telecommunications Inc.
in a $731 million stock deal. This was Malone's preferred way to shape deals to
avoid unnecessary taxes.

So, when in 1999 the AT&T/TCI merger was completed, AT&T had
purchased TCI in the deal. To follow the Tribune's ownership path, in 2000,
AT&T sold the Tribune to the MediaNews Group, triggering a lawsuit by the
McCartheys on behalf of the Kearns family. They dropped the suit in 2007
and never reclaimed ownership of the newspaper. After MediaNews Group
declared bankruptcy in 2010, the Tribune ownership went to Alden Global
Capital, a New York hedge fund, and then in 2016 to Paul Huntsman, president
and CEO of Huntsman Family Investments. As of 2022, Huntsman was board
chair of the Salt Lake Tribune, a nonprofit print newspaper with an online
edition and a web advertising arm.[357]

From start to finish, the 1999 merger happened in 10 days, personally
negotiated between AT&T's Michael Armstrong and Malone. Although a
typical timetable for Malone and TCI, even with multi-billions at stake, it
was a mind-blowing time frame for Armstrong and AT&T, a company with a
historically and notoriously slow decision-making process. Malone said that
Armstrong was the only AT&T chairman who had impressed him.[358]

After the AT&T/TCI merger, AT&T and Liberty Media were Wall
Street favorites. AT&T stock was near $61 per share, and Liberty Media
stock went from $4 a share to above $69 as a result of Malone's investments
in entertainment provider News Corp., digital set-top box supplier General
Instruments, Internet music provider TCI Music, and other entertainment
and Internet companies. During the week of April 6, 1999, a month after
the merger, Liberty's stock price rose 800%, putting a $9.3 billion market
value on a company that a week earlier was worth $450 million. The tacit
understanding here was that whatever video programming services Liberty

---

357   Brief history of the Salt Lake Tribune can be found here: https://www.sltrib.com/
news/2016/04/22/a-brief-history-of-salt-lake-tribune-owners-since-its-birth-with-photos-of-the-
paper-through-the-years/
358   Malone, interview with Tim Larson.

had a stake in had preferential access to AT&T's 14 million broadband cable subscribers nationwide.[359]

Liberty under AT&T remained entrepreneurial because even though Malone sold both TCI and Liberty to AT&T, his make-or-break requirement of the merger was that Liberty Media be spun off as a tracking stock – a special equity offering issued by a parent company that tracks the financial performance of a particular segment or division. This was separate from AT&T and, furthermore, Malone could maintain complete control over its management and direction. In short, after the merger, Malone, as Liberty's chairman, still had virtual control over all of its assets, which included various levels of ownership. Consummated on March 9, 1999, it was the largest telecommunications merger, up to that time.

The merger finally gave AT&T access to local telephone markets. But things changed on Wall Street after a time as AT&T stock plummeted to $16 and Liberty stock to $12 by early 2001. This was a result of investors' concerns that AT&T would have to spend billions to upgrade TCI's cable-television systems before it could offer digital interactive cable and Internet and telephone services at an affordable price. Malone blamed Armstrong's thinking for the decline, and the dispute between the two went public. Malone, as AT&T's largest single stockholder (at roughly 1%) had some time-tested advice for Michael Armstrong, as reported in *Variety*:[360]

> Your [Armstrong's] strategy is sound, but your structure stinks, and it's killing the stock price. The problem is that some investors like growth, some like earnings, but nobody likes a muddy mix of the two. AT&T is a mix: Long-distance is judged on earnings; cellular and cable is valued on growth. It's a mistake to enslave yourself to earnings and, frankly, AT&T is in that trap. (You're) trying to grow in cable and wireless, where competitors don't pay a bit of attention to earnings, and make earnings on consumer long-distance. They're valued on earnings and imposing huge drags on earnings. It's

359   Business Week, July 6, 1998, cover story.
360   Marc Graser "Malone Can't Leave Biz Alone," Variety, April 3, 2000.

irrational. … Issue more tracking stocks of the sort created for Liberty
Media. Liberty loses piles of money yet has a $43-billion market
value.[5]

Malone's advice to Armstrong seemingly struck a responsive chord.
AT&T underwent a massive restructuring in late 2001 and separated into three
companies operating four main businesses --business, consumer, wireless and
broadband. On July 10, 2001, Malone resigned from AT&T's board, a month
before his scheduled departure, because he was excluded from participating in
the Comcast talks to purchase AT&T broadband, the old TCI. Among other
things, Malone believed that the Comcast offer was "insufficient." In addition,
on August 10, 2001, Malone exercised his option to spin-off Liberty Media, "to
allow the media investment vehicle to raise capital on its own, use its stock as
currency in acquiring, merging or partnering with other companies, and help
the public markets to better value the company."

Malone personally prospered from TCI, much of his wealth resulting from
his controlling ownership of Liberty Media, Inc.[361] He had created great value
for TCI in his run with the company. In turn, TCI created great value for its
principal investors. Besides Malone, charter founders of TCI also accumulated
significant wealth. With his TCI stock holdings and investments, Magness was
identified in 1994, two years before he died, as the second wealthiest person in
Colorado, one of only two billionaires in that state, with net worth estimated
at easily more than $1 billion. The Gallivan-managed Kearns-Tribune
Corporation held its 8% share of TCI stock for 30 years and its $330,000
investment had appreciated to about $300 million by 1996. Hatch, the largest
original CTI (later, TCI) investor in 1964 at $1.1 million divested TCI for assets
and cash valued at $50 million. Hatch was forced to divest either TCI or KUTV
because of FCC cross media ownership rules in effect at the time. He chose
to divest of TCI but might have financially fared even better if he divested of
KUTV. He was locally connected and devoted to the television station so chose
to relinquish his TCI holdings. In addition, the "hard-ass" cohort members
who built TCI with Malone were all multi-millionaires, as were some of their

---

361   Tele-Communications, Inc., (Denver), TCI Annual Report, 1994, 4.

vested secretaries and assistants.[362]

TCI no longer existed by that name after the AT&T/TCI merger, but it had a glorious 45-year roller coaster ride, starting from Memphis Cable in Texas through Bozeman and Denver and finally to AT&T. It is clear that the Utah partners, the Standard Corporation and the Kearns Tribune, and their entrepreneurial visionaries, Hatch and Gallivan, along with Magness who founded TCI, above all others, were undeniably responsible for TCI's evolutionary success. Magness also is inseparable from TCI's long history and entrepreneurial culture, and Malone is inseparable from TCI's recent past and Liberty's future:[363]

> [Malone's] personality and influence are so powerful that they are a market force of their own." John, as we all know is a couple cuts above the good business people we all know. … [He] tends to take a longer-term view, and financial markets don't. … Never bet against John… that's a formula for going broke. He has been and will continue to be one of the smartest investors there is.

But Malone's own words may better provide a clue to his thinking about Liberty's future. He named his company Liberty because it represented freedom for him – from a lot of things, to do a lot of things. Malone explained:

> Yes, that's why it's called Liberty. It was freedom. Liberating. So, to this day, Liberty frees me, first of all, from a huge number of employees. Liberty is 24 people with a $50-billion market cap. And total flexibility in what it wants to do – no regulatory problems, no political problems. Lots of balance sheet flexibility. A quick-decision process.[364]

Since 2001, Malone has exponentially grown Liberty, a holding company for a variety of investments in cable and entertainment, including, as Sirius XM's largest stockholder in 2018, a $3.5 billion Pandora purchase, betting on

---

362   The Denver Post, 2 October 1994, 1 (H).
363   Broadcasting and Cable, "Special Report: No Triumph for Liberty," November 27, 2000, 28.
364   Malone, interview with Tim Larson.

the future of streaming.[365] Malone's Liberty Media, which is worth upwards of $24 billion, has in addition to its media investments ventures into sports, auto racing, ranching and more. He also owns 2.2 million acres of land, reportedly making him the single largest private landowner in the U.S. And at $6.5 billion, his personal wealth was ranked 95th on *Forbes* 400 U.S. Richest list in 2020. It is a fitting postscript to a remarkable story about a Utah-grown venture that was among the earliest examples of successful cable operations not just in the state but also of the nation.

---

365   See https://markets.businessinsider.com/news/stocks/john-malone-cable-cowboy-media-dealmaker-2017-8#also-read-23

EPILOG

In 1990, KLO's John Webb in Ogden told me that local broadcasting could not survive under the restrictive FCC ownership rules in effect, allowing an owner no more than one AM, one FM and one television station in the same market.[366] His prescient supposition at the time seemed incredulous because the FCC had, since its inception in 1934, held dear its idealized view of locally diverse broadcast station ownership. Thus, it was difficult to imagine a single owner licensed to or controlling multiple broadcasting station operations in a Utah market or in any other U.S. local market.

Various government entities from early on have guarded the number of broadcasting station licenses a single ownership unit could hold. As such, the ownership of the 10 pioneer Utah radio and three television broadcasting stations engaged here were governed by the "one-to-a-customer" and "duopoly" ownership rules attributable to a given market.[367]

In 1954, the FCC put into effect what came to be dubbed the "Rule of Sevens:" No single ownership unit nationwide could own more than seven AM, seven FM and seven television stations, and no more than one of each in the same market. Also included were restrictive regulations on cross-media ownership.

In 1970, there were more than 6,800 U.S. radio and 847 television broadcasting stations. Local broadcasting markets were controlled by a minimum of 1,100 different ownership units regulated under the FCC's "Rule of Sevens" legacy.

In 1995, there were 11,800 radio and 1,532 television stations, controlled by a minimum of 1,950 different ownership units governed under the FCC's ownership rules as they had evolved.[368]

---

366   John Webb, Conversation with Tim Larson (circa 1990).
367   https://en.wikipedia.org/wiki/Duopoly_(broadcasting).
368   FCC News: Station Totals as of March 31, 1995.
https://docs.fcc.gov/public/attachments/DOC-302055A1.pdf

The Telecommunications Act of 1996 revised radio station ownership restrictions in a manner that allowed marketplace-driven growth among group owners. It was the first significant overhaul of telecommunications law in more than 60 years, effectively amending the Communications Act of 1934. It was the first time the internet was included in broadcasting and spectrum allocations, resulting in a dualistic re-regulation of the telecommunication industry market structure.

By the 2020s, there were an estimated 1,661 U.S. television stations and 15,445 radio stations. [369] Major media corporations owned more than 50% of the radio stations, and there was no limit to the number of television stations nationwide a single owner could control as long as they stayed below the 39% maximum nationwide audience reach and limited themselves to two television stations in the same market.[370] However, this rule limiting TV station ownership in the same market or nationally is easily overcome by employing a Local Marketing Agreement (LMA), a local management contract where one company agrees to operate a television station owned by another party. To wit: Nexstar and Sinclair own, operate, program or provide sales and services to around 200 U.S. television stations each, exceeding the 39% maximum. This includes Nexstar's owed KTVX and KUCW in Salt Lake City, plus LMAs in other Utah cities.   And Sinclair owns KUTV and KJZZ in Salt Lake City and KMYU in St. George.

Few people, including broadcasting station owners and regulators, predicted the monumental transformation of the radio and television broadcasting market structure and the concentration of media ownership

---

369   Statista: Number of Commercial Television Stations in the United States:
https://www.statista.com/statistics/189655/number-of-commercial-television-stations-in-the-ussince-1950/
https://www.statista.com/statistics/252235/number-of-commercial-radio-stations-in-the-us/
370   FCC Broadcast Ownership Rules:
https://www.fcc.gov/consumers/guides/fccs-review-broadcast-ownership-rules; All sorts of creative ownership and operating contracts, however, have significantly breached this 39% maximum boundary through Local Marketing Agreements (LMA), also referred to as Management Services Agreements (MSA), Time Brokerage Agreements (TBA), Joint Sales Agreements (JSA) or some other shared services agreement.

initiated by the Telecommunications Act of 1996, signed by President Bill Clinton and made law on February 8, 1996.

Utah radio and television broadcasting stations depend heavily on commercial advertising or underwriting support for survival. Utah's local market structure is a microcosm encapsulating in miniature the characteristic qualities of the national broadcasting industry comprising 300 other local U.S. media markets. With the merger of media corporations, including print media, and the convergence of broadcasting cable, satellite, telephony and other telecommunication entities with Internet platforms, the 1996 Act pulled down barriers to entry and deregulated ownership rules. This accelerated deployment of advanced U.S. information technologies, to let anyone enter any communications business and to let any communications business compete in any market against any other.

As a result of the Telecommunications Act of 1996 and associated regulations since then, most mass media markets have evolved to be oligopolistic, with few sellers, both nationally and in Utah. "And while the horizontal and vertical concentration of ownership has increased exponentially, resulting in higher advertising rates, listener choice arguably has not increased. High concentration of media ownership reportedly has reduced the diversity of viewpoints and created a potential conflict of interest, the risk of bias, the spread of misinformation and even the suppression of information inimical to the public interest and democracy."[371]

U.S. broadcasting, sparked by the Telecommunications Act of 1996, transformed into a national highly concentrated market structure, where a few cross-media sellers accounted for most of the sales and controlled a majority of America's highly potent information sources.[372]

As media groups and conglomerates exponentially grew and merged over several decades, four corporations came to own not only broadcasting

---

371   The Telecommunications Act of 1996 and Radio Market Structure:
*https://www.tandfonline.com/doi/abs/10.1207/s15327736mel103_2?journalCode=hmec20
372   Media Cross Ownership in the U.S.:
https://en.wikipedia.org/wiki/Media_cross-ownership_in_the_United_States

and cable operations, but all print, digital, advertising, outdoor media and motion pictures. This resulted, by the 2020s, in 90% of American media ownership vested in four major corporations, down from six in 2016. The four corporations based on media holdings, market capitalization and household and customer reach are Comcast, Walt Disney, AT&T, and ViacomCBS. [373]

Comcast Corporation is a multinational American telecommunications conglomerate.[374] Its NBC Universal division markets consumer television services through its television networks, O&O television stations and channels, sports group companies and International network outlets. Its Comcast Cable Communications division, doing business as Xfinity, markets consumer cable television, internet, telephone and wireless services. Comcast's broadcasting and cable television operation is second worldwide, as measured by revenue, only to AT&T. It is the largest Internet service provider in the U.S., and the nation's third-largest home telephone service provider. Comcast Corporation has large broadcasting, cable television and pay-tv operations. It has 12 NBC network O&Os and operates 38 other over-the-air television stations and transmits its programming to at least 226 affiliated stations, reaching 97% of U.S. households. It owns several television networks in addition, including Telemundo, TeleXitos, and Cozi TV. And it has multiple cable-only channels including MSNBC, CNBC, Oxygen and Bravo, to name only a few.

Disney is an American diversified multinational mass media and entertainment conglomerate.[375] It provides studio entertainment and Disney consumer products, as well as operates interactive media and the Disney media networks, including among many other companies: ABC, ESPN (80%), Touchstone Pictures, Marvel, Lucasfilm, A&E (50%), The History Channel (50%) and Lifetime (50%). These are in addition to its ubiquitous parks and recreation operations worldwide.[376]

373   Biggest U.S. Media Conglomerates
https://www.google.com/search?client=firefox-b-1-d&q=Top+4+us+media+group+owne
rs; https://www.investopedia.com/stock-analysis/021815/worlds-top-ten-media-companies-
dis-cmcsa-fox.aspx: Wikipedia: Media Conglomerate: https://en.wikipedia.org/wiki/Media_
conglomerate
374   Wikipedia: Comcast. https://en.wikipedia.org/wiki/Comcast
375   Wikipedia: The Walt Disney Company:
https://en.wikipedia.org/wiki/The_Walt_Disney_Company
376   TitleMax: Every Company Disney Owns

ViacomCBS was formed with the merger of the CBS Corporation with a reincarnated Viacom in 2019.[377] It has film, television, and digital media operations nationally and internationally. Its stable of companies include Paramount Pictures, the myriad of CBS companies including the CBS Network, MTV, Nickelodeon, BET, Comedy Central and Showtime, among many others. The company estimates it operates 170 networks and reaches 700 million subscribers in 160 countries, as of 2021. CBS Television has 17 O&O over the air television stations, reaching 97% of all U.S. households through its 215 CBS network affiliated stations.

Warner Media is a multinational mass media and entertainment conglomerate owned by AT&T. [378]The company has film, television and cable operations, as well as entertainment, programming and media assets, including HBO Cinemax, Warner Media News and Sports, and Warner Bros. consisting of DC Comics, family friendly Turner assets, and a 50% interest in The CW television network, among others.

Radio broadcasting industry trends

The radio broadcasting industry comprises stations, networks, and syndicates that provide audio through AM, FM and satellite channels, sans radio operators that function solely online. To summarize:

> Radio operates with low profit margins and the medium has experienced moderate growth amid fierce competition for advertising dollars from alternative digital formats. As such, radio stations have lost listeners and advertising revenues to podcasts and music streaming services among the newer forms of audio entertainment delivered through internet-connected devices. Over-the-air radio broadcasters have widened their reach and engaged listeners by simulcasting programming online, by achieving economies of large

https://www.google.com/search?client=firefox-b-1-d&q=What+media+outlets+does+Disney+own.

377   Wikipedia: ViacomCBS: https://en.wikipedia.org/wiki/ViacomCBS
378   Wikipedia: WarnerMedia: https://en.wikipedia.org/wiki/WarnerMedia

-scale operations with multiple but diversely programmed radio
stations in the same market and by operating a national stable of
stations, sometimes numbering in the dozens or even hundreds.
Experienced radio station managers seem to correlate with
profitability by attracting a covey of local and national advertisers
with the widest-reaching media format in the U.S.[379]

Television broadcasting industry trends

In Utah as well as in any other media market, television broadcasters
operate station facilities that deliver audiovisual program content to the public
via over-the-air transmission, sans television operators that provide online-
only content. To summarize:

> Although linear viewership has declined and competition for
> advertising dollars is vigorous, television advertising expenditures
> from key buying industries --U.S. cable networks, advertising
> agencies, affiliated networks and consumers, to a lesser extent – have
> grown slightly over the years. As such, TV advertising revenues have
> been sustained at relatively profitable rates for the stations' products
> and services, including national, regional and local advertising,
> grant funding and public access, network affiliate and cable system
> compensation. Additionally, as the customer viewing experience
> evolves, digital distribution and the engagement of large media
> companies likely will help television broadcasters fare better than
> other legacy media industries, like radio broadcasting. [380]

Final thoughts

Whether the media market structure transformation since the passage
of the Telecommunications Act of 1996 and the advent of the digital stage,
resulting in a concentration of ownership vested in a few large media

---

379   Wikipedia: WarnerMedia: https://en.wikipedia.org/wiki/WarnerMedia
380   IBISWorld: https://www.ibisworld.com/united-states/market-research-reports/television-
broadcasting-industry/

companies, is in the public interest or essential to the broadcasting industry's survival is not adjudicated here but is left for government regulators, observant of local market concerns, to determine. The radio and television pioneers highlighted in this book were clear about their obligations to serve the public interest. But the market structure has so dramatically changed that regulators have seemingly yet to seriously address the issue or even acknowledge its importance.

There are intriguing parallels between the experiences of the Utah pioneers from the period stretching from the 1920s to the 1950s and those today who look to the digital media landscape. In the early days of radio, Salt Lake City newspapers and institutions such as the Church of Jesus Christ of Latter-day Saints became partners in the nascent stages of Utah broadcasting. The digital stage now is beginning to display signs of future potential in Utah. In 2022, for example, Deseret Digital Media, which operates KSL.com and Utah.com, recently relocated most of its operations from downtown Salt Lake City to the Silicon Slopes campus in Lehi, Utah. The move underscores how a media institution with deep roots now has added being a tech company as part of its identity.

These events constituting a new media stage likely will be the story for future historians to examine to determine how Utah will be affected by the ever-developing market forces in the broadcasting and mass communication industry. After all, Utah continues as the fastest-growing state in the nation with a nearly 24% population increase during the period from 2010 to 2023.

APPENDIX

How ownership evolved in Utah's
pioneering broadcasting legacy

One reason for a detailed history of the pioneering efforts, first in radio stations and then in the television and cable counterparts is to preserve the facts and accuracy of the stories surrounding the visionaries and entrepreneurs who built the state's broadcasting industry over the last 100 years. Of course, as in so many other markets and industries, the chain of ownership, its transfers and buyouts, have evolved and changed dramatically. Sometimes, that evolution obscures the footprints of Utah's broadcasting pioneers. To clarify how ownership has evolved, events affecting the group of 10 pioneer radio stations followed by a discussion of Utah's first three television stations and the cable enterprise that became TCI are summarized. The Appendix closes the book with a census of the present-day broadcasting portrait in Utah, including the number of stations operating and the programming formats that highlight the state's broadcasting industry.

Ownership dates in this chapter were gathered from reliable sources, and indicate when a change in ownership either was first granted or when the change went into effect. These dates most often are not distant from each other so should not result in significantly different markers for ownership change. It is the hope that future historians studying Utah's broadcasting industry will find the information clarifying and helpful in expanding upon the history and charting subsequent generations of broadcasting activities.

Radio stations

The following summarizes the operating frequencies and the dates of the first license issued for each station according to FCC documentation.

Frequency	kHz operating frequency	1st License Date
1160 kHz KSL	1160, since 3/24/41	4/21/22 as KZN
1320 kHz KDYL	1320, since 4/24/41	5/08/22, now KNIT
1430 kHz KLO	1430, since 3/28/41	1/05/25 as KFUR
750 kHz KEUB	750, since 1986	11/17/36, now KOAL
590 kHz KSUB	590, since 10/16/46	8/18/37
570 kHz KUTA	570, since 6/19/41	8/2/38 now KNRS
610 kHz KVNU	610, since 4/29/47	1/24/39
960 kHz KOVO	960, since 5/6/48	10/23/39
1280 kHz KNAK	1280, since 1/26/46	6/4/45, now KZNS
910 kHz KALL	910 from 1945-2003	1/21/46, KWDZ from 2003

The following section details the evolutionary chain of ownership for each of the ten pioneer radio stations, starting with a description of each station's ownership as of 2022.

KSL (FORMERLY KZN and KFPT), 1922, SALT LAKE CITY
BONNEVILLE INTERNATIONAL CORPORATION (BIC)

Bonneville International Corporation (BIC) has 14 radio stations located in Seattle, Phoenix, Denver and Salt Lake City, plus 8 stations managed under a Local Marketing Agreement, and a TV station in Salt Lake City. BIC touts itself as a premier broadcasting and media company, which provides its advertisers with effective ways to connect with audiences.

Under ownership of The Church of Jesus Christ of Latter-Day Saints, the Radio Service Corporation (RSC) was KSL's licensee from 1925 until August 16, 1963, when KSL, Inc. became the licensee. On August 1, 1964, the Corporation of the President of the Church of Latter-Day Saints turned KSL control briefly to KSL, Inc. and then over to the newly formed Bonneville International Corporation. On February 15, 1967, BIC's control was then transferred from the Corporation of the President of the Church to the Deseret Management Corporation.

The LDS Church through its for-profit arm, the Deseret Management Corporation (DMC), which is wholly owned by the Deseret Management Corporation Reserve Trust, ultimately owns KSL:[381]

> The Trustees of the DMC Reserve Trust are appointed (and subject to removal) by the First Presidency of the Church, which consists of each succeeding President of the Church and counselors appointed by the President. Thomas S. Monson, the President of the Church, died on January 2, 2018. He was replaced as President of the Church on January 16, 2018, by Russell M. Nelson. This notice is being provided to the Commission as has been done on numerous occasions over the last several decades following the death of the President of the Church.

As earlier noted, KSL, Utah's first and oldest sustained radio broadcasting station, was licensed as KZN on April 21, 1922, and its first official broadcast aired on May 6. The KZN call sign evolved to KFPT in 1924 and then to KSL in 1925. The KSL call sign has identified the station for nearly 100 years, as has the 1160 kHz operating frequency since 1941. Except for a couple of years preceding 1924, KSL has de facto been locally owned and operated by the same ownership unit since its founding: The Church of Jesus Christ of Latter-Day Saints.

Permission to increase to 50 kilowatts power was granted on November 17, 1931. And, on October 1, 1936, KSL was given a construction permit to update transmitting equipment, install a new antenna and substantially increase power from 50 kilowatts to 500 kilowatts. This huge power increase never was realized, leaving WLW in Cincinnati the only U.S. station licensed to ever broadcast using 500 kilowatts.

Two radio pioneers, John Cope and Lionel Cornwell, were early involved in what became KSL. Likely the three most important individuals in KSL's business evolution are Earl J. Glade, Ivor Sharp and Arch Madsen.

---

381   Letter Via Hand Delivery to Marlene H. Dortch, Secretary, Federal Communications Commission, Office of the Secretary, Re: Bonneville International Corporation KSL (AM), Salt Lake City, Utah (FIN 6375), et al. Ownership Information, Accepted/Filed Jan 17, 2018.

Call Sign and Date   *Owner and/or Licensee*[382]

KZN (1922-1924)	Deseret News/LDS Church
KFPT (1924-1925)	Radio Service Corporation, John Cope and Family
KSL (1925-1928)	Radio Service Corporation -LDS Church
KSL (1928-1945)	Radio Service Corporation -LDS Church/Kearns Tribune
KSL (1945-1963)	Radio Service Corporation-LDS Church
KSL (1963-1964)	KSL Inc., LDS Church
KSL (1964-1967)	Bonneville International Corporation, LDS Church
KSL (1967-present)	Deseret Management Corporation. Bonneville International Corporation, licensee

KDYL, 1922, SALT LAKE CITY
VICTOR A. MICHAEL JR., OWNER; KONA COAST RADIO, LICENSEE

In 2022, Victor A. Michael, Jr., became the Kona Coast Radio Company registered principal while also a broadcast consulting engineer. The 1320 frequency now carries the KNIT call sign in Salt Lake City. KNIT, originally KDYL, is the only Kona Coast Radio owned AM station, after separating from Salt Lake City's KJJC-AM (1230) in 2019.[383] Vic Michael Radio purchased KFNZ, 1320 (when it was not on the air in Salt Lake City) in October 2017 and changed the KFNZ call sign to KNIT.[384]

After engineering adjustments, KNIT returned to the air in 2019. Michael reportedly paid $100,000 in August 2017 for KFNZ. It is noted that KDYL AM (1320 kHz), was the most valuable asset in a sale with KDYL FM and television stations in 1953, which netted over $2 million for its owners, primarily Sidney Fox, which today would be comparable to nearly $21 million.

KNIT offers Christian programming, as a Your Network of Praise (YNOP) affiliate. YNOP also has affiliates in 41 Montana FM stations, six FM outlets in

---

382   FCC: https://licensing.fcc.gov/cgibin/prod/cdbs/forms/prod/getimportletter_exh.cgi?im port_letter_id=44622&.pdf): (radio-locator https://radio-locator.com/Info/KSL-AM)
383   KNIT Wiki: https://en.wikipedia.org/wiki/KNIT_(AM)
384   radio-locator: https://radio-locator.com/info/KNIT-AM

Idaho, three FM outlets in North Dakota, four FM outlets in Wyoming and the single AM Salt Lake affiliate.[385]

KDYL, Utah's second longest sustained AM radio station was first licensed to the *Salt Lake Telegram* newspaper company on May 8, 1922, with its first official broadcast occurring on May 10. KDYL operated at several frequencies but mainly at 1290 until 1943 when it began operating at 1320 kHz, which it has done so for more than 80 years. Over time, there have been nine call sign changes, seven different owners and at least six program format changes since its beginning in 1922.[386]

As noted elsewhere in the book. Arthur L. Fish's entrepreneurial efforts were instrumental in the founding of KDYL. Ira J. Kaar, a radio amateur, built and operated the station when it first aired (and to whom this book is dedicated). Sidney S. Fox, Philip Lasky and John Baldwin are the prominent people responsible for developing KDYL in its formative years, 1925 to 1953.

Call Sign and Date	Owner and/or Licensee
KDYL (1922-1925)	The Salt Lake Telegram
KDYL (1925-1953)	Intermountain Broadcasting, Inc., Sidney S. Fox
KDYL (1953-1959)	TLF (Time-Life-Fortune) Broadcasting, Inc. (6/25/53)
KCPX (1959-1983)	Columbia Pictures Co., Inc. 11/4/59, (2/21/59 KCPX call sign first used)
KBUG (1983-1987)	Crossroads Broadcasting, Group Owner, Price Broadcasting,
KCPX (1987-1988)	Group Owner: Price Broadcasting
KMEX 1988-1989)	Group Owner: Price Broadcasting (8/1/88 (KMEX call sign 1st used)
KUTR (1989-1992)	Group Owner: Price Broadcasting
KCPX (1992-1992)	Group Owner: Price Broadcasting
KCNR (1992-1996)	Group Owner: Price Broadcasting (8/11/92: KCNR call sign first used)

---

385   YNOP.org: http://www.ynop.org/stationlist.html
386   Wikiwand: https://www.wikiwand.com/en/KNIT_(AM)#/KDYL

KFNZ (1996-2001)   Citadel bought KFNZ in 1997 (8/30/96, KFNZ call
                        sign first used)
KFNZ (2001- 2011)   Citadel Broadcasting merged with Cumulus in 2011
KFNZ (2011-2017)   Cumulus Broadcasting Co. acquired KFNZ on
                        2/27/17; KFNZ operating on 1320 kHz was dark from
                        2017 to 2019
KNIT (2017 to present) Kona Coast Radio,

KLO (formerly KFUR), 1925, OGDEN
CAPITAL BROADCASTING (KLO BROADCASTING CO.)

KLO is licensed to Capital Broadcasting, which is owned by Matt Webb,
longtime KLO owner John Webb's son, and other family members.[387] KLO
Broadcasting also owns and operates two FM stations, KBZN and KSGN in
Ogden. In 2012, Capital Broadcasting purchased KJQN and began to simulcast
KLO's programming on 103.1 FM.[388] The FCC approved the purchase and
KJQN changed its call letters to KLO-FM. KLO hosted several interim owners
from 1970 to 1990 when the senior Webb acquired ownership, and it has
remained in the family to the present.[389]

KLO, Utah's third longest sustained radio station, was first licensed as
KFUR to the Peery Building Company and the Redfield Electric Company on
January 5, 1925. The Peerys owned "Ogden's Amusements," including theaters
and a dance hall. The station first aired programming on January 28 of that
year. On April 11, 1929, the KFUR call sign was officially changed to KLO,
and the Peery Building Company license was transferred to the Interstate
Broadcasting Company and Earl J. Glade. A.L. Glasmann of the *Ogden
Standard Examiner* began assuming Interstate Broadcasting ownership in 1931
and took complete ownership in 1934.

---

387   John Webb obituary:
https://www.legacy.com/obituaries/saltlaketribune/obituary.aspx?n=john-creer-
webb&pid=171520284&fhid=4557
388   Capital Broadcasting, SLC local: https://secure.utah.gov/bes/details.
html?entity=1061341-0142
389   KLO Wiki: https://en.wikipedia.org/wiki/KLO_(AM)

Call Sign and Date	Owner and/or Licensee[390]
KFUR (1924-1925)	Peery Building Company and The Redfield Electric Company
KFUR (1925-1929)	Peery Building Company
KLO (1929-1934)	Peery Building Company & Earl J. Glade.
KLO (1934-1953)	Interstate Broadcasting Corporation (A.L. Glasmann)
KLO (1953-1963)	The Interstate Broadcasting Corporation
KLO (1963-1970)	Utah Radio Inc. (A.L. Glasmann, group owner)
KLO (1970)	Transfer control from Cecil B. & Joyce Heftel to Richard B. Wheeler (Joyce Heftel was A.L. Glasmann's daughter.)
KLO (1970-1974)	Radio Ogden, Inc. & Richard B. Wheeler, president
KLO (1974-1979)	KLO Broadcasting Company, Robert Davis, president
KLO (1979-1990)	KVOC Inc., Fred Hildebrand, president
KLO (1990-2014)	KLO Broadcasting Company, John Webb, president (John Webb died June 26, 2014.)
KLO (2014-present)	KLO Broadcasting Co., Capital Broadcasting Co. Licensee, Matt Webb, KLO General Manager & Capital owner with other family members and a family trust.

As discussed earlier, the 1927 Federal Radio Act set radio station quotas for each state, and Utah had exceeded its quota with KSL, KDYL and KLO. So no new Utah radio broadcasting stations were licensed until the new Communications Act of 1934 authorized the FCC to exceed a state's quota if the public interest would be served by granting a license for a station not exceeding 100 watts of power. The following seven stations among several applicants met those criteria and were licensed by the FCC in the late 1930s and into the 1940s.

---

390   History Card KLO: https://licensing.fcc.gov/cgi-bin/prod/cdbs/forms/prod/getimportletter_exh.cgi?import_letter_id=43081&pdf

KEUB (now KOAL), 1936, PRICE

EASTERN UTAH BROADCASTING COMPANY

The Tom Anderson family members control the Eastern Utah
Broadcasting Company.[391] KOAL, Utah's fourth longest sustained radio
broadcasting station, was first licensed as KEUB (Eastern Utah Broadcasting)
by the FCC on November 17, 1936. Sam G. Weiss was the first Utah applicant
to obtain a 100-watt Utah radio broadcasting license, after 11 years without
a new Utah radio license being granted. Weiss, according to local records,
launched KEUB on October 30, 1936, likely with FCC approval, 18 days before
it officially was issued its FCC license. A FCC History Card for KEUB could
not be located to determine if the November 1936 licensing date is correct.
Weiss was the owner/manager of the station, Frank Carman, who later opened
KUTA in Salt Lake City, was the engineer, and Jack Richards was the program
director. KEUB originated at 1420 kHz, changed to 1450 in 1943, to 1230 by
1947, and to 750 kHz in 1986.

Weiss owned nearly all the stock in the Eastern Utah Broadcasting
Company, Inc., until the FCC approved a transfer of the KEUB license to
Jack Richards in 1939. Richards owned the station until his death in 1986
at age 90, and Tom Anderson, who had been with KOAL for decades, and
whom Richards adopted when Anderson was 40 years old, eventually
assumed principal ownership of the station until his death in 2012.[392] Eastern
Utah Broadcasting continued control of KOAL, with Virginia Anderson
as transferee a year later.[393] Virginia Anderson died in 2015 and Anderson
siblings Paul Anderson, Kelly Lane and Christina Oliekan assumed control.

---

391   Paul Anderson, email to Tim Larson, December 20, 2021, giving names of Eastern Utah
Broadcasting principals.
392   Tom Anderson Obituary: https://www.mitchellfuneralhome.net/obituary/6011605
393   Virginia S. Anderson Obituary:
https://www.legacy.com/us/obituaries/saltlaketribune/name/virginia-anderson-
obituary?id=21573164

Call Sign and Date	Owner and/or Licensee
KEUB (1936-1939)	Eastern Utah Broadcasting Sam G. Weiss
KEUB (1939-1945)	Eastern Utah Broadcasting Company, Inc., Jack Richards & A.W. McKinnon, president, Carbon Emory Bank of Utah
KOAL (1945-1986)	Eastern Utah Broadcasting Company Jack Richards
KOAL (1986-2013)	Eastern Utah Broadcasting Company; Tom Anderson, President, died on September 27, 2012; transfer of control from Tom Anderson (deceased) to Virginia S. Anderson on July 29, 2013.
KOAL (2013-2016)	Eastern Utah Broadcasting Company, Inc., Virginia S. Anderson. Anderson died on December 12, 2015.
KOAL (2016-present)	Eastern Utah Broadcasting Company, Owners are Anderson siblings Paul Anderson, Kelly Lane and Christina Oliekan

KSUB, 1937, CEDAR CITY
CHERRY CREEK RADIO LLC, (CC-ST. GEORGE IV, LLC), SUBSIDIARY

Headquartered in Greenwood Village, Colorado, KSUB Group Owner Cherry Creek Media, through its Cherry Creek Radio subsidiary (CCR-St. George IV, LLC), owns 53 small market radio stations in nine states. Included are 11 Utah stations, five of them in Cedar City, Utah, and six in St. George, Utah.[394] Of the 53 owned stations, just nine are AM stations, with two of them in Utah, each partnered with an FM station. James English became the general manager and marketing manager for the 11 Utah Cherry Creek Radio stations in both Utah cities. He had decades of executive experience and was touted as understanding the need for community engagement and partnership, according to his professional biography.[395]

KSUB (Southern Utah Broadcasting), was Utah's fifth longest sustained

---

394   Utah.gov: https://secure.utah.gov/govpay/checkout/select.html
395   James F. English Linkedin: https://www.linkedin.com/in/james-f-english-36706416

radio broadcasting station. Leland M. Perry and Harold Johnson, Cedar City residents, doing business as the Johnson and Perry firm, were the original applicants and owners of KSUB.[396] On October 27, 1936, the FCC issued Johnson and Perry a construction permit to operate a 100-watt station at 1310 kHz. With FCC approval, opening day was July 3, 1937, a month before it received its official FCC license on August 18. Tragedy, however, struck on July 5, 1938, as KSUB prepared to celebrate its first anniversary. Johnson was killed in a hunting accident.[397] This left Perry with sole financial responsibility for the station that personally plagued him for the next two decades. KSUB has operated at 590 kHz since October 16, 1946.[398] Howard Johnson's Granite District Radio Broadcasting Company assumed station ownership from 1959 to 2006, when Cherry Creek assumed ownership.

Call Sign and Date	Owner and/or Licensee[399]
KSUB (1937-1940)	Harold Johnson & Leland Perry doing business as Johnson & Perry
KSUB (1940-1944)	Southern Utah Broadcasting, Licensee (Leland Perry, principal owner)
KSUB (1944-1957)	Radio Service Corporation of Utah, Licensee (also KSL owner at the time) & Southern Utah Broadcasting of Utah
KSUB (1957-1958)	W. Arthur Jones, Lanell N. Lunt, Durham Morris, Loren C. Miles
KSUB (1958-1959)	Beehive Telecasting Corporation
KSUB (1959-2006)	Granite District Radio Broadcasting Company, Howard D. Johnson, president, died August 5, 1989.
KSUB (2006-present)	George IV LLC, Group Owner: Cherry Creek Radio, LLC

---

396   KSUB Wiki: https://en.wikipedia.org/wiki/KSUB
397   Harold Johnson obituary & gravesite:
https://www.findagrave.com/memorial/20720678/howard-d-johnson
398   radio-locator: https://radio-locator.com/info/KSUB-AM
399   FCC.gov:
https://licensing.fcc.gov/cgibin/prod/cdbs/forms/prod/getimportletter_exh.cgi?import_letter_id=44239

KUTA, 1938, SALT LAKE CITY
iHEARTMEDIA, INC. (iHEARTMEDIA/IHEART)

iHeartMedia, Inc., operates its radio stations through its iHeart Division (formerly Clear Channel Radio). Clear Channel at one time operated more than 1,200 U.S. radio stations.[400] But iHeartMedia, Inc./iHeart Radio, Inc., since emerging from bankruptcy in May 2019, now with over 850 stations, is said to reach more than 90% of Americans each month and is the largest radio station group owner in the U.S. It has six stations in Utah, including KNRS AM (formerly KUTA) and KWDZ AM and four FM stations. Citicasters Licenses, Inc., is the broadcast licensee for the iHeart owned stations in Utah and for most other owned stations across the U.S.[401]

KUTA, Utah's sixth longest sustained broadcasting station, was first licensed on August 22, 1938. Jack Powers, Frank C. Carman, David G. Smith and Grant Wrathal, doing business as the Utah Broadcasting Company, were the owners. Wrathall and Carman were radio engineers, but it was Carman who had the most experience constructing a Utah radio station, having engineered KEUB/KOAL in Price, Utah, prior to helping to establish KUTA. Carman essentially assumed ownership of what began as KUTA, then KLUB, and operated it for several decades until selling his holdings and retiring to his home in Oregon in 1985. In addition, over the years, Carman operated stations in Idaho, Montana and Oregon.

KUTA originated using 1500 kHz at 100 watts in 1938, which increased to 250 watts in 1940, and eventually to 570 kHz at 5 kilowatts in 1941.

---

400   KNRS Wiki: https://en.wikipedia.org/wiki/KNRS_(AM)
401   KNRS /KUTA Call Sign History:
fcc.gov/cgibin/ws.exe/prod/cdbs/pubacc/prod/call_hist.pl?Facility_id=63818&Callsign=KNRS

Call Sign and Date	Owner and/or Licensee[402]
KUTA (1938-1945)	Utah Broadcasting Company, Frank Carman, et al.
KUTA (1945-1956)	Utah Broadcasting & Television Company, Frank Carman, et al.
KLUB (1956-1958)	Frank C. Carman, Licensee, / KLUB Broadcasting Co.
KLUB (!958-1971)	KLUB Broadcasting Company, Inc., Licensee
KLUB (1971-1985)	Carman Corporation
KLUB (1985-1989)	Sun Mountain Broadcasting
KISN (1989-1998)	Sun Mountain Broadcasting, (KISN 1st used on 5/15/89)
KNRS (1998-1999)	Jacor Communications, (KNRS 1st used on 1/9/98)
KNRS (1999-2009)	Clear Channel Communications, Inc., Citicasters, Licenses L.P.
KACP (2009-2010)	Clear Channel Communications, Inc., Citicasters, Licenses L.P (KCAP 1st used on 9/1/09)
KNRS (2010-present)	iHeart Media, Citicasters Licenses, Inc. KNRS again used starting on 12/23/10

KVNU, 1939, LOGAN
SUN VALLEY RADIO INC. (D/B AS CACHE VALLEY MEDIA GROUP)

Sun Valley Radio, Inc. operates 10 Utah stations, which, among them, serve the Logan, Tremonton, Bear Lake, northern Utah, southern Idaho, and western Wyoming areas.[403] Two of the stations — KVNU 610 and KLGN 1390 are AM outlets — and the other eight are FM outlets.[404] The two AM stations simulcast their respective programs on FM stations. M. Kent Frandsen owns Sun Valley Radio, Inc. and is its president. Besides the 10 Cache Valley Media Group stations in Logan, the Frandsen family owns and operates 10 Sandhill Media Group stations in Idaho, eight Canyon Media stations in Southern Utah,

---

402   FCC: https://licensing.fcc.gov/cgibin/prod/cdbs/forms/prod/getimportletter_exh.cgi?import_letter_id=43095&.pdf
403   Sun Valley Radio Group d/b as Cache Valley Media Group, M. Kent Frandsen registered agent: https://secure.utah.gov/bes/details.html?entity=1154160-0142
404   Cache Valley Media Group Utah Stations
https://www.cachevalleymediagroup.com/stations/

and two stations in Evanston, Wyoming.[405]

KVNU is Utah's seventh longest sustained radio broadcasting station. KVNU's parent company, Cache Valley Broadcasting Company, was formed on August 8, 1935, more than three years before it obtained its official FCC license on January 24, 1939.[406] Seymore Levi "Hap" Billings, Jr. served as president and owned 24% of the company. Several others owned the remaining shares. KVNU's first test broadcast was on December 20, 1938, a year before it was issued a formal FCC license.[407] The delay in part was due to issues about tower height and nuisance discrepancies, as concerning the station's studio address and location in the license application.[408]

KVNU opened as a 100-watt station operating at 1200 kHz, moved to 1230 kHz on March 24, 1941 at 250 watts, and then moved to 610 kHz on April 29, 1947 at 1 kilowatt. In 1939, Henry F. Laub became a 17% owner of Cache Valley Broadcasting and over the years became a principal owner, until in 1946 he grudgingly turned control of his share of the company over to the Bullen family, which owned and operated KVNU for the next 50 years.[409] Reed Bullen was the general manager for the majority of those years, followed by his son Jonathan who served as general manager until the Bullen family sold the station to the Sun Valley Radio Group in 1996.

405   The Frandsen Family:
https://archive.sltrib.com/article.php?id=14655900&itype=storyID
406   KVNU Wiki: https://en.wikipedia.org/wiki/KVN
407   FCCInfo.com:
https://www.fccinfo.com/CMDProEngine.
php?sCurrentService=AM&tabSearchType=Appl&sAppIDNumber=1346874&sHours=D
408   KVNU History
https://en.wikipedia.org/w/index.php?title=KVNU&action=history
409   Cache Valley Media Group: https://www.cachevalleymediagroup.com/stations/

Call Sign and Date	Owner and/or Licensee[410]
KVNU (1939-1946)	Cache Valley Broadcasting Company, Seymore, "Hap" Billings, president, Henry Laub, VP, and Reed Bullen, secretary/treasurer and manager of the corporation
KVNU (1946-1966)	Cache Valley Broadcasting Company, Transfer of the license in 1946 from the Henry F. Laub family: H.F, John H., Clair M., and Emma K. Laub, and Adrian W. Hatch, to the Herschel Bullen family: Herschel (45%) and Reed Bullen (32%), and the remainder to Helen, Herschel Keith, and T.H. Bullen and Dan B. Shields. (Herschel Bullen died on 2/2/66.)
KVNU (1966-1979)	Cache Valley Broadcasting Company, Helen Bullen, president and Reed Bullen GM. (Reed and Helen were Herschel Bullen's son and daughter)
KVNU (1979-1983)	Cache Valley Broadcasting Company, Helen Bullen, President, Jonathan W. Bullen, GM (Jonathan was Reed Bullen's son.)
KVNU (1983-1989)	Cache Valley Broadcasting, Jonathan Bullen, president,
KVNU (1989-1996)	Reed Bullen, licensee
KVNU (1996-1996)	Cache Valley Media Group (Reed Bullen died October 9, 2005 at 98)
KVNU (1996-present)	Sun Valley Radio Group (Cache Valley Media Group)

KOVO, 1939, PROVO
BROADWAY MEDIA LS, LLC

Broadway Media is a Salt Lake City-based company owned by Dell Loy Hansen, also owner of several businesses including, up until 2021, the Real Salt Lake professional soccer team franchise. Broadway Media was originally founded as Simmons Media that operated KOVO from 2004 to 2014 before turning control over to Broadway Media, which operates nine Salt Lake

---

410   FCC History Card:
https://licensing.fcc.gov/cgi-bin/prod/cdbs/forms/prod/getimportletter_exh.cgi?import_letter_id=45360&.pdf

City area stations: seven FM outlets including the station with the long-time morning drive time show *X-96's Radio from Hell*, and two AM outlets, KOVO at 960 kHz and KALL at 700kHz (not at its original 910 kHz).[411] One of the FM stations, U92 operating at 92.5 kHz, airs an electronic dance music format supplied by an EDM program provider. Broadway Media, in addition to its Salt Lake City radio stations, sponsors entertainment and special events businesses from its Salt Lake City offices on Broadway Street (300 South in downtown Salt Lake City)., likely an easy pick for the company's name. Broadway Media also owns KALL, in Salt Lake City, as discussed below.

KOVO is the eighth longest sustained Utah radio station. Clifton A. Tolboe's "Citizens Voice and Air Show" business in 1938 outdid another applicant in an FCC comparative hearing to determine who should be awarded the construction permit for the station. KOVO first aired using a faulty technical system on September 21, 1939, but it didn't receive its formal FCC license until a month later (October 23). Under Tolboe's ownership, KOVO launched in 1939 on 1210 kHz at 100 watts of power, then moved to 1240 kHz at 250 watts on March 24, 1941, and up to 1 kilowatt at 960 kHz on May 6, 1948, where it has remained to the present.[412]

Tolboe and his first station manager, Arch Madsen, were the two prominent people in KOVO's early operations, as discussed earlier in the book.

Call Sign and Date	Owner and/or Licensee
KOVO (1939-1956)	KOVO Inc. Clifton A. Tolboe, trading as Citizens Voice & Air Show, Licensee: KOVO Broadcasting Company
KOVO (1956-1973)	KOVO Inc., Ashly Robison and Glen Shaw
KOVO (1973-1975)	Transfer of license corporation for Ashley Robison & Glen Shaw to Sidney S. Gilbert, receiver
KOVO (1975-1976)	First Media Corporation, subsidiary of Marriott Corporation
KAYK (1976-1980)	First Media Corporation, Group Owner
KDOT (1980-1985)	First Media Corporation, Group Owner

411   Broadway Media Radio stations: http://broadwaymediagroup.com/radio-stations/
412   KOVO Wiki: https://en.wikipedia.org/wiki/KOVO

KFMY (1985-1990)   First Media Corporation

KFMY (1990-1994)   The Great Stock Company

KOVO (1994-2004)   The Great Stock Company

KOVO (2004-2014)   Simmons Media Group, Simmons-SL Group owner

KOVO (2014-present)   Broadway Media LS, LLC

KNAK, 1945, SALT LAKE CITY
JAZZ COMMUNICATIONS, LLC, LICENSEE
(SMITH ENTERTAINMENT GROUP)

The Larry H. Miller (LHM) Communications Corporation obtained what became KZNS in 2012 from the Simmons Media Group, which had since 1982 owned the station operating at 1280 kHz.[413] LHM sold "The Zone" Sports Network (1280 KZNS along with KZNS FM 97.5) to the Smith Entertainment Group (SEG) in May 2021.[414] Bonneville International Corporation (BIC) then took over the management and operations of Jazz Communication Sports (for the Utah Jazz NBA franchise), which included the broadcasting rights for the Utah Jazz basketball games.[415] BIC's KSL began airing select Jazz games, reaching a larger audience on KSL 1160 AM and on KSL 102.7 FM.[416]

The LHM Communication Group also purchased KXIV television in 1993, and then later changed the call sign to KJZZ, in reference to the Miller owned JAZZ NBA basketball team. On February 20, 2009, Larry H. Miller passed away at the age of 64 from complications associated with diabetes. His wife, Gale Miller, assumed the chairwoman of the Larry H. Miller Group when he died. The group sold the television station in 2016 to the Sinclair Broadcast Group that owns or operates a stable of about 200 television stations nationwide. The Miller Corporation in 2021 also sold the Utah Jazz franchise to Qualtrics co-founder Ryan Smith and now holds only a 20% ownership stake in the team.[417]

---

413   Larry H. Miller Group of Companies: https://www.lhm.com/companies/
414   KZNS AM Wiki: https://en.wikipedia.org/wiki/KZNS_(AM); KZNZ-FM Wiki: https://en.wikipedia.org/wiki/KZNS-FM
415   KSL takes over management of The Zone Sports Network, to simulcast ...
416   FCC.gov: https://licensing.fcc.gov/cgibin/prod/cdbs/forms/prod/getimportletter_exh.cgi?import_letter_id=45435&.pdf
417   Operation of the Zone: https://radioinsight.com/headlines/213496/bonneville-to-take-over-

KNAK (now KZNS) is Utah's ninth longest sustained radio station. It was built by Howard D. Johnson during WWII, and was first licensed on June 4, 1945 to Granite District Broadcasting. It has been on the air since February 1945, the only Utah station to begin operations during WWII.

Johnson, his wife, and members of her family, the Miners, owned Granite District Broadcasting, incorporated in 1940. Members of the extended Johnson family, principal owners of Granite District Broadcasting, owned KNAK from its inception until 1976. Howard was a talented radio engineer, who before and after KNAK helped set up technical infrastructure for some 30 radio stations in Idaho, Wyoming, Nevada, Colorado and Utah, including KOVO in Provo, KSVC in Richfield, KBUH in Brigham City, KVOG in Ogden, KJAM in Vernal, among others, and even owned KSUB in Cedar City for an extended time. Howard Johnson died on August 5, 1989.

KNAK operated on 1400 kHz at 250 watts originally, then moved to 1280 kHz at 500 watts on January 26, 1946, and to 1 kilowatt during the daytime in October 1947.

Call Sign and Date	Owner and/or Licensee[418]
KNAK (1945-1973)	Granite District Radio Broadcasting Company, Howard D. Johnson
KNAK (1973-1975)	Granite District Radio, Howard D. & Lucille M. Johnson transferred station to son Jerold W. Johnson, trustee.
KNAK (1975-1976)	Granite District Radio, Group: WMS Corporation -Arthur Powell Williams and Virginia M. Williams, as a Family Group
KWMS (1976-1978)	Granite District Radio Broadcasting Company, Arthur P. Williams, President

---

operations-of-1280-97-5-the-zone/
418   FCC.gov:
https://transition.fcc.gov/fccbin/q?call=kzns&arn=&state=&city=&freq=530&fre2=1700&type
=0&facid=&class=&list=1&ThisTab=Results+to+This+Page%2FTab&dist=&dlat2=&mlat2=&sl
at2=&NS=N&dlon2=&mlon2=&slon2=&EW=W&size=9

KWMS (1978-1982)	Granite District Radio Group: WMS Corporation, Arthur P. Williams
KDYL (1982-2001)	Simmons Family Inc., Roy W. Simmons, president
KZNS (2001-2012)	Simmons Media Group (Roy Simmons died on May 9. 2006)
KZNS (2012-2021)	Larry H. Miller Communications Corporation
KZNS (2021-present)	Jazz Communications Licensee, (Smith Entertainment Group; Ryan Smith, Qualtrics CEO)

KALL, 1945, SALT LAKE CITY
iHEART MEDIA, INC, (FORMERLY CLEAR CHANNEL)

In 2001, Clear Channel sold KALL to Mercury Broadcasting but kept the rights to the KALL call sign and continued to program the station. The station had at least five different company owners from 1992 to 2003 when Disney bought KALL and changed the call sign to KWDZ, operating at 910 kHz.[419] With KWDZ reflecting the station's new owner's namesake (Walt Disney). Clear Channel then moved the KALL call sign to its station at 700 kHz. Clear Channel (CC Media Holdings) changed its name to iHeartMedia, Inc. in September 2014.

KALL 910, Utah's tenth longest sustained radio station, was granted a license on January 21, 1946.[420] It was issued to Abrelia S. Hinckley, George C. Hatch and Wilda Gene Hatch as a partnership. Hinckley was Robert Hinckley's wife and essentially a surrogate for him in the KALL application. Robert Hinckley was close to President Truman and seemingly wanted to avoid a perception of favoritism for the KALL license, although behind the scene, KALL was, in fact, favored. KALL was the only radio station in Utah granted a construction permit to use scarce resources during WWII, but it didn't go on the air until September 30, 1945, less than a month after the war officially ended on September 2. As noted elsewhere in this chapter and the

---

419   KWDZ Wiki: https://en.wikipedia.org/wiki/KWDZ
420   KALL Wiki: https://en.wikipedia.org/wiki/KALL

book, KNAK was the only Utah station allowed to go on the air during WWII because Howard Johnson, its engineer, did not use scarce resources to build the station.

Various companies owned by the Hatch/Glasmann family --for example, Wilda Gene Hatch was a Glasmann family member-- completely controlled KALL from 1946 until it was sold in 1992 to Apollo Broadcasting, except for a time from 1946 to 1954 when the Kearns-Tribune Corporation had a 50% interest in the station.

Call Sign and Date Owner and/or Licensee[421]

KALL (1946-1953)   Abrelia Hinckley, George & Wilda Gene Hatch (50%) and the Telegram Publishing (50%). License assigned to Salt Lake Broadcasting Company, Inc. on 6/27/46. The Telegram Publishing sold its 50% share of KALL to apply for a television station in Salt Lake City, finalized in 1954

KALL (1953-1970)   Intermountain Network, Inc., Transfer of control to George C. Hatch & the Intermountain Network, Inc. on 7/3/53.

KALL (1970-1978)   Communications Investment Corporation, George C. Hatch

KALL (1978-1992)   Salt Lake Broadcasting Company, George C. Hatch

KALL (1992-1995)   Apollo Radio Partners

KALL (1995-1997)   Regent Communications

KALL (1997-1999)   Jacor

KALL (1999-2001)   Clear Channel (now iHeart)

KALL (2001-2003)   Mercury

KWDZ (2003-2015)   Disney/ABC, the KALL call sign was moved to 700kHz in 2003

KWDZ (2015-2018)   iHeartMedia (formerly Clear Channel)

KWDZ (2018)   KWDZ on 910kHz (formerly KALL) went dark, and iHeart surrendered the license on April 25, 2018 and the

---

421   KALL History Card:
https://licensing.fcc.gov/cgibin/prod/cdbs/forms/prod/getimportletter_exh.cgi?import_letter_id=45278&.pdf

FCC cancelled it on June 26, 2018.

Television stations and cable network

Each of the chapters about the three Utah pioneer television stations documents the sequence of activities leading to ownership succession for each station. For the most part, the same principals who began the KDYL, KSL and KUTA AM radio stations, respectively, founded the first three Utah television stations. The tables for each television station outline the ownership succession. The same applies to the chapter about Telecommunications, Inc. (TCI).

KDYL TV

Date	**Owner and/or Licensee**
(1948-1951)	Intermountain Broadcasting Corporation, Sidney S. Fox, president
(1951-1953)	Intermountain Broadcasting & Television Corporation, Sidney S. Fox, president.

KTVT TV:

(1953-1959)	Intermountain Broadcasting & Television Corporation (Time Inc. 80%, G. Bennett Larson (20%) G. Bennett Larson, president

KCPX TV:

(1959-1959)	Columbia Pictures Electronics Company, Inc.,
(1959-1975)	Screen Gems, subsidiary of Columbia Pictures Industry Inc.

KTVX TV:[422]

(1975-1984)	20th Century Fox Film Corporation. Licensee: United Television, Inc. In 1981 United Television merged with Chris Craft Industries
(1984-2001)	United Television, Inc.
(2001-2001)	Fox Television Station, Inc. Subsidiary of News Corporation

---

422   KTVX Wiki: https://en.wikipedia.org/wiki/KTVX

(2001-2007)	Clear Channel Communications, Inc.
(2007-2008)	Newport Television, subsidiary of Providence Equity Partners
(2008-2012)	Newport Television
(2012-present)	Nexstar Broadcasting Group

KSL TV

Date	**Owner and/or Licensee**
(1949-1962)	Radio Service Corporation of Utah
(1962-1964)	Church of Jesus Christ of Latter-Day Saints. Licensee: Radio Service Corporation of Utah
(1964-1965)	KSL Inc.
(1965-1977)	Bonneville International Corporation (98.2%), Arch Madsen, president. BIC is a subsidiary of the Deseret Management Corporation owned by the LDS Church, Licensee: KSL Inc.
(1977-1983)	Bonneville International Corporation (100%), BIC owned by the Deseret Management Corporation, LDS Church. Licensee: Bonneville International Corporation
(1983-2008)	Bonneville International Corporation. Licensee: Bonneville Holding Company
(2008-present)	Bonneville International Corporation. Deseret Management Corporation is parent company, LDS Church. Licensee: Bonneville International Corporation

KUTV TV

Date	**Owner and/or Licensee**
(1954-1956)	Kearns –Tribune Corporation/*Salt Lake Tribune* (50%) and Utah Broadcasting Corporation/Frank C Carman (25%) & Grant R. Wrathall (25%)
(1956-1967)	*Ogden Standard Examiner*/A.L. Glassman (51%), and *Salt Lake* Kearns-Tribune Corporation/*Salt Lake Tribune* (35%), and Salt Lake City Broadcasting (KALL)/George and Wilda

	Gene Hatch (14%). Gene Hatch was Glassman's daughter
(1967-1972)	The Standard Corporation/*Ogden Standard Examiner*/ A.L. Glassman (80%), and *Salt Lake* Kearns-Tribune Corporation/*Salt Lake Tribune* (35%), and Salt Lake Broadcasting Company, Inc./George and Wilda Gene Hatch (20%).
(1972-1993)	The Standard Corporation/*Ogden Standard Examiner*/A.L. Glasmann (80%), and Communications Investment Corporation (20%), George Hatch president. Licensed to KUTV Inc.
(1993-1994)	KUTV L.P. George Hatch Family (60%), VS&A (Veronis Suhler & Associates investment fund) (40%)
(1994-1995)	NBC (88%) George Hatch Family (12%)
(1995-2000)	CBS/GroupW, then CBS Inc. Licensee: KUTV Associates
(2000-2007)	CBS Corporation/CBS Inc. (Viacom Television Station Group)
(2007-2011)	Cerberus Capital Management (Four Points Media Group)
(2011-present)	Sinclair Broadcast Group

Telecommunications, Inc. (TCI)

Date	Ownership[423]
(1958- 1965)	Community Television, Inc., Standard Corporation/Kearns Tribune Corporation
(1965-1969)	Community Television of Utah/Western Microwave
(1969-1997)	Telecommunications, Inc., including Liberty Media
(1997-1999)	Telecommunications Inc. merged with the Kearns-Tribune Corporation publisher of *The Salt Lake Tribune*, including Liberty Media
(1999-2002)	AT&T/ATT Broadband and Internet Services, excluding Liberty Media, which took on newer TCI business as TCI Ventures

---

423   Telecommunications, Inc.: https://en.wikipedia.org/wiki/Tele-Communications_Inc

(2002-present)   Comcast[424]

With the history of the pioneer radio stations in Utah extensively covered through the end of World War II, the following timeline, segmented in decades, summarizes key developments in Utah radio.

Number of Utah radio broadcasting stations over the decades

1945: KNAK and KALL round out the first ten AM Utah radio broadcasting stations.

1950: The number of radio broadcasting stations grows to 20 (17 AM, 3 FM), with 3 FM stations added, including KSL-FM in 1946, and KDYL-FM in Salt Lake City in 1947 and KOPP FM in Ogden in 1947.

1960: Utah has 35 radio broadcasting stations (29 AM, 6 FM). Three educational, non-commercial FM stations join the ranks: KVSE in 1952 (KUSU call sign by 1953 at a different frequency) at USU in Logan, Salt Lake City's KUER at The University of Utah and Provo's KBYU at Brigham Young University, the latter two were licensed but neither is listed in the Broadcasting Yearbook that year as on the air. The KDYL-FM call sign had changed to KCPX.

1970: Utah numbers reached 43 (30 AM 13 FM), with some over-the-air listener reach enhanced using translators across Utah.

1980: There were 72 Utah radio broadcasting stations (33 AM, 39 FM), where FM radio broadcasting stations outnumbered AM stations for the first time.

1990: Utah numbers jump to 86 (39 AM, 47 FM). In addition to the 47 FM stations, there are a dozen more Utah FM stations with approved construction permits or licenses but are not yet on the air.

2000: Utah counts 96 radio broadcasting stations. The AM stations

---

424   Comcast: https://en.wikipedia.org/wiki/Comcast

plateau at 39, but the FM stations surge to 57, with additional translator distribution.

2010: Radio broadcasting station numbers total 107 in Utah. The AM stations number 38, one less than the decade before, and the FM stations increase to 69. Digital signals are introduced, which means if they chose, there could have been at least three more FM program services for each of these stations beyond the 69 main FM frequencies.

2022: With digital operations in full force, Utah broadcasting station numbers totaled 148 (40 AM, 108 FM, including 6 low power outlets). The number of AM stations remained constant over three decades, but numbers of FM outlets significantly increased. Six of Utah's radio broadcasting stations were nonoperational or temporarily dark in 2022. This included, at one time, KWDZ, the station now on 1320, which was originally KDYL, one of the 10 pioneer stations.

Present-day market structure of Utah radio broadcasting

The 148 Utah radio stations do not account for digital subchannels, which operate by a method of transmitting more than one independent program stream simultaneously from the same digital radio on the same radio frequency channel. A station may be included in more than one entry in the numbers below. The 148 stations can be summarized in the following breakout:[425]

- 71stations owned by in-state corporate owners
- 36 stations licensed to out-of-state corporations
- 11 identified as Christian radio outlets
- 5 owned by Utah cities or sheriff's agencies
- 4 owned by public school districts
- 4 owned privately
- 1 owner identified as Hare Krishna outlet
- 56 different Utah cities have a radio station
- 79 radio stations within listening range of Salt Lake City
- 9 stations in Salt Lake County

---

425   https://radio-locator.com/cgi-bin/locate?select=city&city=Salt%20Lake%20City&state=UT

- 15 stations in Davis County
- 6 stations in Utah County
- 5 stations in Tooele County
- 4 stations in Weber County
- 43 stations in Washington County and St. George municipal area
- 28 stations in miscellaneous Utah counties
- 6 full powered Public Radio stations
- 7 non-profit stations
- 13 low power stations
- 18 stations licensed to colleges and universities (six to The University of Utah, with 32 additional translator stations; seven to Utah State University, with an additional 30 translator stations; two to Brigham Young University, with an additional five translator stations; and one each to Southern Utah University, Utah Tech University and Snow College.

Utah radio broadcasting station formats

Due to simulcasts, syndicated, network and multiplex programming carried on group owned stations and among owners of multiple stations across the state, there are far fewer different programing formats aired than there are Utah radio broadcasting stations. For example, there are, as presently noted above, 32 University of Utah and 30 Utah State University translator/satellite stations repeating programs transmitted to more than 200 Utah cities from their main stations, thereby blanketing the entire state as well as parts of neighboring states.

There are dozens of named radio formats and subcategories nationwide, but they fall into several broad categories in Utah:[426]
- 31 Adult Contemporary/MOR/Alternate
- 28 News/Talk/Information
- 21 Religious/Christian, including 2 Catholic and 1 Hare Krishna
- 20 Country

---

426   List of Radio Stations in Utah: https://en.wikipedia.org/wiki/List_of_radio_stations_in_Utahž

- 9 Variety
- 8 Public Broadcasting
- 7 Classic Hits
- 6 Mexican/Spanish
- 6 Oldies
- 6 Rock
- 5 Sports
- 1 Jazz

It will be a formidable project to see how local radio and television outlets will be able to sustain and thrive on a unique community identity in the decades to come.

Index

launch, 309

ownership changes, 313-16

KVNU, 5, 146, 199-212, 354-56

beginnings, 201-203

Bullen family legacy, 208-211

programming, 203-208

L.H. Strong Motor Company, 199-200

LaFount, Harold, 115-17, 294

Larson, G. Bennett (Ben), 93-94, 227, 279-84, 286

Lasky, Philip, 89-104

Latter Day Saints University (LDSU), 26, 27, 31-32

Latter-day Saints, The Church of Jesus Christ of (LDS), 3, 47, 59, 61, 65-67, 69-72, 119, 226, 229, 296-99, 341-42, 345

Laub, Henry F., 206-207

Lee, J. Bracken, 156, 162-63

Lee, Joe, 107, 216

Lehman, Kynn, 107-108

Lewis, B. Rowland, 143

Liberty Media, 331-35

Lieurance, Thurlow, 62

Lindow, Lester W., 228-29

Logan Republican newspaper, 208

Logan, 'Waxin Wayne', 237

Lomack, Stan, 254

Lucas, Will, 265

Luddy, Barbara, 107

Madsen, Arch L., 5, 72, 144-49, 177-84, 187, 190-92, 215-225, 228-29, 256

Magness, Bob, 6, 322-26, 328, 334

Mailander, Harold, 35, 76, 80, 90

Malone, John T., 6, 326-35

Marbel, Eddie, 101-102

Marconi Company, 11-13

Marconi, Guglielmo, 11-12

Marcroft, Bill, 253, 263-64, 313

Mardikian, George, 95

Mares, Eliseo, 102

Marvin, C.F., 57

Matheson, Scott M., 177

McCollom, Julian G., 19, 26-27

McDonald Chocolate Company, J.G., 62

McKay, David O., 72. 229

McKinnon, A. W., 153, 161-62

McQuarrie, Zelda, 289

Meadow Gold Dairy Company, 263, 321

Meyer, Lynn, 261

Mid-Utah Broadcasting Company, 223

Miller, Cutler (Cut) L., 34, 177, 178-84, 190-91

Miner, L. John, 239

Miner, Lawrence A., 230

Miracle Diamonds, 105-106

Mitchell, Doug, 313

Mitchell, 'Skinny' Johnny, 107-108

Moab Broadcasting and Television Corporation (MTBC), 318

Moelris, Russell, 18

Morgan, George B., 123

Morris, Durham, 184

Morrison Brothers, 143-44

Morse, Samuel, 10

Mulcock, S.E., 63

Mullens, Wesley, 112

Murdoch, Lennox, 188-91

Murdock, Abe, 176

Mutual Broadcasting System, 102, 124, 163-64, 221, 234, 236, 254-55, 261

National Association of Broadcasters, 71, 114

National Broadcasting Company (NBC), 94-95, 117, 124, 131, 144-46, 159,193, 219, 234, 241,248, 257, 277-78, 281-86, 310, 315, 318, 340, 364

Negroponte, Nicholas, 317

Nelson, Mary L., 265

Neslen, C. Clarence, 63

Newhouse Hotel, 78-80

Provol, George, 96, 100-101, 278

Provol, Hazel, 281

Provol, Robert, 96, 100, 101

Public Interest Convenience and Necessity clause (PICAN), 43-44, 128, 157

Public Interest Convenience or Necessity clause (PICON), 39-40, 114

Quaal, Ward, 228

Quinn, Elwyn, 102

quota system, radio stations, 126-140

Radio Act of 1912, 17, 41-42, 86

Radio Act of 1927, 4, 42-43, 86, 114, 127

radio amateurs, Utah, 17-37, 75-76, 142-43, 171, 179-80, 199-200

Radio Club of Salt Lake City, Utah, 17

radio developments, Utah, post-1945, 365-68

Radio Service Corporation (RSC), 3, 47. 62-67, 70, 84, 193, 223, 293, 296-99, 302

Rainger, Danny, 253, 276-78, 281-86

Rawlings, Calvin W., 98-100, 287-88

RCA (Radio Corporation of America), 12, 275

Redfield Electric Company, 111-12

Redfield, Carl, 111

Reeder, J.A., 203-204

regulatory policy, early radio, 40-44

Remy, Mel, 237

Reynolds, W.D., 89-90

Richards, Jack, 5, 158-66, 220

Riesen, Phil, 267

Riley, Bill, 253

Robinson, J.W., 221

Robison, Ashly, 227-28

Rocky Mountain Broadcasting System, 149

Rogers, Ted, 102

Rolly, Paul, 265-66

Roosevelt, Franklin D., 12, 209, 247, 248-49

Salt Lake Herald, 13, 73

Salt Lake Telegram, 46-47, 73, 75, 77-80